The Cold War 1949–2

Covering the development of the Cold War from the mid-twentieth century to the present day, *The Cold War 1949–2016* explores the struggle for world domination that took place between the US and the Soviet Union following the Second World War. The conflict between these two superpowers shaped global history for decades, and this book examines how this conflict developed into a nuclear arms race, spurred much of the wider world towards war and eventually resulted in the collapse of the Soviet Empire.

In this accessible yet comprehensive volume, Martin McCauley examines not only the actions of the US and the Soviet Union but also the effects upon and involvement of other regions such as Africa, Central America, Asia, Europe and the Middle East. Key themes include the Sino-Soviet relationship and the global ambitions of the newly formed People's Republic of China, the rise and fall of communism in countries such as Cambodia, Angola and Ethiopia, the US defeat in Vietnam, the gradual unravelling of the Soviet Union and the changing shape of the post–Cold War world.

Providing a wide-ranging overview of the main turning points of the conflict and illustrated throughout with photographs and maps, this is essential reading for all students of the Cold War and its lasting global impact.

Martin McCauley is a prolific author and broadcaster who has a wealth of experience in Soviet, Russian and international affairs. He was at the University of London for over thirty years, and his recent publications include *Origins of the Cold War*, 4th edition (2015), *Russia, America and the Cold War*, 2nd edition (2008), *Stalin and Stalinism*, 3rd edition (2008) and *The Rise and Fall of the Soviet Union* (2008).

The Cold War 1949–2016

Martin McCauley

Routledge
Taylor & Francis Group

LONDON AND NEW YORK

First published 2017
by Routledge
2 Park Square, Milton Park, Abingdon, Oxon OX14 4RN

and by Routledge
711 Third Avenue, New York, NY 10017

Routledge is an imprint of the Taylor & Francis Group, an informa business

© 2017 Martin McCauley

British Library Cataloguing-in-Publication Data
A catalogue record for this book is available from the British Library

Library of Congress Cataloging-in-Publication Data
Names: McCauley, Martin, author.
Title: The Cold War 1949–2016 / Martin McCauley.
Description: Oxon ; New York, NY : Routledge, 2017. | Includes
  bibliographical references and index.
Identifiers: LCCN 2016056845 | ISBN 9781138999008 (hardback :
  alk. paper) | ISBN 9781138999015 (pbk. : alk. paper) |
  ISBN 9781315213309 (ebook)
Subjects: LCSH: Cold War. | World politics—1945–1989. |
  World politics—1989–
Classification: LCC D843 .M3344 2017 | DDC 909.82/5—dc23
LC record available at https://lccn.loc.gov/2016056845

ISBN: 978-1-138-99900-8 (hbk)
ISBN: 978-1-138-99901-5 (pbk)
ISBN: 978-1-315-21330-9 (ebk)

Typeset in Galliard
by Apex CoVantage, LLC

Visit the eResources: http://www.routledge.com/9781138999015

Contents

Illustrations

Maps

Foreword

Greek mythology holds that Zeus once released two eagles at each end of the earth and ordered them to fly towards each other. A sacred stone, called the omphalos – the navel of the world – was placed where the eagles met. China saw itself as the resting place of the omphalos, the centre of the earth; then the Persian Empire; then the Ottoman Empire. The prominence of Western Europe from the sixteenth century led to the belief that the omphalos resided in the great European capitals. Eurocentric history saw Ancient Greece giving birth to Rome, Rome to Christian Europe, Christian Europe to the Renaissance, the Renaissance to the Enlightenment, the Enlightenment to political democracy and the Industrial Revolution. In the twentieth century the omphalos resided in Berlin but that soon passed; then Moscow and Washington claimed possession of the sacred stone. Will the twenty-first century see it again move back to Beijing?

Communism was the greatest challenge to the US and its allies in the second half of the twentieth century. Communism, wearing Chinese garb, is the great challenge of the present century. Terrorism is a secondary challenge. Communism, represented by the Soviet Union, China, Eastern Europe and a host of Third World countries, was easily comprehensible. Its ideas and ideals could be traced back to the European Enlightenment in the eighteenth century. It was a secular religion and its goal the kingdom of heaven on earth. Terrorism, with its suicide bombers, by way of contrast, is almost incomprehensible as its practitioners prefer the promise of heaven after death to living on earth. It presents a great intellectual challenge, probably a greater intellectual challenge than the ideas and ideals of Karl Marx.

On reflection, it is clear that the thinking of the rulers in the Kremlin was informed by the tenets of Marxism, but their actions were those of traditional Russian politicians engaged in their country's influence and security. Except for a few years after the October Revolution, national interests took precedence over international interests. Protecting the revolution at home was given the highest priority.

Security is of the greatest concern to Russia during its history of a thousand years and more. The Mongols ruled Russia from 1240 to 1480. The country was invaded by a European power three times in just over a century: in 1812 by Napoleon, in 1914 by Kaiser Wilhelm, and in 1941 by Adolf Hitler. In contrast, modern American insecurity was only in the mind. Its geographical location ensured that it has never known invasion and occupation since gaining independence from Britain. Culture is also a significant factor in international behaviour. One can see the Soviet Union's attitude and actions as a continuation of the imperial Russian tradition. Blessed (or cursed) with few natural frontiers, Russia was always on the move. So was the US until the French and Spanish had been vanquished. The collapse of the Soviet Union left the US as the sole superpower and for a decade or so afterwards, inebriated with the wine of victory, believed it could shape the world according to its own norms.

The searing experience of lost wars in Afghanistan and Iraq has changed all that. Nowadays Washington is reluctant to become embroiled in conflicts far from its shores. If there is such a thing as the Obama Doctrine it consists of retreating from a world mission and concentrating on domestic affairs. How things have changed.

The other factor which is changing the global balance of power is China. The US is still the only superpower and militarily is the greatest force on the planet, but Beijing has proclaimed the China Dream which amounts to the Middle Kingdom ascending to the throne of world dominance. It still declares itself a communist power but its communism is unrecognisable from the version practised by the Soviet Union and its empire. It is single-party rule politically but economically it is capitalist. Just as the Soviet Union introduced a state and ideology unknown to the world in 1917, the Middle Kingdom is developing a system unknown hitherto. The commanding heights of the economy are in the state's hands and thus it can be labelled state capitalism. However, the much more dynamic part of the economy consists of small- and medium-sized enterprises (SMEs). Can these two coexist or will capitalism, as represented by the SMEs, eventually devour communism? Capitalism, after all, in order to flourish requires some elements of democracy. That is the experience of the last two centuries. Or will communist China evolve in such a way as to overturn the historical record? Xi Jinping and his team face a fascinating challenge as they turn the Middle Kingdom into a global powerhouse.

The Cold War during the second half of the twentieth century embraced the whole world; the Third World, especially, paid a heavy price for this. A nuclear war could not be fought by the superpowers so they engaged in proxy wars. This book spells out the genesis and conclusion of these conflicts. The Cold War was fought on many planes: political, economic, military, cultural, sporting, ideological, architectural, religious – indeed there was no aspect of human endeavour which was excluded. It is an intriguing story, and the reader can experience some of the highs and lows of the various contests.

So the old Cold War is over but there is a new Cold War between old adversaries: Russia and the US have reignited the enmity which existed under Soviet communism. This reveals that Marxism was not the dominant feature of the old conflict. Had it been so, everything would be sweetness and light between Moscow and Washington today. Great power rivalry was and is a constant factor. Relations between the old enemies have reached a point where the US 2015 National Military Strategy judges Russia to be the greatest security threat. How has it come to this in a short span of twenty-five years?

We already have a new Cold War between Russia and the US, but there is another simmering in the background: the one between China and the US. So the US is faced with a two-front Cold War, but by far the greater threat emanates from the Middle Kingdom. Make no mistake: China regards the US as a declining power and itself as a rising power. The Middle Kingdom is no longer a game player diplomatically; it is a game changer. The Silk and Maritime Roads (One Road, One Belt) and the Asian Infrastructure Investment Bank, to name only two initiatives, are testimony to China's ambition and ability. China shares the Soviet view about small states: they should concede to large states. One can see this now being manifested in the disputes in the South China Sea. Beijing has to beware of hubris or overconfidence which can lead to disaster.

The threat of terrorism is quite a different matter. It has not been given prominence in this book as it is a phenomenon of the present decade. The Islamic State (or ISIS or ISIL) is a new arrival on the world political stage. Its thinking is Salafist, a fundamentalist interpretation of Sharia. It proclaimed a caliphate in June 2014 and called on all Muslims to acknowledge Abu Bakr al-Baghdadi as their leader. It has been remarkably successful in attracting foreign fighters to its cause in Iraq and Syria. Some are university graduates. It claims to be the main protector of Sunnis in the Middle East and beyond. It has affiliates in many other states and is regarded as a mortal foe by Saudi Arabia and the Gulf States. Iran, the leading Shiite power, is now engaged in fighting it in Iraq. The fear of European states is that jihadis may return home and wreak havoc throughout the continent. Moscow, especially, is concerned that radicals may penetrate Central Asia and then spread to Russia. Boko Haram ('Western education is forbidden') in Nigeria rejects all Western state models and wishes to establish a Muslim world free of outside influences.

What will emerge from this rejection of all things Western? A new form of state and society? The Western model of democracy and a free market economy is no longer attractive to many people throughout the world. What will take its place? Increasing conflict seems inevitable.

Martin McCauley
April 2016

I am deeply indebted to Jukka Renkama, Christopher Lee and David McCron for valuable assistance in compiling this volume.

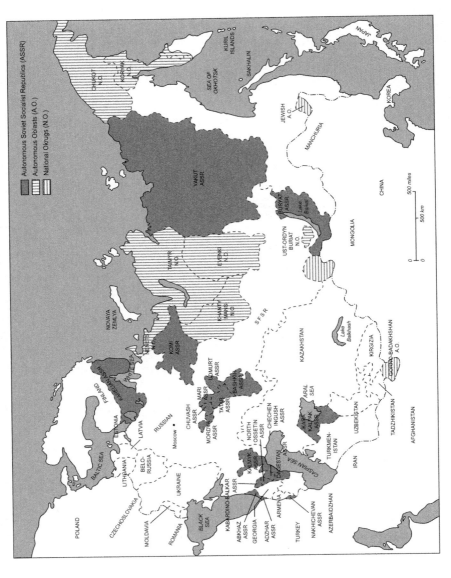

Map 0.1 Political-administrative map of the USSR until 1991

1   Origins of the Cold War

A static power declines but a dynamic power expands. Is this statement a sophism, in other words false, or does it reveal the underlying causes of the monumental conflict which engulfed the Soviet Union and the US for over four decades after 1945? Both the US and Russia were revolutionary powers. They possessed universal visions of how to improve the lot of humankind. From a Marxist perspective, to be a static power meant that one's state was in decline. The goal of communism required an expansionary policy and this would continue until the goal of a communist society had been achieved worldwide. Likewise, the US understood that its prosperity depended on what happened outside its borders. President Harry Truman put it very succinctly:

> If communism is allowed to absorb the free nations then we would be isolated from our sources of supply and detached from our friends. Then we would have to take defense measures which might really bankrupt our economy, and change our way of life so that we couldn't recognize it as American any longer.
>
> (Leffler 1992: 13–14)

Was this just rhetoric to gain popular support for higher taxes to fund the Marshall Plan, extend military help to states facing a communist threat and promote business opportunities abroad, or was it a core belief of the Truman administration? The thrust of this book is that the Americans linked liberty, justice and freedom to a liberal market economy and the right of the individual to self-betterment. By the same token, a communist society was collectivist. The Soviet version had almost eliminated private property and private trade. The state dominated the economy. A small group of decision makers enjoyed the right to decide how the economy developed. In ideology, there was a ruling party and a ruling ideology. This party had a monopoly of political power. No dissenting voices were permitted. Where the American way was pluralistic and there were myriad economic decision makers, the Soviet way was to mobilise the population from the top down.

In 1945 no one could say for certain which revolutionary path, the Soviet or the American, would prove victorious. Europe was in ruins. Germany, its leading economy, was in total collapse. The same applied to Japan. Korea and South East Asia were economic cripples. There was a widespread feeling in Europe that old-style capitalism was finished. It had led the continent into a disastrous, fratricidal war. The new order would have to attend to the people's demands for economic and social change. President Truman was warned in 1945 that if actions were not taken to alleviate the suffering in Europe, the whole region could fall to communism. Desperate people were willing to adopt desperate solutions. However, it was only in 1947 that large-scale economic programmes, such as the Marshall Plan, got under way. Likewise, in Japan, in 1947, the US switched from nurturing reform of political and economic institutions to reviving the Japanese economy. This was based on securing raw materials (Japan is a resource-poor country) in East and South East Asia and markets in the US. Hence, we can say that in 1947 key economic decisions were taken which conditioned political and military policy decisions. In order for the market economy to develop, stability and security were essential. The task of the politicians and military was to provide this. The Americans perceived that political and military actions would be ineffective without rising living standards. Marx and his latter-day apostle Lenin had recognised this decades before. What became known later as consumerism would decide the titanic battle between the two revolutionary models. It was only in the 1970s that the Americans could feel that they had won the contest economically.

The opening of the archives in the former Soviet Union, Eastern Europe and China has resulted in a flood of publications. Has recent scholarship solved problems such as who was responsible for the Cold War; why it broke out; whether it was an accident or entirely predictable; whether it could have ended in the 1950s or the 1960s had the opportunities been grasped, given the massive arsenals on both sides; why a nuclear war did not break out; and why it ended as it did? Did the military confrontation between the superpowers destroy the Soviet Union or was its collapse due to other factors? The answer is that the more there is published, the more opaque the problems become. Monocausal answers are no longer acceptable. What is clear is that the conflict was immensely complex and worldwide. Asia came into the equation in the 1950s, Africa in the 1960s, and Latin America was embroiled in the same decade with Castro's revolution in Cuba.

Euphoria consumed the Soviet Union in 1945 as it had won a titanic struggle with Germany which few observers in 1941 had thought possible; the Soviet Union was now the most powerful country in Europe. Stalin held to the old concept that the more territory one controlled the more secure one was. The Red Army had fought its way through Eastern Europe to Berlin, and there was a Soviet zone of Germany and a Soviet sector in Berlin. The Soviet Union had no intention of retreating from these territories. Churchill thought of launching an attack on the Soviet Union on 1 July 1945, in alliance with the German Wehrmacht, to force it back to its own frontiers. It was labelled Operation Unthinkable, and it proved to be unthinkable as President Truman would have none of it. Stalin could feel secure in what was soon labelled his Soviet Empire because he believed President Roosevelt had recognised Eastern Europe as a Soviet sphere of influence. The Soviet *vozhd* sought two objectives in his dealings with the Allies: to be recognised as an equal and for Soviet security needs to be met. Access to the Soviet zone of Germany ran through Poland so the government there had to be well disposed towards Moscow. Roosevelt thought Eastern Europeans would have to learn to live with the new reality.

Roosevelt died on 12 April 1945 at a critical juncture in relations between Moscow and the Allies. A post-war settlement had to be agreed upon which satisfied all the victors. Roosevelt might have pulled off this difficult balancing act but his successors could not. First of all, President Truman, a newcomer to foreign affairs, did not regard Stalin as an equal and did not regard Eastern Europe as war booty for the Soviet Union. On these two vital questions he was poles apart from Roosevelt.

There are many theories about the reasons for the Cold War (Halliday 1983: 24–28):

- *The Soviet threat.* All the conflicts and crises originated with the Soviet Union and were caused by Soviet expansionism. This in turn was part and parcel of Marxist-Leninist ideology which envisaged the world victory of socialism over capitalism. Hence, one state is blamed for all the problems that arise in international relations.
- *American imperialism.* This is the mirror image of the previous view, with Washington the root of all evil, emanating from predatory, expansionist capitalism. Again responsibility is ascribed to the actions of one state with the other trying to avoid armed conflict. Capitalism is viewed as requiring confrontation and military production to survive.
- *The superpowers theory.* Developed by the Chinese in the 1960s to demonstrate that Moscow had departed from the true Marxist-Leninist path, this view regards the superpowers as colluding and competing in an attempt to rule the world. This underlines the break between Beijing and Moscow and reveals Chinese insecurity. In the 1970s there is rapprochement with the US, which in turn alarms Russia.
- *The theory of the arms race.* The build-up of nuclear weapons had reached proportions where it appeared to be out of control. Both East and West were responsible. Hence, the stopping and reversing of the arms race was of paramount importance. This theory was especially popular among those in the peace movement.
- *North-South theory.* Proponents of this view perceive the main conflict in the world as that between North and South, between rich and poor nations and

between dominant and dominated states. The contest for the leading position in the Third World is the motive behind all conflict.

- *West-West theory.* World politics is dominated by conflicts among rich capitalist states. The Russian-American conflict is a smoke screen for the real conflict: that between the US, Japan and the European Union. The origins of Cold War II are to be found in the increasingly sharp conflicts among rich capitalist states. These, in turn, promote and exacerbate conflicts within the Third World.
- *Intrastate theory.* The domestic policies of states determine their foreign policy. Changes in foreign policy are related to movements in internal power relations, new economic weaknesses and alterations in social composition. Politicians use international events to resolve internal tensions and overcome domestic competitors.
- *Class conflict.* This is based on the Marxist analysis of class conflict as the motor of change. Tension is the product of the ebb and flow of social revolution. The conflict between capitalism and communism is expressed in tensions between the superpowers. The revolutionary movement in the Third World inevitably sucks in the superpowers.

There are three main explanations for the origins of the Cold War:

1   The orthodox or traditional
2   The revisionist
3   The post-revisionist.

The orthodox or traditional

The expression 'Cold War' first appeared in 1946 and became common currency in 1947, and from 1950 was taken over by both sides of the Iron Curtain and used worldwide. The term originated with Herbert B. Swope who joined Bernard M. Baruch in the US delegation to the UN atomic energy commission in 1946 (he borrowed it from George Orwell). The objective of the commission was to prevent the spread of atomic weapons. During the negotiations Swope concluded that East and West were already in a Cold War and the danger was that it could become a nuclear war.

On 9 August 1945, after the second atomic bomb had been dropped on Nagasaki, President Truman warned of the danger of a Third World War and it would be a nuclear war.

Truman was unaware that Stalin knew of the Manhattan Project, hence Stalin was not surprised when the US president informed him at the Potsdam Conference of the successful test explosion. His spies were providing vital intelligence about nuclear research. On 20 August 1945, eleven days after Nagasaki, Stalin signed a decree appointing Lavrenty Beria, his feared secret police (NKVD) chief, as head of the nuclear programme.

FINLAND

Vyborg

Leningrad

Jallinn

SWEDEN

ESTONIA

0   500 mls
0   300 km

Riga   LATVIA

LITHUANIA

Konigsberg   Kaunas   Vilnius

Minsk   SOVIET

UNION

GDR   Stettin
Since 1949   annexed by
Poland from
Germany   Bialystok

Bremen

Berlin   Pinsk

Bonn   SILESIA   Poznan   Warsaw

Erfurt   Dresden

GFR   Breslau   POLAND

Prague   Cracow

Nuremberg   CZECHOSLOVAKIA   Przemysl

Lvov   GALICIA

Munich   Chernovtsy

SWITZ.   Uzhgorod   BESSARABIA

AUSTRIA   Vienna   Kishinyov

HUNGARY   Budapest   Jassy

Trieste   ROMANIA

Belgrade   Bucharest

ITALY   YUGOSLAVIA

BULGARIA

Sofia

Tirane

ALBANIA

GREECE   TURKEY

FRANCE

GFR: German Federal Republic (West Germany)
GDR: German Democratic Republic (East Germany)

Map 1.1 The Soviet Union in Eastern Europe

In the US, the first plan for a nuclear war was drafted in December 1945, and Operation Totality envisaged that a Soviet conventional attack would lead to thirty atomic bombs being dropped on Soviet cities. This would provide enough time for the US to mobilise its conventional forces. Several more plans to counter a Soviet conventional attack were drafted between 1946 and 1948. By 1947, the US had thirteen atomic bombs, but this rose to 700 in 1949, and the Strategic Air Command was formed in March 1946.

In the Soviet Union, most resources went into atomic bomb research and the air force. As in the US, air power was regarded as primary in a future conflict. In 1947, a biological weapons facility was set up at Zagorsk, near Moscow, and the State Committee on Defence established a nuclear weapons department, headed by the brilliant physicist Igor Kurchatov. The first atomic explosion occurred in August 1949 (almost a carbon copy of Fat Boy dropped on Nagasaki) with twenty-two kilotonnes of explosives, near Semipalatinsk, Kazakhstan.

Truman thought he had two aces up his sleeve: the atomic bomb and credits to rebuild the shattered Soviet economy. These could be deployed to force concessions and allow American policy to prevail. Even before the war was over Moscow had asked for credits, and the point was made that this would provide markets for post-war US industry. The Soviet view was that peace would be accompanied by an economic crisis as millions of servicemen and women would have to be found jobs. Capitalism would spawn conflict as countries fought for markets, and the task for the Soviet Union was not to become enmeshed in these wars but to benefit from the fallout.

Soviet ideology was accorded great significance in Western analyses of Soviet aims. Marxism-Leninism envisaged the whole world becoming communist. Hence it was aggressive and eager to expand, and this was regarded as the main reason for the Cold War. Stalin's speech of 9 February 1946 blamed the capitalist powers for the war – an orthodox Marxist analysis – and warned the Soviet people that the way ahead would be hard. He talked of three five-year plans (fifteen years) to restore Soviet economic and military power, but the speech was misread by some as hostile. In reality, Stalin was saying that every sacrifice had to be made to rebuild the country. The inability of Western negotiators to achieve their aims led to frustration, and this fuelled the belief that Moscow was to blame. Some intellectual respectability was provided by George F. Kennan in his 'Long Telegram' of 22 February 1946, followed by his 'Mr X' article in *Foreign Affairs*, in July. The Soviet response soon appeared and Nikolai Novikov, the Soviet ambassador in Washington, sent a 4,000-word report to Stalin concluding that 'American monopoly capitalism' was aiming at world domination.

Winston Churchill weighed in with his Iron Curtain speech of 5 March 1946. President Truman was in the audience in Fulton, Missouri, and had seen some drafts of the speech. However, it did not resonate with the American public at the time but the old warrior, out of office, knew how to shock his listeners.

The concept of containment and then rollback emerged, but because nuclear war was unthinkable, the only weapons which could be used were words. In the propaganda war, the Soviets proved themselves past masters of the art but the Americans did have an ace: jazz. It was a winner everywhere, and the Soviet Army even had a jazz band. Not surprisingly, Louis Armstrong took France by storm.

Another indication of the coming Cold War was the exchanges in the UN Security Council on the Iran Crisis of early 1946. The Soviets had to leave Iran by 2 March 1946 but had promoted the appearance of Azeri and Kurdish autonomous republics in the north west of Iran, and they also wanted a large oil concession in 1946. Exchanges were relatively polite but the divisions between the Soviet Union and the US and UK became evident. France and China, the other permanent members of the Security Council, tended towards neutrality. The autonomous republics were crushed by the Iranian army, and this episode drove Iran into the American camp. A similar scenario was played out in Turkey, where Moscow demanded territorial concessions and, as a result, Turkey turned to the US for support. An attempt by the Soviet Union to acquire a foothold in Libya was rebuffed by the West.

The capital of the Kurdish autonomous republic was Mahabad; Qazi Moham-mad was president and its military commander was Mullah Mustafa Barzani, whose son, Masoud Barzani, was born in Mahabad, in August 1946. He is now the president of Iraqi Kurdistan. Mustafa Barzani and others fled north, across the Araks river, into the Soviet Union, where they remained until 1958. Barzani thanked Khrushchev for the assistance they had received. While in the Soviet Union, Kurdish language newspapers appeared in Erevan, Tbilisi, Moscow and Leningrad and radio broadcasts began in Erevan. Messages of 'Leninist interna-tionalism' and 'equality of peoples' found considerable resonance in Kurdish communities, especially in Turkey.

Had the UK not intervened in Greece after the war the communists almost certainly would have come to power by military means. The economic weakness of the UK led to appeals to Washington to intervene and stem the communist tide, and the Truman Doctrine was the response. Any country threatened by communism would receive American aid. The Soviets were seen as helping the Greek communists but, in reality, it was the Yugoslavs who were extending aid. Stalin opposed this policy. Truman had to use apocalyptic language to get his message across: if Greece and then Turkey went communist, the world would soon be going red. The same rhetoric was applied to Western Europe which was run-ning out of US dollars to pay for vital imports. The European Recovery Programme, or Marshall Plan, had to be couched in language which would exclude the Soviet Union, and Moscow ensured that no satellite country joined. As the Soviets had opted out of the Bretton Woods agreement (1944), which had established the International Monetary Fund and the World Bank, they cut themselves off from Western loans. To compensate they took enormous amounts of war reparations from their German zone and the other countries under their control.

The communist seizure of power in Czechoslovakia in February 1948 – masterminded by a Soviet official, Valerian Zorin – appeared to confirm the belief that the Soviet Union was an expansionary, aggressive power.

Stalin regarded Germany as the acid test of Allied cooperation. He assumed that it would go communist in the long term so there was no need to force events in the short term. His main objective was not ideology but security as the *vozhd* feared a resurgent Germany might seek revenge for its defeat in 1945. The first objective, therefore, was to ensure that the country was not remilitarised, and second, for the country to remain neutral. Western frustration at the lack of progress in agreeing to a pan-German government led to the decision to issue a new currency, the Deutsche Mark, in the western zones and in the western sectors of Berlin. Restrictions on Western access to Berlin began in March 1948 and a full blockade was proclaimed in June 1948. The Soviet commandant informed Stalin that Berlin could not be provisioned from the air; preliminary US and British analyses agreed with this, but President Truman refused to accept it, and the airlift began. At first, it brought in goods for the garrisons and then for the West Berlin public. It transformed his political fortunes and portrayed him as a strong leader capable of standing up to Stalin. Without it he would probably have failed to be re-elected. The airlift turned the Amis (as the Berliners called the Americans) and the British into heroes. By the time the blockade was lifted in May 1949 the decision had been taken to set up a separate West German state and a military alliance, the North Atlantic Treaty Organization (NATO). Without the blockade the latter might not have come into being as many Americans opposed such a military commitment to Europe.

So why did Stalin allow the blockade to last so long? The longer it lasted the greater the damage caused to the Soviet position in Europe and internationally. First, he did not think the city could survive, and he also had the Tito affair to deal with. The Yugoslav leader wanted to proceed rapidly to a socialist economy; Stalin regarded this as inopportune but the main point was that Tito was promoting a Balkan confederation. He declared himself a loyal follower of Stalin but this availed him nothing, and he was expelled from the Communist Information Bureau (Cominform) in June 1948. A witch hunt for alleged Titoists in Eastern Europe began and show trials were held.

In the Soviet Union there was the Leningrad affair. Andrei Zhdanov, Stalin's deputy for party affairs and head of the Central Committee apparat, died in August 1948; he had headed and was patron of the Leningrad clan. Georgy Malenkov took over his role, but without a patron the Leningraders were exposed. Nikolai Voznesensky, head of the state planning commission (Gosplan), Aleksei Kuznetsov and Pyotr Popkov and other officials were charged, in February 1949, with trying to turn the Leningrad organisation into a power base. As such it was an 'anti-Leninist faction'. In October 1950, Voznesensky, Kuznetsov, Popkov and three other leading officials were shot. Another 200 were sentenced to between ten and twenty-five years in prison and over 2,000 others were sent into exile. All the evidence had been fabricated. The same happened to Molotov's Jewish wife, Polina Zhemchuzhina, who was accused of being involved with anti-Soviet Jewish organisations. Stalin instructed Molotov to divorce her which he did; in January 1949, she was expelled from the party and sent to prison, but she was released on Stalin's death and the couple were reunited. Molotov was dismissed as foreign minister in March 1949. Zhemchuzhina's disgrace initiated an anti-Jewish campaign which saw the murder, on Stalin's orders, of Solomon Mikhoels, a leading Yiddish theatre director, in January 1948. The members of the Jewish Anti-Fascist Committee were arrested. A campaign was launched, in January 1949, against 'rootless cosmopolitans'. This was a clear reference to Jews and many were dismissed from their jobs and arrested. A letter sent to Stalin reveals how widespread distrust of Jews was: 'Just as the entire German people bear responsibility for Hitler's aggression, so too the Jewish people must bear responsibility for the actions of the bourgeois cosmopolitans.' Trials between May and July 1952 resulted in all but one of the members of the Anti-Fascist Committee being shot, and Stalin came to regard Jews as subversives towards the end of his life. He told top party officials in late 1952: 'Any Jew-nationalist is an agent of American intelligence . . . Jew-nationalists believe that their nation was saved by the US (there you can become rich, a bourgeois, etc.). They feel they have an obligation to the Americans' (Khlevniuk 2015: 286).

In 1949, Edward R. Stettinius, Roosevelt's secretary of state at Yalta, produced an analysis which included criticisms of US policy after Roosevelt's death. Charles E. Bohlen took great exception to these comments, and he told Stettinius that all those involved in formulating policy towards the Soviet Union agreed that the Cold War had originated in the 'character and nature of the Soviet state' (Costigliola 2012: 7) and in its ideology. He did not accept that the Truman administration bore any burden of responsibility for the tensions in US-Soviet relations. Bohlen spelled out the generally accepted view: 'Yalta proved the impossibility of expecting agreements with the Soviet Union to provide solutions to the post-war world.' Stettinius's view that Yalta was a good starting point, which had been dissipated by mutual suspicion on both sides, was absolutely false. Bohlen's vehement defence of the prevailing wisdom leads one to the conclusion that there was some substance to Stettinius's criticisms.

The Soviet analysis of the origins of the Cold War was almost a mirror image of the Western view. It was articulated by Andrei Zhdanov, in September 1947, in Poland, on the occasion of the founding of the Cominform. He divided the world into two camps: the peaceful communist one and the aggressive Western one. Countries such as India and Indonesia were not included in either.

The revisionist

Many of the documents published in the *Foreign Relations of the United States* covering the war and its immediate aftermath undermined the simple good guy-bad guy interpretation of the origins of the conflict. This permitted a new school of thought to reject the traditional view as a self-serving capitalist exposé based on a profound misconception of Soviet domestic and external reality. The early revisionists are to be found among the critics of Truman's foreign policy such as the former vice presidential candidate Henry A. Wallace, and among European opponents of Western integration and in the 'neutral' movement (between the US and the USSR) of the late 1940s. The writings of William A. Williams, whose first major publication appeared in 1959, had a seminal influence; the protests against the Vietnam War and the rise of the 'New Left' in the late 1960s and early 1970s completed the process. Books by Walter LaFeber (1968, new edition 2006) and Gabriel Kolko (1972) argued that American policymakers were following a capitalist agenda in opening up Eastern Europe and the rest of the world to American companies, and they saw this as being in the US national interest. Gar Alperovitz (1985) went even as far as arguing that the decision to drop the atomic bomb on Japan was an attempt to intimidate Moscow. The fact that the US enjoyed an atomic monopoly before 1949 is also regarded as a major reason for the Cold War.

At first sight, the revisionist school's analyses are reminiscent of a Soviet or Marxist-Leninist viewpoint. Washington was responsible for the Cold War, and it pursued an expansionary political and economic policy with total disregard for legitimate Soviet political, economic and security interests – in other words, imperialism in action. This led to its rejection by the traditionalists and other critics of the regime, but the Left loved it. The revisionists gave succour to those who opposed Eisenhower's foreign policy.

The post-revisionist

The orthodox and revisionist viewpoints found some common ground in the 1970s. The basic premise was that the perceived threat from the other side was exaggerated and thus led to misguided policies; a rapid arms race was one of the results. The Cuban Missile Crisis of 1962 had brought the world within a hair's breadth of nuclear war. Détente emerged and there was an East-West German easing of tension. The 1972 Anti-Ballistic Missile Treaty (ABM) revealed that an agreement could be reached on limiting the expansion of nuclear weapons. This led to the view that failures in communication between East and West had given rise to the Cold War, so if mistrust could be overcome the conflict could be put to rest. The end of the Cold War in 1991 came about not because of the military superiority of one side or the other but by a change in perception on the Soviet and American sides. Gorbachev concluded that the Soviets could not win the arms race, and as they had enough conventional and nuclear forces to defend themselves, what was the point of adding to these arsenals? However, conclusions about the end of the Cold War differed. Gorbachev regarded it as a victory for common sense – a draw if you like – but the Americans perceived it as a political and military victory.

An important point to make about the Cold War is that its origins lay in the Stalin period. Stalin was the most formidable leader the Soviet Union ever produced, and he played a weak hand brilliantly. None of his successors was in the same league and none of them ever acquired the power wielded by him. They had to debate policy with their Politburo colleagues, but Stalin's security gains proved to be a Pyrrhic victory. He left his successors a flawed legacy, especially a resentful empire in Eastern Europe, and it rapidly became an economic burden. Kennedy and Khrushchev might have reached a rapprochement as the latter needed to cut Soviet defence expenditure. One of the reasons for Khrushchev's dismissal in 1964 was his reckless risk-taking, and a major complaint was that he had failed to consult his colleagues when taking critical security and domestic decisions. The consequence of his risk-taking was to reinforce the traditionalist view about Soviet expansionism. The Soviet leader was so unpredictable that the rational response was to increase military spending. The breakthrough came in the Brezhnev era as he was a consensus-building, low-risk leader; this promoted the post-revisionist view that agreements could be reached to cool the Cold War. So it is not surprising that the 1970s decade was the heyday of the post-revisionist interpretation. In some ways this was surprising as the 1970s saw the expansion of communism in Africa and elsewhere aided by Soviet and Cuban military power. Détente ended in 1979 with the Soviet invasion of Afghanistan. The traditionalist viewpoint appeared again to be the rational one, but all this ended under Gorbachev.

A major weakness of the post-revisionist argument, based on the failure of communication, is that it excludes the power political aspect. It is not regarded as a power struggle for world dominance, conducted on a global scale – one that was based on escalating and de-escalating tension until one side or the other won. Khrushchev's policy of peaceful coexistence was not a peace offering and only referred to relations with the West, and the battle for influence in the rest of the world went on unabated. Peaceful coexistence was strongly contested by China, for instance, which regarded it as kowtowing to the West and thereby a betrayal of Marxism. To Mao Zedong the contest between capitalism and communism was a war of the worlds, one that had to be fought to the death.

The fact that the death of Stalin did not signal the end the Cold War reveals that it had deeper roots which can be traced back to Imperial Russia's role in Europe. Imperial Russia regarded itself as the natural defender of Orthodox Christians in the Balkans. Russia ruled Warsaw and a sizable portion of Poland before 1914. The Crimean War (1854–6) was fought by Britain and France to prevent Russia taking over the Straits, which would have given it access to the Mediterranean, but the other great powers also wished to deny it this control. The irony is that if Russia had remained on the Allied side until November 1918, it would have secured these waterways. Russia had no natural frontier with Eastern Europe and had suffered various invasions – in 1812 by Napoleon and in 1914 and 1941 by Germany. Hence security on its western front was always a top priority. As the wry Czech joke goes, Russia always regards a good neighbour as one it occupies.

2 Cold War
1949–53

The dropping of the atomic bombs on Japan had a dual purpose: force the Japanese government into an early surrender and intimidate the Soviets and make them, in the words of Secretary of State James Byrnes, 'more manageable' when discussing the post-war world (Burr and Kimball 2015: 12). The dominant US position led to the practice of nuclear threat diplomacy. Nuclear weapons were deployed, their use was threatened and nuclear alerts were carried out to coerce adversaries into concessions or to cease activities which were judged inimical to US interests. Hence nuclear policy was both a deterrent strategy but also one to coerce and intimidate.

The US administration concluded that in order to ensure its continued wellbeing, no adversary or coalition of adversaries could be allowed to dominate Europe and Asia. This led to the policy of establishing foreign bases worldwide to cope with military threats and the risk of being cut off from raw materials and foreign markets. It was natural to conclude that the Soviet Union was becoming the greatest military threat to American power. Despite the fact that President Truman abhorred the use of nuclear weapons because of their indiscriminate destruction of military targets and civilians, he and his military advisers set out to ensure that the US was capable of waging a nuclear war successfully. It was thought that the threat of conventional or nuclear bombing would undermine the enemy's resolve and thereby secure victory. Immediately after the nuclear attack on Japan, the air force was thinking of forming a group which could drop atomic bombs on any part of the planet and, as a result, the Strategic Air Command (SAC) was set up in March 1946. A secret agreement with the Royal Air Force to construct nuclear storage sites at two air bases was concluded. SAC assumed the key role in US nuclear thinking, but by the end of 1947 there were only eighteen B-29s capable of carrying nuclear bombs and only thirteen bombs which could be used. By late 1948, there were thirty B-29s and fifty-six bombs available, but this was far short of the 200 needed to destroy key Soviet targets. During the Berlin blockade, bombers were based in West Germany and England but were not capable of carrying atomic bombs, and it was a game of bluff as the Soviets could not be sure that atomic weapons would not be used. The Berlin crisis also led President Truman to agree to the use of nuclear weapons in the first instance, as he concluded that deploying sufficient conventional armed forces would be prohibitively expensive and would ruin the US economy (Burr and Kimball 2015: 13–17).

Scientists and politicians wrestled with the problem of what would happen when the Soviet Union developed its own atomic bomb. Bertrand Russell, the famous British mathematician, advocated a nuclear strike against the Soviets in October 1946, and by 1948 he was proposing a preventive war to eliminate a Soviet nuclear threat. John von Neumann, the founder of game theory and a leading nuclear scientist, in 1950, said: 'If you say bomb them tomorrow, I say why not today? If you say today at five o'clock, I say why not one o'clock?' (Trachtenberg 1991: 104). George Kennan, in June 1950, commented that a war with the Soviet Union before it had built up its nuclear arsenal might, in the long term, 'be the best solution for us' (Trachtenberg 1991: 103). Charles Bohlen, of the State Department, also ruminated about what Americans might think in the future about not acting in the present.

The Berlin Blockade was the first time since 1945 that a military conflict between the Soviet Union and the West could have erupted. Washington had a plan for a preventive war (First Strike), with thirty-four atomic bombs being dropped on twenty-four Soviet cities if the crisis escalated. The atomic First Strike would provide the time to mobilise conventional forces. On 10 May 1949, the blockade was lifted by Moscow and the crisis passed but it had major ramifications. The danger from the East led to the formation of the North Atlantic Treaty Organization (NATO) on 4 April 1949. Truman regarded it as a 'gamble', and George F. Kennan and Charles Bohlen believed it to be a mistake. Would it get through Congress? It did with an overwhelming majority, as Stalin had frightened the Americans into guaranteeing the security of the Western Europeans.

With the blockade over, the West attempted to overturn communism in Albania in December 1949. It was a disaster because Kim Philby, a Soviet agent in British intelligence, then in Washington, revealed what was being planned. The explosion of the Soviet atomic bomb in August 1949 ended any hopes of military action to remove a communist regime. The bomb also demonstrated the inadequacy of US military planning which had assumed that its nuclear monopoly protected it against a Soviet conventional attack. Washington now had to spend to bring its conventional forces up to the levels of the Soviet. This was not popular, and Truman still hoped for some accommodation with Moscow, but the war in Korea ended such dreams. NSC-68 was the result and it envisaged a massive increase in defence spending. This led President Truman to lament on

9 December 1950: 'I have worked for peace for five years and six months and it looks like World War III is near. I hope not.'

The Korean War was the first time that the use of nuclear weapons was seriously considered. Washington incorrectly concluded that the North Koreans had initiated the conflict without consulting Moscow and worried that the latter might intervene. The Americans hesitated to use nuclear weapons against another Asian nation, but the entry of China changed the situation. President Truman, on 30 November 1950, stated that the US would deploy 'every weapon we have' against Chinese and North Korean civilian and military targets. Worldwide opposition forced him to retract his words and declare that the atomic bomb would not be used. Nine atomic bombs were deployed in Guam, but the North Koreans and Chinese paid no attention. As a result, the president gave up threatening a nuclear strike because the enemy did not believe him.

President Eisenhower and Secretary of State John Foster Dulles had no such qualms about the use of nuclear weapons, and it became integral to their military thinking as they regarded the atomic bomb as just another weapon. Control of nuclear weapons passed from the Atomic Energy Agency to the Department of Defense in April 1953. The president came to believe that his threat to use nuclear weapons had played a 'decisive part in terminating the Korean War' (Burr and Kimball 2015: 22). This is almost certainly incorrect, but that is irrelevant because the president believed it, and it strengthened his conviction that nuclear threats were an effective way of conducting diplomacy.

The People's Republic of China

In February 1949, the People's Liberation Army (PLA) took Beijing, and in October it secured the last remaining key city in the south, Guangzhou. Chiang Kai-shek's only option was to decamp to Taiwan.

So why did Mao defeat Chiang? Even in 1949 Chiang had more troops than Mao. Chiang, in Taiwan, analysed the reasons for his defeat. The Guomindang or Nationalists had not learnt enough from Mao. 'Disdaining the dialectic was the reason why we lost,' mused Chiang. The Guomindang should have adopted democratic centralism, set up a youth movement and made workplace cells the basic building block of the party. The Leninist model was thus superior to the American model of democracy and a liberal market economy. Mao found it astonishing that the US military did not intervene to save the Nationalists. The communist tactic of unleashing a class war in the countryside (ironically pioneered by the Nationalists) was a great success. The Guomindang could never control inflation. This can be illustrated by the following: in 1940, 100 yuan bought a pig; in 1943 a chicken; in 1945 a fish; in 1946 an egg; and in 1947 one third of a box of matches. Neither could corruption be tamed.

Just before the People's Republic came into being, Mao outlined three major goals: set out a separate stove; put our house in order before inviting guests; and one-sidedly follow the Soviet Union. The first two goals implied that the task was to remove the influence and impact of imperialism in China. A long list of imperialists had ruled China. The Jin and Yuan dynasties ruled from 1115 to 1368. A Han Chinese dynasty, the Ming, took over from 1368 to 1644. Then China again succumbed to foreign rule, the Manchu Qing dynasty lasting until 1911. Hence over the previous thousand years, a Han Chinese dynasty only ruled for about a quarter of this period. Britain, the US, Russia, Italy, Germany, Portugal, France and Japan had all occupied parts of China. The years between 1839 and 1949 are known in China as the 'century of humiliation'. Soon the Soviet Union was to join the league of imperialists. For Mao, it was time the Han Chinese took control of their destiny. The third goal allowed China to join the communist commonwealth and hence the world of the future.

The People's Republic of China was proclaimed by Mao Zedong in Tiananmen Square on 1 October 1949. Why was 1 October chosen and not 25 September, for instance? The Qing dynasty was toppled in October 1911 and the Bolsheviks seized power during October, so October had symbolic significance. The new national flag was red or communist but also identified with China's red earth. The four yellow stars which surrounded the larger star in the left-hand corner represented the national unity of the classes in society: the bourgeoisie, the petit bourgeoisie, the workers and peasants. The new order in China would be communist, nationalist and pro-peasant.

Mao declared that China was no longer 'on its knees' and it would stop kowtowing before foreigners. The task was to destroy the old world and create a new one. China had accounted for 30 per cent of the world gross domestic product (GDP) as late as 1820 – an amount greater than the GDP of Europe and the US combined – and was still the largest world economy in 1860.

Taking power was a stupendous achievement and modernisation would now follow a communist and not a capitalist model, but Mao had no understanding of economics, at least in the sense of raising living standards. The goal was to make China militarily strong enough to be able to stand on its own feet. The 'century of humiliation' had come to an end, and henceforth China would seek to develop in a way which corresponded to Chinese characteristics. Foreigners, first and foremost the Soviet Union, still possessed concessions on Chinese soil, and persuading them to leave was an important task.

China, economically, was in a poor state with the vast majority of the population below the poverty line. Investment and know-how would mainly have to come from one source: the Soviet Union. Capitalism had not industrialised China, and in 1952 industrial output accounted for less than 3 per cent of GDP. The state would now industrialise the country, but American capital and expertise would not be accepted.

In order to gain the maximum advantage from the Soviet connection, Mao had to be obsequious to Stalin. He had played this game during the 1930s when he knew that the *vozhd* could have removed him with a flick of his finger. The Stalinist model was de rigueur if he wanted the boss's support. In the early stages – until the mid-1950s – it was the Leninist model which was more relevant:

Map 2.1 The People's Republic of China

a single dominant party claiming the monopoly of power; democratic centralism to ensure a power vertical; a ruling bureaucracy; a cadre party where iron discipline was enforced; the ruthless use of terror to eliminate opposition in the party and outside; a powerful secret police to strike fear into opponents; a military devoted to the party; the commanding heights of the economy in state hands; state control of foreign trade; and predominantly private agriculture with market prices being regulated by the state. Lenin had provided a master plan of how to take and keep power, but Mao pretended that he had learnt it all from Stalin.

Mao's problem was that Stalin had no intention of developing China into a state which could challenge the hegemony of the Soviet Union in the communist world. The risk for Moscow was that China, not the Soviet Union, would become the beacon of hope for Asia and the developing world. Mao could turn into an even more formidable Tito. Hence the master's first priority was Soviet security.

Mao kept on asking for permission to visit Moscow but Stalin kept him at arm's length. On 26 April 1948, Stalin agreed that Mao could come to Moscow but retracted his invitation on 10 May. On 4 July 1948, he informed the *vozhd* that he was about to leave Harbin and fly to the Soviet capital. A reply came ten days later, but he was told that because of the harvest, leading comrades would leave in August and remain away until November, so the end of November would be an appropriate time for the Chinese leader to come to Moscow (Mao saw through this flimsy excuse). Mao informed Stalin that his bags had been packed, leather shoes acquired and a thick woollen coat made, and he kept on asking for an invitation. On 28 September 1948, he wrote that on a 'series of questions it is necessary to report personally to the Central Committee and the *glavny khozyain* (big boss)'. Stalin agreed he could come in late November, but the visit was postponed, and on 14 January 1949 Stalin again suggested Mao postpone his trip. Anastas Mikoyan, the *vozhd*'s diplomat for all seasons, was dispatched to tell Mao that such a visit would be understood in the West as one to receive instructions. This 'would lead to a loss of prestige for the Communist Party of China (CPC) and would be used by the imperialists and the Chiang Kai-shek clique against the Chinese communists'.

Mikoyan stayed in China from 30 January to 8 February 1949. The talks were wide-ranging and Mao went out of his way to portray himself as a 'humble student of Stalin'. Mikoyan viewed the Chinese revolution as an event of worldwide importance and believed that the CPC's experience enriched Marxism. Mao asked for military aid, a loan of $300 million and Soviet specialists to help run the country. Mikoyan advised the nationalisation of Japanese, British and French but not American property. Mao wanted Outer Mongolia to unite with Inner Mongolia (which was part of China) but Mikoyan retorted that Outer Mongolia was already independent. If they did unite in the future, they would form an independent state. Moscow regarded the 1945 Sino-Soviet Treaty as an unequal one and was willing to withdraw its forces from Port Arthur, but the Changchun Railway, on the other hand, had been built with Russian money and was therefore not part of the unequal treaty.

In August 1945, Chiang Kai-shek, the Guomindang leader, had been forced by the US to sign a thirty-year Sino-Soviet Treaty of Friendship and Alliance, along with other agreements. These stemmed from accords reached at the Yalta conference in February 1945, which awarded the Soviet Union territories lost as a result of the Russo-Japanese War of 1904–5. The Chinese Changchun Railway would be jointly owned and operated by China and the USSR; Outer Mongolia was recognised as a Soviet satellite and it became the People's Republic of Mongolia; the Port Arthur naval base was to be jointly used by China and the Soviet Union; and a long-term lease on the port of Dalian was agreed. In return, Stalin recognised Chiang as the leader of China and advised the CPC to submit to him. The geopolitical aim of reclaiming all that Tsarist Russia had lost in north east China took precedence over supporting the CPC, and the latter was advised not to expect Soviet assistance in its struggle for power. In June 1948, a request for arms to launch an attack in Manchuria was turned down by Moscow. However, the Soviet Union stepped up economic aid, including restoring railway lines and building bridges. The CPC supported the expulsion of Yugoslavia from the Cominform.

A CPC delegation, led by Liu Shaoqi, arrived in the Soviet Union on 26 June 1949 and left on 14 August. This was the first high-level delegation to the Soviet Union since Mao had achieved supremacy in the CPC. In late June, Mao declared that the CPC's policy of 'leaning to one side' (the Soviet Union) while Liu was in Moscow (actually he had decided on this policy a year earlier). The political base for the alliance was being laid.

The Chinese would get a $300 million loan at 1 per cent interest, and the first group of specialists were ready to leave for China. Stalin hoped the CPC would accept more responsibility for assisting national democratic movements in colonial and semi-colonial states since the Chinese revolutionary experience would be highly relevant to these countries. The boss proposed a division of labour: China would concentrate on the East and the Soviet Union on the West. Despite these fine words, the Korean War was to demonstrate that Stalin had no intention of affording China primacy in Asia. The USSR would assist China in constructing an army, air force and navy, but Stalin made clear that he would not support an attack on Taiwan as it could trigger a Third World War. In May and June 1949, a US diplomat discussed US-China relations with a senior communist official. Nothing came of these talks as Mao had already decided to side with the Soviet Union (Shen and Xia 2015: 11–37).

In the euphoric days after the founding of the People's Republic, Mao waited for the invitation of invitations: a summons from the *vozhd*. None came and so on 8 November he sent a telegram saying he would like to come and would put the Sino-Soviet Treaty of 1945 at the top of his agenda. Zhou Enlai, now number three in the party hierarchy and foreign minister, was dispatched to tell the Soviet ambassador that Mao would like to pay his respects to Stalin on his seventieth birthday, on 21 December 1949. He was thinking of spending four months away – one month negotiating a new Sino-Soviet treaty with Stalin, two months in Eastern Europe and a month relaxing at a Soviet spa. Stalin grudgingly agreed but made clear it was not to be a state visit. Mao would be visiting Moscow as one of a group of communist leaders all cackling about how wonderful the master was. Mao left Beijing on 6 December 1949 by train and arrived in Moscow ten days later. The station clock dramatically struck twelve as he arrived, but Mao did not take with him his number two (Liu Shaoqi) or his number three (Zhou Enlai). He was greeted by Molotov and Bulganin, the latter resplendent in his marshal's uniform. Stalin received Mao in his Kremlin office later that evening, but when he met Stalin, Mao excluded his own ambassador as he expected to be humiliated and wanted to ensure that no one witnessed his discomfort.

The brief Stalin received described Mao as

> unhurried, even slow . . . He moves steadily towards any goal he sets, but not always follows a set path, often with detours . . . is a natural performer; is able to hide his feelings and can play whatever role is needed.

The Chinese leadership referred to Stalin as the 'old man'. During the first meeting Mao did not present a list of demands. He just requested advice and listened attentively to the Boss's remarks. Responding to Mao's question about the Sino-Soviet agreement, Stalin made clear that he preferred to retain the accord but was willing to make concessions in favour of the People's Republic. Annulling it could permit 'England and America' to reconsider the treaty's provisions awarding the Kurile Islands and southern Sakhalin Island to the USSR. Mao did not see through this obfuscation at the time but he did later. Stalin said that aid would be extended to the infant state, but Mao had not achieved his main objective, annulling the Sino-Soviet agreement; this would have to wait until later. Stalin even said that Mao's collected writings would be published in Russian.

Mao was ensconced in a dacha – bugged, of course – about 30 km from Moscow. All he could do was fume and look out at the snow. A succession of minions came to see him, and their task was to draw up a psychological portrait of the new Chinese Emperor. Mao complained about the food and the bed, but every now and then he was given a little treat. On one occasion he was taken to a collective farm to gaze at some cows. He was keen to meet other communist leaders but Stalin ensured he only met the Hungarian chief. On 21 December, he was seated on Stalin's right at the birthday festivities in the Bolshoi Theatre and was the first foreign guest to speak. The audience roared: 'Stalin, Mao Zedong!' Mao responded with: 'Long live Stalin, Glory to Stalin.' The Hungarian Party leader thought the ovation reached heights that the Bolshoi had seldom experienced. Then Mao returned to his dacha. He became so frustrated that he shouted at one of Stalin's aides that he had come to Moscow to negotiate not to 'eat, shit and sleep' and talked about returning to China a month early.

Mao met Stalin on 24 December, but the *vozhd* would not discuss another pet theme: the arms industry. Further, Mao's birthday on 26 December was ignored. Mao then decided to call Stalin's bluff. He shouted – in order to ensure it was heard – that he was ready to do business with the US, Britain and Japan. Diplomatic relations were established with London on 6 January 1950, and a rumour was leaked to the British press that Stalin was holding Mao under house arrest. Stalin engaged in a volte-face and began to negotiate seriously. Zhou Enlai and other officials were summoned to Moscow but they were instructed to take their time and come by train.

Only on 22 January 1950 did talks between Stalin and Mao and his team get under way – in the boss's Kremlin office. A Sino-Soviet Treaty of Friendship, Alliance and Mutual Assistance was agreed on 14 February 1950 and various other agreements were also signed. The Soviet Union lost almost all the gains it had achieved at Yalta and in the Sino-Soviet treaty. The Changchun Railway and Port Arthur, instead of passing to the USSR for thirty years, were to be returned by 1952. Property leased in Dalian was to be returned to China immediately and thereby the USSR lost its only ice-free port on the Pacific. The People's Republic renounced all claims on Outer Mongolia. A $300 million loan was extended, at 1 per cent interest, over five years, and to go on defence. The Soviet Union would begin building fifty large industrial projects and in return, Mao conceded – through gritted teeth – that Manchuria and Xinjiang were Soviet spheres of influence. The Soviets were to exploit their industrial and raw material wealth and Moscow also had the right to acquire 'surplus' tungsten, tin and antimony for fourteen years. This prevented China from selling these valuable products on the world market for dollars until the mid-1960s. Deng Xiaoping told Mikhail Gorbachev, in 1989, that of all the unequal treaties signed with Tsarist Russia and the Soviet Union, this was the most painful. China not only had to pay the wages of Soviet engineers – often ten times what a Chinese engineer earned – but had to compensate their home enterprises for the loss of their labour as all Soviet citizens were outside Chinese jurisdiction. This was reminiscent of the days of European imperialism, but the Soviet Union did agree to a treaty guaranteeing to intervene if China were attacked by Japan or its allies, in particular the US. At the signing ceremony, Stalin warned Mao that any leader who imitated Tito would soon be replaced.

Mao told Stalin that the People's Republic needed up to five years to consolidate and restore the economy. How many years of international peace would prevail? Stalin was very optimistic and pointed out that Japan and the US would not invade China. Peace might even last twenty-five years or even longer, so a military alliance between the two countries was not needed.

Stalin did pay his respects at a reception at the Metropol Hotel on the evening of 14 December to mark the signing of the treaty. He wanted it to be held in the Kremlin, but Mao demurred and eventually Stalin gave in. A handwritten invitation arrived addressed to Stalin and his wife, and this revealed that the Chinese knew nothing of the *vozhd*'s private life. As was customary, there were lots of toasts proposed and responded to. Stalin hosted a farewell luncheon on 16 February, and the Chinese delegation left the next day by train (Khlevniuk 2015: 288–93).

Throughout the negotiations Stalin addressed Mao as Gospodin (Mr.) and refused to call him comrade. This was deeply insulting to the Great Helmsman and revealed that the *vozhd* was not certain that he was a communist. He even referred to him as a 'margarine' communist.

So why did Stalin make so many concessions to Mao? He was wary of China going its own way and Mao turning into another Tito, and Sino-American relations might develop in a manner inimical to Soviet interests. He abandoned his strategic interests in north east China, but it occurred to him that there were ice-free ports and naval facilities in Korea.

The Korean War

In 1945, Korea was divided along the 38th parallel. Japanese forces surrendered to the Red Army in the North and to the Americans in the South. In the North, the Soviets installed a thirty-three-year-old Red Army officer, Kim Il-sung (literally 'Become the Sun Kim'), and in the South, the Americans installed a seventy-year-old professor, Syngman Rhee, who had spent thirty-three years in exile in the US. Skirmishes between North and South were the order of the day, and both sides concluded that the only way to reunite Korea was by military force. Stalin was cautious and his instructions to Soviet representatives in the North, in May 1947, were: 'We should not meddle too deeply in Korean affairs.'

Kim Il-sung visited Moscow in March 1949 to ask for help in taking over South Korea but Stalin declined. He kept Kim in check until he had the atomic bomb, the communists had taken over China, and Korean units fighting with the Chinese Red Army – amounting to about 50,000 troops with their weapons – had returned to North Korea. To increase the pressure on the *vozhd*, Kim even hinted of reorienting his country's policy towards China. Only the Soviet Union could provide the North with weapons, and the Chinese were also dependent on Soviet military assistance. Perhaps reverses in Western Europe could be compensated for in the East. Soviet occupation forces began to leave North Korea in late 1948, and US forces left South Korea in June 1949.

On 12 January 1950, Dean Acheson, US secretary of state, articulated a new Asia policy as Washington was washing its hands of Chiang Kai-shek's Guomindang. On 30 December 1949, the National Security Council had concluded that the 'strategic importance of Formosa [Taiwan] does not justify overt military action', and President Truman made it clear that the US would not extend military aid to Chiang. Acheson then went on to state that the greatest threat to the People's Republic was the Soviet Union which was detaching Outer Mongolia, Inner Mongolia, Manchuria and Xinjiang from China and annexing them to the Soviet Union. He also stated that the integrity of China was in America's national interest irrespective of China's communist ideology. The secretary of state was, in fact, proposing a new Sino-American relationship (Kissinger 2012: 119–20). Stalin reacted as if stung – Acheson's intention – and sent foreign minister Andrei Vyshinsky and Vyacheslav Molotov to inform Mao and ask for a rebuttal of the

Acheson 'slander', but Mao merely asked Xinhua, the Chinese news agency, to publish a rebuttal. Acheson went on to define the US military defence perimeter in the Far East. It ran from the Aleutians through Japan and the Philippines. South Korea and Taiwan were not mentioned, nor was Vietnam. This was not an innovation as he was merely reiterating what General Douglas MacArthur had stated in March 1949. The Soviet ambassador in Pyongyang sent a telegram about Acheson's speech and reported that Kim Il-sung had asked repeatedly for a meeting with Stalin to discuss the reunification of Korea. In September 1949, the Soviet Politburo had expressly prohibited the North Koreans from engaging in any military measures near the 38th parallel. On 30 January 1950, Stalin changed his mind saying he would talk to Kim Il-sung. If North Korea won the war the whole of Korea would fall under Soviet control. If it lost the war, the situation would be so tense that the Chinese would request that Soviet troops remain in Port Arthur and Dalian.

Kim flew to Beijing, on 13 May 1950, to report on his talks with Stalin, reporting that the Soviet leader had approved his plans to attack the South. Mao wondered if the US would intervene, but Kim thought that even if it did, the North would have occupied the South beforehand. Mao offered to deploy three armies along the Sino-Korean border, but Kim waved this aside saying his own forces did not need any help (Chen 1994: 112). Mao asked Zhou Enlai to cable Moscow and seek Stalin's confirmation of Kim's narrative. The *vozhd* replied that the decision to go to war was to be taken by China and North Korea, but if there was disagreement, they should postpone the attack. Kim returned to Pyongyang on 16 May with Mao's support for war – or at least this is what he told Stalin. Stalin did not think the US would intervene but he was wrong, and so were US policymakers who believed that China would not intervene. Mao saw the US intervention in South Korea as an act of war against Asia and it was thus inevitable that China would join the war sooner or later. What was Mao's objective and why did he intervene when he did?

Mao's goal was a pre-emptive strike to take US military planners by surprise and thereby sow confusion about China's intentions. China saw very quickly that North Korea would lose the military conflict and set about preventing this. Chinese strategy normally exhibits three characteristics: meticulous analysis of long-term trends; careful study of tactical options; and detached exploration of operational decisions (Kissinger 2012: 135). The Chinese had intended to invade Taiwan just before the Korean War but the US fleet prevented this. They could then switch these troops – over 250,000 – to the Sino–North Korean border, and these moves were in place even when the North was winning in the South. The Chinese military believed it could defeat the Americans, who they calculated could only deploy half a million soldiers while the PLA could muster four million. China also had logistical advantage and they calculated that most of the world would support them. A nuclear attack was discounted. Zhou Enlai thought that if the US won in Korea it would move against Vietnam, so it had to be blocked in Korea.

On 25 June 1950, the North Koreans crossed the 38th parallel and initially were unstoppable. The Americans acted immediately as they regarded the offensive as a plan to expand communist influence which would eventually embrace Europe. The Americans managed to get a UN mandate from the Security Council; this was possible because the Soviet delegate had been boycotting the UN Security Council. A UN coalition, including US, Britain, Turkey and twelve other nations, turned the tide. The Northern gamble to take over the South before large numbers of American troops arrived failed, but despite taking most of South Korea by September the communists could not administer the killer blow. MacArthur invaded at Inchon (predicted by the Chinese) and crossed into North Korea, took Pyongyang and most of the North, and it appeared the Americans would sweep Kim Il-sung into the sea.

On 1 October, Stalin requested that Chinese volunteers dressed in North Korean uniforms intervene north of the 38th parallel, but he remarked he had not informed the North Koreans of this. The *vozhd* was willing to pledge military support and, if there was going to be a major international war, it would be better to fight it now before Japan recovered its military might. Was Stalin serious about launching a war against the US? No. The balance of forces was still against the USSR, and Stalin's aim was to tie US forces down in Korea and prevent a US-dominated Korea and Japan emerging as a 'new' NATO in East Asia.

On 11 October, Zhou Enlai and Lin Biao – who had refused command of the North East Border Defence Army – arrived at Stalin's villa on the Black Sea. Zhou and Lin had orders to inform Stalin that without Soviet supplies, China might not commit itself to the planned invasion. The *vozhd* made it clear that the Soviet air force was not ready to provide air cover for invading Chinese troops. On 13 October, Stalin told Kim:

> We feel that continuing resistance is pointless. The Chinese comrades are refusing to take part militarily. Under these circumstances you must prepare to withdraw all troops and military hardware. Draw up a detailed plan of action and follow it rigorously. The potential for fighting the enemy in the future must be preserved.
>
> (Khlevniuk 2015: 296)

Stalin proposed that Kim set up a Korean government in exile in Manchuria, something which was bound to annoy Mao. The Soviets informed the Americans that if General Douglas MacArthur halted at the 38th parallel, they would convince the North Koreans to cease fighting and agree to a UN delegation entering to organise a general election.

On 18 October 1950, over 180,000 Chinese troops crossed into Korea under night cover and took UN forces completely by surprise, obliging them to retreat. It has been called the greatest ambush in modern warfare. The Soviet air force would defend Manchurian airspace but not Korean. On 1 November, the Soviet air force took part in a battle over the Yalu River (the border between China and North Korea). On the same day, MiG fighters shot down two F-82 planes and anti-aircraft guns another two, but the Soviet side suffered no losses. Peace negotiations could have begun after the Chinese defeated the UN forces in North Korea, but Mao did not want peace. The coalition defeat underlined the catastrophic misjudgement of Chinese military potential by General MacArthur. The Chinese took Seoul, the South Korean capital, in early 1951, but the South counterattacked and it appeared no side would win.

Kim asked Mao for a ceasefire in June 1951, but China wanted the war to wear down the Americans and their allies. The longer the war lasted the more arms factories he could ask for from Moscow. In February 1953, the new US president, Dwight D. Eisenhower, warned China he might use the atomic bomb; this was great news for Mao, so he asked Stalin for an atomic bomb. On 28 February 1953, Stalin decided that the war had to end, and on 5 March 1953 he was dead.

Mao did not bother to go to the funeral and Zhou Enlai went instead. He then moved into Eastern Europe. Harry Pollitt, the chief of the Communist Party of Great Britain, asked him for a $5,500 donation to refurbish Marx's grave in Highgate Cemetery, in London. The Chinese had better things to do with their money.

An armistice was signed on 27 July 1953. China sent three million men into Korea and lost about 400,000 and the coalition counted 142,000 dead including 30,000 Americans. The Soviet air force won the air war, and twelve Soviet air divisions were deployed with 72,000 airmen involved in combat. The Soviets claimed they shot down 1,097 enemy planes and anti-aircraft guns accounted for another 212, with the Soviets losing 335 planes and 120 pilots. Among the dead was Mao's eldest son. Moscow provided the Chinese with hundreds of MiG warplanes.

The war came at an inappropriate time for China as it needed all its resources to develop the country. There was also the risk that war could lead to greater internal opposition, but it also permitted Mao Zedong Thought to be emphasised, with the Americans – and by extension capitalism – clearly the enemy. Widespread purges were carried out during the Korean War and as many as five million may have been executed. The Korean War resulted in forced grain requisitions, and millions starved as grain was taken by force to feed the military. However, on balance, it was a great victory for Mao and the People's Republic as, for the first time in a century, China had come out of a war victorious and this swelled national pride. The communists could now boast that they could defend the motherland against any foreign devil and, as a result, Mao's prestige reached a record high.

Between 1950 and 1953, China imported technical equipment worth 470 billion roubles, or 69 per cent of what had been ordered; this permitted the construction of forty-seven industrial projects. The 19th Congress of the All-Union Communist Party (Bolsheviks) – it was renamed the Communist Party of the Soviet Union (CPSU) at the Congress – in October 1952 increased the assistance. Over the years 1950 to 1953, 1,093 technical experts worked in China, and the number involved with Chinese projects in the USSR rose by 30,000.

The Soviets designed about 80 per cent of all projects, provided 80 per cent of the equipment and provided technical materials free of charge. Over the same period, Moscow sent 120,000 books and reference materials and 3,000 scientific documents free of charge. Thousands of Chinese students and specialists went to the Soviet Union to study. The Soviets, therefore, provided the science and technology base which permitted the Middle Kingdom to industrialise rapidly (Shen and Xia 2015: 89–90).

The war poisoned Sino-American relations for almost two decades, and it ensured that Beijing had to look to Moscow for support. Just after the outbreak of the Korean War, the US Seventh Fleet moved into the Taiwan Strait; this prevented the PLA from launching an attack to take the island. It also made it possible for Chiang Kai-shek to develop the island into an anti-communist fortress. If Taiwan was protected, Tibet was not. The US stood aside as Beijing invaded and the UN General Assembly refused to debate the Chinese takeover.

The People's Republic could not move to socialism without Stalin's say-so. Mao sent Liu Shaoqi to Moscow, in October 1952, to attend the 19th Congress to ask Stalin if China could start building socialism. The *vozhd* said it could but it had to proceed 'gradually', and he advised Mao not to rush collectivisation.

The Korean War led many Americans to fear that a war against the Soviet Union was inevitable. Even Henry Kissinger viewed the USSR, at that time, as a revolutionary power which, inevitably, would have to fight the US because it was the bulwark of capitalist democracy. When war came, thought Kissinger, the best location would be the Middle East rather than the vast plains of the Soviet Union where the Soviets had a strategic advantage. Washington had to avoid being sucked into wars on the Soviet periphery, such as Korea, where the Americans had limited or no ground forces. Hence the policy of containment of the Soviet Union around the world would not be effective and the only way of achieving real deterrence was the threat of a nuclear war with the US. The devastation of Korea would encourage small states to purchase neutrality in order to divert Soviet forces elsewhere. Western Europeans needed to expand their defence budgets to give the impression they were willing to fight. Limited American ground forces would be deployed there and diplomatic aid would be guaranteed (Ferguson 2015: 315–17).

Eastern Europe

In January 1951, a meeting took place between the Soviet leadership and top officials from the eastern bloc. The Soviet side was represented by Stalin and several members of the Politburo and military. Eastern European countries sent their party leaders and defence ministers (only the Polish Party leader was absent). General Sergei Shtemenko, chief of the General Staff of the Soviet armed forces, spoke about the growing threat from NATO and the need to counterbalance it by increasing the military capability of the socialist countries. The Soviet satellites were told to increase greatly their military might within three years and to create a military-industrial complex to make this possible. Shtemenko laid down specific targets for each country.

The Polish defence minister, Marshal Konstantin Rokossovsky, pointed out that such an expansion was planned for 1956 and therefore could not be realised by 1953. Other states also doubted their ability to attain such targets, but Stalin stood firm and insisted the goals be reached. Rokossovsky's point about 1956 was fine, said Stalin, providing he could guarantee that war would not break out before 1956. Because he could not, the original plan was to be implemented.

Stalin was preparing for an eventuality which included a military confrontation. The Soviet military, reduced to 2.3 million by 1949, had grown to 5.8 million by 1953. Military expenditure grew by 60 per cent in 1951 and 40 per cent in 1952, but these are estimates and the actual outlay may have been higher. Investment in the civilian economy, on the other hand, only grew by 6 per cent in 1951 and 7 per cent in 1952.

Highest priority was afforded nuclear weapons, rocket technology, jet bombers and fighters and an air defence system for Moscow. During his last year, Stalin was determined to surpass the defence capacity of his adversaries. In February 1953, he launched major programmes in aviation and naval ship construction. There were to be 106 bomber divisions by the end of 1955 – instead of the thirty-two in 1953. This involved constructing 10,300 new planes over the period 1953–5 and increasing naval and air force personnel by 290,000. The naval expansion involved the building of medium and heavy cruisers by 1959. Soviet military bases were established in Kamchatka and Chukotka, near the maritime boundary with the US (Khlevniuk 2015: 297–8). Did this huge military build-up presage a Soviet pre-emptive strike against the West? Given Stalin's state of mind in 1953, anything was possible.

In early 1951, Stalin proposed the holding of another Cominform conference and to nominate Palmiro Togliatti, the general secretary of the Italian Communist Party (PCI) as the general secretary of the Cominform. But Togliatti declined the offer and no conference was held. What was behind Stalin's proposal? Was he contemplating encouraging Western European communist parties to attempt to seize power?

Spies

During the 1930s, the Cambridge spies (Guy Burgess [leader], Kim Philby, Donald Maclean, Anthony Blunt and John Cairncross) – dubbed the Fabulous Five – provided Stalin with voluminous material. The talent spotter, recruiter and mentor of the spy ring (he did not recruit Philby) was James Klugman who was a CPGB functionary and had spent time at Mao's base camp at Yan'an and played a decisive role in convincing Churchill to support Tito and the communist Partisans (*The Spectator*, 5 December 2015). Burgess, for instance, forwarded 4,604 documents (over twice as many as Blunt) before 1939, but Stalin suspected that they were a plant, having been so detailed and informative. The Soviets received so much intelligence material they could not cope with all of it. The wartime material was invaluable to Stalin as it provided him with British and American negotiating positions at all the Big Three meetings, and American spies sent US analyses and goals as well. Burgess and Maclean defected to the Soviet Union in 1951 and Philby in 1963. Blunt confessed in 1964 and was granted immunity and John Cairncross admitted spying in 1951 but was not prosecuted.

It was not all one-way traffic. Wilfrid Mann, a brilliant British physicist involved in the Manhattan Project, spied for the Soviet Union but was turned and worked for the CIA. In 1951, he joined the National Bureau of Standards as the head of its Radioactivity Section. For the next thirty years he was the most influential radionuclide meteorologist in the world.

The Fab Five caused enormous damage to Western intelligence but Britain owes a huge cultural debt to them. They 'changed the country beyond all recognition by wrecking the smug assumptions of the post-war ruling class, shaking the intelligence community to its foundations and ushering in a new world: less comfortable and complacent and above all, less clubby'. The establishment was deeply shocked, often unwilling to believe that men born to privilege, educated at public schools and Cambridge, could possibly be communist spies. Burgess was at Eton, Maclean at Gresham's, Philby at Westminster and Blunt at Marlborough, all of whom were members of the most prestigious clubs. (Cairncross was the exception and studied at Glasgow University, the Sorbonne before going to Cambridge.) Class protected them from suspicion. Philby described the 'genuine mental block that stubbornly resisted the belief that respected members of the establishment could do such things'. He understood this mentality and exploited it ruthlessly. The archives reveal the slow realisation that the service 'had fallen victim to its own ingrained assumptions about class, background, education and social status'. The old boy network has never recovered from this catastrophe, and the scandal did much to undermine deference to wealth, accent and privilege. The Fab Five accidentally made Britain a more egalitarian country.

> [The] best symbol of the transformation wrought by the Cambridge spies is James Bond himself. Ian Fleming was a clubman but 007 is not. While 'M' takes Bond to lunch at the fictional Blades club, Bond is not a member. An orphan at 11, Bond has no father to ease him into the right clubs.

He is classless and independent, and this stands out in *Spectre*, the 2015 film. He defends the establishment but is outside it, and he becomes the perfect post-war spy (*The Times*, 23 October 2015).

The Briton who possibly became the most famous Soviet spy was Rudolf Ivanovich Abel. He was born William Fisher in Newcastle upon Tyne in 1903. His father, Genrikh Fisher, was a metal worker in St Petersburg and a Marxist who had moved to Germany and then England. William was proficient in English, French, German and Russian. The family moved back to Soviet Russia in 1921, and William joined the Red Army as a radio operator and translator. He joined the OGPU, secret police, and was posted to Oslo and London during the 1930s and became involved in radio deception. He entered the US in 1948 as part of a spy ring in New York City. He did not have diplomatic cover and worked at various jobs while running agents. By then, he was known as Rudolf Abel. The name was that of a dead KGB colonel. Eventually, he was betrayed by an associate in Brooklyn and arrested in 1957, but he avoided the electric chair and was imprisoned and then exchanged in February 1962 – as KGB Colonel Vilyam Fisher – for Gary Powers at the Glienicke Bridge, which connected West Berlin to Potsdam, in the German Democratic Republic (GDR). Abel died in 1971 and was honoured on a Soviet postage stamp. He is the subject of the 2015 Steven Spielberg film, *Bridge of Spies*, and Abel is brilliantly played by Mark Rylance.

The most successful Soviet spy in Israel was Avraham Marek (Marcus) Klingberg, an internationally acclaimed expert on chemical and biological weapons who, as deputy director of Israel's secret Ness Ziona biological weapons research centre, had access to all Israel's top secrets in this clandestine field. It is reasonable to assume he handed all these secrets on to 'Viktor', his Soviet handler (they met in the Russian Orthodox Church in Tel Aviv); Moscow, in turn, passed the information on to Arab countries. Israel admits that Klingberg did more harm than any other spy in the country's history. After the Soviet Union and Israel severed diplomatic relations in 1967, they met in Switzerland and at international conferences. Born in Warsaw in 1918, into a Hassidic Jewish family, Klingberg studied medicine at Warsaw University, and when Germany invaded, he moved to the Soviet Union and completed his medical studies in Minsk. He served in the Red Army at the front but was sent to Perm to study epidemiology and became chief epidemiologist in Belarus. The war over, he returned to Warsaw and began working for the Polish government. He married another communist, and in 1946 they moved to Sweden (they could not obtain a US visa), where he established contact with Soviet intelligence; in 1948 they emigrated to Israel. A brilliant research scientist, he became an officer in the Israeli army and then joined the Israel Institute for Biological Research which, it is believed, manufactured poisons used by Mossad, the Israeli secret service. He went on research visits to the US, Norway, London and Oxford, where any information he was able to glean about biological and chemical warfare weapons was passed on to Moscow. He was unmasked by a double agent in 1983, kidnapped by Israel security, tried and given the maximum sentence of twenty years, but he then simply disappeared. In fact, he was imprisoned under a false name and kept in solitary confinement for ten years. In 1993, after the collapse of the Soviet Union, Israel admitted that he was being held prisoner and in 2003 he was released. In his memoirs, *Der Letze Spion (The Last Spy)*, published with Michael Sfard and Wiebke Ehrenstein in 2014, he argued that he was always motivated by Marxism and that, scientifically, the sensitive material he had access to should be shared internationally. His grandson commented: 'He remained a communist to the end and faithful to communists and Russia' (*The Times*, 8 December 2015).

The Office of Strategic Services (OSS) was set up on 13 June 1942 and headed by 'Wild Bill' Donovan to provide mainly intelligence about Germany, and it was wound up on 20 September 1945. The CIA appeared on 18 September 1947. As there was an urgent need for information about the Soviet Union, a Research and Analysis Division was set up staffed by many prominent academics, including leading Marxists such as Paul Sweezy, Franz Neumann and Herbert Marcuse – the OSS's leading analyst on Germany. The latter concluded that the only credible opposition to Nazism in Germany were the communists. Finding out what was happening in the Soviet Union was a problem, as copies of *Pravda* and *Izvestiya* arrived in Washington six weeks late. Due to lack of Soviet data, they used German material to estimate what was happening on the Eastern Front. They correctly predicted that the Wehrmacht could not win at Stalingrad because of the insuperable logistical problems, but they did foresee the looming problem of dealing with the Soviet Union after the war. It was pointed out that the USSR would be a growing power, the US a satisfied power and Britain a declining power. Concessions to Moscow should be made in order to secure peaceful coexistence. One of the best British sources turned out to be the Japanese ambassador in Berlin whose reports to Tokyo were decoded by Bletchley Park (where Enigma was deciphered). The ambassador reported that Stalingrad was the greatest German defeat since Napoleon had smashed the Prussians at Jena in 1806. The Soviets provided London and Washington with very sparse information about what was happening on the Eastern Front.

Towards the end of the war, thoughts turned to acquiring the Wehrmacht's intelligence network on the Eastern Front. Lt Colonel Reinhard Gehlen, senior intelligence officer of the Wehrmacht on the Eastern Front, became a German star. He proved no more accurate at predicting where Red Army attacks would occur than the General Staff and was sometimes completely wrong. The reason his reputation grew was his skill in recruiting agents behind the Soviet front line who provided valuable information which influenced how the Wehrmacht was deployed. The conclusion is that he was one of the most influential intelligence officers on either side during the war. On the other hand, the latest information suggests he was brilliantly misled by Soviet intelligence. One of his key agents was Aleksandr Demyanov, codenamed Max who, in reality, was an NKVD officer feeding him information, some of which Stalin himself authorised. One of the ways the Soviets built up his credibility was to report his group had conducted railway sabotage near Gorky (now Nizhny Novgorod), and newspapers duly report this canard. Max provided a constant flow of reports about the Red Army's order of battle and strategic intentions, and Berlin was overjoyed to receive such valuable material. Stalin was taking a huge risk in providing some accurate information about the battle plans of the Red Army, presumably to secure even greater military advantage elsewhere.

Gehlen, once he had perceived that Germany would be defeated, concluded that the next conflict would be between the Soviet Union and the West. He therefore gathered all the material of his intelligence apparatus and ensured it was not destroyed. After defeat, he offered the Americans his services including all his personnel and files; Washington welcomed him with open arms. The Gehlen Bureau later became an important part of the CIA's operations in Europe. This delighted the NKVD (it became the MSS in 1946 and the KGB in 1954) and the GRU (military intelligence) to no end. After all, they controlled almost all his sources and were aware of most of the others (Hastings 2015: 223–38, 544–5).

In 1944, the young American physicist Ted Hall, working on the Manhattan Project, told his NKVD handler that 'There is no country except the Soviet Union that can be entrusted with such a terrible thing' (Hastings 2015: 524). Around fifty of the scientists in Britain and the US provided atomic secrets to Moscow, and it was the greatest espionage coup of the war for the NKVD and GRU. It did not affect the war against Germany and Japan but it had a formative influence on the atomic age.

In 1940, Soviet scientists concluded that an atomic bomb from enriched uranium was feasible, and on 16 September 1940 Donald Maclean – one of the Fabulous Five of British spies – forwarded a report to Moscow on a project codenamed Tube Alloys. In August 1941, Klaus Fuchs, a German-born physicist and committed communist, was recruited by a GRU agent. In March 1942, Beria sent Stalin a report on British atomic research, mainly supplied by John Cairncross.

Robert Oppenheimer, now leading the Manhattan Project, met the NKVD *rezident* in San Francisco and told him of Einstein's 1939 letter to Roosevelt about the Germans working on an atomic bomb. He may also inadvertently have provided hints about the US project. In January 1943, Bruno Pontecorvo, an Italian-born British subject, reported to the NKVD about the first nuclear chain reaction, and by July 1943 Moscow had received 286 classified US documents on the Manhattan Project. In Britain, Melita Norwood, recruited in 1937, was providing vital information (she was only unmasked in 1999 but not prosecuted) and proved to be Moscow's most important atomic spy in Britain, but Soviet spies could get it wrong. On 1 July 1943, the NKVD station in New York reported that 500 individuals were working on the Manhattan Project, but the correct figure was 200,000, which was to rise to 600,000 if all subcontractors are added. In late 1943, Klaus Fuchs was transferred to the US and began to provide regular weekly reports on progress. The Washington *rezident's* office received 211 rolls of classified documents in 1943, 600 in 1944 and 1,896 in 1945. These included valuable material on radar, wireless technology, jet propulsion and synthetic rubber which permitted Soviet industry to advance. Beria became suspicious about the flow of classified material because it was so easy to obtain. Twelve days before the US bomb was assembled at Los Alamos, Fuchs and Pontecorvo provided descriptions of the bomb to their handlers. When the first Soviet atom bomb was detonated, in August 1949, it was very similar to the 'Fat Man' plutonium bomb dropped on Nagasaki.

American security gradually improved and Julius Rosenberg was sacked from Los Alamos because of his Communist Party membership. After the war, a

Soviet specialist estimated that the FBI had only uncovered half of the Soviet network (Hastings 2015: 524–35).

In January 1950, the confession of Klaus Fuchs that he was a communist spy led to an intensive investigation by the US and British authorities. He had handed over 246 pages of secrets between August 1941 and October 1942 and a further 324 pages by November 1943. Another British spy, Alan Nunn May, acquired 142 pages on the Manhattan Project and passed them on to his Soviet contact. Another key scientist, never identified, supplied about 5,000 pages of secret documents (Haslam 2011: 62). Bruno Pontecorvo defected to the Soviet Union in September 1950, and he had worked on the British atomic bomb at Harwell under Sir John Cockcroft.

Fuchs identified Harry Gold as his courier and he was arrested in the US in May 1950; the latter revealed that David Greenglass was another source. His sister, Ethel Rosenberg, and her husband, Julius Rosenberg, were arrested and accused of passing atomic secrets to the Soviet Union. Greenglass's wife Ruth was in fact a spy, but Greenglass, in order to save his wife, identified Ethel Rosenberg as a spy. Allegedly, she had typed some documents for her husband, but she was innocent because Greenglass's wife had typed the documents. Julius and Ethel Rosenberg were executed in April 1953; they were the only US civilians to suffer such a fate for passing Manhattan Project secrets to Moscow. Greenglass served time in prison and the charges against his wife were dropped, but he never expressed remorse for his false testimony which led to his sister being sent to the electric chair. He said he expected to be remembered as the spy who 'turned his family in'. Others were more successful in covering their tracks; Alger Hiss, for example, fooled his interrogators.

In February 1950 the revelations about spying were seized upon by the junior senator from Wisconsin, Joseph McCarthy, who declared dramatically that he had evidence that the State Department was replete with communists. He claimed to have a list of no fewer than 206 members of the Communist Party of the USA in the Department. Allegedly, there were communists in the military and elsewhere. He argued that Truman was soft on communism and had 'lost' China, but the claims were dismissed by the Truman administration. The witch hunt for communists, labelled McCarthyism, reached hysterical heights, and it revealed the deep insecurity of the US facing a Soviet Union with nuclear weapons. It is worth noting that the House Un-American Activities Committee (HUAC), in hearings involving Hollywood (up to 1958) heard evidence from seventy-two 'friendly witnesses' who identified 325 film people as present or past communists.

One of the puzzles about espionage is why so many British and American specialists spied for the Soviet Union; they appeared to regard the Soviet Union as an earthly paradise in the making but ignored all the information about how brutal the Stalin regime was. Many of them were well off and, in the case of several of the British spies, from a privileged background.

NSC-68

National Security Council Report No. 68 (NSC-68) established a framework for US defence which lasted for most of the Cold War. Paul Nitze chaired the committee, which drafted the report after President Truman had requested it in January 1950; the president approved it in 1951. The dramatic language adopted was typical of the era. The 'issues that face us are momentous involving the fulfillment or destruction not only of the Republic but civilization itself.' It called for a rapid increase in defence spending to contain the expansionary policies of the Soviet Union. Hence it can be called a military response to Kennan's diplomatic vision of containment, but rollback or offensive military action was excluded. Kennan opposed the massive increase in military spending. The goal was to build a coalition of nations to prevent the advance of communism; if this was not achieved then the Soviet Union could develop to the point where no coalition of the willing could successfully oppose it. Hence it expected the USSR to rapidly expand militarily and economically. There were those who regarded this as much too optimistic but the Korean War won over many. Secretary of State Dean Acheson acknowledged that the war provided the critical impetus; Truman opposed a rapid expansion of the military budget but gave in. In 1950 defence accounted for 5 per cent of GDP and climbed to 14.2 per cent in 1953. The military-industrial complex was gathering momentum. This term is associated with President Eisenhower, who used the expression in his Farewell Address on 17 January 1961. He had originally intended to say military-industrial-congressional complex as a result of some congressmen, including his successor as president, who kept harping on about a missile gap which had to be closed at all costs (Ferguson 2015: 463n).

There was an alternative to the use of military force: psychological warfare (PW). The concept surfaced in 1950 and was promoted by William Yandell Elliott III, who participated in the setting up of Radio Liberty, which targeted the Soviet Union. He also favoured cultural exchanges to bring young people to the US to imbibe the American experience, and they were to be trained to run their own countries. Hearts and minds also had to be won at home as it was unwise just to rely on US values, such as the free market, to carry the day. The first time PW was deployed was during the Italian elections of April 1948 to prevent communists and socialists winning a majority. Financial aid permitted the Christian Democrats to engage in black propaganda such as warning Italians that if the communists took over, all males would be deported to the Soviet gulag! Frank Sinatra and other Hollywood stars wrote to their relatives warning them of the dire consequences of a communist victory. The Christian Democrats won 305 seats, a clear majority. An Office of Special Projects (later the Office of Policy Coordination [OPC]) was set up. The OPC specialised in founding front organisations: the National Committee for a Free Europe, which ran Radio Liberty; the Free Trade Union Committee; Americans for Intellectual Freedom; and the Congress for Cultural Freedom, to name only a few. PW was hugely popular and every agency wanted to get involved, but this resulted in confusion. A Psychological Strategy Board (PSB) was set up in 1951 to speak with one voice, but this was never achieved as some wanted to wipe communism from the face of the earth and others merely to engage in coexistence; the net result of all its activities was rather disappointing (Ferguson 2015: 263–4). President Eisenhower was a cautious conservative but he had a heart of steel. He defined PW as the struggle for the minds and wills of men and American values had to beat Soviet values. George Kennan had pointed out that a revolutionary state such as the Soviet Union was permanently insecure and that the battle of ideas would continue until one side won and took over the world.

During the Korean War, in 1951, the PSB sent Henry Kissinger to South Korea to write a report on civil-military relations. He concluded that military officers had to be alert to the fact that civil affairs were of critical importance in achieving political and military objectives. He next went to Germany, where he found a pervasive distrust of the US and propaganda did not work because it was too reminiscent of Goebbels. In the western zones, Americans were perceived as more brutal and arrogant than Russians and were inconsiderate, insensitive and cynical. The Soviets were much more successful because they stressed peace and the unification of Germany. The Americans would not win until they emphasised the 'psychological component' of their political strategy. The solution was to found a 'university, large foundation, newspaper and similar organization'. Germans and Americans needed to work together in joint projects and establish a community of interests in study groups, cultural congresses, exchange professorships and intern programmes, under non-governmental auspices (Ferguson 2015: 270–1). PW would then carry the day. Nowadays, this is called 'soft power'.

Some wondered that if Moscow was willing to use force in an attempt to reunite Korea, could the same policy be adopted in Germany? More NATO troops were needed in Europe. Konrad Adenauer, the West German chancellor, began talks about founding a new German army in 1950, but it was not until November 1955 that the Bundeswehr appeared; this was because of opposition by other European powers, especially the French. General Dwight D. Eisenhower was named Supreme Allied Commander in Europe, and more US divisions were expected to be moved there.

Japan's fortunes changed as well, as it had supplied the lion's share of the provisions needed by the UN forces in Korea. In September 1951, a peace treaty was signed in San Francisco which envisaged American withdrawal by May 1952. All belligerent states signed except the Soviet Union, China, North Korea and other communist states. The US retained some military bases and Japanese security was guaranteed by Washington. The Philippines, Japan, Australia and New Zealand signed security pacts with the US, and in Europe, Greece and Turkey joined NATO. The Americans then turned their attention to the Middle East. Stalin could decipher the Soviet Union being surrounded by a ring of states who owed their security to Washington (Cohen 1993: 58–80; LaFeber 1993: 99–145).

Germany

Stalin regarded Germany as the key country in Europe, but he did not envisage it being divided into two states – one communist and the other capitalist – so his German policy was always pan-German. His major objective was to ensure Germany never again threatened Soviet security and this could be achieved in various ways. The favoured option was that Germany become a neutral, demilitarised state. The four occupying powers would still retain responsibility for ensuring that Germany never became a military threat but the Berlin Blockade transformed the situation. It led to the formation of the Federal Republic of Germany (FRG) in the west and the German Democratic Republic (GDR) in the east. The FRG was gradually integrated into Western Europe, and this ensured it would develop as a capitalist state and be under American influence.

Stalin's response was the note of 10 March 1952, which proposed a German peace treaty and a united, neutral, demilitarised Germany. Freedom of speech and assembly were guaranteed, and all occupation forces would leave within a year of the signing of a peace treaty. The note was made public by the Soviets, a move which compromised diplomatic negotiations. This has led many historians to view the note as an attempt to sway the West German public and halt the integration of West Germany in Western Europe. West Germany was to be included in the European Defence Community (EDC), but it never came into existence because the French National Assembly voted against it. A further note followed on 9 April and other notes came on 24 May and 23 August. The Western response was dominated by Konrad Adenauer, the West German chancellor, who regarded it as insincere and as a delaying tactic to prevent the integration of West Germany in the EDC and other European institutions. He was also aware that a united Germany almost certainly would elect a social democratic government, and his Christian Democratic Union–Christian Social Union party would thus lose its majority in a pan-German parliament.

The failure of the Western powers to respond positively to the notes gave rise to a heated controversy about a 'missed opportunity' to reunify Germany. The valid point was made that Stalin's sincerity should have been put to the test. It is striking that Winston Churchill, again British prime minister, did not argue in favour of negotiations to test Soviet intentions; the US administration was also lukewarm and deferred to Adenauer.

Soviet archives reveal that the origin of the 10 March 1952 note goes back to 1951. It was regarded as a delaying tactic, and Stalin only consented to it being sent after being assured that it would be rejected. There is no indication that Moscow was willing to sacrifice the GDR to obtain a united, neutral Germany which would have been capitalist.

Culture

Stalin loved watching films until the early hours, and members of the Politburo were required to attend. Stalin sat alone in his row behind everyone else. One visitor, the director of the film, was searched fifteen times before he was allowed to sit down. Then Stalin's secretary brought him a message. 'What's this rubbish?,' he commented, but the director thought he was commenting on his film, fainted and was carried out. And 'they didn't give him a new pair of pants for the ones he had soiled, either,' commented the Boss. Among Stalin's favourites were *The Great Waltz* about Johann Strauss, which he saw dozens of times. He loved the *Tarzan* films and saw every one – so did everyone else. The Red Army had seized many American films in Berlin, including those starring Johnny Weissmuller, and they were gradually released to the public. Boys would wear Tarzan haircuts and utter war cries which were said to be so piercing that they disturbed cattle on the collective farms and kept cows from giving milk! Some Russians believed Tarzan was a real person. So pervasive was the Tarzan cult that the party stepped in and started a campaign against it. Mikhail Chiaureli's *The Fall of Berlin* (*Padenie Berlina*) was a seventieth birthday gift for Stalin in 1949. The hero and heroine are summoned to meet Stalin in his white tunic in a beautiful garden, where Stalin is carrying a hoe and listening to the birds singing. The Germans then attack, and Stalin and his generals confer during the defence of Moscow. Hitler, the corpulent Göring and the limping Goebbels (he had a club foot) are chatting with diplomats from Japan and the Vatican. The Führer rants and raves in Russian, and Göring is chatting to an American who toasts the imminent fall of Stalingrad. Shostakovich's music accompanies the Soviet victory. At Yalta, the cunning, double-chinned Churchill puffs on a cigar, and Roosevelt nods as Stalin unfolds some maps. The battle of Berlin is dramatic, with everyone looking up as Stalin's plane lands in Berlin; this is followed by quasi-religious scenes of adoration. The only problem is that Stalin did not go to Berlin. The film was widely distributed in Western Europe, but it was only in 1952 that it hit America. The *New York Times* dismissed it as a 'deafening blend of historical pageantry and wishful thinking'. Stalin alighting in Berlin was like a 'Gilbert and Sullivan frolic'. However, there were American critics who regarded it as a 'masterpiece of cinema art' (Caute 2003: 143–7). I saw the film in the 1950s and it made a great impression on me, especially the scene where Stalin descends from his plane like God from Heaven. After Stalin's death it was lambasted by the critics. Shostakovich took his revenge on Chiaureli and claimed he could not tell a piano from a toilet bowl.

The Conspiracy of the Doomed (1950) was widely distributed. A US ambassador, MacHill – villains in Soviet Cold War–era films were usually call Mac something – arrives to arrange a crop failure to overthrow the communist government (apparently Czech). The suave diplomat is also plotting the assassination of the deputy prime minister. A devious cardinal – probably modelled on Cardinal Minszenty, Primate of Hungary – tells everyone the drought is God's punishment for forsaking Him. It turns out that there is no grain shortage – it was being hidden by kulaks all along and workers take over and chant: 'Stalin, Stalin'. The ambassador curses everyone and flies away. The film never reached the US but this did not stop some American critics rubbishing it based on Soviet reviews. Nevertheless, it is regarded as one of the two best Cold War films produced in the Soviet Union.

They Have a Native Land (1949) tells the story of Soviet children captured in Germany by the British and Americans and some are put on a ship for New York. They 'want to send them to be cannon fodder in a new war', the voiceover explains. Frau Wurst ('Mrs Sausage') asks a British officer for a slave girl with blue eyes and the officer obliges, but all ends happily as the children are returned to the Motherland. The British and Americans all speak impeccable Russian – they were in counter-intelligence, of course.

What message came through Soviet Cold War–era films? The Soviet Union defeated Germany and Japan without any help from the US and Britain; it did so despite an Anglo-American conspiracy to help Germany and Japan; victory was due entirely to the leadership of Stalin. The Anglo-American conspiracy appeared time and again, but Roosevelt was always held to be innocent. *The Secret Mission* (1950) drew protests from London and Washington. Americans are shown running away from a German offensive in January 1945. Montgomery shouts into the telephone: 'I won't help the Americans. They can go to the devil.' Churchill appeals to Stalin for help and complains the Americans are ready to negotiate a separate peace with Germany. Heywood, a US senator, says: 'We held up the second front for two years to cheat the Russians.' Himmler replies: 'We have left the Western front deserted.' German troops are shown surrendering to the Americans in ceremonial order. How this fits with the beginning of the film, which showed Americans fleeing in panic, is not explained. Vice President Truman is presented as the person who sent Heywood to inform Hitler about the forthcoming Soviet offensive, and the German industrialist Krupp promises Heywood that he will preserve his military factories in West Germany but destroy those in East Germany before the Soviets arrive. Krupp thanks Heywood for all the raw materials he received to continue his war production. Heywood goes to the Balkans to meet Hitler supporters and he is told that if things get too hot to go to Yugoslavia where he will be safe. This was the film's swipe at Tito. In the last scene, Churchill promises a new world war and expects it to cost the lives of half of the world's population before it ends. No wonder the British and American governments were outraged at the total falsification of history. The film was a runaway success in the Soviet Union.

Silvery Dust (1953) deals with the African American question and is set in the American South. White racists are willing to sacrifice blacks in pursuit of a 'death ray'. Blacks are sentenced to the electric chair but the Ku Klux Klan moves in to execute them themselves. A general intervenes, and the blacks are put in a laboratory cage and expected to die from 'silvery dust', but peace partisans raid the laboratory, rescue the African Americans and warn the white racists that they will face a people's court one day. The American delegate even complained in the UN Security Council about the 'extravagant fictions in which all the villains are Americans. For many years the Soviet Union has been busy at just this sort of thing.' The Soviet representative commented that he had encountered dozens of American films which contained outrageous slanders against the Soviet Union.

Cold War films, he admitted, presented superficial 'psychological portraits' but overall reflected the reality of the 'imperialist conspiracy'.

The Woman on Pier 13 was one of the first 'Red Menace' (1949) films to be favourably reviewed. It concerned communist manipulation of labour on the San Francisco waterfront; the party ruthlessly disciplines its members. *I Was a Communist for the FBI* (1951) has a leading communist committing a fictitious murder. To 'bring communism to America we must incite riots' is a comment. Communists are portrayed as the sworn enemies of African Americans, workers and Jews. In *My Son John* (1952) a wholesome American mother has two sons fighting in Korea 'on God's side', but the third one, John, is a red and she hands him over to the FBI. Informing on family members as a civic duty appears in many American Cold War movies. John decides to confess but his party comrades murder him before he can; however, he had taped his confession beforehand in which he confessed he was a traitor and a communist spy. *Walk East on Beacon* (1952) praises the FBI for protecting Americans from communism. They uncover a vast network of spies trying to steal the secrets of a path-breaking new computer. *Big Jim McLain* (1952) starred John Wayne as an agent who deals with communists on the Honolulu waterfront. Big Jim's assistant is murdered, and the communist plan is to paralyse communications and halt the flow of war matériel to Korea. Big Jim has a punch-up with the bad guys before they are arrested.

An arts festival held in West Berlin in 1951–2 revealed how seriously the State Department took cultural competition with the Soviet Union. *Porgy and Bess* was a hit with Berlin audiences, and the Boston Symphony Orchestra and others gave concerts; the Americans enthused that US prestige had risen more in one month than in the previous seven years.

A Soviet cultural festival took place in Paris in April 1952. Works by Prokofiev, Ravel, Copland, Rachmaninov and Richard Strauss were played; Stravinsky, who had fled to Paris in 1939, returned to conduct his own work. Works by composers banned under Hitler were performed. In December 1952, six Soviet musicians ventured as far as Edinburgh to give a concert in a half empty Usher Hall, and listeners were very impressed by their technical skill.

Jazz was all the rage in the Soviet Union after 1945. The Red Army even had a jazz band and the Communist Party set up its own. Then during the *Zhdanovshchina* jazz was banned not only in the Soviet Union but also in Eastern Europe. It was derided as 'black music' and, in 1949, all saxophones were confiscated, and many jazz musicians ended up in the gulag. Many American jazz bands toured Europe and Japan. Louis Armstrong took France by storm and the Pope thanked him. The Voice of America and the US army in Germany and Austria broadcast jazz to an adoring audience. Jazz in Moscow was seen as a narcotic, a way to dope workers and hypnotise the will by machine rhythm. Paul Robeson maintained that the 'real' Negro music was spirituals and the blues.

Soviet art concentrated on three genres: the portrait, mainly of political and military leaders (there was a famous one of Marshal Zhukov on a white horse backed by Berlin burning); historical themes, displaying the evolution of the new socialist state; and genre painting (workers, collective farmers bring in the harvest, parades for peace, and joyous folk festivals in which everyone is depicted as smiling, healthy and moving forward). Needless to say, the leading figure portrayed was Stalin, always receiving the thanks of a grateful people. Artists in the satellite countries had to follow suit. East German art copied Soviet art, and the only thing that was different were the costumes (Caute 2003: 152–77, 394–6, 444–6, 516–17).

3   To the brink and back
1953–62

Stalin was reported dead on 5 March 1953. The people mourned, and some were even crushed to death trying the see the *vozhd*. Others celebrated, first and foremost Lavrenty Beria, but the last years of Stalin were replete with fear. At the 19th Party Congress, the Politburo was replaced by the Presidium with twice as many members as before. Was Stalin preparing a purge of the old guard to make way for a new, younger Stalin cohort? Dmitry Shepilov, a member of the Central Committee of the party and later editor of *Pravda*, attended the Congress which he found awe-inspiring but Stalin's behaviour troubled him. He was condescending towards his closest colleagues and hurled accusations at them. Marshal Kliment Voroshilov was guilty of 'espionage'; Vyacheslav Molotov and Anastas Mikoyan had 'capitulated to American imperialism'.

> Could all this be a product of Stalin's schizophrenic paranoia? . . . To question Stalin or try to object – these outlandish ideas did not occur to anyone. The pronouncements and views of the genius Stalin could only be reverently and rapturously acclaimed.
>
> (Shepilov 2007: 235)

In January 1953, *Pravda* had announced the discovery of a Doctors' Plot. Since 1945 several leading politicians had allegedly been murdered by a group of doctors, most of whom were linked to a Jewish organisation run by the Americans. One of those accused confessed that he had been ordered to 'eliminate the leading cadres of the Soviet Union', and this included Comrade Stalin. The newspaper assured readers that documentary evidence to prove these heinous crimes was available. Ministries were accused of slackness and the Komsomol of lacking vigilance, and Stalin devoted a lot of time to the fabrication of evidence against the 'wrecker doctors'. Their patrons were to be found in the Ministry of State Security.

The minister, Semyon Ignatiev, suffered the full force of Stalin's foul-mouthed insinuations which included calling officers 'hippopotamuses' and he was going to 'drive them like sheep and hit them in the mug'. Several leading doctors who treated the Kremlin elite were arrested in October and November 1952, and Stalin told investigators to use torture. The Minister informed Stalin that two of his most skilled torturers had been assigned to the case but there was resistance to the brutal methods being deployed. A Party Presidium meeting, on 4 December 1952, passed a resolution on the work of the Ministry of State Security.

> Many Chekists [Ministry of State Security officials] hide behind . . . rotten and harmful reasoning that the use of diversion and terror against class enemies is supposedly incompatible with Marxism-Leninism. These good for nothing Chekists have descended from positions of revolutionary Marxism-Leninism to positions of bourgeois liberalism and pacifism.

In a closed session, Stalin made clear what he wanted done. 'Communists who take a dim view of intelligence and the work of the Cheka, who are afraid of getting their hands dirty, should be thrown down a well head first' (Khlevniuk 2015: 308). Rumours swirled around Moscow about possible pogroms and the expulsion of Jews from Moscow and other cities. No evidence has come to light that Stalin was planning anything comparable. Then suddenly, on 23 February 1953, the whole campaign was dropped. Shortly after Stalin's death, the so-called plot was acknowledged as a fabrication, and the deputy Minister of State Security was indicted and executed.

After Stalin's death a collective leadership of Malenkov, Molotov and Beria would 'prevent any kind of disorder or panic', but the collective leadership could only last until a new, strong leader took over. Tension was relaxed at home and abroad. Georgy Malenkov had already talked about peaceful co-existence in 1952 and now promised the Soviet population higher living standards; and he held out an olive branch to Tito and assured the capitalist world of the Soviet Union's peaceful intentions. Beria launched a few initiatives of his own, proposing the promotion of non-Russians (he himself was a Georgian) in non-Russian republics. He also released many from the gulag, and they flooded back to Moscow demanding justice and compensation for their ordeal, and he even toyed with the idea of a unified, neutral Germany which meant sacrificing the German Democratic Republic (GDR). The uprising in East Berlin and elsewhere in the GDR, on 17 June 1953, took him to Berlin. While he was there Khrushchev organised a cabal against him; the day after he returned, he was arrested and executed along with some of his subordinates later in the year. The intriguing question remains: had Beria become dominant in Moscow, would Germany have been united and the situation in Eastern Europe transformed? The uprising in East Berlin ensured that the GDR could not be sacrificed. As Khrushchev later argued, it could have led to the unravelling of the Soviet position in Eastern Europe.

Lost opportunities

When Stalin died there was a new president in the White House, Dwight D. Eisenhower, a war hero and former commander of allied troops in Europe. He was a rara avis (a rare bird), a world politician who was a modest man. There was also a new secretary of state, John Foster Dulles – he was not a modest man. He had served under Truman and regarded himself as an expert on foreign affairs. Eisenhower's vice president was Richard Nixon, who had made his name as a communist-bashing lawyer.

If the Cold War could be attributed to Stalin, it could now be expected to end. The *vozhd* did not think his minions were up to the task of running the great country he had created. Stalin and Molotov decided foreign policy so his successors would be faced with challenges which would be novel to them. Khrushchev, with Stalin safely dead, commented that the Boss had laid too much store on military might and, needless to say, his former colleagues blamed the *vozhd* for all the failures of the post-war era – the Korean War, the Berlin Blockade and the estrangement of Iran and Turkey. However, the new leaders shared one of Stalin's maxims: the bloodletting of the war had accorded the Soviet Union a preeminent position in Europe and this permitted Moscow to determine the fate of Europe.

Churchill sensed that with a new collective leadership in Moscow there was an opportunity to negotiate a better relationship, so he proposed a four-power meeting to Eisenhower. The new US president was hesitant but Secretary of State Dulles was unequivocal. No good would come out of negotiating with communists. Again the 17 June uprising in East Berlin, where the Soviets had used tanks to put down the rebellion, muddied the waters. The day after its suppression, at a National Security Council meeting, Eisenhower commented that the events 'provide the strongest possible argument to give to Mr Churchill against a four power meeting'. An allied foreign ministers' meeting did take place in Berlin in January and February of 1954 but there was no agreement on the German question. A further meeting in Bermuda did not take place but the foreign ministers convened again, in Geneva, from April to June 1954. Whereas the previous meeting had dealt with Europe, this meeting focused on Korea and Indochina. This was the occasion when Dulles ostentatiously refused to shake Zhou Enlai's hand.

One of the reasons for the lack of interest in détente by the Eisenhower administration was that it could have jeopardised German rearmament because reunification was to be based on the country becoming neutral. The prevailing view in Washington was that the Soviets were waxing strong while America was falling behind but, in retrospect, this was nonsense and analyses which argued that the Soviet threat was diminishing were ignored. All in all, a great opportunity was missed to engage with the new, inexperienced Soviet leadership which also wanted to reduce tension with the capitalist world. Another problem was that there was an interest group that could benefit from exaggerating Soviet military potential: the military-industrial complex.

Khrushchev takes over

Georgy Malenkov appeared the natural successor to Stalin. He was head of the party and the government but offered to relinquish one of these posts on 14 March and chose to remain as prime minister, a position which permitted him to chair Party Presidium meetings. Beria was feared by all and he was close to Malenkov but the latter was not a natural leader – just like Molotov – and the others were afraid he could be manipulated. The comrade with leadership qualities turned out to be Khrushchev. The latter learnt about foreign policy from Mikoyan and he learnt fast. Molotov, again foreign minister, remained fixed in Stalinist mode and was incapable of launching the new initiatives the country needed.

With Beria out of the way, Khrushchev was elected First Secretary of the party in September 1953. In September 1954, Malenkov lost the right to chair Party Presidium meetings, and in November all documents from the Council of Ministers appeared under the signature of Nikolai Bulganin, his deputy. Malenkov had to resign in February 1955 and confess that he had underestimated the need to promote heavy industry over light industry; he was also accused of stating that nuclear war would mean the end of civilisation. The view was that the leadership could hold such a view but it should not be revealed to the general public. The removal of Malenkov meant that the opportunity for détente had passed as Khrushchev followed Stalin in believing that more military might meant more security.

Khrushchev had little formal education but possessed considerable peasant cunning (this is meant as a compliment). His lack of formal education led Viktor Sukhodrev, his English language interpreter, to castigate him as 'uneducated, uncouth, a peasant if you will'. In his memoirs, he recounts translating Khrushchev's claim that Soviet citizens had no interest in owning a house or a car and mumbling to himself: 'I want a car! I want a house!' Sukhodrev also interpreted for Gorbachev at summits with Reagan and Bush. Gorbachev's language was a challenge as it 'was frequently very convoluted and it was hard to really find out what he was trying to say because he used too many words to spell out something simple that he had in mind' (this is a clever parody of Gorbachev speak) (*The Times*, 29 May 2014).

Khrushchev and China

The Soviet leader regarded China as very important and agreed repeatedly to Chinese requests to increase aid but ignored the views of technical experts that such a vast aid programme was beyond the country's capabilities because, to him, it was a political question first and foremost. His first foreign visit was to Beijing in September and October 1954 to mark the fifth anniversary of the founding of the People's Republic. It was deeply symbolic to Mao as it was the first time a Soviet leader had visited the Middle Kingdom. Khrushchev hugged and kissed the Great Helmsman – which greatly offended him – and provided huge gifts which included, among other things, fifteen new industrial projects; a loan of 520 million roubles for military enterprises; the transfer of all Soviet stock in joint Sino-Soviet companies in Xinjiang and Dalian; the construction of a railway from Urumqi to Alma Ata; and withdrawal of Soviet troops from the Port Arthur naval base (and Dalian) ahead of schedule and returning the base to the Chinese free of charge. On the other hand, Khrushchev did not make any concessions on Mongolia. Mao grasped the opportunity to ask for more Soviet specialists to be sent. Overall, he concluded that Khrushchev was a weak leader and needed Chinese support.

The number of Soviet technical experts rose 46 per cent in 1955, 80 per cent in 1956 and 62 per cent in 1957, and Moscow also provided 31,440 technical documents and a huge number of other technical aids. During the Chinese First Five-Year Plan (1953–7), Beijing received about 50 per cent of the aid to socialist countries, and this permitted an annual growth rate of 11.3 per cent. Aid to the Middle Kingdom was about 7 per cent of Soviet national income – a heavy burden for a state struggling to improve living standards.

Whereas the First Five-Year Plan had been drafted by Soviet specialists, the Second Five-Year Plan (1958–62) was drawn up by the Chinese. It involved a request for 188 new industrial projects and help to establish a nuclear industry. Mikoyan visited China in April 1956 and agreed to fifty-five Soviet projects and the construction of a railway from Lanzhou to Antigay in Kazakhstan. In May, Chinese planners arrived in Moscow to discuss the 188 projects and asked for assistance in undertaking another 236 projects but were told that their plans were too ambitious. Eventually, the Soviets agreed to assist the Chinese in designing 217 new projects. Soviet specialists were provided in non-technical areas, including government, law and security, and they also helped draft the new Chinese constitution.

Estimates of Soviet loans during the 1950s are as high as $2.7 billion with 95 per cent of loans during the Korean War going to the military. In March 1961, Khrushchev offered a loan of a million tonnes of grain and half a million tonnes of Cuban sugar to alleviate the famine at that time, and Beijing accepted the Cuban sugar. In 1964, China paid off all existing Soviet loans and hence declared it had no foreign debts (Shen and Xia 2015: 103–10).

Eisenhower's New Look

The Korean War had drained US resources, and Eisenhower wanted to link increases in military expenditure to the growth of the economy. The Soviet threat was economic as well as military, and this had to be borne in mind.

The atomic stockpile grew from 169 weapons in 1949 to 823 in 1952. By 1956, hydrogen (or thermonuclear) weapons were part of the nuclear arsenal; one could wipe out an entire city. Eisenhower's New Look policy, adopted on 29 October 1953, was based on four criteria:

- Defence expenditure was not to undermine the dynamism of the US economy; and therefore increases in one part of the armed services had to be accompanied by cuts elsewhere.

- Nuclear weapons were the main deterrent.
- The CIA was to engage in covert actions against pro-Soviet regimes.
- Defences of allies were to be strengthened and friends won abroad.

As a consequence, the Strategic Air Command was given greater prominence and land and naval forces cut. Local wars, using nuclear weapons, could be fought but a nuclear war against the Soviet Union was now unthinkable. The president was to be the sole judge of when nuclear weapons could be used, but gradually he moved away from regarding them as a weapon of first resort. Threatening a nuclear attack became a salient part of diplomacy known as brinkmanship. There was even discussion of a preventive war after the Soviet Union became a nuclear power in 1949 but this was ruled out in late 1954. Europeans, especially, opposed nuclear war because the continent would inevitably be devastated.

Figure 3.1 President Dwight D. Eisenhower

Courtesy of the Library of Congress Prints and Photographs Division, Washington, DC 20540 USA, LC-USZ62-13034.

The first time that brinkmanship and the threat of a nuclear strike were tried was in March–May 1954 when the French, at Dien Bien Phu in north western Vietnam, appealed for air strikes to break the Viet Minh siege. The French wanted to strengthen their position at the Geneva talks, which began in April, and then leave Vietnam with some honour, but the Americans wanted to defeat the Viet Minh because they saw them as a proxy for the Chinese. Plans for a nuclear strike were drafted but eventually discarded because it would have had a very negative effect on US standing in the world, and its military efficacy was also doubtful. Brinksmanship and nuclear threats thus failed to save the French. At the Geneva conference, Vietnam was divided in two along the 17th parallel with elections to reunite the country in two years' time. The Americans decided to extend aid to the South Vietnamese government and thus began US military involvement in Indochina.

The next test for brinkmanship and nuclear threats was the Taiwan crisis of 1954–5. The US aimed to keep the Chinese guessing about their military intentions, and Henry Kissinger dubbed this the 'uncertainty effect'. Mao Zedong also met brinkmanship with brinkmanship, but what the Americans did not fully grasp was that Mao was trying to draw the Soviet Union into a nuclear confrontation with the US. An example of this was in September 1954, when John Foster Dulles was flying to Manila for the formation of the South East Asian Treaty Organization (SEATO) – which involved the US, UK, France, New Zealand, Australia, the Philippines, Thailand and Pakistan – and China began shelling Quemoy and Matsu. Mao was aware that SEATO was to contain China.

In total, President Eisenhower was called upon to launch nuclear strikes five times:

- In April 1954, to aid the French at Dien Bien Phu; the argument was that nuclear weapons should be made available to the French;
- In May 1954, when France was on the verge of defeat;
- In June 1954, when rumours circulated that China was about to intervene in the Indochina War;
- In September 1954, when China began shelling the islands of Quemoy and Matsu;
- In November 1954, when long prison sentences were handed down to a dozen captured US pilots; Marshal Zhukov intervened at Eisenhower's request and they were released.

On 23 November 1954, Dulles and the Taiwanese ambassador initialled a defence treaty between the US and Taiwan which included the Pescadores Islands, but it did not mention Quemoy and Matsu and other territories close to the Chinese mainland. It was inevitable that Mao would attempt to retake some of these small islands. On 18 January 1955, China invaded the Dachen and Yijiangshan Islands, not covered by the treaty, and the US reacted by evacuating Guomindang forces. But Mao ordered the People's Liberation Army (PLA) not to fire at the

Americans. Dulles hurled threats at the enemies of the US and, in February 1955, during a visit to Thailand, he stated the US was ready to go to war to counter the 'expansionist aims and ambitions of China'. On 15 March 1955, Dulles warned that the US would deploy nuclear weapons to counter any new communist offensive, and it was not a paper tiger. President Eisenhower, the next day, thought that tactical nuclear weapons were no different from a bullet or anything else (Burr and Kimball 2015: 23–37).

Mao beat a hasty retreat and made it clear that China did not want war with the US. His aim had been to show China's potential, and the crisis was put to rest. It had achieved its objective by placing the People's Republic at the centre of world politics. Mao made Moscow fear that it might be drawn into a nuclear confrontation with the US, and this underlined Mao's foreign policy strategy of creating tension with both superpowers simultaneously. Khrushchev complained to Mao that he did not understand Chinese policy. If the aim of shelling the islands was eventually to capture them, why was this not done? Khrushchev did not grasp that Mao did not want to take the islands but preferred to be able to shell them so as to create Taiwan crises in the future. He knew he could shell the islands with impunity whereas an attack on Taiwan would have provoked a massive US response.

After the first Taiwan crisis, Sino-American relations made little progress as China would only discuss the withdrawal of the US from Taiwan, and the US required China to renounce the use of force to solve the Taiwan question. There were 136 meetings between US and Chinese ambassadors (mostly in Warsaw) between 1955 and 1971, and the only agreement reached was to permit citizens trapped by the civil war to return home (Kissinger 2012: 160). It really was a dialogue of the deaf. One of the reasons for stagnant US relations with China during the 1950s was that the State Department was dominated by Soviet specialists – most Chinese specialists had left in the aftermath of the witch-hunt to discover who 'lost' China. The Soviet specialists were convinced that any rapprochement with China risked war with Soviet Union (Kissinger 2012: 200) – unfortunately, a false judgement.

Dulles was credited with inventing brinkmanship. He commented:

> the ability to get to the verge without getting into the war is the necessary art. If you cannot master it, you inevitably get into a war. If you try to run away from it, if you are scared to go to the brink, you are lost.
>
> (*Life*, 30 January 1956)

Dulles said there was a change under Eisenhower 'from a purely defensive policy to a psychological offensive, a liberation policy which will try and give hope and a resistance mood within the Soviet Empire'. As regards communist dominated countries, the US must demonstrate that it 'wants and expects liberation to occur'. He regarded containment as 'futile, negative and immoral'. Churchill had a low opinion of his diplomatic skills (Mosley 1978: 65):

He is the only bull I've ever met who carries his own china shop around with him . . . he is a dull, unimaginative, uncomprehending, insensitive man. I hope he will disappear . . . he is a terrible handicap . . . he preaches like a Methodist minister and his bloody text is always the same . . . nothing but evil can come out of meeting [with the Soviets] . . . I am bewildered. It seems that everything is left to Dulles. It appears that the President is no more than a ventriloquist's doll.

(Larres 2002: 310)

Nevertheless, Eisenhower thought Dulles was the best secretary of state the US ever had, but he had to reprimand him at times and told him not to use the expression 'instant retaliation' in his speeches. Eisenhower stated 'peace is our objective and we reject all talk of and proposals of preventive war'. After Sputnik 1 the churches called for 'massive reconciliation' instead of 'massive retaliation'. Dulles commented, in 1957, that there had been a shift in the balance of power in the world, and that shift had been in favour of communism. It should also be mentioned that Eisenhower thought he knew as much or even more than Dulles about foreign policy. Even though Dulles was normally bellicose about communism, he came to believe that a 'peaceful evolution' would eventually lead to communist states collapsing. Peace would result in their final demise, and he was right. When Dulles died he was succeeded, in April 1959, by the fragile Christian Herter.

Despite the bellicosity, Eisenhower's strategy can be regarded as subtle and nuanced, resting on seven pillars (Ferguson 2015: 344–5):

- Feasibility of deterrence;
- The necessity of a secure 'second strike' capability;
- The abandonment of forcible 'rollback' of the Soviet Empire as a US goal;
- The recognition of the long-term character of the Cold War;
- The strengthening of US alliances in Europe and Asia;
- The pursuit of realistic forms of arms control;
- Bombing would not achieve these goals and had to be accompanied by diplomacy, psychological warfare and covert operations.

The key question, of course, was: would nuclear weapons be used in any conflict? Eisenhower did not believe that fighting a limited nuclear war was feasible because it would inevitably escalate, and there was also the point that US allies in Western Europe did not want any war to go nuclear for the simple reason that they would be wiped out.

General Douglas MacArthur, reflecting on the 1950s, commented (MacArthur 1965: 186):

Our government has kept us in a perpetual state of fear – kept us in a continuous stampede of patriotic fervor – with the cry of grave national emergency. Always there has been some terrible evil at home that was going to gobble us up if we did not blindly rally behind it by furnishing the exorbitant sums demanded. Yet, in retrospect, these disasters seem never to have happened, seem never to have been quite real.

A sobering comment by a top military man.

The Geneva spirit

Moscow had always linked Germany and Austria and, in the latter, there were Soviet, US, British and French zones, and Vienna was divided into sectors. Shortly after Stalin's death Khrushchev raised the question of Soviet troops leaving Austria, but Molotov strongly objected and as foreign minister ensured there was no progress for about two years. What forced Molotov's hand? The imminent accession of West Germany to the North Atlantic Treaty Organization (NATO). The Soviets did not want Austria and West Germany coming together to form a union (Anschluss) similar to that in 1938 so Molotov offered a peace treaty and withdrawal of forces if the country became neutral like Sweden or Switzerland and the peace treaty was signed in May 1955. There was another bonus for Moscow as neutrality meant that NATO forces could not move to Italy through Austria and would now have to go via France.

During an official visit, the Austrian chancellor, Julius Raab, handed a gift to Nikita Khrushchev, the Soviet Party leader. It was an original letter by Karl Marx providing information about revolutionary exiles in London, Paris and Switzerland. He received the equivalent of $25 for each missive. In other words, Marx was a paid agent of the Austrian secret service but there is no record of how Khrushchev reacted to this information.

This was the high point of Soviet détente at the time. Hopes were raised that a four-power meeting in Geneva, in July 1955, would resolve the German and other questions. Khrushchev was already top dog in Moscow but had no official state position to permit him to attend the summit. Bulganin was prime minister and formally headed the Soviet delegation. However, when Bulganin was asked a question, Khrushchev butted in and answered it, and this revealed who was now boss. Marshal Zhukov had pressed Eisenhower to attend, and he did, but the marshal was unusually sombre at the meeting. A reason for this may have been his discovery that the US had a plan – Operation Dropshot – which envisaged dropping 300 hydrogen bombs on Soviet targets and destroying 85 per cent of the Soviet Union's industrial capacity. Dulles thought that Soviet power could be rolled back. The Geneva 'spirit' dissipated quickly as no progress was made on bringing East and West together, and the conclusion that Khrushchev drew was that the capitalists were as afraid of war as the Soviets. He told the French foreign minister that the whole of Germany would soon fall into the Soviet lap like a 'ripe plum'. The Americans assessed Khrushchev as a leader who acted on emotion – a sharp contrast to the sober, calculating Stalin. Khrushchev, on the other hand, knew how far Dulles would go. In his memoirs, he says that the secretary of state was aware of how far he could push the Soviet Union and never went too far. An example was the Middle East crisis of 1958 involving Syria and Lebanon when Dulles stepped back from the brink of war. US and British troops pulled back, partly under the pressure of world opinion but also partly as the result of Dulles's prudence.

Diplomatic relations were established between the Soviet Union and the Federal Republic of Germany in September 1955. The German chancellor, Konrad Adenauer, conceded that the Soviets would not agree to a united Germany. Why did Moscow agree to diplomatic relations? They needed German technology and know-how. The remaining German prisoners of war were repatriated, some choosing to go to the GDR.

Khrushchev liked to tell a joke about Adenauer:

> Adenauer likes to speak in the name of the two Germanies and to raise the German question in Europe as though we couldn't survive without accepting his terms. But Adenauer does not speak the truth. If you strip him naked and observe him from the rear, you can see clearly that Germany is divided into two parts. However, if you look at him from the front, it is equally clear that his view of the German question never did stand up, doesn't stand up and never will stand up.

The first Soviet ambassador to Bonn was Valerian Zorin, who had masterminded the communist coup in Prague in February 1948, but he was so unsuccessful that he was withdrawn in July 1956. This indicated that there was no need to worry about a German-Soviet rapprochement which could lead to a German withdrawal from NATO. Bulganin and Khrushchev were invited to Britain in 1956, and the visit was a success.

> Khrushchev is in a foul mood. He comes into the Kremlin and spits on the carpet. 'Tut, tut', says an aide, 'that is uncouth behaviour.' 'I can spit on the carpet as much as I like. The Queen of England gave me permission.' 'How come?,' asks the incredulous aide. 'Well, I spat on the carpet in Buckingham Palace and the Queen said: "Mr Khrushchev, you can do that in the Kremlin if you wish but you can't behave like that here."'

The Geneva spirit led to the flowering of US-Soviet cultural exchanges with the Soviet pianist Emile Gilels and the violinist David Oistrakh delighting American audiences; Gershwin's *Porgy and Bess* was staged in Moscow. The New York, Chicago and Los Angeles Symphony Orchestras gave concerts, and pianist Van Cliburn and violinist Isaac Stern wowed Soviet audiences. Igor Moiseev's Folk Dance Company, the Beriozka Dance Troupe, and the Bolshoi Ballet toured the US.

Poland and Hungary in 1956

Khrushchev's Secret Speech at the 20th Party Congress, in February 1956, rocked communism in Eastern Europe to its foundations. He highlighted the dangers of unlimited power in the hands of one man which had resulted in Stalin dealing brutally with those who disagreed with him; he was capricious and despotic, and this was labelled the cult of personality. Foreign policy after 1945 resulted in complications for the Soviet Union because it was decided by one man. The Congress resolution underlined a new policy: peaceful coexistence, peaceful transition and peaceful competition, and thus a peaceful transition from capitalism to socialism was possible. The Secret Speech – so called because it was delivered to a selected group of delegates at the Congress – did not remain secret for very long. On 1 March, the Communist Party of the Soviet Union (CPSU) Presidium printed 150 copies of the speech, and Soviet embassies handed them to the Central Committee of the Communist Parties. The Polish Party printed copies, and a Reuters journalist was slipped a copy in March. Eventually, it was published by the CIA for worldwide consumption.

The speech caused consternation in Georgia (Stalin was Georgian). After the contents became known there was a mass wreath laying at Stalin's statue in Tbilisi. Demonstrations grew and tens of thousands, carrying portraits of Stalin, demanded the resignation of Khrushchev, Malenkov and Bulganin and their replacement by Molotov. The demonstrations spread to all cities in Georgia and were, eventually, bloodily suppressed. At least a hundred were shot by Soviet Army soldiers in Tbilisi.

The release of tens of thousands of Soviet prisoners – many of them political – in 1956 added to the excitement in Poland. Violence exploded in Poznań, in June 1956, when factory workers came out and demanded higher wages and an end to food shortages; soon half the city was involved in demonstrations. Communist Party buildings were fired at and set on fire. The communist leadership ordered the military and police to shoot workers; over 150 died and hundreds of others were injured. One of the architects of the massacre was Józef Cyrankiewicz, the prime minister, who was a great toy collector – apparently, a whole room in his apartment was full of them, and he was said to spend hours playing with them. Cyrankiewicz, in the eyes of Edward Ochab, party leader from March to October 1956, was a weak man who had been broken during his time in Auschwitz.

Khrushchev, three members of the Soviet Presidium and the commander of Warsaw Pact forces, Marshal Ivan Konev, flew into Warsaw unannounced. When he saw Edward Ochab, he shook his fist under his nose and began screaming abuse. The Polish leader asked him not to make a scene at the airport and that everyone should repair to the Belvedere where foreign guests were received. Khrushchev wanted a plenum of the PUWP, the Polish Communist Party, which was to propose Władysław Gomułka as the new leader, cancelled. Ochab (reminiscing in 1981) told Khrushchev this was out of the question and that the plenum would go ahead.

I've spent a good few years in prison and I'm not afraid of it; I'm not afraid of anything. We're responsible for our country and we do whatever we think fit, because these are our internal affairs. We're not doing anything to jeopardise the interests of our allies, particularly the interests of the Soviet Union.

Khrushchev countered by saying that they'd come as friends, not as enemies. Ochab replied: 'We don't use such methods towards our friends . . . We'll not back down . . . and Polish affairs will be decided by our Politburo.' The Soviet leader complained that the Polish Politburo was taking decisions without consulting him. Ochab, rather cheekily, asked: 'Do you consult us about the make-up of your Politburo or your Central Committee?' Ochab described the discussions with the Soviet leaders as 'bitter and difficult' (Toranska 1987: 76).

Khrushchev ordered Soviet troops in Poland to halt their move towards Warsaw, and Gomułka warned Khrushchev that Poles would resist Soviet military intervention. The growing crisis in Hungary was also a contributory factor in staying the hand of Moscow. Mao, who shortly before had spoken of Soviet great power chauvinism, reported to a meeting of his Politburo that he had received a letter from the Polish leadership asking for help. 'The relations between the USSR and Poland are no longer those between teacher and pupil. They are relations between two states and Parties.' Mao summoned the Soviet ambassador to his bedroom (contrary to protocol) and told him: 'We resolutely condemn what you are doing. I request that you immediately telephone Khrushchev and inform him of our view. If the Soviet Union moves its troops, we will support Poland.'

Khrushchev invited representatives of socialist countries, including China, to come to Moscow for consultations. It was logical for Mao to oppose Soviet military moves in Poland because if Khrushchev had used force and Mao had acquiesced, it would have set a precedent as Khrushchev could have used the same tactic to intervene militarily in China and remove Mao. The Great Helmsman again summoned the ambassador to his bedroom and told him that he was greatly displeased by Khrushchev's anti-Stalin policy (Pantsov 2015: 179).

Gomułka managed to get compensation for additional coal deliveries, and he also succeeded in getting the Polish born Soviet Marshal Konstantin Rokossovsky (Rokossowski in Polish), minister of defence since 1949, to pack his bags and return to Moscow. On his return, despite having had eight teeth knocked out by the NKVD while under arrest in 1937, he refused to participate in Khrushchev's anti-Stalin campaign. He commented: 'For me, comrade Stalin is sacred.'

A decisive factor in allowing the Poles to choose their own communist leader was Gomułka's promise to remain loyal to Moscow and the Warsaw Pact Organisation.

One of the reasons why the previous party leader, Edward Ochab, had failed was because he had fallen out with the Roman Catholic Primate of Poland, Stefan Wyszyński. The Primate had entered into a secret agreement with the communists in 1950, which permitted the Church to own property, separated

Church and state and permitted the Church to select bishops from a list of three drawn up by the state. Wyszyński was arrested in 1953, and Ochab made the mistake of cancelling the agreement about the appointment of bishops. Gomułka was much cleverer, and he released the Primate and restored him to office. Wyszyński appealed to Poles to forget about heroics and lead a normal life. It was a remarkable tandem. Religious instruction was provided in schools on demand, masses were crowded and Poland became the most religious state in Europe with a new state-Church social contract emerging. How different things were in Hungary. When the Primate, József Mindszenty, was released from prison, in 1956, he sided with the insurgents and thereby fuelled the civil war.

Pax, from the 1950s, an official Catholic party, was represented in parliament, controlled its own press and publishing house, educated children and built many churches. From 1956, it was replaced by Znak which also sat in the Sejm and from which many oppositionists emerged, including Tadeusz Mazowiecki who became prime minister in 1989. From the 1960s onwards, the Church was permitted to engage in a huge construction programme of churches, seminaries and sanctuaries, unprecedented since the eighteenth century. The prevailing Modernism did not apply to ecclesiastical designs (Hatherley 2015: 192–3).

Poles hoped that the second coming of Gomułka would herald a new political, social and cultural dawn for the country. They were to be bitterly disappointed as Gomułka turned into a narrow-minded communist bureaucrat who dissipated the legitimacy he enjoyed in 1956. Initially, he got on well with the intelligentsia but gradually it resented the censorship and encouraged student revolts. The regime began to identify the Jewish origins of many of those involved and ugly anti-Semitism appeared; this was to result in the expulsion of many Jews in 1968. Gomułka, according to Ochab, was afraid of democratisation because it would open the door to 'hostile elements' (Toranska 1987: 84).

> He simply had a nationalistic mania. But I'd never suspected he would go as far as an anti-Semitic campaign. Still, he shouldn't be seen in an entirely negative light; you can't judge him solely on the basis of his nationalistic mania, his autocratic aspirations, his lunacies – I think they were symptoms of a disease: megalomania and persecution mania. Such manias tend to flourish in the difficult circumstances in which our government is developing.

Ochab states that his disgust at the anti-Semitic campaign led to his resignation from all his party and state posts. He died on 1 May 1989, when communism in Poland was on its last legs.

Events in Hungary took a much more tragic turn in 1956. Both the reformers and conservatives looked to China for support but the embassy locked its gates and refused contact with everyone. When members from the former Rákosi government sought refuge, the doorman told them to go to the Soviet embassy.

Anastas Mikoyan had travelled to Budapest in July 1956 to insist that Mátyás Rákosi depart as communist leader, and Khrushchev had him flown to Moscow and put under house arrest there. Mikoyan also met and considered János Kádár as the new leader but Ernö Gerö was chosen. The Kremlin was aware that picking a Jew, Gerö (né Singer), to succeed another Jew, Rákosi (né Rosenfeld) would make it difficult for the party to win over the population. Gerö had spent much time in the Soviet Union and was regarded as a 'Moscow' communist, not a national communist, and Khrushchev later conceded that they had picked the wrong comrade. The party permitted the reburial of László Rajk, a former minister of the interior, who had been executed as a Titoist. Hungarians now regarded him as a martyr. On 23 October, thousands lined the streets of Budapest, and Rajk's widow was told by Imre Nagy that Stalinism would soon be buried there too. Nagy, a popular prime minister from 1953–5, was readmitted to the party.

Liu Shaoqi and other members of the Chinese delegation flew to Moscow on 23 October and engaged in eight days of discussions with Khrushchev and other members of the Presidium. On several occasions, the first on 24 October, Liu and Deng Xiaoping attended Presidium meetings. Khrushchev explained to them that whereas the Polish crisis had been an intra-party dispute, the Hungarian concerned the overthrow of communist power.

Students issued a manifesto calling for Soviet troops to leave Hungary and 'Comrade Imre Nagy' to become prime minister. On 23 October, the huge Stalin statue which dominated central Budapest was toppled. Khrushchev instructed Gerö to appoint Nagy prime minister immediately but Gerö then made a hard line speech which infuriated many. Soviet troops and tanks moved into Budapest the next day and fighting broke out. Pál Maléter, a colonel in the Hungarian army, became the face of opposition to Soviet domination. Imre Nagy was appointed prime minister on 24 October and remained in office until 4 November.

On 28 October, the Kremlin ordered its troops out of Budapest to be replaced by Hungarian troops. It appeared that Khrushchev had conceded that a reform communist could run Hungary, and Maléter became minister of defence in a coalition government which included members from the reformed Social Democratic Party and Smallholders' Party. This was a national government, and it also included János Kádár, the new leader of the Communist Party.

Mao did not comment on events until 29 October, when he phoned Liu and told him Moscow should loosen its grip on the Eastern European states and that peaceful coexistence should extend to socialist state to state relations. Also on 29 October, in consultation with Liu, Khrushchev agreed to draft a statement, which was to be published the next day, declaring full equality between the Soviet Union and Eastern European states. When the security situation became more desperate, Khrushchev and Liu changed their minds and agreed to resort to force, but Mao intervened and recommended that events should be allowed to 'go further'; the Soviets then decided not to use force.

Anastas Mikoyan and Mikhail Suslov, in Budapest, approved the appointment of Kádár and the composition of the coalition government, but they were taken aback by Nagy's statement that the government would begin negotiations with the Soviets to remove their armed forces from Hungary. Resistance fighters began hanging hated policemen and communists from lamp posts in Budapest.

On 30 October, the Soviet Presidium accepted the five principles of peaceful coexistence proposed by the Chinese:

- Respect for sovereignty and territorial integrity;
- Non-aggression;
- Non-interference in internal affairs;
- Equality;
- Peaceful coexistence.

This revealed that the Chinese view that the Hungarian crisis should be resolved peacefully had prevailed. The Soviet Party Presidium decided thereupon to withdraw all Soviet troops from Hungary and all socialist states and to work towards a peaceful solution. On the same day, the Soviet Presidium adopted a declaration which stated that 'countries of the great community of socialist states can base their mutual relations only on the principle of . . . non-interference in one another's domestic affairs.' However, the situation changed dramatically, and Khrushchev changed his mind and declared: 'troops will not be withdrawn from Hungary and Budapest and will take the initiative in restoring order in Hungary.' On the evening of 31 October, as the Chinese delegation were at the airport en route to Beijing, Khrushchev and the Presidium explained the reversal of the decision to resolve the situation peacefully. The Chinese concurred that force was necessary (Pantsov 2015: 180–2; Shen and Xia 2015: 172–6). Hence in Poland and Hungary, China played an important role.

On 1 November, Kádár voted in favour of Hungarian neutrality as a member of the coalition government, but the same evening he flew to Moscow and was accompanied by Ferenc Münnich, a 'Moscow' communist. The next day, they met the Soviet leadership but not Khrushchev, who was in Eastern Europe briefing leaders on the reasons for the deployment of force. Kádár was unaware that the Soviets had picked him as the next Hungarian leader and told them that he had voted for neutrality and was against military force. On 3 November, Kádár changed sides and became Moscow's comrade in Budapest and in doing so betrayed his own comrades. Because the Communist Party had lost all authority, he became prime minister. The Communist Party, eventually renamed the Hungarian Socialist Workers' Party, would have to be rebuilt, and once that had been achieved he would again become party leader.

On 2 November, Khrushchev and Mikoyan flew to see Tito on Brioni to explain why they had decided to use force. Hungary was withdrawing from the Warsaw Pact and was to become neutral, but if Hungary left the 'socialist camp' Stalinists in the Soviet Union would receive a massive boost. Hungarian minorities in Romania and Slovakia, if Hungary became independent, would lobby to return to Hungary and thereby undermine the existing communist governments. There was a window of opportunity afforded by the Anglo-French attack on the

Suez Canal which was then under way. Under this cover the Soviet Army could get away with using massive force. The Soviets misread the Suez attack, thinking it was American-inspired. As such, an invasion of Hungary could now follow to suppress the Revolution.

The intervention was wholly Soviet but it was packaged as a Warsaw Pact intervention. An 'invitation' was extended by the Hungarian coalition government and collective support came from other Warsaw Pact countries.

The suppression of the Hungarian Revolution took four days (4–7 November 1956); over 2,000 died and 20,000 ended up in hospital. Subsequently over 100,000 were arrested on 'counter-revolutionary' charges. Several hundred were executed. Over 100,000 fled Hungary and formed a Western diaspora which was not well disposed to the Soviet Union, to say the least. The communists were pleased to see them go.

Imre Nagy sought refuge in the Yugoslav embassy and was assured safe passage when he left the embassy on 23 November but was immediately arrested and taken to Romania. He remained under house arrest until 1958 when he was tried in Budapest and hanged. Maléter and another rebel were also hanged. It was long believed that these deaths were ordered by Moscow but this was not the case. It was Kádár who wanted the executions as he regarded Nagy as a dangerous political opponent. At his trial, Nagy stated that he knew one day there would be a new trial which would rehabilitate him and that he would also be reburied. He was remarkably prescient as all these things later occurred.

Communist regimes did adjust after 1956, and they introduced reforms which made contacts with the West easier. Vice President Richard Nixon was given an enthusiastic welcome in Warsaw in 1959, and there were even slogans such as 'Long Live America'.

The events of 1956 proved that the Communist Party of the Soviet Union was still a Leninist party. It would shed the blood of workers to stay in power, and this reality had a profound impact on Eastern Europe. Violence would be ineffective against the regime, and opposition would have to be more subtle. If economic prosperity could be achieved, then dissent would have little impact, and this meant that the greatest threat to communist power would result from failure to raise living standards. There was severe repression in Hungary in the late 1950s as the communists strengthened their grip, and Kádár, a morose, miserable comrade at the best of times, turned out to be a suitable choice of a defeated nation. He and Yuri Andropov, who had been Soviet ambassador in Budapest in 1956, and later head of the KGB, got on very well. What a peculiar friendship! The story goes that Andropov's wife was kept awake by the screams of prisoners being tortured which led to her suffering a deep depression.

In other parts of Eastern Europe, national communists dominated, and this was the case in Romania, Bulgaria, Albania, Yugoslavia and Poland. All the leaders wanted to have the power of Stalin and discovered that the best way to achieve this was to pose as saviours of their nation. As time was to show, Romania and Albania were to join Yugoslavia in distancing themselves from Moscow.

The suppression of the Hungarian Revolution had a dramatic effect on communism worldwide as droves of comrades in Europe and elsewhere abandoned the party. Some of those who left stated that they remained Marxists but were no longer communists. Those who remained demonstrated that they were willing to accept that Leninism – the use of brute force to suppress dissent – should not be revised.

The Berlin crises

The Polish and Hungarian crises had revealed divisions in the Soviet leadership, and the bill to maintain Soviet power in Eastern Europe was increasing by the day as Poland had to be given loans and Budapest had to be repaired. The other important lesson was that the West would not intervene militarily. The US had considerable strategic superiority but it was not aware of this at the time.

In July 1955, President Eisenhower announced that the US would launch an artificial earth satellite, but the Soviet Union got there first with the success of Sputnik 1 (meaning 'fellow traveller') in October 1957. It was an enormous propaganda coup for Moscow. Moscow was now ahead in space, and plans got under way to launch the first human in space. Sputnik was a tremendous shock, and a wave of near hysteria swept the US. The governor of Michigan expressed his dismay in verse (Andrew and Mitrokhin 2005: 6):

> Oh, Little Sputnik, flying high
> With made-in Moscow beep
> You tell the world it's a Commie sky
> And Uncle Sam's asleep

West Germany joined NATO in 1955, and in 1956 began to contemplate producing its own nuclear weapons. How would Khrushchev, in 1958 prime minister as well as First Secretary, respond? He returned to Stalin's tactic: force the Western allies out of Berlin and thus began the second Berlin crisis. In November 1958, a note was sent to the Western allies accusing them of grossly violating the Potsdam Agreement on Germany; West Berlin was being turned into a mini-state, and this undermined the unification of Germany. The Soviet Union would transfer its occupation rights to the GDR, and West Berlin might become a Free City. The allies had to abandon West Berlin within six months. The US moved nuclear weapons to West Germany in such a way that the Soviet military mission in Frankfurt-am-Main, West Germany, could monitor events. The Americans also created a fleet of nuclear bombers which were permanently airborne and ready to strike when necessary. Khrushchev engaged in brinkmanship and thought the Allies would not go to war over Berlin, and his military told him it could take the city in six to eight hours. As during the crises in Poland and Hungary, Anastas Mikoyan was the voice of reason and encouraged Khrushchev not to provoke conflict. He was sent to Washington in January 1959, but nothing was achieved. Then the Soviet Union signed a peace treaty with the GDR.

Khrushchev and Eisenhower met at Camp David, Maryland, in September 1959, during his visit to the US. The US president was hoping to agree to a ban on nuclear testing and move towards verification but such was the mutual distrust that nothing came of these initiatives.

To President Eisenhower's great relief, he was never called upon to sanction the use of nuclear weapons. As a soldier, he was aware that after the first salvo of nuclear weapons, there would be such devastation that the 'fog of war' would be such as to make planning for a second stage valueless.

In his memoirs, Khrushchev conceded that he had been forced to

> economise drastically in the building of apartments, the construction of communal services and even in the development of agriculture in order to build up our defences. I even suspended the construction of subways in Kiev, Baku and Tbilisi so that we could redirect these funds into strengthening our defences and attack forces.
>
> (Khrushchev 1971: 545)

Khrushchev was very impressed by American agriculture on his visit, especially the role of maize. On his return he ordered maize to be planted as the solution to the fodder problem. This earned him the nickname of Comrade Kukuruznik ('Comrade Maize'), and he was lampooned far and wide.

> The Soviets land on the moon. The Kremlin asks: 'What do you see?' 'Well, there's a short, bald man planting maize!'

The failure of maize was one of the reasons for his removal in October 1964. He gave the impression that the Soviet Union was ahead in rocketry, also in intercontinental ballistic missiles (ICBMs), but this was a fiction and sooner or later the Americans would rumble him. Eisenhower was criticised for the 'missile gap' which had opened up with the Soviet Union. Khrushchev's brinkmanship was based on false premises because he hoped that Soviet advances in rocketry would solve all his security problems within a few years. American overflights were aimed at discovering the real state of affairs but Soviet missiles could not bring them down.

On 1 May 1960, the US spy plane U-2 was shot down over Sverdlovsk (now Ekaterinburg). Captain Gary Powers was on a mission from Pakistan to Norway to photograph several highly sensitive nuclear sites in the Urals. At a height of 20,000 metres he felt safe, but three hours into the mission and over the Urals the autopilot failed. Instead of staying within the narrow speed and altitude ranges, it began pitching up and slowing down. Should he attempt to return to base or carry on? He decided to carry on. That meant another six hours flying, and he had to fly the aircraft manually and still operate the huge cameras under it.

The Soviets had no MiG aircraft which could fly higher than 17,500 metres but there was a new Sukhoi (Su-9) which was being delivered, unarmed, from the factory. One of the delivery pilots was ordered to fly the aircraft without pressure suit or helmet. 'Your mission is to intercept the target and ram it,' his commander told him – a suicide mission. The Su-9 climbed and attempted to approach Powers from the rear at Mach 2 (twice the speed of sound). The pilot was travelling about a thousand miles an hour faster than Powers, but he could not find the U-2. Ground control ordered him to cut his afterburner and he fell to earth. Two MiGs scrambled above Sverdlovsk but could not reach Powers, so the only hope now was to launch missiles. Three were fired but only one ignited and it took off the U-2's tail and the wings also went. Powers went into a vertical spin. He managed to extricate himself and landed by parachute. He should have destroyed the cameras and the aircraft but he put his own safety first. Miraculously, he survived and the only person to die was a Soviet pilot who had been sent up to intercept Powers but had been hit by a stray Soviet rocket.

The Paris summit, which opened on 16 May, collapsed two days later, and Eisenhower's proposed visit to the Soviet Union was cancelled. The U-2 incident dashed the hopes of a comprehensive Test Ban Treaty as the centrepiece of disarmament talks between the superpowers. It also ended the prospect of an end to the Cold War. President de Gaulle was personally affronted by Khrushchev's behaviour and the failure of the Paris summit, and the outcome was that he turned away from the Soviet Union for five years and sided with the US on international relations.

After Castro seized power in Cuba, a band of Cuban exiles was set up in Nicaragua and funded by the CIA. Eisenhower did not give them the go-ahead to attack Cuba, but under Kennedy they formed the core of the April 1961 attack at the Bay of Pigs. The president was informed by his Joint Chiefs of Staff that the invasion had a 'fair chance' of success. Kennedy assumed this meant it was quite likely to succeed while the chiefs actually meant it had a 25 per cent chance. Greater precision would have avoided this misunderstanding and prevented the fiasco which resulted.

Khrushchev deduced that Kennedy was a weak president, and the Bay of Pigs debacle revealed that he was not at all intelligent, and it followed he would wilt under pressure. Kennedy met Khrushchev in Vienna in June 1961 and came off second best. He was warned not to engage in polemics with a master such as Khrushchev but he failed to follow this advice. This strengthened Khrushchev's resolve to force concessions in Berlin and, more daringly, in Cuba. Walter Ulbricht had been advocating stemming the tide of refugees to West Germany for some time, as socialism could not be built in the GDR if skilled personnel walked away. A wall was needed, and he had asked for one to be built at a Warsaw Pact meeting in March 1961 but was flatly turned down. Khrushchev eventually agreed, and the Berlin Wall went up on 13 August 1961 – the anniversary of the birth of Karl Liebknecht, one of the founders of the Communist Party of Germany (KPD). The Soviet leader did not think he was risking war, and to remind everyone of Soviet power, nuclear tests resumed. This underlined the fact that the Soviet leader believed nuclear threat diplomacy was effective and he had been practising it since the Suez crisis when he had incorrectly concluded that his threat to launch a nuclear attack on US bases in Britain had forced the Anglo-French pull out of Egypt.

The Western powers accepted the Wall but one dangerous incident did occur. On 27 October 1961, ten US and ten Soviet tanks faced one another at Checkpoint

Charlie for sixteen hours. The reason was the refusal of the GDR authorities to allow a US diplomat access to East Berlin; he had insisted that he could enter without any passport checks. Khrushchev was attempting to end free access to East Berlin by the Western powers. Kennedy sent his brother, Robert, to inform a Soviet official that if the Soviets removed their tanks, the Americans would do the same within twenty minutes. Dean Rusk, secretary of state, instructed General Lucius Clay, the president's personal representative in Berlin, that entry to Berlin was not a 'vital interest' and would not justify the use of force to 'protect and sustain' it. The next morning, the Soviet tanks withdrew, followed by the US tanks half an hour later. At the 22nd Party Congress, then in session, Khrushchev announced that he was withdrawing his Berlin ultimatum. The crisis revealed that Kennedy was willing to make concessions by back channel contacts to conceal from the public that he had backed down.

In November 1958, a secret military organisation, Live Oak, had been set up by the three Western military powers for the defence of Berlin. During the afore-mentioned crisis, they sent military vehicles along the autobahn to Berlin to discover if the GDR or Soviet authorities would interfere with the traffic. Had they done so, it would have led to escalation and possibly to nuclear war. From a conventional point of view, the Western military position in West Berlin was untenable, and the only way to defend the city was by deploying nuclear weapons. The West had made it clear that any attempt to blockade Berlin, as in 1948, would lead to escalation. General Clay, from his experience in 1948, was convinced that Khrush-chev was bluffing and would not risk nuclear war; he turned out to be correct but no one could be certain, least of all the president. It was a baptism of fire for him and prepared him for an even greater test the following year. The Berlin crisis also confirmed in Kennedy's mind that a limited nuclear conflict – for example, over Berlin – was not credible. A nuclear conflict would be all or nothing.

There were incidents in 1962 when Soviet aircraft interfered with flights to West Berlin. This led to the US sending jet fighters to accompany US aircraft. The second Berlin crisis can be said to have ended in October 1962. This was when the Cuban Missile Crisis was resolved, and this underlined the fact that the two crises were interlinked. Had Khrushchev got his way in Berlin and Cuba, the geopolitical map of the world would have been redrawn. NATO would have turned out to be a fig leaf, and Bonn would have been in Moscow's pocket. The stakes for Kennedy were that high, and because of this the US was prepared to fight a nuclear war over Berlin and Cuba.

The Cuban Missile Crisis

On 29 June 1960, Khrushchev received from the KGB an alarming piece of intelligence about US military intentions (Andrew and Mitrokhin 2005: 38).

> The Pentagon is convinced of the need to initiate a war with the Soviet Union as soon as possible. Right now, the USA has the capability to wipe out Soviet missile bases and other military targets with its bomber forces.

But over the next little while the defence forces of the Soviet Union will grow . . . and the opportunity will disappear . . . As a result of these assumptions, the chiefs at the Pentagon are hoping to launch a preventive war against the Soviet Union.

Khrushchev took this totally false analysis at face value and, on 9 July, warned the US that the Soviet Union had rockets with a range of 13,000 km and could defend Cuba if the Pentagon dared to intervene there. Raúl Castro, visiting Moscow later that month, conveyed Fidel's gratitude for Khrushchev's speech. Was this misleading report the genesis of the plan to place medium range missiles on Cuba?

On 29 July 1961, Aleksandr Shelepin, head of the KGB, presented to Khrushchev a grand plan to create circumstances in different parts of the world which would divert American attention and tie it down during the settlement of a 'German peace treaty and West Berlin'. National liberation movements, armed by the KGB, were to launch attacks on 'pro-Western reactionary governments'. Top of the list, together with Cuba, was the establishment of a second communist state in Nicaragua. The Frente Sandinista de Liberaciòn Nacional de Nicaragua (FSLN), headed by Carlos Fonseca Amador, guided by the KGB and the Cubans, was to attempt this. A revolutionary front, headed by Cuba and Nicaragua and directed by the KGB, would become active in Latin America. The KGB was providing thousands of dollars through its embassy in Mexico City. Sandinista guerrilla groups were also being trained in Honduras and Costa Rica and other guerrilla groups appeared in Colombia, Venezuela, Peru and Guatemala. Peru became a disappointment because the most effective guerrilla group was the Sendero Luminoso (Shining Path) which was Maoist. This was a constant problem for Moscow as it battled to counter the appeal of the extreme left Maoists.

American advantage in intercontinental ballistic missiles (ICBMs) was 9 to 1, and the Soviets only had twenty-five delivery vehicles to hit the US, but the Americans did not know this at the time. Because a Soviet ICBM could reach the US, the Cuban missile crisis was more about power and prestige than about missiles. The US had already stationed missiles in Turkey. It occurred to Khrushchev that if the Soviet Union could place medium- and intermediate-range nuclear missiles in Cuba, they could strike at many US cities. The CPSU Presidium accepted this in May 1962, and shortly thereafter a small delegation was sent to Havana to seek Castro's approval. The latter commented later that had it only been about Cuba's defence he would have rejected the missiles, but in a show of solidarity with the Soviet bloc he agreed. Khrushchev concluded that the Americans would accept the missiles if they were installed before the (mid-term congressional) elections in November. This was based on his own judgement as he had not requested an intelligence report on the likely reaction of the US. Anastas Mikoyan was unhappy, saying that the Americans would never tolerate it and he, as usual, had a better nose for superpower relations. He was to prove, as in domestic policy, the voice of reason who had to rein in the wild risk-taking of the First Secretary.

In April 1961, the Americans had attempted in the Bay of Pigs to overthrow Castro's regime; Moscow thought they would try again and they were right. It was called Operation Mongoose. Secret Operation Anadyr was launched, and even the Soviet ambassador in Washington was not informed. Five missile regiments with modern medium-range missiles were dispatched; about 42,000 troops were involved. Soviet ships docked 183 times to deliver 23,000 tonnes of military ordnance. In October, Soviet troops had 152 nuclear missiles as well as Ilyushin Il-28 bombers and the most modern nuclear submarines armed with submarine-launched ballistic missiles (SLBMs) as well as nuclear torpedoes. The Americans only discovered the arsenal on 15 October as a result of U-2 overflights, and it would have taken longer if the Soviet troops had thought of camouflaging the launch sites. The Soviets, therefore, had carried out a brilliant secret mission under the noses of the Americans. President Kennedy found himself confronted with a painful dilemma: accept the presence of the missiles, bomb the sites or negotiate them away. His military favoured a surgical strike, but when he asked if they could guarantee 100 per cent success, they were silent. Kennedy rejected a military in favour of a diplomatic solution. Nevertheless, SAC had 912 bombers on fifteen-minute ground alert with every bomber carrying three or four thermonuclear bombs. By early November, when the crisis was abating, SAC had increased the number of bombers on alert from 652 to 1,479 and nearly 3,000 nuclear weapons were ready for launching. One hundred and eighty-two ICBMs were ready to be fired as were all 112 Polaris missiles. Soviet bomber and missile forces were also on high alert. Both sides threatened massive retaliation.

On 22 October, Kennedy demanded that Khrushchev remove the military installations and return the missiles to the Soviet Union; on 23 October he discussed an all-out nuclear exchange with his advisers; on 24 October he announced a quarantine of Cuba; on 24 October DEFCON (Defense Readiness Condition) 2 was set in motion – this was one step from imminent nuclear war. On 25 October, Soviet ships heading for Cuba were turned back, and the US placed a quarantine zone around the island. The most dangerous day was 27 October, when everything could have gone pear- or rather plume-shaped when a Soviet submarine almost fired a nuclear torpedo. On the same day, a U-2 reconnaissance aircraft drifted into Siberian airspace in error, and Soviet MiGs were scrambled to shoot it down; fortunately F-102As got there first and guided the US plane safely to Alaskan airspace. Had the MiGs shot it down, the Soviets might have interpreted it as the last reconnaissance flight before American missiles rained down on the Soviet Union.

On 28 October, Khrushchev announced, after a secret exchange of letters, that the missiles would be transported back to the Soviet Union. Kennedy agreed not to attack Cuba and to withdraw US missiles from Turkey, but the latter part of the deal was not to be made public.

Khrushchev did not need to judge whether Kennedy was bluffing or not. As the Soviets had broken the American codes, he could read all American communications, and when he found out that Kennedy had placed US forces worldwide on full alert – one step from going to war – he was shocked and gave in.

Figure 3.2 President John F. Kennedy

Courtesy of the Library of Congress Prints and Photographs Division, Washington, DC 20540 USA, LC-USZ62–13035.

Castro was not involved in the negotiations and learnt of the climb down from the radio. When an official reported what he had heard, it took Castro about five minutes to take it in. He berated the Soviet leader as a 'bastard, an idiot without balls and a homosexual'. To say that the Cuban leader was livid would be an understatement. The KGB chief in Havana warned Moscow that 'one or two years of especially careful work with Castro will be required until he acquires all the qualities of Marxist-Leninist Party spirit' (Andrew and Mitrokhin 2005: 40–6). The volatile Cuba leader was proving a hot potato for Moscow to handle and would increasingly become so in the future.

Anastas Mikoyan, the comrade for all seasons, was dispatched to explain to Castro that the decision had been right. Mikoyan was not the only one who thought that the world had been a hair's breadth from a Third World War. The experience exposed the danger of the lack of direct links between Moscow and Washington, and the telephone hotline was the result.

On 2 November 1962, Gervase Cowell, an intelligence officer in the British embassy in Moscow, received a phone call. The call consisted of three short blows of breath, and a minute later the phone rang again. Once more there were three short blows of breath. Cowell was the officer who was running Colonel Oleg Penkovsky, one of the most important Soviet agents ever recruited. The calls were the prearranged signal to announce that a Soviet nuclear attack on the West was imminent. At the time Britain's nuclear armed V-bombers were still on high alert.

What did Cowell do? He pondered and then did nothing! He did not even inform his ambassador or London, as he concluded that Penkovsky had been arrested (he had been taken on 22 October) and that the information had been beaten out of him. What an extraordinary stunt to pull! Did Khrushchev give the go ahead? Had Cowell misjudged the information, the sky could have been black with nuclear missiles. What would have happened had a CIA officer received the call? It does not bear thinking about.

It is now clear that the Berlin crisis and Cuba were linked (as were Vietnam and Laos). On 16 October, Dean Rusk, US secretary of state, commented that 'Berlin is . . . very much involved in this . . . for the first time. I'm beginning really to wonder whether maybe Mr Khrushchev is entirely rational about Berlin' (*International Security*, Vol. 10, no. 1, 1985:177).

In January 1963, a joint US-Soviet note to the UN Secretary-General officially ended the Cuban conflict. Both the US and USSR concluded, on the basis of the Cuban crisis, that nuclear war would devastate their countries. On 20 June 1963, a hotline was established between the US and the USSR. During the crisis, it had taken Washington up to twelve hours to receive and decode a 3,000-word message from Moscow. By the time Washington had drafted a reply, a tougher message from Moscow had arrived, and this made for confusion. The hotline was never a telephone line. At first, teletype equipment was used, then replaced by facsimile units in 1988 and since 2008 by a secure computer link over which messages are exchanged by email.

What impact did the Cuban crisis have on the average American? Tom Hanks, in *Bridge of Spies* (2015), plays James Donovan, a lawyer who defends Rudolf Abel, a Soviet spy later exchanged for Gary Powers. He reminisces:

> I was six and I remember the way every adult I knew was carrying around this thing, which was fear. I didn't know the world was any bigger than Redding, California, but it was the beginning of this reality that carried right through to the 1970s – that the Third World War was inevitable, round the corner. It could be staved off for a while, but not for ever – and we might lose.
>
> (*The Sunday Times*, 15 November 2015)

Khrushchev goes

Khrushchev loved travelling. In 1963 he spent almost half the year away from Moscow and, in 1964, an astonishing 150 days abroad. His opponents struck when he was on holiday at Pitsunda, on the Black Sea, on 12 October 1964. He received a phone call from Leonid Brezhnev and was summoned to a meeting of the Central Committee which was to discuss agriculture and 'some other matters'. He had been told by his son, Sergei, that there was a plot under way but had given it little thought.

No one met him at the airport – ominous. Furious, he rushed to the Kremlin and barged into the room where the Presidium was in session. 'What's going on here?,' he thundered. 'We're discussing Khrushchev's removal from office,' Suslov calmly replied. 'Are you crazy? I'll have you all arrested here and now.' Khrushchev stormed out of the room and rang Marshal Rodion Malinovsky, the minister of defence. 'As Commander-in-Chief I order you to arrest the conspirators at once.' Malinovsky countered that he would only carry out the orders of the Party Central Committee. Rebuffed, Khrushchev then rang Vladimir Semichastny, chair of the KGB. Again he declined, stating that he was bound to carry out the orders of the Central Committee.

Who stood to gain most from the removal of Khrushchev? Leonid Brezhnev and Nikola Podgorny: the latter became president of the Soviet Union when Brezhnev became the new First Secretary. According to Vladimir Semichastny, head of the KGB, Brezhnev had proposed the assassination of the First Secretary on several occasions. A car or plane crash could be arranged. Semichastny avers that he rejected all these suggestions.

There were many accusations:

- Khrushchev had tried to develop a new cult of personality.
- He had ignored the elementary rules of leadership, giving his colleagues insulting, obscene names.
- He had presided over the economic decline of the country; labour productivity was down.
- The US was economically further in front than ever.
- Five-storey apartment blocks were less efficient than 9–12 storey blocks.
- Twenty years after the war, agriculture was in such a mess that ration cards had to be reintroduced and 860 tonnes of gold sold to import food from capitalist countries, and living standards in the countryside had not improved.
- Economic aid to the Third World was a failure; Guinea received considerable Soviet investments but 'we were pushed out'; in Iraq, the Soviet Union was involved in over 200 projects; despite this, the new leader was an enemy of the Soviet Union and communists; the same happened in Syria and Indonesia; large amounts of aid and arms were sent to India, Ethiopia and other countries.
- He banged his shoe at the United Nations.
- He turned his son-in-law, Aleksei Adzhubei, whom he had made editor in chief of *Izvestiya*, into his unofficial foreign minister.
- He was guilty of adventurism (high risk-taker) in foreign policy and had brought the country to the verge of war on several occasions: during the

Suez crisis the Soviet Union was within a hair's breadth of war; on Berlin he issued Kennedy an impossible ultimatum to make Berlin a 'Free City': 'we are not foolish enough to think it is worth starting a war to make Berlin a Free City'; the Cuban missile crisis forced the country into a shameful retreat.

- He called Mao Zedong an 'old boot' and Castro was a 'bull who would charge any red flag'; he threatened to drive foreign opponents 'three metres into the ground'; he told the West German ambassador: 'We'll wipe all you Germans off the face of the earth.'
- He was ignorant, incompetent, caddish and an adventurer in domestic and foreign policy.

(Pikhoya 1998: 212–14)

Kissinger has characterised Khrushchev's foreign policy as that of the quick fix: the explosion of a super-high-yield thermonuclear device in 1961; the succession of Berlin ultimata; the Cuban Missile Crisis in 1962. His aim was to achieve a psychological equilibrium in negotiations with a country that Khrushchev, deep down, knew was considerably stronger (Kissinger 2012: 162).

Figure 3.3 Henry Kissinger and Andrei Gromyko
© SPUTNIK/Alamy.

Culture

The death of Stalin in 1953 resulted in a deep exhalation of breath by the literati. The conformity and fear of the Stalin years now gave way to reflection about the past and why writers and the population had remained silent. The first breakthrough novel was Ilya Ehrenburg's *The Thaw* (1954), which gave its name to the first part of Khrushchev's dominance of Soviet politics. It relates the story of a tyrannical 'little' Stalin boss and his wife's voyage from conformity to eventually leaving him. The spring thaw symbolises the thaw in cultural life but also her emotions. Ehrenburg, a prolific wartime author, went on to write several other novels and memoirs. The diversification of culture and language undermined the staid conformity of the Stalin era. Uniformity, coherence and apparent stability would never be the same again. Terms such as sincerity and genuine, prevalent in the 1920s, were again discussed passionately. The more conservative elements in the literary hierarchy took umbrage at the pace of change, and a vigorous debate unfolded in the most popular journals, with *Novy mir* publishing the new wave and *Oktyabr* the traditional perceptions. A startling move was to publish Alexander Solzhenitsyn's *One Day in the Life of Ivan Denisovich* in *Novy mir* in 1962 (his whole sentence is treated as a day because each day was the same). It brought the experience of the camps (gulags) to a wide Soviet and international audience. It was a sensation and, even more surprising, its publication had been personally approved by Khrushchev.

Soviet cinema began producing entertaining films, and one won the Palme d'Or at the Cannes Festival in 1958. Ballet was a Russian passion; the greatest ballerina was Maya Plisetskaya, but she was under a cloud in the post-war years because she was Jewish. Her father, a dedicated communist, had been executed in the purges, and her mother was sent to the gulag. Her interpretation of the *Dying Swan* (by Saint-Saëns) was enough to bring tears to anyone's eyes. She danced for Stalin and Mao Zedong at the Bolshoi on the occasion of the dictator's seventieth birthday, and as the daughter of a disgraced family, she was afraid to look Stalin in the eye. She reappeared in *Swan Lake* (by Tchaikovsky) at the Bolshoi in 1956. After the first act, the audience exploded. The KGB tried to dampen the enthusiasm and dragged members of the audience out screaming, kicking and scratching, but after the performance the KGB retreated and conceded defeat to the exultant audience. She was then permitted to travel abroad in 1959 and was feted worldwide. She always returned to Moscow despite pleas by her Western friends to defect. She confessed that, of all the great theatres in the world where she had performed, she loved the Bolshoi the most.

Fashion made a comeback during this period. Normally there were no dresses on sale, only material, so girls had to make their own dresses. This gave rise to a semi-independent clothes industry based in seamstresses' homes. Designs were inspired by Western films and magazines. I was always struck by how well girls were dressed in Moscow and how badly men were attired.

The Virgin Lands scheme, launched by Khrushchev to increase grain output, was a Komsomol project – over 300,000 volunteers were mobilised – mainly in northern Kazakhstan and western Siberia in 1954. Conditions were so primitive that many of them returned home. 'It seemed that if we did a little bit more, and a little bit more, we would find ourselves in paradise,' the pioneer Viktor Mikhailov remembered. 'We thought we were bringing the future to this country.' Tens of thousands of students, soldiers, lorry and combine harvester drivers, and equipment were transported there annually on a seasonal basis. A combine harvester brigadier commented:

> We didn't have enough machinery. We started harvesting in August and stopped when the snow came. Then we tried to complete the work in spring. Sometimes we just piled the grain up in the fields. Not enough lorries and no roads.
>
> (Swanson 2008: 131–2, 142)

Artists were also sent and instructed to paint the reality of life and the successes of the venture. This genre produced some striking canvasses and showed young people battling to bring in the harvest. What is even more illuminating are the colours displayed, as they are vivid, bright and quite different from the staid northern Expressionism. These paintings changed Soviet art and launched a new era of realism.

Socialist Realism died after 1985 with the advent of *perestroika* and *glasnost*. There were four categories of art forbidden in the USSR: anti-Soviet; religious; erotic; and formalist and satirical. In 1987, anti-Soviet art appears and, by 1990, all the other taboos had gone. One artist commented: 'Our generation which grew up in the 1930s and 1940s believed absolutely in the purity of revolutionary ideas, it believed in the transforming power of art' (Swanson 2008: 209), but disillusionment and cynicism begin to surface under Khrushchev.

From the mid-1950s a group of Soviet philosophers and experts began developing the concept of 'universal values'. They were not overturning the class basis of society but pointed out that some of the values of a capitalist society could be regarded as universal values. This was innovative and surfaced again under Gorbachev.

The Sixth World Youth Festival, in June 1957, changed Soviet perceptions of the outside world forever. About 30,000 foreign guests (myself included) attended from 131 countries. Many famous Western artists performed including the folk singers Ewan MacColl and Peggy Seeger who were ardent Marxists. Arthur Scargill, the communist miners' leader, was also there and a brass band welcomed him. The CIA funded some American participants, and they were expected to ruffle the feathers of Soviet communism. There were numerous concerts (I attended operas and ballets in the Bolshoi), theatre productions and so on. We also visited a collective farm (*kolkhoz*), and as ever we were accompanied by the KGB. I was also introduced to the Soviet black market. I was invited to meet a few Russians – in the evening when it was dark – behind one of the buildings where we were housed. A young Russian, speaking impeccable English, acted as interpreter. Would I sell him some British pounds? I took it as a KGB trap and declined, but when I mentioned it to our guide, she blanched and warned me not to mention the incident ever again. The black marketeers were genuine and living proof that the planned economy had spawned a functioning black market. Afterwards I went on trips to Kiev and Leningrad. Khrushchev, in a resplendent white suit, threw a huge party for 12,000. About 120,000 other Soviet citizens came to Moscow to take part in the festivities and to see and meet foreigners for the first time. On a darker note, during a visit to the magnificent Moscow underground, the Metro, a bust of Stalin was still in place. Without thinking, I asked my guide: 'Why is that criminal still here?' She burst into tears. Khrushchev's denunciation of Stalin the previous year was obviously still very painful for her.

If the festival made a great impression on the foreigners, this was nothing compared to the impact on young Russians and other Soviet citizens. Cut off from the outside world for decades, they had the chance to mingle and chat with Westerners and other foreigners. When I asked about the victory of Khrushchev over his rivals – the Anti-party group – the response was: 'Tell us, as you know more about Soviet politics than we do.' Endlessly curious, young Russians had an insatiable thirst for knowledge about the outside world, and it became obvious that their knowledge of the outside world was very limited, to say the least. Andrei Grachev, an adviser to Gorbachev, called the festival 'the Woodstock in Moscow'. He was sixteen at the time, spoke English, wore a checked shirt and spoke loudly, hoping people would take him for an American cowboy! Grachev compares the impact of the festival as tectonic as the launch of Sputnik 1 the same year. The two events broke the 'hermetically enclosed political system, creating the first fissures in the hull of the Soviet Titanic'. Evgeny Evtushenko, recently expelled from the Moscow Institute of Literature for 'individualism', commented that he had broken Soviet rules. He had kissed the lips of an American girl, and many of his friends were doing the same thing in streets and parks. This was unheard of behaviour in such a conservative society (Tony Cash, *East-West Review*, Vol. 14, no. 1, spring/summer 2015, pp. 13–16).

There were many Eastern European participants at the festival as well, and they took home the impression that the Stalinist monolith was developing cracks. Polish theatre, to cite only one example, began to push back the boundaries of what was possible.

4 The US and the Soviet Union in the Third World

The US regarded colonialism as a phase of history when European powers ruled the world. The European colonial powers in 1945 were a ragged bunch clinging to America's coat-tails to survive the coming onslaught from communism. The Dutch had to be forced out of what became Indonesia (speaking Dutch was banned); the French, bedraggled and defeated, were quitting Indochina; but the British had the willpower to confront and defeat the Malayan communist insurgency which began in 1948. When India was granted its independence in 1947 it was inevitable that Britain would quit Asia.

So post-1945 became the post-colonial era. But how did the new states view themselves and what form of government and economy would they choose? They all shared one burning ambition: to throw off the shackles of colonialism and take control of their own destiny. Their cultures and traditions were now to flourish without alien influences.

There were two great development models: the American and the Soviet. Could the Third World come up with its own model? The American model was capitalist and thereby based on market competition; the Soviet model eliminated the market and was predicated on planners replacing the market.

The American model

- Urban-based growth in both the private and state sectors;
- Import of advanced consumer goods and the latest technology and become part of a global capitalist market and alliance with the world's number one state;
- Democracy, involving a multi-party system;
- A free press and the rule of law;
- Secure property relations needed to protect ownership;

- Law of contract to promote business activity and enforce contracts;
- Independent courts to adjudicate disputes.

The main drawback of this model was the perception of post-colonial elites that the US was replacing the former European colonial powers. Another was that the post-colonial states did not want to become dependent on the US as their goal was to become successful independent states, choosing alliances whenever they gauged them advantageous. Another downside is that capitalism promotes inequality, as those who innovate swim to the top and inevitably acquire political influence. Foreign corporations tend to work with enterprising locals, and they then form an elite, leaving the vast mass of the population behind. The argument is that capitalism promotes economic growth and that the fruits of this trickle down to those below. This takes time, but locals wanted a tangible increase in their living standards immediately.

The Soviet

- Politics dominated by a single Communist Party which would promote economic growth through central planning (annual and five year plans, etc.)
- Mass mobilisation would provide the labour force for rapid economic transformation
- Emphasis would be placed on heavy industry (steel, iron, machine building, energy, etc.) and light and consumer goods industries would receive less investment;
- The resources for investment would come from depressing living standards in the short term and loans from Moscow;
- Huge infrastructural projects would advance the economy;
- The planned economy would operate according to prices set by planners and would not be subject to the market (supply and demand);
- Trade would be promoted with communist states;
- Soviet and Eastern European specialists would help to develop the economy;
- The military, police and security services would be trained by the Soviets and Eastern Europeans;
- All the necessary equipment would be supplied;
- The goal of social justice would be achieved because the means of production (factories, land, etc.) would be owned by the people (in reality, the state);
- Some African leaders thought that capitalism was too complex for their fledgling states and favoured a centrally directed, non-market model;
- Private trade would gradually be taken over by the state.

A major disadvantage was that the Soviet Union was viewed as less developed economically than the US; its consumer and investment goods were regarded as inferior to American and other Western products; the exception to this was the military sector.

Common to both models was the emphasis on education and science and technology. Knowledge-based growth would be accorded a high priority.

After independence, many leaders were attracted to the Soviet model (such as Indonesia and India) because it concentrated political and economic power at the centre and promoted the emergence of a dominant party. New elites could form around a dominant leader who would act as a patron, and political and economic decision making would be concentrated at the centre. The Soviet experience revealed that once a leader was in place he was there for life or when someone overthrew him. There was no mechanism for an orderly succession (China introduced one after Mao's death). The Soviet model was particularly attractive in Africa where tribes are the dominant form of social grouping. A dominant leader from a minority tribe could emerge and legitimise his rule by arguing that he was promoting social justice and modernisation. A Marxist analysis is based on class, but some African states (e.g. Tanzania) pointed out that there are no classes there. There is only the tribal chief and his subjects. The Soviet model was based on heavy industry as the key to economic growth. The drawback here was although African was rich in raw materials, they had not been exploited. So, in the short term, they would have to be imported. A machine building industry needs to be built up to manufacture the equipment for heavy industry, so a cadre of skilled engineers has to be trained in communist countries.

India is an interesting case study. Jawaharlal Nehru, Indian prime minister from Indian independence in 1947 to 1964, studied law at the University of Cambridge and was influenced by George Bernard Shaw and other socialist intellectuals who belonged to the Fabian Society. Nehru set out to implement Fabian socialism in India. It involved the nationalisation of the steel industry, transport, electricity generation and mining. Private economic activity and entrepreneurship were discouraged and property rights downplayed. Economic life was dominated by state planning, licences were issued to regulate work and taxes were high. One of the results of this socialist experiment was that India's share of world trade slumped and abject poverty was a feature of Indian life. It was only in the 1980s that free market reforms were introduced and the Indian economy then began to grow rapidly, lifting many out of poverty. Many Indian leaders were educated at British universities where socialist – often Marxist – economics was in vogue. This applied to other leaders of the Third World who had been educated in Britain such as Julius Nyerere, president of Tanzania from 1964 to 1985, who also implemented Fabian and African socialist ideas. He had read economics and history at the University of Edinburgh. He enforced collectivisation, and when peasants resisted, he burnt down villages. The result was economic decline, corruption and food shortages. When Tanzania tried market economics, it recorded impressive growth: gross domestic product (GDP) rose 40 per cent between 1998 and 2007.

Kwame Nkrumah studied at the London School of Economics where socialist economics was dominant. On returning to Ghana, he rushed through 'forced industrialisation', complete with state enterprises and ten-year plans. The inevitable result was low growth, corruption and heavy debt. Zulfikar Ali Bhutto, at various times president and prime minister of Pakistan, studied at the University of California, Berkeley and Oxford. Once he had gained power, he declared that 'socialism is our economy' and began nationalising the steel, chemical, cement and banking industries along with flour, rice and cotton mills. Economic growth plummeted. British academics, therefore, bear some of the responsibility for the poor economic performance of former colonies. An exception to the rule is Lee Kuan Yew, who studied at the University of Cambridge and the London School of Economics. When he returned to Singapore, he rejected the socialist economics he had imbibed and built one of the most successful economies in the Third World.

The International Monetary Fund (IMF) provides funds to governments which have short-term liquidity problems. The World Bank invests in infrastructural projects. Both institutions are based in Washington and are controlled by the US. The head of the World Bank is always an American, and the IMF is always headed by a European, usually French. The IMF provided resources for France and Portugal to resist challenges in their colonies, and without these funds, decolonisation would have begun earlier. In the new Third World states, the World Bank and IMF favoured those states which adopted the American model. They became powerful instruments in the hands of the US and often influenced private bank lending as well. When the US left the gold standard in 1971, it became easier for Third World states to access loans. The rapid rise in oil prices after 1973 made more funds available as the oil-rich states sought to invest their new-found wealth, but the Third World fell into the trap of accepting cheap loans and gradually became heavily indebted. US banks were happy to lend to Third World states assuming that Washington would bail them out if these states defaulted on their debts. The newly independent states were often dependent on exporting raw materials, but prices fell as technology advanced. The US aim was to create an international environment which promoted convergence between communism and capitalism, but the opposite occurred. Hence US policy made it more difficult for developing states to raise living standards as so much wealth had to be used to service debt. This, inevitably, contributed to the growth of left-wing movements.

US aid was always based on political and military criteria. Israel was top of the list for US aid – this was a far cry from 1948 when Czechoslovak arms, agreed with the Soviet Union, had been of critical importance in the foundation of the state. The Israelis declared an 'unbreakable alliance with our great friend and the defender of mankind – the Soviet Union'. This changed very quickly and, a year later, Zionism was declared to be an imperialist plot to subvert the Soviet Union (Andrew and Mitrokhin 2005: 222–3). Zionism continued to be seen in this light until the late Gorbachev era. As regards US aid, Egypt was second only to Israel. Then came sub-Saharan Africa and South Vietnam.

The difficulties of constructing new, post-colonial states led to considerable instability in the Third World in the 1950s and 1960s. New leaders found themselves under attack from the left, often from Marxist movements. Marxism proved very attractive in Africa especially in Portuguese colonies (Mozambique, Angola, Guinea-Bissau and Cape Verde), Zimbabwe and South Africa.

The oil weapon

The First World was not as powerful as it thought. The Third World discovered that it had something which was crucial to the development of advanced economies: oil. The power of oil as a weapon was revealed in 1973. OPEC (Organization of the Petroleum Exporting Countries) was set up in Baghdad in 1960 and consisted of Third World oil producers. It was an attempt to compete with the 'seven sisters', the powerful Western oil companies. After the US came to the rescue of Israel during the Yom Kippur War of October 1973, Saudi Arabia used oil to reset global politics. Angered by Israeli's successful counterattack and push into Arab territory, Riyadh announced a complete oil embargo against the US. To ensure that Washington felt economic pain even if oil slipped in through the back door, Saudi Arabia – followed by the OPEC cartel which it dominated – cut production ultimately by 25 per cent, and between September 1973 and March 1974 the oil price quadrupled. Sheikh Yamani, the Saudi Arabian oil minister, declared: 'What we want is a complete withdrawal of Israeli forces from occupied Arab territories and then you will have the oil.' The Saudis thus launched what became known as the 'oil weapon'. Henry Kissinger, US secretary of state, referred to these démarches as 'political blackmail' and as the 'most important of our century'. The Saudi oil minister spelled out the geopolitical implications by referring to a 'new type of relationship' where 'you have to adjust yourself to the new circumstances'. The US secretary of state adjusted, Israel retreated back east of the Suez Canal and the embargo was lifted, but global politics would never be the same again. Saudi Arabia, as the swing producer, had demonstrated that it possessed the power to drive up inflation and break economies, regardless of politics in the West. That threat has been Saudi Arabia's entry pass to the global political stage, and it is still there today, but that entry pass is only valid as long as Riyadh is the swing producer. It was the first time that a group of relatively weak states had provoked such dramatic changes in the lives of the vast majority of people on the planet. The consequence eventually was a world economic crisis, but the raising of the oil price was only one factor. The US had abandoned the gold standard in 1971, and as a consequence the Bretton Woods system collapsed. Thereby the long period of economic growth in the developed world ended. In West Germany driving was banned on Sundays, and the autobahn was given over to pedestrians and cyclists. GDP there fell by 1.5 per cent, and unemployment climbed above one million.

The sharp rise in the oil price spurred research into alternatives, and nuclear power was promoted. This aroused considerable opposition because it was associated with the Cold War. The Iranian Revolution of 1979 cut the amount of oil available on international markets, and in 1981, the price of a barrel rose to $41 and kept on rising. As a result, Western Europe turned to the Soviet Union for oil. It was bonanza time for Moscow, and the Soviets became more and more reluctant to export oil at low Comecon prices to Eastern Europe. One estimate puts the Soviet subvention to the region in the ten years after 1973 at $118 billion, and this covered oil and other raw materials. The GDR, for example, exported the cheap Soviet oil and gas to Western markets at a handsome profit and, needless to say, the Soviets were not amused. In January 1989, a GDR delegation travelled to Moscow to ask for an extra two million tonnes of oil on top of the seventeen million expected. The Soviet leadership regarded this as brazen cheek and threatened to deliver less than seventeen million. The oil producing Gulf States and Saudi Arabia amassed huge dollar reserves, and per capita income was above that of the US. However, the vast wealth did not trickle down, and the average Arab remained poor.

The downside of the oil bonanza for the Soviet Union was that it put off the need to launch economic reforms. It was at precisely this moment that the Soviet economy began to decline, but this was only realised later. The high oil and gas prices halted necessary reforms for a decade.

The Soviets rediscover the Third World

After Stalin, Soviet leaders resolved to deal with Third World states at the level of government. Sukarno's Indonesia, Nasser's Egypt and Nehru's India were high on the list of priorities. Why? They were viewed as anti-Western and radical. Khrushchev's first important foreign trip was to Beijing in 1954, and he went on to Burma (Myanmar), India and Afghanistan the following year. The welcome in India was so effusive that crowds almost crushed him to death. Everywhere he stressed the Soviet Union's willingness to cooperate with non-socialist countries economically and militarily, and their common enemy was colonialism and imperialism. Stalin's view of the Third World was blinkered, but now Moscow should reach out to non-socialist parties and national movements. New institutes for the study of Africa and Latin America were set up, and the KGB and GRU (military intelligence) were to roam the Third World collecting useful information.

In 1960, at the United Nations, Khrushchev talked up the alliance with national liberation movements as the best way to spread communism around the world. Together with the Soviet Union, a bright economic future beckoned. Sputnik 1 had shocked the Americans and astonished the world, and Yuri Gagarin was the first man in space in 1961. Social revolution was like an irresistible tide which would drown capitalism and lead to global communism within a generation. The self-confidence of the Soviet Union was boundless. How would the US respond? (Westad 2005: 66–72).

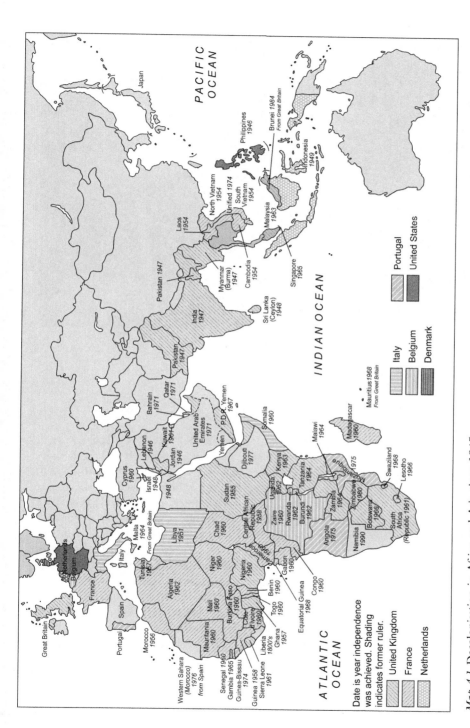

Map 4.1 Decolonisation in Africa and Asia since 1945

After Odd Arne Westad, *The Global Cold War* (Cambridge University Press, 2011, p. 88).

Figure 4.1 Valentina Tereshkova and Yuri Gagarin
© Heritage Image Partnership Ltd/Alamy.

Bandung and the Non-aligned Movement

Both Moscow and Washington competed to attract Third World states to their side. They regarded it as a zero sum game: a country which joined the other side was a loss, but many Third World states did not wish to become embroiled in Cold War politics and preferred to forge their own identities. Could they reject East and West and, through solidarity, become a force in the world? Five Asian states – Indonesia, India, Pakistan, Burma (Myanmar) and Sri Lanka – launched an initiative which grew into the largest gathering of Asian and African countries ever assembled; they convened in Bandung, Indonesia, in April 1955. France had just been evicted from Indochina, and many African colonies were on the road to independence. Twenty-nine countries were represented, including the People's Republic of China, but the Soviet Union was not invited although most of its territory lay in Asia. They counted 1.4 billion people, over half of the world's population, and the goal was to articulate a common ideology which would supersede capitalism and communism. Sukarno, the Indonesian leader, spoke of fusing nationalism, Islam and Marxism into a new moral ideology. Morality, he claimed, was better understood by Third World countries because they had suffered the indignities of colonialism. Jawaharlal Nehru, the Indian prime minister, rejected the efforts of Iraq, Iran and Turkey to label Soviet control of Eastern Europe as colonial, and Zhou Enlai promoted peaceful coexistence and non-alignment. The meeting did not endorse the armed struggle of the national liberation movements but called for an end to apartheid in South Africa and support for Palestine.

The Bandung conference was viewed with mounting distrust in Washington. The Third World was moving left, and Dulles even thought of organising an anti-Bandung conference of pro-Western states but dropped the idea quickly. Nikita Khrushchev warmed to the prospect of declining Western influence, but the desire for independence worried him as this would make it more difficult for the Soviet Union to promote its agenda in the Third World as local Communist parties might be seen as taking orders from a foreign power. He was further disconcerted by the meeting on Brioni Island, Yugoslavia, of Nehru, the Egyptian leader Nasser and Tito. Khrushchev was aware that Tito had no intention of ever subordinating himself to Moscow. A nightmare scenario would be hordes of Titos running the Third World.

What about economic cooperation after Bandung? It turned out to be very disappointing. Why was this so? One reason was that Third World countries had complementary economies – they wanted to export primary products and import technology which was best sourced from the First World. Another difficulty was the lack of credit available to trade among themselves as Western banks concentrated on promoting trade between the Third and First Worlds. Third World states favoured barter agreements among themselves because they had so little hard currency.

In September 1955, Nasser signed an arms deal to procure large quantities of Soviet arms via Czechoslovakia. This move came as a tremendous shock to the West. The KGB made Nasser aware of British plans to assassinate him just before the Anglo-French attack on Suez in October 1956. The crisis brought home to Third World countries the need to procure military hardware, and the main source was the Soviet Union and its Eastern European satellites. Nasser began supporting the armed struggle in north Africa much more directly and, in Algeria, the Front de Libération Nationale (FLN), the national liberation movement, was recognised as a de facto government by much of the Third World.

In the 1960s, the New Left in Europe, harbouring guilt for Europe's imperial past and present, began to identify with national liberation movements which promised a new, exciting future for those involved. It also promised to undermine the bourgeoisie in the West. They saw the Third World as the future, many Americans joined this bandwagon and the Soviet Union was viewed as conservative and having lost its revolutionary teeth.

Algeria became independent in 1962 after eight years of bitter civil war which cost the lives of a million Muslims and led to the expulsion of about the same number of French settlers (*les pieds noirs*). Ahmed Ben Bella, its leader, became the spokesman for the Third World. China recognised the FLN in 1958 and the Soviet Union in 1960. The pro-Soviet Algerian Communist Party thought that another revolution was necessary to correct the errors of the first. An attempt by the KGB to conclude an intelligence agreement with the new government failed.

Many national liberation movements had offices in Algiers, and Algeria provided weapons and military training for the struggle to liberate Africa. Among those who were inspired were Nelson Mandela and the African National Congress along with Yasir Arafat, and al Fatah received considerable support from the FLN.

Ben Bella was given a hero's welcome in Havana during the Cuban missile crisis and echoed Castro's judgement that Khrushchev had 'no balls'; when he returned to Algiers, he berated the Soviet ambassador for the climb down. When a border conflict between Algeria and Morocco broke out in October 1963, Cuba came to Algeria's aid, not the Soviet Union. It sent tanks and combat troops, but these were not needed. The tanks had been provided by the Soviet Union and were not to be used in Third World countries, but Castro had ignored this. As the US would not sell arms to Algeria, the Soviet Union stepped in and provided substantial quantities. Ben Bella was feted in Moscow, in May 1964, but he was overthrown a year later in a military coup.

Twenty-five countries gathered in Belgrade in 1961 to establish the Non-alignment Movement (NAM). National self-determination, mutual economic assistance and neutrality were the founding principles, and Algeria was the country to emulate. The meeting took place during the Berlin crisis, and the leaders of all states present sent identical letters to Khrushchev and Kennedy, warning about the potential for war and arguing for a peaceful outcome. The Third World saw itself as having arrived on the international stage.

The Sino-Indian Border War of October 1962 – provoked by the Indians establishing outposts on the Chinese side of the border which had been delineated under British rule whereas Beijing was protecting the outer limits of the Chinese Empire – and Indo-Pakistani War three years later (Moscow and Washington had to step in to broker a peace in both conflicts) badly dented India's image. Bandung had underlined that disputes should be resolved through diplomatic channels. China's aim was not to start a general war but to launch a decisive attack and then retreat so as to bring India to the negotiating table and even returned captured Indian heavy weaponry. During the June 1967 war between Israel and Egypt, Third World solidarity availed Nasser little, and he had to rely on Soviet arms to reequip his armed forces. The defeat was humiliating; the conflict was virtually decided during the first three hours when the Israelis destroyed 286 of 340 Egyptian combat aircraft on the ground, thereby leaving the ground forces without air cover during the battles in the Sinai desert. The KGB only discovered what was going on from Western news reports! This failure led the KGB to recruit academics and other specialists, among whom was Evgeny Primakov, and over 20,000 Soviet advisers were sent to Egypt.

The Organisation of African Unity (OAU) was set up in Addis Ababa, Ethiopia, in 1963. Ben Bella was the main speaker.

The high hopes of the NAM and OAU were dashed by the harsh economic realities of the 1960s and 1970s. The Soviet model became more attractive as the American model and local efforts failed to generate the economic growth expected. The increasing economic and military might of the Soviet Union seemed to prove that the Soviet model was the one to choose for rapid economic advancement. Moscow had chosen to support nationalist movements in the 1960s, and gradually Marxism began to spread among Third World elites in the 1970s. Moscow could now engage ideologically with these new currents and the Cuban revolution added substance to the view that the future was bright – the future was communist. China sidelined itself during the mayhem of the Cultural Revolution (1966–76). The Soviet model was now the only game in town (Westad 2005: 97–109).

US interventions in the Third World

Why did the US intervene so often?

- It possessed the capability.
- Often intervention was viewed as defensive – to counter left or communist regimes; a major goal was to promote democracy but not if it helped communists to come to power; the US strongly opposed former colonial powers clinging on to their colonies – the exception was Malaya, where the UK was fighting a communist insurgency; Indochina was a struggle between colonialism and revolutionary nationalism; the armed struggle there gradually sucked in the US; it was the most effective way of exerting influence; the communist insurgency in the Philippines was crushed by 1953; China revealed the shortcomings of the American democratic model: Chiang Kai-shek resisted efforts to promote democratic government and transparency; instead he prioritised the military struggle against the communists; when the Americans withdrew military support, the communists won.
- NSC-68 made the US responsible for imposing order throughout the world.
- Eisenhower, speaking in 1950, feared the US was in deep trouble in the Third World; even before the outbreak of the Korean War he confided: 'I believe that Asia is lost with Japan, Philippines, the Netherlands East Indies (Indonesia) and even Australia under threat; India itself is not safe'(Chandler 1981: 1092).
- Vietnam was of key importance; opposition to French colonial rule gradually gave way to concerns about the rising influence of Ho Chi Minh, the North Vietnamese leader; Washington accepted the status quo and waited for non-communist nationalists to emerge (they never did); Eisenhower provided the French with $500 million annually in their conflict with the Viet Minh (League for the Independence of Vietnam);
- Vice President Richard Nixon, in December 1953:

If Indonesia falls, Thailand is put in an almost impossible situation; the same is true of Malaya and its rubber and tin; the same is true of Indochina;

if Indochina goes under communist domination, the whole of south east Asia will be threatened, and that means the economic and military security of Japan will inevitably be endangered also.

(Chandler 1981: 58)

- This became known as the Domino Theory – 'You have a row of dominos set up. You knock over the first one . . . What will happen to the last one is the certainty that it will go over very quickly,' was how Eisenhower put it; it took root in American minds and led to intervention on a global scale; hence the US became responsible for protecting the world capitalist system; this led to it being willing to intervene politically, economically and militarily anywhere communism was perceived to be a threat; this involved backing dictators if they were threatened by a communist insurgency.

Iran

Iran was of special relevance to the West because of its oil; the British had very lucrative interests there, but sooner or later the Iranians would want to be master in their own house. In 1953, the government, headed by Mohammad Mossadeq, nationalised the oil industry. John Foster Dulles, secretary of state, warned President Eisenhower that this undermined the US position in the Middle East. Even more threatening, nationalisation might be a prelude to revolution and the Soviet Union would then secure these valuable assets and, if Iran went communist, other states in the Middle East would go red as well. The US ambassador regarded Mossadeq as not 'quite sane'. When Sir Anthony Eden, Churchill's foreign secretary, visited Eisenhower, he found him obsessed by the fear of a communist Iran.

Operation Ajax to remove Mossadeq was given the go ahead in June 1953 as a joint American-British undertaking. The young Shah, Mohammed Reza Pahlevi, did not want to be associated with this anti-constitutional démarche. Bribing local officials and helping to stage anti-Mossadeq demonstrations finally turned the tide, and the military went over to Colonel Fazlollah Zahedi, who had been hiding in the CIA mission, and Mossadeq was arrested. The coup was the first time the CIA had toppled a government abroad, and the belief grew that if it could do it in Iran, it could do it elsewhere on the planet. It did – in Guatemala – and even considered assassinating foreign heads of state who supported the 'wrong' side.

In 1957, the CIA and Mossad – the Israeli intelligence service – helped the Shah set up an intelligence and security service, SAVAK, which gained a reputation for brutality. In 1959, Iran and Israel signed a secret agreement on intelligence and military co-operation (Andrew and Mitrokhin 2005: 170). The KGB countered by forging documents which purported to show that Dulles denigrated the Shah and the US was plotting to overthrow regimes of which they disapproved. The Shah was taken in by all the forgeries.

Iran's nuclear programme

On 8 December 1953, President Eisenhower delivered a speech at the UN General Assembly which was later dubbed his 'Atoms for Peace' speech. The president talked about nuclear energy being capable of providing abundant electrical energy to power the world. The US would provide the research reactors, fuel and scientific training to those nations which wished to establish a civilian nuclear programme. To ensure nuclear materials were not surreptitiously transferred to making weapons, what became the International Atomic Energy Agency (IAEA) was set up under UN auspices. The 'Atoms for Peace' programme became a key factor in the Cold War as the superpowers offered to share nuclear expertise with their allies.

One of the first countries to take up the offer was Iran and, in 1957, a nuclear cooperation agreement was signed. In 1959 the Shah set up the Tehran Nuclear Research Centre at the University of Tehran, and in 1967 the US delivered a five-megawatt nuclear reactor together with the highly enriched uranium needed to fuel it. Iran signed the Nuclear Non-proliferation Treaty in 1968, becoming one of the first states to do so. Iranian students went to the US to be trained, and it took the country about a decade before it had a team of nuclear scientists capable of making full use of the research reactor.

In 1974, the Shah announced ambitious plans to build twenty-three nuclear power reactors during the next twenty years. In order to carry out this programme, the Shah requested that the Massachusetts Institute of Technology (MIT) accept and train young Iranian scientists and engineers. However, Washington suspected that the Shah's real intention was to create a nuclear weapons programme and reduced the flow of sensitive technology. Uranium can be separated – spent fuel – and used for nuclear weapons; for this reason, the US opposed Iran's plans to build a nuclear reprocessing facility. President Jimmy Carter prevented the Shah from getting the necessary technology and from obtaining it elsewhere. Eventually the Shah only signed one deal with a foreign company – West Germany's Kraftwerk Union (a Siemens subsidiary) to build reactors at Bushehr. The Iranians formed a special group to collect the technology required to make a nuclear device (*RFL/RL Iran Report*, 9 July 2015). In 1979, the Shah was deposed, and Ayatollah Khomeini took over and acquired all the installations and expertise which had been built up. Since then, Iran has continued its efforts to build a nuclear bomb. So, unwittingly, Uncle Sam became the father of the present Iranian nuclear programme.

The US was not the only state which helped Iran develop its nuclear programme. China, between 1985 and 1997, was Iran's principal nuclear partner. China provided four small teaching and research reactors, including one utilising heavy water, the key to producing plutonium and fissile material. China also provided Iran with uranium and chemicals to extract plutonium. Chinese engineers also worked with the Atomic Energy Agency of Iran, the official body responsible for implementing regulations and operating nuclear energy installations, to design a facility to be used to enrich uranium. It also helped to produce tubes and mining, and China may have helped with the centrifuge design supplied by Abdul Qadir Khan, the Pakistani scientist, who had a global black market proliferation network.

China joined the IAEA in 1984 and signed the Non-proliferation Treaty in 1993. China turned down an Iranian request for a team to observe a Chinese nuclear weapons test – an Iranian military source revealed this in 1996.

The US and China reached an agreement, in October 1997, according to which China was not to sell nuclear power plants, heavy water reactors and heavy water production plants and not to engage in any nuclear cooperation with Iran in the future. This resulted in it cancelling the delivery of two 300-megawatt power plants and a single twenty-seven-megawatt reactor.

In 2002, an Iranian opposition group revealed the existence of the Natanz enrichment facility, and Iran's nuclear file was passed to the UN Security Council. China supported the latter's resolutions sanctioning Iran in 2006, 2007, 2008 and 2010.

On 14 July 2015, the Joint Comprehensive Plan of Action, agreed between the P5+1 group (US, UK, Russia, China, France and Germany) and Iran opened a new chapter in Iran's nuclear relations with the rest of the world. The agreement foresees the lifting of sanctions (except those relations to human rights and terrorism). Assets worth about $100 billion will be unfrozen, and Iran's aim is to increase its oil exports rapidly.

In 2014, Iran and Iraq each provided 9 per cent of China's oil imports and thus were the Middle Kingdom's fourth most important supplier. In the same year, Iran exported goods worth $24.3 billion to China, and foreign direct investment was $702 million in 2012. On the other hand, Saudi Arabia provides 16 per cent of China's crude oil imports. China's preferred option is stability in the Middle East and opposes regime change in Iran as Beijing perceives this to be Washington's policy goal. The Middle Kingdom is at present involved in building six nuclear reactors in Pakistan and twenty-six worldwide (*China Brief*, Vol. 15, No. 14, 17 July 2015).

Syria

Growing Soviet influence in Syria led the US and Britain, in September 1957, to consider a plan to assassinate three top men in Damascus: Abd al Hamid Sarraj, head of Syrian military intelligence; Afif al Bizri, chief of the Syrian General Staff; and Khalid Bakdash, leader of the Syrian Communist Party. A joint CIA-MI6 operation envisaged frontier incidents and border clashes being staged to provide a pretext for Iraqi and Jordanian military intervention. Syria had to be seen to 'appear as the sponsor of plots, sabotage and violence directed against neighbouring governments. The CIA and MI6 should use their capabilities in both the psychological and action fields to augment tension.' Operations in Jordan, Iraq and Lebanon were to be blamed on Damascus. A Free Syria Committee was to be

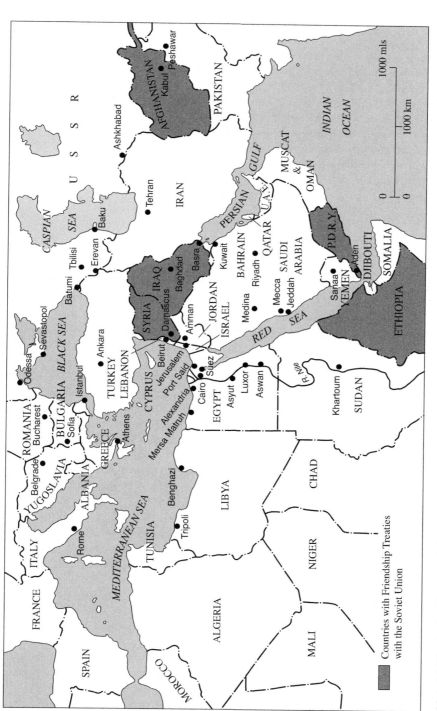

Map 4.2 The Soviet Union and the Middle East

set up and armed, and the CIA and MI6 would instigate internal uprisings – for instance by the Druze in the south – to help free political prisoners held in the Mezze prison and stir up the Muslim Brotherhood in Damascus. The Baath-communist government would be replaced by an anti-Soviet one, but this would be unpopular and repressive measures would need to be used.

Kermit Roosevelt, CIA director for the Middle East, was a major influence behind the plan and had first deployed his skills in Iran in 1953, when Mossadeq had been removed. Eisenhower and Macmillan backed the plan. It failed because Syria's Arab neighbours refused to take action, and an attack from Turkey was deemed unacceptable (*The Guardian*, 27 September 2003).

Egypt

In 1952, an Egyptian coup removed King Farouk, and the new leaders promised radical reform; Arab unity was another goal. Gamal Abdel Nasser, who had planned the overthrow of the monarchy, seized power in 1956, and his principal aim was to remove British influence. He had told Dulles in 1953 that the main enemy in the Middle East was British imperialism, not Soviet communism. He wanted the US to remain inactive as Arab nationalism overcame its domestic and external enemies. The main domestic enemy in Egypt was the Muslim Brotherhood. Nasser had played a leading role at Bandung; he forged a close association with Tito, and he was aware that he had to put together alliances if he were to succeed in the Middle East. The two immediate problems were taking control of the Suez Canal from the British and French and returning the Palestinian refugees to their lands and possessions. He nationalised the canal in July 1956 and began negotiations with Moscow for assistance and arms. In October, Israel attacked followed by British and French troops. President Eisenhower was furious and complained he had been double-crossed. After a week the British were within reach of their military objectives, but Washington forced a ceasefire and withdrawal of foreign forces. The British pound came under pressure and less oil was moved to Europe. Khrushchev assumed that the Americans supported the Suez adventure and that if military force could be used in Egypt it could also be deployed in Hungary. Khrushchev used the Suez crisis to threaten to intervene militarily and direct nuclear missiles at US bases in Britain. This was the first time the Soviet Union had engaged in brinkmanship and nuclear threats. Khrushchev incorrectly thought that this had forced the British and French to withdraw and concluded that nuclear threats were an effective diplomatic tool. This was put to a severe test during the Cuban Missile Crisis.

Nasser lost the war but won the peace; his standing in the Middle East rose and with it Soviet influence, as Britain and France ceased to be major players in the region.

The Eisenhower Doctrine was announced in January 1957. It promised regimes which were under threat from communism economic and military support. The president was concerned to stem the advance of pan-Arab nationalism in the Middle East and the loss of prestige there of the West in the aftermath of the Suez crisis. The nationalists could link up with communists and thereby strengthen the Soviet position in the oil-rich region. The first test came in 1958 when the US sent 14,000 soldiers and marines plus air force and naval support to support the Lebanese president; US forces stayed three months and then withdrew when the president's term of office expired. In Iraq, the pro-Western king was assassinated, the new leaders entered into an alliance with the Iraqi Communist Party and Iraq began negotiations with Moscow for military aid. The British sent troops to Jordan to prop up the Hashemite monarchy there. Moscow warned local communists in the Middle East to be circumspect, and this turned out to be justified. In Iraq the Baath party – which declared itself to be socialist – eventually moved brutally against communists as did Nasser in Egypt. Increasing US support for Israel stoked Arab resentment as Washington began to work with Tel Aviv to counter Soviet influence in the region.

In South East Asia, the US kept 15,000 Chinese (Guomindang) troops in Burma (Myanmar) for possible use against the People's Republic and to exert pressure on the left wing government in Rangoon (now Yangon). In Cambodia, Washington supported rebellions against Prince Sihanouk because of his coop-eration with the left and the People's Republic of China, and the Americans also paid for the armies in Laos and South Vietnam which were to counter the rise of the Viet Minh and the Left.

However, it was in Indonesia, the most populous Muslim state in the world, that the US concentrated greatest efforts to change the direction of the regime. Sukarno wanted more rapid economic growth, and a parliamentary system gave too much influence to existing elites. In 1957, he requested a loan from the US but was turned down, so Khrushchev stepped in and provided $100 million for military hardware. Sukarno then declared that there would be guided democracy overseen by four parties, one of which was the Indonesian Com-munist Party (PKI). The Americans decided to support separatist movements, especially in Sumatra and Sulawesi. Weapons were delivered, and US, Guomin-dang and Filipino pilots flew combat missions from Sumatra bases, and Dulles thought it might be possible to land US troops there. The aim was to break up Indonesia, but Sukarno was able to mobilise military and political support and survive. The capture of a US pilot, shot down on a bombing mission, proved that the US was involved and inflamed Indonesian opinion. The rebels fragmented, but the US continued to support them in northern Sumatra.

Hence during the Eisenhower era, Washington developed a strategy which involved intervening in countries regarded as going left wing. This was viewed as a halfway house towards communism. The obverse of this was that Third World countries became more resistant to the American model.

Africa

Africa was a problem for Washington in the 1950s and 1960s. As dedicated anti-colonialists, they opposed British, French, Belgian and Portuguese rule there. But were these tribal societies ready for self-rule? Would civil war and chaos follow a precipitate withdrawal of the Europeans? Africans could be quickly seduced by Marxism and lead to the rapid expansion of Soviet influence there. In the US, African-Americans lived in a segregated society deprived of many human rights. The natural ally of the US was South Africa. After winning a whites-only election in 1948, the Afrikaners replaced English with Afrikaans (the word means 'African' in Afrikaans) as the first national language. They also imposed strict segregation (apartheid) in a country in which 80 per cent of the population was black. The Eisenhower administration developed a good relationship with Pretoria. The police killing of Africans at Sharpeville in 1960 changed the relationship at a time when the civil rights movement was under way in the US.

The Kennedy administration viewed Africans as adolescents but dropped the idea that socialism did not fit the 'African tribal mentality', so America had to intervene in black Africa and not leave the continent open to Soviet influence. The CIA began backing Holden Roberto's Frente Nacional de Libertação de Angola (FNLA) (National Front for the Liberation of Angola) and Eduardo Mondlane's Frente de Libertação de Moçambique (FRELIMO) (Front for the Liberation of Mozambique).

The Belgian Congo (Belgium had acquired the mineral-rich colony in 1908) was home to over 200 tribes. Brussels concentrated on exploiting the riches and paid little attention to the locals. It became independent of Belgium on 30 June 1960, and Patrice Lumumba, head of the Movement National Congolais (MNC) (Congolese National Movement), was elected prime minister. He was a dapper dresser and had a taste for women, beer and the Congolese equivalent of marijuana. The US had acquired Congolese uranium to develop their nuclear arsenal and, although no longer dependent on the Congo, Washington set out to ensure the Soviet Union did not gain access to the uranium. In May 1960, the head of the CIA, informed President Eisenhower that Lumumba was being supported by the Belgian communists. There were no institutions in the country; it began to break up, and Lumumba was faced with a military mutiny. The mineral-rich Katanga province seceded, partly in response to Belgian prompting. Lumumba asked the UN to intervene and expel the Belgian military. The request was turned down, and Lumumba retorted that he was turning to Moscow for help, but this was akin to dancing with the devil. This enraged the Americans who rated Lumumba worse than Castro. Lumumba went to Washington and made a determined defence of his country's sovereignty and the right to choose its allies. Eventually it was decided the best option was to assassinate Lumumba and replace him with a military general, Joseph Mobutu – a 'completely honest and dedicated man' – in the opinion of the US ambassador.

It is still uncertain who ordered the liquidation of Lumumba: the CIA or Mobutu. The assassins were not CIA agents, but it supplied the weapons they used. (The same modus operandi was deployed to assassinate Generalissimo Rafael Trujillo, leader of the Dominican Republic, in May 1961.) Lumumba was captured by Congolese soldiers in December 1960; he was handed over to his archenemies, the Katangans, who tortured him for five hours and then took him into the jungle and shot him in January 1961. His body was buried in a shallow grave with one arm protruding. He was disinterred, dismembered and the body parts dissolved in battery acid. The Belgian responsible for this pulled out two of his teeth as souvenirs. They were capped with gold (Gerard and Kuklick 2015: 194).

The ramshackle Mobutu regime managed to get rid of the Soviet, Eastern European and Chinese advisers who had clustered around Lumumba. When Mobutu visited Washington in 1963, Kennedy told him that he had saved the Congo from communism, but the brazen military intervention and the removal of a hero to many Africans were bound to stir up anti-American and anti-Western emotions throughout the continent. Che Guevara, unknown to the Americans, had headed a Cuban group to assist Lumumba and remarked later that he had learnt a lot about the weaknesses of counter-insurgency strategies there. An unresolved mystery concerns the death, in a plane crash in September 1960, of UN Secretary-General Dag Hammarskjöld, who was on his way to negotiate a ceasefire between UN and Katangan forces. Some speculated that the plane crash was not an accident and that it had been shot down.

Under Mobutu, who became the richest and most corrupt man in Africa, the country was renamed Zaire in 1971, and in 1997 it became the Democratic Republic of the Congo.

Latin America

The Monroe Doctrine (1823) claimed Latin America as the US' zone of influence, and European powers were to stay out of the region. The great inequality of wealth fostered the development of communist parties, and Washington began to be concerned lest Moscow order local communists to hold up the export of strategic raw materials.

Stalin dismissed Latin American states as the 'obedient army of the US', and until the late 1950s, the Soviets only maintained three embassies in the subcontinent: in Mexico City, Buenos Aires and Montevideo. Small subsides were disbursed to local Communist Parties but nothing like the money and resources extended to parties in the West and Asia.

The first time that the US intervened directly was in 1954 in Guatemala. The president, Jacobo Arbenz, legalised the Communist Party, and it began to acquire influence. He made land reform (91 per cent of arable land was owned by large landowners) the centrepiece of his programme of social justice. The CIA began to arm and train Guatemalan opposition groups in Honduras. President Eisenhower gave the go-ahead for US aircraft to attack Guatemalan military bases. The military changed sides and removed Arbenz. Most communists escaped abroad, including Che Guevara, who was there to study developments. Dulles thought that dictators were the best leaders to work with in 'adolescent' Latin American states.

It was Castro who awakened Soviet interest in the subcontinent which was, and is, traditionally anti-American and anti-capitalist. The lead in expanding contacts with Latin America was taken by the KGB rather than the Ministry of Foreign Affairs, and this remained the pattern while Andrei Gromyko was foreign minister. Mikhail Suslov, number two in the party and therefore the chief ideologue, shared the KGB's enthusiasm for the Third World. Boris Ponomarev, head of the international department in the Party Secretariat, dealt with the leaders of the national liberation movements in the Third World. He was very conservative, and Khrushchev thought he was as 'orthodox as a Catholic priest'. Gromyko despised Ponomarev who returned the favour. The KGB, Suslov and Ponomarev viewed the great contest between the Soviet Union and the US, that between capitalism and socialism, as being won by whomever was victorious in the Third World.

A boost to these views was the declaration, in the new party programme adopted in 1961, that the 'liberation struggles of oppressed peoples is [*sic*] one of the mainstream tendencies of social progress'. A grand plan to use national liberation movements and the forces of anti-imperialism as a pincer movement to envelop the US was conceived, headed by the KGB.

In Brazil, in 1964, President João Goulart caused concern because of his radical economic and social agenda, and as he had also recognised Cuba and other communist countries, he had to go. President Lyndon Johnson saw him as a dangerous radical who should be removed by any means possible. The US banked on the military removing him, and it eventually did – sweetened, of course, by American largesse. The new president, Castelo Branco, did not follow the political and economic advice of a legion of American advisers. He was more concerned with dealing with his political enemies, and Brazil remained a military dictatorship until 1985. The Brazilian military became a close strategic ally of the US, and in 1965 Brazil helped Washington to invade the Dominican Republic. In 1966, Uruguay was warned that if the wrong person was elected, the country would face a Brazilian invasion (Westad 2005: 111–52).

The US made some accidental gains without any direct involvement. Military coups in the mid-1960s in the Congo, Indonesia, Algeria and Ghana took these countries out of the Soviet orbit. A key factor was the inability of the Soviets and Chinese to intervene militarily. They could in Vietnam, for instance, because it had a common border with China.

5 The Sino-Soviet schism

In 1954, Khrushchev left the Chinese perplexed after his first visit to Beijing. Ignoring protocol, he hugged and kissed Mao – which the Chinese regarded as scandalous behaviour – played the buffoon, promised a lot and distributed presents like a rich uncle. A loan of 520 million roubles was extended, many industrial enterprises were to be built and there was even a promise to help China's nuclear scientists. Khrushchev's largesse backfired because the Chinese read his behaviour as a sign of weakness.

The first clear articulation of the Chinese road to socialism was in December 1955 when Mao praised the uniqueness of the Chinese experience and implied that China would adopt its own economic model (Schram 1989: 113).

> We had twenty years' experience in the base areas and were trained in three revolutionary wars; our experience was exceedingly rich . . . Therefore, we were able to set up a state very quickly and complete the tasks of the revolution . . . Our population is very numerous and our position is excellent. [Our people] work industriously and bear much hardship . . . Consequently, we can reach socialism more, better and faster.

In April 1956, he went a step further and argued that China's road to socialism was superior to that of the Soviet Union. He pointed out that the Soviet Union's inability to attain the pre-1917 grain production and the disequilibrium of heavy and light industry in some Eastern European countries were phenomena not present in China.

Deng Xiaoping was the deputy head of the Chinese Party's delegation to the 20th CPSU Congress, held in Moscow in February 1956. A letter from Mao praising Stalin to the skies was read to the Congress, but the Chinese were taken aback as speaker after speaker ignored Stalin and merely quoted Lenin. Zhu De, the leader of the Chinese delegation, was told by Khrushchev that the collectivisation of Soviet agriculture resulted in food production long remaining below 1913 levels; this underlined that the leadership did not understand the peasantry.

The Chinese were excluded when the secret speech was delivered during the night of 14–15 February. On the evening of 17 February, a messenger arrived to inform the Chinese of the contents of the secret speech. The Chinese interpreter translated some and summarised the rest into Mandarin; when he had finished, the messenger took the report back with him. When the CPSU Presidium reprinted the speech on 1 March, Deng secured a copy, and he and the others reported to Mao at Zhongnanhai – the Chinese Kremlin – on 3 March. Communist Party of China (CPC) officials informed party members orally about the contents, and the party also produced a Chinese translation, together with other materials, and distributed it. Information about foreign reaction to the speech and on Stalin was also provided for party cadres.

At a Politburo meeting on 12 March, Mao commented: 'First, he lifted the lid; second he made a mistake.' He meant that Khrushchev had dropped his blind faith in Stalin, and this implied that other parties could think and act as they thought fit. The mistake he made was to attack Stalin, a figure of 'great international importance', without consulting other parties first. He also implied that the international communist movement was now in a mess and did not agree with Khrushchev on peaceful coexistence. At a Politburo meeting later in March, he stated that Stalin had been 30 per cent wrong but 70 per cent right. It was inevitable that Stalin made mistakes because he was the first leader to create a socialist country. An article was published which summarised the Politburo discussions and made clear the CPC's confidence in socialism. It underlined the historical achievement of the 20th Congress and its courage in denouncing Stalin's personality cult, and it also provided a detailed analysis of Stalinism. All the blame for the Soviet Union's mistakes in the post-war years should not be put down to the cult of the personality. Stalin believed that he was always right and that he was the only person defending the interests of the Soviet Union and, as a result, he had lost touch with reality and the masses. *Pravda* printed a Russian translation and distributed 200,000 copies. The Chinese analysis was widely praised in Eastern Europe and elsewhere in the communist world.

On 31 March, Mao spent several hours talking to Pavel Yudin, the Soviet ambassador, and was careful to mention that Stalin's policy towards China had been 'basically right', but then he went on to enumerate many of Stalin's errors. When Mikoyan arrived to discuss the Stalin question, the Chinese defended the Boss but made clear that the two parties fundamentally agreed on the issue. Mao later told Politburo members that there were right and wrong kinds of personality cults. He was later to accuse the Soviet leadership of lacking 'revolutionary morality' for praising Stalin to the skies one day and consigning him to hell the next. Another conclusion was that the new Soviet leader was not a 'leader and teacher'. Mao could now develop Marxism with Chinese characteristics, but this did not mean that he was considering taking a different path. Could the Stalinist model of development be refashioned to ensure faster economic growth? Could China outpace Soviet industrialisation by, for instance, increasing steel production at a much greater tempo? Here was sown the seeds of the disastrous Great Leap Forward policy and the mad rush to up steel output in 1958. The debunking of Stalin led Mao to conclude that he could correct his own mistakes and achieve economic paradise first (Pantsov 2015: 167–72; Shen and Xia 2015: 145–52). On 5 April, Mao presented his carefully considered comments on Stalin and the personality cult to the general public.

On 10 November 1956, Tito delivered a speech which blamed Soviet leaders for the crises in Eastern Europe. Mao had been thinking of penning an article on the international situation since the 20th Party Congress, and it appeared on 29 December 1956. It was widely praised; *Pravda* printed 20 million copies of it and expressed 'great satisfaction' with it. It provided an in-depth analysis of the current state of Marxism-Leninism and the road ahead for the international communist movement. At a New Year's Eve party in the Kremlin, Khrushchev hugged, kissed and proposed a toast to the Chinese ambassador and told him he 'totally agreed' with the article. The Hungarian Party loved it, but the Poles were lukewarm.

Khrushchev invited Zhou Enlai and a Chinese delegation to Moscow in January 1957 to cement the new relationship and to help solve the problems with Eastern Europe. The Yugoslav ambassador commented that China had begun to play the role of an intermediary or arbiter between Moscow and the other communist states. Zhou stressed two factors: support for Kádár and unity within the socialist camp. On 10 January, the Soviet, Chinese and Hungarian delegations held talks in Moscow and denounced Western attempts to undermine the unity of the socialist camp. Zhou insisted that the Soviet Union was the leader of the socialist camp, but several parties were unwilling to accept this. On the other hand, he stressed that all parties were equal and no party should force its views on others. The Soviets were aware of the rumours before the Polish and Hungarian crises that China, Poland and Yugoslavia would form an anti-Soviet front.

When Zhou visited Poland he attempted to reconcile the conflicting views between Warsaw and Moscow but without much success, with the Poles simply informing him they took a different line. Mao saw Gomułka as a rightist and revisionist but also a nationalist who opposed great power chauvinism in foreign policy. Nevertheless, China needed Poland as an ally.

In Hungary, Zhou and Kádár agreed on almost all issues, and Sino-Hungarian relations were thus much smoother than Sino-Soviet and Sino-Polish relations. Kádár asked for a 200 million rouble loan, 50 million of which was to be in foreign currency. Zhou promised 100 million roubles in foreign currency and 100 million roubles' worth of goods and materials. In the event, China only provided a loan of about 60 million roubles. So dangerous was the internal situation that the Soviet Army was put in charge of Zhou's security during his visit.

Back in Moscow, Zhou began to criticise Soviet policy. The Communist Party of the Soviet Union (CPSU) had failed to provide a comprehensive analysis of the present situation; the current leadership had not assumed personal responsibility for Stalin's mistakes; and it had failed to coordinate responses with fraternal parties. Khrushchev responded by saying that it was not necessary to consult the Eastern Europeans on the Stalin issue. Zhou told him that moving Soviet troops towards Warsaw during the Polish crisis was a mistake. Khrushchev's response was that it should not have happened but was not a mistake. Zhou's understanding was that the problem with the Soviet leadership was that it placed Soviet interests first and Soviet leaders often overstepped the mark and adopted short-term policies. Unsure of their position in the international communist movement, they resorted to political and military intimidation to maintain control. The Soviets often admitted their mistakes for tactical reasons but were not convinced they had made these mistakes; even more important, they did not learn from their mistakes. Needless to say, Khrushchev was mortally offended and commented to Mikhail Suslov, his chief ideologue, 'we cannot accept Zhou's lecture.' At the farewell reception, Khrushchev did not say a word. The broadcast version of the final communiqué was not the complete one agreed by both sides (Shen and Xia 2015: 181–8).

So why did Zhou and, by extension, Mao launch such a penetrating and critical analysis of CPSU behaviour? China did not wish to become an ally of the Soviet Union nor did it intend to become an ally of any other country. A Westerner, and indeed a Soviet, would have expected Beijing to seek a closer relationship with Moscow, given the fact that Khrushchev was bending over backwards to accommodate the Chinese. He had involved them in resolving the Polish and Hungarian crises and was helping to modernise the Middle Kingdom. This was deploying Western or Soviet logic but not Chinese. The Soviets could not anticipate what Beijing's reaction to a proposal would be or anticipate what its next move would be. Part of the problem was that China wanted to be treated as an equal, but Khrushchev refused to do so. To him, economically and militarily, the Soviet Union was vastly superior, so why treat the Middle Kingdom as an equal superpower? The Sino-Soviet relationship was reminiscent of the difficulties encountered by the US in dealing with the Soviet Union in and after 1945. China saw itself as unique and, therefore, was unprepared to be lectured by any other power.

The defeat of the Anti-party group in June 1957 sent shock waves through the communist world. The Chinese did not react, and some Soviet students in Moscow even said that they would wait for Mao to comment as he was always right, and some oblast party secretaries had to call on the KGB to restore order, so great was the tumult. Khrushchev was very nervous about the Chinese response and sent Mikoyan to win them over. They initially opposed the expulsion of Molotov and the others from the Central Committee but eventually changed their mind. As a sweetener, the Soviets agreed to provide advanced nuclear technology to the Middle Kingdom. In October, the dismissal of Marshal Georgy Zhukov as minister of defence caused many waves at home and abroad, and Mao accepted his removal after Mikoyan explained that Zhukov had threatened to weaken the party's control over the military.

The Moscow conference

During the Chinese civil war, Mao was so enthusiastic about the Cominform that Stalin thought he was interested in forming a Cominform of the East. In early 1949, communist parties in Burma (Myanmar), Malaya and Indonesia proposed to the CPC a Cominform of the East, but Mao turned it down as the civil war was still his priority. Liu Shaoqi, during a secret visit to the Soviet Union in June to August 1949, proposed to Stalin that a victorious China join the Cominform. The *vozhd* brushed it aside by saying it was 'utterly unnecessary' and instead proposed a coalition of East Asian Communist Parties. The outbreak of the Korean War brought this to nought. In April 1956, Mikoyan, after visiting India and Burma, floated the idea of Communist Parties jointly publishing a journal and setting up a liaison bureau. Mao was not in favour and proposed a conference to settle differences among the various Communist Parties. On 18 April 1956, *Pravda* announced that the Cominform would be dissolved and its journal would cease publication, and stated a successor organisation would be welcome.

After the Polish and Hungarian crises, China again turned to the idea of a conference and hoped that the League of Communists of Yugoslavia (LCY) would be a co-sponsor. Tito thought it was a démarche to devise a single policy for all communist states. As such, Yugoslavia's hard-earned independence would be put at risk, so Yugoslavia would not co-sponsor it and Tito would not attend. The CPC declined to be the sole sponsor, and the CPSU had to assume the role. The Chinese insisted that the final communiqué be agreed beforehand, and a draft was accepted which took into account about a hundred changes to the original Soviet draft; it became a working paper at the conference. A sticking point was whether a socialist takeover could be peaceful or violent with the French (PCF) favouring violence while the Italians (PCI) and British (CPGB) were for a peaceful transition. The Chinese seizure of power had been violent, but the 20th CPSU Congress had laid down a peaceful transition to socialism.

In November 1957, the largest-ever conference of Communist Parties convened in Moscow with sixty-four Communist Parties and twelve ruling parties attending. The conference marked the high water mark of Sino-Soviet relations, and Mao, the initiator of the meeting, was in his element. This demonstrated that the CPSU and CPC were now treated as equals. There was considerable opposition to the phrase 'the socialist camp led by the Soviet Union' as the Poles, Yugoslavs and Italians rejected it. Eventually the 'socialist camp, led by the Soviet Union', was adopted mainly due to Mao's insistence that there had to be a head. Some wanted the 'camp led by the Soviet Union and China', but Mao rejected this, arguing that the Middle Kingdom was too weak economically to lead. Khrushchev only realised later why the Chinese had insisted on a leader. It was because the leader could be replaced, and that meant China would eventually take over. This was an example of Chinese culture which the Soviets failed to grasp.

During his speech, Mao used the expression: 'The East wind prevails over the West wind.' This meant that capitalism was being left behind and that he regarded this as permanent. In private, Khrushchev insisted that the Soviet Union was only temporarily ahead of the US in military and some other areas, but the tremendous American strength in science should not be underestimated. Gomułka told Mao the capitalist countries were behind (due to Sputnik 1 and 2), but it was incorrect to assume they could never match such feats. Despite asking that Molotov not be mentioned, Mao did himself and spoke of a 'two-line struggle' in the CPSU. This expression was taken to mean that there were two factions within the Soviet Party, and this inevitably annoyed the Soviet leadership. Khrushchev boasted that the USSR, in fifteen years, would overtake the US, and Mao immediately responded that China would overtake Britain in steel production in fifteen years.

Another aspect of Mao's speech which aroused indignation were his views on nuclear war:

> Let us imagine, how many people will die if war breaks out. Out of a world population of 2.7 billion, one third – or even half – may be lost . . . Imperialism would be destroyed and the whole world would become socialist. In a number of years there would be 2.7 billion people again and definitely more.

The Poles and Czechoslovaks were appalled by this because they calculated they would be wiped out. When he returned to Beijing, he commented: 'Out of the world population of 2.7 billion, 900 million would survive. It is easier to get things done with 900 million, a good trade for the end of imperialism and permanent world peace' (Shen and Xia 2015: 241–70).

As the LCY delegation was in Moscow for the fortieth anniversary celebrations of the Soviet Union, Khrushchev and Mao attempted to convince them to attend the conference and sign the final statement. They made it clear that they had no intention of joining the socialist camp, especially one led by the Soviet Union. Khrushchev tried to get them to change their minds, and when they demurred he resorted to insults. Mao, on the other hand, was much more subtle and told the Yugoslavs that the CPC would not accept the leadership of any other party, including the CPSU, and it was not important if they did not sign the final statement, as the Russians liked signing documents but it caused China no harm. The LCY did not attend the Moscow conference. In the end, the Moscow declaration was such a compromise that each party interpreted it in its own way. Hence unity in the socialist world receded into the background.

Nuclear weapons

During Mao's visit to Moscow, in January 1950, Stalin showed him a film of the explosion of the first Soviet nuclear bomb which had occurred in August 1949. He intended to demonstrate to the Great Helmsman the destructive power of nuclear weapons and the ability of the USSR to extend a nuclear umbrella over all socialist states, including China. Despite this, Mao decided that he would not rely on the Soviets for security and that China would develop its own nuclear weapons. While Zhou Enlai was in Moscow, in July 1954, he was instructed to inform Soviet leaders that China would attack and liberate Taiwan. The attack was launched on 3 September and thus began the first Taiwan crisis which lasted until 1955. It led to the US threatening to use nuclear weapons against the Middle Kingdom.

Stalin would not share nuclear secrets with any other socialist state, but when Khrushchev visited Beijing in September–October 1954, Mao mentioned that he hoped the Soviet Union would aid China to develop its own nuclear weapons programme. The Soviet leader tried to fob Mao off with the argument that his country needed to devote all its efforts to developing the economy and not to engage in very expensive nuclear research. Mao wore him down, and a small nuclear reactor for research was promised, but nuclear weapons were off the agenda. Despite this, Mao informed Jawaharlal Nehru, the Indian leader, that China had begun research on an atomic bomb.

In January 1955, the USSR offered assistance to China and several Eastern European countries to enable them to develop a peaceful nuclear power industry. This included experimental nuclear reactors, accelerator design and fissionable material. On 20 January, China and the USSR signed an agreement on prospecting for radioactive elements in China. The uranium discovered would meet Chinese needs, and the surplus would be sold to the Soviet Union. On 18 February, the Chinese minister of defence submitted to Mao a plan for the development of a nuclear weapons programme. Various Sino-Soviet agreements were signed which promoted research in nuclear energy, the provision of equipment and the setting up of a nuclear energy research facility outside Beijing. A nuclear programme covering the years 1956–67 was agreed. A nuclear science research centre was established in Dubna, near Moscow, with the Soviet Union responsible for 50 per cent of the costs and China 20 per cent with other socialist states (except Vietnam) also contributing. It contained the largest synchrocyclotron in the world at that time, and research results were to be shared with all socialist states. Many leading Chinese nuclear scientists worked at Dubna, and one can say the Chinese nuclear weapons industry began to take place there. Due to the extensive Soviet spy network, researchers made use of developments in nuclear research worldwide.

Cooperation expanded during 1956 and 1957, and a railway was built from Aktogai, in Kazakhstan, to Lanzhou, in Gansu province, to provide Soviet equipment for China's experimental nuclear testing sites. The Soviet goal was to develop a comprehensive nuclear industry in China before 1962. By November 1959, China had 6,000 nuclear physicists, up from 600 two and a half years before.

The dilemma which faced Moscow in 1957 was that it had proposed to the UN a nuclear test ban and a ban on the production of nuclear weapons delivery systems, including missiles. It even went so far as to propose the destruction of all hydrogen bombs. This led to Moscow refusing to help China develop a missile programme, but Chinese students would be trained in Soviet universities and institutes in missile technology.

As a reward for siding with Khrushchev in the Polish and Hungarian crises and the Anti-party group, Moscow agreed, in August 1957, to help China develop its atomic, missile and aviation industries. A model of a nuclear bomb would be delivered with blueprints and industrial equipment to enrich uranium would also come. Prior to 1959, Moscow sent surface-to-ship missiles and assisted the Chinese navy in building a missile unit. The plan, before the end of 1961, was to provide the Middle Kingdom with sample missiles, design a test site and train specialists to conduct a nuclear bomb test. Hence the USSR was transferring to China the technology to produce atomic bombs and the missiles to deliver them and this included many Soviet specialists working in Chinese ministries. For example, over a thousand laboured in the Second Ministry of Machine Building. In December 1957, the Soviets delivered two train loads of R-2 surface-to-air missiles (based on the German V-2 missile) and related equipment and 103 specialists to teach the Chinese to launch them. This was not state of the art technology as the R-2 was no longer deployed by the Soviet armed forces. More advanced missiles followed and, in October 1957, a Chinese missile shot down a Taiwanese high-altitude reconnaissance plane over Beijing, and this was their first kill.

In April 1958, before the second Taiwan crisis, Khrushchev informed Zhou that the delivery of the model atomic bomb was being expedited. During the crisis, a US Sidewinder air-to-air missile landed in Zhejiang province but failed to explode. The Soviets asked to examine the missile but the Chinese said they needed time to examine it. Khrushchev was so angry he withdrew his offer to help with the development of the R-12 intermediate range missile (with a range of 1,050 miles). Several months later the Sidewinder missile was delivered, badly assembled and missing a vital component. The First Secretary's response was to go back on his promise to deliver a model atomic bomb by June 1959. Again China had not informed the Soviet Union about its decision to attack Taiwan as Mao had told Khrushchev that Taiwan was a domestic issue. The Soviet leader pointed out on numerous occasions that Taiwan had international implications and hence the two powers should consult one another. In 1958, the Soviet Union requested Chinese support for its proposal to prohibit the development and testing of nuclear weapons but Beijing did not reply. In 1959, Moscow enquired about the Chinese view on nuclear proliferation and China replied that it expected the Soviets to fulfil existing agreements and to 'provide equipment for the production of the final products'.

During the second Taiwan crisis of August–September 1958, President Eisenhower practised brinkmanship by deploying a huge naval and air force presence in the region. In the event of a Chinese invasion – which Eisenhower did not expect to occur – nuclear weapons were only to be used if conventional weapons failed to stem the advance. Mao also engaged in brinkmanship and never intended to invade Taiwan but he wanted to demonstrate to his domestic Chinese audience that he could stand up to the Americans. Washington had assumed that the Chinese shelling of the offshore islands, which resulted in about a thousand people being killed or wounded, was at the behest of the Soviet Union, but this was completely false. When the Americans threatened nuclear retaliation, Khrushchev had to respond in kind. Mao's skill in foreign policy had set the two superpowers at one another's throat. A classic Chinese stratagem: pitting the barbarians against one another. Khrushchev was unaware that whereas the Chinese referred to Europeans who invaded China in the nineteenth century as 'barbarians who came by sea', they regarded the Soviets as 'barbarians who came by land'.

Zhou Enlai explained Beijing strategy to President Nixon in 1972. John Foster Dulles had advised Chiang Kai-shek to abandon Quemoy and Matsu but he demurred and, bizarrely, Beijing advised him not to withdraw. This was signalled by firing shells on odd days and not shelling on even days and holidays. 'They understood our intentions and stayed', commented Zhou. This was Chinese strategy at its most subtle!

After the Taiwan crisis, Khrushchev regretted having signed the agreement to provide a sample atomic bomb but changed his mind on the R-12 missile, and it could be sent. Further nuclear aid would depend on the state of Sino-Soviet relations. On 26 June 1959, with the atomic bomb loaded on a railway carriage, the decision was taken not to proceed. A letter was sent to the CPC stating that in light of the ongoing negotiations between the Soviet Union, the US and Britain on a nuclear test ban treaty in Geneva, the Soviet Union could not provide a sample atomic bomb at present. On the other hand, the Soviet Union continued to supply missile and related advanced technology, and Soviet specialists travelled to the Middle Kingdom to instruct the Chinese in electronic and optical instruments, missile guidance computers, infrared ray technology and other topics. Needless to say, Khrushchev's decision to renege on the Sino-Soviet nuclear agreement angered the Chinese, and they set about developing nuclear weapons on their own. The codename for the first atomic bomb, '596', was a reminder of the 'shameful' date – in June 1959 – when the Soviet Union went back on the agreement to support China's nuclear programme. The two sides fell out and, in February 1960, the Chinese concluded that Moscow had decided not to help them with the development of nuclear weapons. By August 1960, all Soviet experts had been withdrawn and took their blueprints and equipment with them (Shen and Xia 2015: 207–29).

The Chinese tested their first atomic bomb on 16 October 1964 at Lop Nur, in the Gobi desert, Xinjiang province. China thereby became the fifth nuclear power on the planet after the US, USSR, Britain and France. This led to Mao fearing a possible US nuclear attack, and he ordered the relocation of over a thousand enterprises from the east coast inland. China's first hydrogen bomb was exploded on 17 June 1967.

Presumably Khrushchev's decision to renege on the nuclear agreement was based on the fear the Chinese could embroil the Soviet Union in a nuclear conflict with the US. The Soviet leader was aware that China would sooner or later develop nuclear weapons. From his point of view, later was preferable to sooner. When the British, in Hong Kong in the late 1950s, picked up information that China was mining uranium ore, there was the fear that the Middle Kingdom would develop a dirty bomb and explode it in, perhaps, Siberia. This might then provoke a nuclear war between the Soviet Union and the US.

In July 1958, Pavel Yudin, the Soviet ambassador, presented Mao with a proposal that the USSR and China establish a joint Pacific Ocean submarine and naval fleet. Mao wanted to know who would command it, but the ambassador did not know. This annoyed the Great Helmsman especially, as he had previously received a request from the Soviet Ministry of Defence to construct jointly with China a long-wave radio station to track nuclear powered submarines and ships of the Soviet Pacific Fleet. The Chinese leadership regarded these moves as encroaching on Chinese sovereignty. On 22 July 1958, Mao gave Yudin a dressing-down:

> You do not trust the Chinese at all, only the Russians. Russians are superior while the Chinese are inferior and careless. So you want a joint venture? Since you want a joint venture, let us discuss everything – army, navy, air force, industry, agriculture, culture and education. Is this OK? Maybe we should give you the entire Chinese coast of over ten thousand kilometres, while we only keep a guerrilla army. You possess only a little nuclear power, yet you want to control us.

Mao continued to vent his spleen and to condemn Soviet policy all day long. This, despite maintaining that the two sides agreed on almost everything. No wonder the Soviets were 'greatly depressed' and realised they had no understanding whatsoever of Chinese policy as they had overestimated the role of ideology but underestimated the differences which separated the two countries' national interests. When Yudin reported to Khrushchev, he omitted Mao's contention that if the fleet question could not be resolved, there was no point in the First Secretary coming to Beijing. Yudin's explanation was that he did not wish to sow discord between the two leaders.

Khrushchev flew in to smooth the ruffled feathers and denied that the Soviets had proposed a joint fleet and blamed his ambassador for all the misunderstandings. Mao was rude to Khrushchev but relented and agreed to the long-wave radio station, but it had to be financed entirely by China and no loans would be accepted to do this. Eventually it was built, and the Soviets did use it for a short time. Deng Xiaoping had become the leading specialist on Sino-Soviet relations and was a brilliant polemicist. According to the Chinese interpreter, he 'unmasked the attempts of the CPSU to undermine the sovereignty of China and to control the Communist Party of China'. The next day they moved to the swimming pool where Khrushchev was like a fish out of water. Nights were no relief because he was eaten alive by mosquitos. Mao commented that his treatment of the Soviet leader was like 'sticking a needle up his arse' (Pantsov 2015: 193–4; Shen and Xia 2015: 307–19).

On 30 October 1958, the Soviet Presidium resolved to 'cut back trade but not sharply with China'. Khrushchev could not conceal his irritation at the lack of respect extended him by Mao who now described him as the 'big fool'. On 1 December, the Soviet leader vented his anger at Chinese policies during a meeting with US Senator Hubert Humphrey. Mao was incensed as the intra-communist conflict now had an international audience. At the 21st CPSU Congress, in January 1959, Khrushchev took aim at 'egalitarian communism'. By this he meant the Great Leap Forward and the People's Commune Movement (1958–61).

Khrushchev's *amour propre* was piqued by Mao regarding himself as preeminent in Marxist philosophy and theory and the discoverer of a new route to communism. The Soviet leader, on the other hand, was only known for his fascination with maize. In July 1959, in Warsaw, Khrushchev openly criticised communes for the first time, and the Polish press published the speech but omitted the attack on the communes. *Pravda*, on the other hand, published the complete speech, and Mao found it intolerable that the Soviet leader should denigrate his great discovery in public. At the time, he was under pressure from his own cadres, some of whom regarded the communes as an 'artificial product', a waste of money and a political rather than an economic initiative. Despite this, the Soviet Union continued to deliver industrial goods and materials and agreed, in 1959, to assist the Chinese in building 125 new enterprises (Shen and Xia 2015: 284–99).

There was another issue which irked Mao. In 1958, Khrushchev asked about the availability of Chinese labour for logging in Siberia (Talbott 1974: 249).

> You know, comrade Khrushchev, for years it's been a widely held view that because China is an underdeveloped and overpopulated country, with widespread unemployment, it represents a good source of cheap labour. But you know, we Chinese find this attitude very offensive. Coming from you, it's rather embarrassing and if we were to accept your proposal, others . . . might think that the Soviet Union has the same image of China as the capitalist West has.

Khrushchev travelled to Beijing in September 1959 to mark the tenth anniversary of the People's Republic. He had just come back from seeing President Eisenhower and a trip round the US, and the Soviets had been stunned by the level of material wealth. Peaceful coexistence was in the air, and the Chinese did not like it. Khrushchev and Chinese Foreign Minister Marshal Chen Yi ended up shouting at one another. Chen called peaceful coexistence 'opportunism and time-serving'. The Soviet leader countered: 'Look lefty. Watch it comrade Chen, if you turn left, you may end up going to the right. The oak is also firm but it breaks.' Mao weighed in: 'we . . . attach to you one label – time servers. Please accept it.' Khrushchev refused to accept it:

> we take a principled communist line. Why may you criticise us and the senior brother may not censure you? . . . it turns out you may censure

us and we may not. You do not tolerate objections, you believe you are orthodox and this is where your arrogance reveals itself . . . Take back your political accusations or we will downgrade relations between our Parties.

Khrushchev was so annoyed he left Beijing the next day, and the shouting match with Chen Yi continued until he boarded the plane. On arrival in Moscow, he briefed the Presidium and then ordered that the minutes of the discussions with the 'Chinese friends' should not be sent to the archives but be destroyed. (The preceding quotations are from the Chinese archives.) The split between the two leaders was now reality.

In December, Mao informed the Politburo that Khrushchev was a

poor Marxist . . . His world view is empirical, his ideological method is metaphysical. He is a great power chauvinist and a bourgeois liberal . . . he does not understand Marxism-Leninism and his knowledge is superficial; he does not understand the method of class analysis and is like a correspondent of a news agency who turns in whichever direction the wind blows.

He also called him an 'extreme subjectivist-idealist'. The following month, Mao called for open polemics against the CPSU in the press.

Mao had really gotten under Khrushchev's skin. In February 1960, at a Warsaw Pact meeting, he began cursing Mao in the presence of the Chinese observer (China had refused to join the Warsaw Pact when it was set up in May 1955): 'If the old man is a fool, then he is no better than a pair of torn galoshes. He should be put in the corner like defective products that are good for nothing.' Kang Shang, called by some as Mao's Beria, answered in kind and then engaged in a heated argument with Khrushchev who claimed that Kang did not have the qualifications to debate with him. Kang's speech was not published in the Soviet Union but was in China. In April, on the ninetieth anniversary of Lenin's birth, the Chinese press accused Moscow of revising and betraying Lenin's legacy.

The Chinese published two articles replete with quotations from Marx, Engels and Lenin. The target was Khrushchev's policy of 'coexistence of the two systems' and his view that a 'peaceful transition from capitalism to socialism' was feasible. The Chinese view remained that war between capitalism and socialism was inevitable. In June, in Beijing at a conference of the World Federation of Trade Unions, Deng subjected 'Soviet revisionism' to withering criticism. Liu Shaoqi expressed the view that the only reason why China had remained within the Soviet bloc was fear of the US. In other words, Beijing and Moscow had never seen eye to eye. On 21 June, in Bucharest at the Romanian Party Congress, Khrushchev shouted at Deng: 'If you want Stalin, you can have him in a coffin. We'll send him to you in a special railway carriage.' He also claimed that 'only madmen and maniacs can now call for another world war.' He told the Chinese that it was clear they wanted to dominate the world. A two-day discussion was held to berate the Chinese with only the Albanians, North Vietnamese and North Koreans dissenting (Pantsov 2015: 204–9).

Mao needed Soviet assistance to build nuclear weapons, but there was no meeting of minds in September in Moscow as the two sides remained far apart. At a conference of eighty-one Communist Parties in Moscow in November 1960, the two sides agreed a joint declaration. The Soviets accepted the Chinese view on the immutability of capitalism and the equality of all Communist Parties. The Chinese accepted the significance of the 20th Party Congress and the need for peace, and then Mao sent the First Secretary effusive greetings to mark New Year 1961. The Soviets relented and provided help on some projects, but one area was excluded: cutting-edge military technology.

In October 1962, Khrushchev needed to ensure that China did not make life difficult for him if a confrontation with the US ensued over missiles on Cuba. China was planning a war with India over its northern border. This had been laid down during British colonial rule, and Beijing did not recognise it. In mid-October, Moscow made it clear that it would stand by India if it became embroiled in a war. The Soviet Union had also just agreed to sell India MiG21s and make it possible for India to manufacture them.

China attacked on 20 October, advanced deep into Indian territory and then withdrew, occupying some disputed areas. China then bit the hand that fed it and accused the Soviets of weakness and selling out to the Americans; Havana was told repeatedly that Moscow was an untrustworthy ally. *Pravda* then commented on the war but omitted confirmation that the Soviet Union supported China.

Khrushchev had a new party statute drafted for the upcoming 22nd Party Congress in November 1961. The era of the dictatorship of the proletariat was over, and the Communist Party was now a party of the whole people. The Soviet Union was to reach the foothills of communism (everyone's needs would be met) in 1980. Zhou Enlai headed the Chinese delegation, and they laid wreaths at the Lenin-Stalin mausoleum. The one to Stalin was inscribed: 'To I.V. Stalin: the great Marxist-Leninist'. Then the Congress decided that Stalin be removed and buried nearby. Khrushchev told Zhou that the Chinese Party's opinion was of no significance. Deng (read Mao) thought that a split between the two countries was looming.

Khrushchev neatly avoided any more transfers of nuclear know-how by signing the Nuclear Test Ban Treaty with the US and Britain in July 1963. It prohibited signatories from providing help to any other power to develop the atomic bomb and nuclear weapons.

In July 1963, Deng headed a Chinese delegation to Moscow with Mao launching a nine-pronged attack. The Soviet leadership was pilloried for denouncing Stalin, revisionism and its love affair with peaceful coexistence. The most violent speech was delivered by Kang Sheng who stoutly defended Stalin (Byron and Pack 1992: 253).

Can it really be that the CPSU . . . had a 'bandit' as its great leader for several decades? From what you have said, it appears as if the ranks of the international communist movement which grew and became stronger from year to year were under the leadership of some sort of 'shit'.

Kang then proceeded to mock Khrushchev by quoting his eulogies of Stalin and recalling their joint efforts to wipe out Trotskyites in the 1930s. The Chinese came out on top as they revealed themselves masters of polemics, and the Soviet and Chinese people now learnt of the chasm which existed between the two countries. Relations were broken off on 14 July 1964. Shortly before his removal, Khrushchev told a Romanian delegation that Mao was 'sick, crazy . . . and should be taken to an asylum' (Andrew and Mitrokhin 2005: 264). In 1964, the People's Republic established diplomatic relations with fourteen African states, and Moscow was appalled to see Soviet leaders replaced by huge portraits of Mao.

Moscow's ability to monitor events in China was crippled by Khrushchev's revealing to Beijing the KGB and GRU's Chinese networks. The Soviets had worked closely with the Chinese, and many Soviet illegals were trained there and sent abroad. Hence the Soviets, after the schism, until the end of the Soviet era, lacked access to the intelligence which they could gather in other countries. Most of the KGB's agents whose identities had been revealed to the Ministry of State Security were either shot or sent to labour correction camps. In Beijing, KGB officers of Mongolian or Central Asian appearance were smuggled out of the embassy in the boots of cars and then let out to read the wall papers and mingle with the crowds.

Mao espoused a Three World Theory: the US and the Soviet Union were the First World; the other capitalist states, the Second World; and the rest, headed by China, the Third World. China was full of revolutionary fervour while the Soviet Union was sated, growing fat and lazy. The Sino-Soviet split allowed Cuba and Vietnam room for manoeuvre and to challenge the US. In 1963, Zhou Enlai and Liu Shaoqi between them visited twenty Third World countries to carry the message that China was on the offensive against capitalism, and aid, civil and military advisers were sent far and wide. One striking example was the building of the railway line from Zambia to Tanzania. Zhou, known as the master diplomat, committed a faux pas in Tanzania in June 1965. He declared that Africa was ripe for revolution, and African leaders were so indignant that no one would welcome him after he left Tanzania. Kenya even refused to allow his plane to refuel on the way home. The KGB forged documents revealing plots against incumbent leaders. This led to Chinese missions in Burundi, the Central African Republic, Dahomey (now Benin), Tunisia and Senegal being closed between 1965 and 1968. The Chinese became close to the Vietnamese and Indonesian Communist Parties. The Soviets began to fear that China was becoming dominant in Africa and Asia. One argument used by Beijing was that the Soviets were Europeans and hence the Third World had to unite against European imperialism.

What was behind Mao's polemics with Khrushchev? Were they really ideological, or was there another motive behind the smokescreen of quotations from Marx, Engels, Lenin and Stalin? When Khrushchev arrived in Beijing in 1954, he came as First Secretary of the CPSU, the world's leading Communist Party, and he expected Mao to acknowledge his primacy. The Soviet leader could not contain his delight at being in such a position of power and behaved outrageously. The conclusion was that Khrushchev was a weak leader and the Chinese could take advantage of this. The denunciation of Stalin at the 20th Party Congress was their opportunity, and this was followed by Khrushchev's espousal of peaceful coexistence with the capitalist world. These were bundled together and labelled revisionism. What did this mean? It was an attack on a move away from the self-sacrifice of the Soviet people. Khrushchev wanted to raise living standards and make life easier, but to Mao this meant becoming more bourgeois. China was still so poor that self-sacrifice was the order of the day. By reviling revisionism in the Soviet Union, Mao made it impossible for any Chinese politician to propose anything similar in China. Capitalism was still the major enemy, and Khrushchev's view that there could be a peaceful transition from capitalism to socialism meant that there was a possibility that defence budgets need not be so high. Mao used revisionism as a weapon to maintain his supremacy in China but also to demand greater sacrifices from the people. Khrushchev's boast that the Soviet Union would reach the foothills of communism in 1980 risked placing the Middle Kingdom in a permanently minor position.

There was also another side to revisionism. It permitted Mao to vent his anger at the way he had been humiliated by Stalin. It was catharsis, but it was also catharsis for the Chinese leadership after the 'century of humiliation' before 1949. Khrushchev could not control his emotions and drank too much, and some of his outlandish comments were made when he was inebriated. Mao used this as a weapon and used Deng, Zhou Enlai, Chen Yi and Liu Shaoqi to attack the Soviet leader like wild dogs. Deng could wind up Khrushchev like a clock.

A sixty-eight-page document listing the sins of the Chinese Party was launched by the Soviets at the Romanian Party Congress. The Chinese countered with their own attack on the CPSU. I was given a copy by a West German communist, and I must say it was brilliant polemics and on a par with Trotsky's silver tongue and pen when attacking Stalin. The CPSU's chief ideologue was Mikhail Suslov, but he was no match for Deng. He was only two years older than Deng, but the latter had boundless energy and wore Suslov down. Deep down the Soviet communists realised they could not win the ideological war, and so they had to achieve economic and military dominance to cope with the challenge of the Middle Kingdom.

China had to pay a price for attacking the hand that fed it. About 2,000 Soviet specialists were withdrawn, they stopped work on 250 projects and Comrade Ivan ceased to be as generous as before. Mao was willing to pay this price, and this reveals that he placed his own interests ahead of those of his country.

The removal of Khrushchev, in October 1964, provided Mao with an opportunity to improve relations with the Soviet Union. Needless to say, he thought that the new leadership under Leonid Brezhnev, as Party First Secretary, and

Aleksei Kosygin, as prime minister, should now engage in a repudiation of de-Stalinisation.

Zhou Enlai headed a delegation to celebrate the anniversary of the October Revolution in Moscow. On 7 November, at a glittering Kremlin reception, Marshal Rodion Malinovsky, minister of defence, approached Zhou. 'We don't want a Mao or a Khrushchev to stand in the way of our relationship,' he commented. Zhou beat a hasty retreat. Then Malinovsky turned to Marshal Ho Lung and said: 'We've got rid of our fool Khrushchev; you can now get rid of yours, Mao. Then we can have friendly relations again.' The Soviet marshal then expressed himself very crudely. 'The uniform I am wearing is Stalin's dog shit. The marshal's uniform you are wearing is Mao's dog shit' (Chang and Halliday 2005: 511).

Zhou made a formal protest, and Brezhnev and his colleagues apologised, saying Malinovsky had not expressed their views and anyway had been drunk. Mao was confirmed in his view that it had been a put-up job when he discovered that the marshal had not been demoted or even disciplined. The Soviets had discovered what they wanted to know: it was impossible to detach Zhou from Mao. No member of the Mao team visited Moscow officially until his death.

The great proletarian Cultural Revolution

The economy reverted to central planning after the Great Leap Forward and People's Commune Movement. Something like 45 million Chinese died of starvation and disease between 1958 and 1961, and this amounted to about 7 per cent of the population. Upwards of three million were simply murdered by cadres because they were unwilling or unable to work (Dikötter 2010: 298). Even over the years 1961–65 when grain was imported, there were still 4.7 million deaths from hunger and disease. Dikötter also estimates that a staggering 40 per cent of China's housing stock was also destroyed. Was Mao aware that people were starving? He was, and he replied that it was better for half the people to die so that the other half could eat their fill.

Mao saw centralisation as producing a self-serving bureaucracy, and the key objective of the revolution was to permit the people to take over. He was aware that social stratification was occurring and that interest groups were emerging, and something had to be done to reverse this trend. He could set out to eliminate a self-serving bureaucracy, but a new hierarchy was needed to replace it, otherwise the country would sink into anarchy. This new hierarchy would wax and become a new ruling bureaucracy. This was the contradiction which Mao never resolved.

Mao believed in permanent class struggle which was needed to protect the party from capitalist pollution, and it had to be purged from top to bottom. There was going to be the 'greatest revolutionary transformation of society, unprecedented in the history of mankind'. The four 'olds' were to be banished: old thought, old culture, old customs, old habits. Books, paintings, temples, statues and other aspects of the old culture were to be destroyed. Libraries were closed, and the only books available were by Marx, Engels, Lenin, Stalin and Mao. Learning was derided, and the popular slogan was 'knowledge is useless,' and so the educated again became a target and all contact with Japan and the West ended.

The destruction of traditional culture and learning during the Cultural Revolution has probably no precedent in modern history as it amounted to China negating its past. The only other example is Pol Pot's destruction of urban elites and culture in Kampuchea, but there was less to destroy in that country.

In June 1964, Mao accused the creative intelligentsia and periodicals of not implementing party policy over the previous fifteen years. 'Capitalist roaders' or leading party officials were a prime target. In December, he told the leadership that there was a danger of revisionism reappearing in the party as there were two factions in the party: a socialist and a capitalist. In January 1965, he decided to remove Liu Shaoqi and others who were taking the 'capitalist road'. Jiang Qing, Mao's wife – but she did not share his bed – was in charge of culture and determined to increase her political influence, but she had a bad press. Her detractors labelled her vindictive, malicious, treacherous and venomous. Some of her enemies put her spiteful behaviour down to sexual frustration, and it was inevitable that she and Deng would fall out.

Mao had a vision and spelled it out to André Malraux in 1965 (Malraux 1967: 373–4):

> The thought, culture and customs which brought China to where we found her must disappear, and the thought, customs and culture of proletarian China, which does not yet exist, must appear . . . Thought, culture, customs must be born of struggle and the struggle must continue for as long as there is still danger of a return to the past.

Mao likened his vision to the smashing of the atom which destroyed the old but released colossal energy to build a new society. After each victory, a new task had to be set, and no one would be permitted to rest. Each cycle would bring China to a higher level of development. What was the goal? 'Classes, state power and political parties will die out very naturally and mankind will enter the realm of the Great Harmony' (Kissinger 2012: 95). Even though Mao wanted to destroy Confucianism with its deference to authority, he was echoing Confucius's own goal of the Great Harmony. He wanted to attain it by other means and, more importantly, more rapidly. He saw himself as Qin Shihuang, who had founded the modern Chinese state, reincarnated. He was the new emperor with a mandate from Heaven. One of the elements of the Cultural Revolution was to purify China of those elements which could lead to the country becoming part of universal culture. Mao's perception was Sinocentric, and he was consumed by an intense vision of the uniqueness of the Chinese people and what they could achieve.

In March 1966, he signalled his intent in an extraordinary attack on the party apparatus (Priestland 2009: 359–60).

> The central Party propaganda department is the palace of the Prince of Hell. The palace of the Prince of Hell should be overthrown and the Little Devil liberated . . . Local areas must produce several more [monkey kings] to create a vigorous disturbance at the palace of the King of Heaven.

April 1966 saw the launching of the purge of traditional culture. Beijing Party secretary Peng, Chief of Staff Luo and others were arrested and declared an 'anti-party group'. Zhou had his reservations but, as usual, sided with Mao. An unprecedented Mao cult developed: everyone wore a Mao badge, pretended to read his *Selected Works* and hung a portrait in their home. In May, students at Peking University accused members of staff, including the rector, of revisionism. Other universities in Beijing and elsewhere joined the witch hunt.

A Cultural Revolution Group formed, headed by Chen Boda and included Zhou Enlai, Jiang Qing and several others. Membership varied over time, but this group set the Revolution in motion on 1 June with a sensational editorial in the *People's Daily*, titled 'Sweep Away All Monsters and Demons.' The people were to cleanse the country of all those harbouring bourgeois values.

In August, the post of party secretary general was abolished and the Secretariat severely weakened. Their functions passed to the Cultural Revolution Group. Deng became Capitalist Roader no. 1 and Liu Shaoqi Capitalist Roader no. 2 in July; they were humiliated in the Great Hall of the People by student activists. Deng was forced into a stumbling mea culpa.

In September 1966, the Red Guards (students from secondary schools and universities) were turned on the real target: party functionaries who 'are taking the capitalist road'. They were to be wiped off the face of the earth. Several thousand were murdered in Beijing and Shanghai, and many others committed suicide. In October, Liu Shaoqi and Deng Xiaoping became the main targets. Mao commented that China had a large population so would not miss a few. However, the rule of the party was not to be put in question; Army personnel took the place of ousted officials and over 50,000 obtained middle- and top-level party positions. Citizens spent hours and days denouncing 'capitalist roaders' and reciting quotations from the *Little Red Book*. 'Great chaos will lead to great order,' commented Mao.

In August 1967, Deng and his wife were again humiliated by Red Guards and spent two years in almost total isolation. They were not permitted to see their children or other relatives. Deng's younger brother committed suicide, and his brother-in-law died in prison. Jiang Qing tried to convince Mao to liquidate Deng, but the situation changed in 1969 and the Dengs could meet their children once a week. They learnt that their son had been pushed off the top of a building and broke his spine, but no hospital would treat him. He was treated later, but by then he was paralysed from the waist down.

During the summer of 1967, the situation appeared to be getting out of hand as the military had stood aside and allowed the various factions to fight it out. Mao then ordered soldiers to intervene, and they embarked on an orgy of killing of the various guard groups. In Jiangxi, using bullets was seen as a waste of money, so the condemned had their ears cut off and were left to bleed to death. In Yunnan, half a million were arrested, and there were 6,979 'enforced suicides'. The executioners celebrated by eating the heart, brains, testicles, penis, flesh and liver of victims, and over 650,000 people died in the mayhem. The Red Guards were officially disbanded in 1968. Foreign embassies were targeted, and the British mission was set alight on 22 August 1967. Mayhem reigned in Hong Kong for a while. Idolatry of Mao turned into hysteria.

The Cultural Revolution was economic madness. Mao was an economic illiterate and regarded poverty and a hard life as essential to the building of socialism. He looked at things from a purely political perspective, and from this vantage point, the policy was rational as it cemented his hold on power for a party and a people who would follow his every dictate. He favoured permanent revolution which involved class struggle and endless campaigns, and this was reminiscent of Trotsky. That way, revolutionary enthusiasm could be maintained, but after each excess he was forced to backtrack – for a while. He feared that a lack of conflict in the country would result in the dictatorship of the bureaucracy. He was a great admirer of Stalin but knew that classical Stalinism produced a ruling bureaucracy, and the product of that bureaucracy was Khrushchev, so he strove to ensure that China did not follow the same Soviet path. He failed, but in failing he paved the way for Deng Xiaoping's market reforms from 1978 onwards. How did Mao manage to hold on to power? He ensured the country was always in a state of emergency and the military stayed loyal to him. By April 1969, 45 per cent of the members of the Party Central Committee were military, compared to 19 per cent in 1956, and the average age of new members was sixty (Kissinger 2012: 110). In 1972, when President Nixon complimented Mao on transforming an ancient civilisation, he responded that he had changed very little. In other words, Chinese tradition and culture were much more deeply embedded than the Great Helmsman had imagined and could not be transformed by a revolution from above.

Moscow was very worried about developments and could not easily reconcile itself to the end of communist unity and its role as the leading interpreter of Marxism-Leninism. The Soviets intervened in the Cultural Revolution and

> supported the Party apparatus against Mao by two methods both related to Vietnam: a) they sought to appeal to Party members to create a unified socialist front against the US on Vietnam. This is one reason . . . why the Soviet Union had been loath to do anything to end the war; b) They used the pretext of arms shipments to Vietnam to strengthen army units thought to be favourable to their point of view. This in turn explained two related developments: i) the ambivalence of Soviet policy as long as there

was a chance of using Vietnam to re-cement socialist unity, the Soviets were reluctant to assist peace efforts and even to relax tension in Europe.

This interpretation of Sino-Soviet affairs was related to Henry Kissinger in Prague in January 1967 by a Czech intelligence official. It made clear why Washington's efforts to achieve a settlement of the Vietnam War by going through Moscow was doomed to fail. It also made clear that the Soviets had backed the party apparatus against Mao, but the Maoists were winning and were 'now desperate to expel the Soviets physically from China. Nothing less than a complete rupture with the Soviet Union will enable them to feel secure' (Ferguson 2015: 745–6). Moscow had burned its boats by siding with the losers.

Conflict on the Ussuri

In November 1967, there were border skirmishes between Chinese and Soviet troops, and the first Chinese fatalities were recorded in January 1968. In February 1969, the People's Liberation Army (PLA) decided to ambush Soviet troops on Zhenbao or Damansky Island, and on 2 March, twenty-nine Soviet soldiers and two officers were killed, and the Chinese lost seventeen men. In all, forty-nine servicemen were wounded, and one captured Soviet soldier was tortured to death. Between 2 and 21 March, the Soviets lost forty-four soldiers and four officers with eighty-five soldiers and nine officers wounded. On 15 March, the Soviets had counter-attacked but had not attained their objectives. The exact number of Chinese casualties is unknown, but the Soviets reported over 800 Chinese dead. Why did the Chinese attack Soviet border guards? The Chinese move was defensive in the sense that its aim was to shock the Soviets into stopping their border skirmishes. The 'offensive deterrence concept involves the use of a pre-emptive strategy not so much to defeat the adversary militarily as to deal him a psychological blow to cause him to desist' (Kissinger 2012: 216). On 21 March, Aleksei Kosygin, the prime minister, attempted to speak to Mao on the telephone, but the operator refused to put the call through, cursing Kosygin as a 'revisionist element'. In August, Soviet troops wiped out a Chinese battalion on the border with Xinjiang, and war became a possibility as over a million soldiers were stationed along the Sino-Soviet border.

There were some Soviets who were in favour of drastic action. Marshal Andrei Grechko, the minister of defence, was one of those who wanted to obliterate China's nuclear potential. In August, a Soviet diplomat asked what the Americans would do if the Soviet Union wiped out China's nuclear installations. How would Washington react if Beijing asked for assistance to repel Soviet attacks? Soviet diplomats posed the same questions in other countries. Moscow then thought of a conventional attack.

During this tense period, Mao set up a study group of four marshals on relations with Moscow and Washington. Marshals Chen Yi and Ye Jianying concluded that the best response would be for China to play the 'US card'. This was because the US would not favour a Soviet conquest of China. This led to secret talks with the Americans which concluded with President Nixon's visit to Beijing in 1972 (Andrew and Mitrokhin 2005: 281). The Soviets engaged in the same exercise but concluded that the main adversary remained the US.

In August 1969, President Nixon, at a National Security Council meeting, argued that the Soviet Union was the more dangerous party and it would run counter to US interests if China were 'smashed' in a Sino-Soviet war. Kissinger put out a directive stating that the US would remain neutral in the case of a Sino-Soviet conflict but would lean towards China to the greatest possible extent. This was revolutionary after two decades of enmity between Beijing and Washington, as capitalist America wanted the second most powerful communist state to survive and would assist it to do so. Recent research indicates that the Soviets came very close to launching an attack, and it was only uncertainty about America's reaction which held them back. Mao expected an attack, on 1 October, the anniversary of the revolution, and ordered all leaders to disperse around the country (except Zhou who was to run the government), and the military was placed on 'first degree combat readiness' alert (Kissinger 2012: 218–20).

Zhou met Kosygin at Beijing airport in late September, and they agreed to seek a negotiated settlement to the conflict. On 11 December, border talks failed again, but on 1 May 1970, Mao received the head of the Soviet border negotiation team and told him that the two sides should only fight with words. An uneasy truce ensued.

The Chinese version is as follows:

> The US had been sending U-2 planes from Taiwan over central and western China and located Lop Nor, in south east Xinjiang, as the nuclear test facility. Washington expected China to test a nuclear device in in 1962 and a nuclear bomb in 1965. President Kennedy feared, in 1961, that a nuclear armed China would gobble up South East Asia. As a result, on 14 July 1963, in Moscow, an American official gave a detailed presentation of China's nuclear potential and proposed a joint attack to eliminate it. Khrushchev refused, stating that China posed no threat. The US considered other options: an attack by Taiwanese and American paratroops, conventional and nuclear bombs.
>
> In August 1964, the US predicted that China would explode its first nuclear bomb in 1965 but the Middle Kingdom exploded it in October 1964. President Johnson called it the 'blackest and most tragic day for the free world'.

In October 1969, all party and military leaders were told to leave Beijing, and Mao moved to Wuhan. Liu Shaoqi ordered 940,000 soldiers, 4,000 aircraft and 600 ships to scatter, airport runways were blocked and workers were given weapons to shoot Soviet air force personnel when they landed. Major archives were moved from Beijing to the south west, and the Chinese were told to prepare for war (*South China Morning Post*, 12 May 2010, quoting a Beijing scholar). An underground city of 85 km² was built under the capital. By the end of 1970, the country's seventy-five largest cities had enough underground shelters to house 60 per cent of the population. Over 1,800 factories were transferred to remote areas to protect them from attack, but economically it was a colossal waste of resources (Dikötter 2016: 212, 214, 218).

Soviet ambassador Anatoly Dobrynin informed Henry Kissinger of Soviet plans to launch a nuclear attack on China and requested the US remain neutral. The White House leaked the story to the *Washington Post*, which wrote that the Soviet Union planned to attack Beijing, Chongqing, Anshan and its missile launch centres at Jinquan, Xichang and Lop Nor.

On 15 October, Henry Kissinger informed Dobrynin that if the Soviet Union launched nuclear missiles at China, Washington would launch nuclear missiles against 130 Soviet cities. President Nixon was also concerned about the effect of a nuclear war on the 250,000 US troops in the Asia-Pacific region.

Nixon viewed the Brezhnev leadership as a collective whose main concern was to stay in power. A collective leadership was less likely to engage in rash judgements. The president rated Mao and Zhou Enlai more highly than the comrades in Moscow. Another explanation would be that Moscow wanted to signal to Beijing that it was serious about ending the border conflict but never had any intention of launching a nuclear attack. Leaking the information to the *Washington Post* provided the Soviet leadership with global publicity, and this is precisely what it wanted.

The People's Republic faced the threat of a nuclear attack five times: once by the US and the USSR in 1963 (if we accept Chinese information on this), three by the US (in 1950, 1955, and 1958) and one by the Soviet Union in 1969.

In January and February 1955, the PLA captured two islands opposite Fujian. The Taiwanese, helped by the US Navy, evacuated 25,000 soldiers and 15,000 civilians to Taiwan and centred their defences on Quemoy and Matsu. On 6 March, John Foster Dulles, the US secretary of state, made it clear that if the PLA took over Quemoy and Matsu, it would be a disaster for Taiwan and the rest of Asia. Nuclear weapons might be used to defend the islands.

In late March, B-36 planes in Guam were loaded with nuclear weapons ready for action. However, there was worldwide criticism of the decision to use nuclear weapons to defend these small islands. The US pulled back and began discussions at ambassadorial level with the Chinese in Geneva later that year.

The next nuclear threat occurred after the PLA launched 45,000 shells at Quemoy on 23 August 1958. The following day, it attacked ships leaving the island for Taiwan and enforced a blockade. Five B-47s were put on standby to launch a nuclear attack on Xiamen airport. However, like President Truman, President Eisenhower decided not to use nuclear weapons to defend the islands and instead rely on conventional weapons.

In October 1969, Deng, his wife and stepmother were exiled to Nanchang. They spent three and a half years there where Deng engaged in 'corrective' labour at a tractor repair plant alongside his wife. Political re-education consisted of reading the works of Mao and newspapers, but their children were permitted to visit them. Mao was shocked when Lin Biao, his anointed successor, suddenly attempted to flee to the Soviet Union, but the plane crashed in Mongolia and all aboard were killed. The KGB severed Lin's head, boiled it to remove the hair and skin and placed the skull in its museum in the Lubyanka (Dikötter 2016: 252).

Mao began to see Deng in a better light, and, in February 1972, his party membership was restored. In February 1973, Deng and his family were rehabilitated and returned to Beijing. A major reason for this was that Zhou Enlai was dying of cancer. He was irreplaceable, and Mao judged that he needed Deng's expertise and experience.

In December 1973, Deng returned to the Politburo, headed the Party Secretariat and became a member of the Central Military Commission. Jiang Qing was not amused as Deng's rise weakened her political influence. Economic difficulties led Mao to appoint Deng deputy prime minister in October 1974, and he was also made chair of the Central Military Commission and Chief of the General Staff. He became a member of the Politburo Standing Committee in January 1975 and began to implement the four modernisations: agriculture, industry, defence and science and technology laid down by Zhou Enlai in December 1964. The goal was to attain the present development level of advanced countries by the end of the century. Jiang Qing and the left (with three others, they were labelled the Gang of Four) began chipping away at Deng's power base.

In January 1976, Mao appointed Hua Guofeng as acting prime minister and head of the Party Central Committee. The next month Hua (read Mao) declared open season on Deng. Jiang Qing called him a 'counterrevolutionary double dealer, a fascist, a representative of the bourgeoisie, a betrayer of the fatherland and an agent of international capitalism in China'. Mao tried to rein her in, but she controlled the press and pilloried him there. Rumours that Zhou Enlai had been a capitalist roader ignited protests which became violent and had to be suppressed. Jiang blamed Deng for heading the 'counterrevolutionary uprising', and he was dismissed from all his posts but remained a party member and was placed under house arrest. When Mao passed away on 9 September 1976, Deng was apprehensive as things could get worse for him.

A secret plan was devised, on 26 September 1976, to depose the Gang of Four by Hua Guofeng. On 6 October, the Politburo Standing Committee convened, ostensibly to discuss Mao's legacy, and two members of the Gang of Four were arrested as they arrived. Another was taken into custody at his home. Jiang Qing was in bed when the troops arrived, and she realised it was a coup. There was some fighting between the military and local radical militias, but the radicals had no hope of success. Ye Jianying, the minister of defence, was offered the top post but declined and passed it on to Hua Guofeng, who thus stepped into Mao's shoes. The Gang of Four were not charged with 'ultra leftism' but 'ultra right opportunism'! (Pantsov 2015: 308).

Within a month after Mao's death, the Cultural Revolution was over. It had devastated the economy and led to between 1.5 and 2 million deaths (Dikötter 2016: xvi), but it had also ruined the lives of millions more.

6 Cuba, Vietnam and Indonesia

Cuban communism is synonymous with the name of Fidel Castro Rus, but when he took power in January 1959, he was not a Marxist. He is one of the many in the disaffected middle class who were to wage war against their own class and background. His father was from Galicia, in Spain, and arrived penniless, gradually clawing his way up the property ladder, and his mother was the housekeeper whom his father later married. Cuba was a democracy in name but not in practice after it had gained independence from Spain in 1898, helped by the US. When presidential elections were due in March 1952, Fulgencio Batista seized power, but he was in cahoots with the American mafia, and a top mafioso, Meyer Lansky, became his chief adviser. These two hoods treated Cuba as their casino and amassed quite a fortune, but when Castro came to power, he confiscated Lansky's hotels, brothels, gambling dens and other houses of ill repute.

The hero of the independence struggle, José Marti (died 1895), was the inspiration for those who sought social justice and independence. Although not a Marxist, he is claimed by both communist and anti-communist Cubans today.

Castro hit it off with Naty Revuelta Clews, a society beauty and the wife of a prominent surgeon. His approach was revolutionary: 'May I indoctrinate you?' She invited him to call at her home any time after five. 'He was the kind of person who couldn't be ignored,' she recalled years later. 'If he was in a room, people paid attention. I too had a certain charm of my own.' The house became the base for Castro's first attempt at revolution as he and over a hundred men attempted to take over the Moncada Fortress in Santiago de Cuba. Those who were not killed were later captured and almost all put to death. This took place on 26 July 1953, and in Cuban revolutionary mythology, it is the beginning of the revolutionary struggle. Castro, through good fortune, was not executed but sentenced to twenty-six years in prison. He was permitted to address the court on 16 October 1963, and his peroration concluded with words which were to become famous: 'Condemn me. It does not matter. History will absolve me.'

Figure 6.1 Fidel Castro arrives in Washington, DC, in April 1959

Courtesy of the Library of Congress Prints and Photographs Division, Washington, DC 20540 USA, *US News and World Report* Magazine Photograph Collection, LC-USZ62–13035.

Enrique Pérez Serantes, Archbishop of Santiago de Cuba, had interceded on Castro's behalf (Castro had been educated in a Jesuit college), and he and others were released after 19 months. As time would tell, the good Father was completely taken in by Fidel. To be fair to the archbishop, Castro was not a Marxist at this time although he had read some Marx and Lenin. He was still searching for a revolutionary ideology which would unite a search for social justice and power for himself. He was to say, in Chile, on 18 November 1971:

> I was a man who was lucky enough to have discovered political theory, a man who was caught up in the whirlpool of Cuba's political crisis . . . discovering Marxism . . . was like finding a map in the forest.

What he really means is that he discovered Leninism. Marxism is an analysis of capitalism whereas Leninism is a road map to power.

Castro thereupon founded his own political group, the 26 July Movement. Fearful of being assassinated by a Batista agent, he and others made for Mexico and there linked up with his brother Raúl, who had embraced Marxism, and Ernesto 'Che' Guevara, the flamboyant Argentinean doctor who was later to be a comrade in arms in taking power. The nickname 'Che' came from a Guarani term for 'hey, you'. Guevara was fired with enthusiasm about revolution and in September 1963 published an influential article on guerrilla warfare. 'Revolution can be made at any given moment anywhere in the world,' he declared. Castro shared his views, but the Soviets were appalled, calling his opinions 'adventurism'. Exporting the Cuban revolution was now on the agenda, and all revolutionary movements could count on Cuban combat troops coming to their aid.

In late 1956, Castro and his comrades were told to leave Mexico and, acquiring a rickety boat called *Granma* (Grandmother), set sail for Cuba. It almost sank en route. The comrades made for the Sierra Madre mountains and proceeded to conduct a guerrilla campaign against Batista's forces. Castro won some middle class support as he was viewed as the leader of a democratic movement.

Castro adopted Mao Zedong's tactics: win over the local peasants, seize and redistribute the property of large landowners, organise the peasants into a fighting militia and continue taking over the countryside. The leaders were middle class, and the peasants made up the foot soldiers.

At a meeting in Caracas, Venezuela, various Cuban opposition groups proclaimed a manifesto and named Castro as their leader. The Communist Party was, however, not a signatory. However, shortly afterwards, the communist leader visited Castro in the Sierra Madre, and Fidel's journey towards Marxism continued.

By the end of 1958, Castro's forces were approaching Havana. On 1 January 1959, Batista scooped up the gold and currency reserves in the Central Bank and boarded a plane for the Dominican Republic. On 8 January, Castro made a long-winded speech – his hallmark – from the balcony of the presidential palace and was greeted with wild enthusiasm. Most Cubans thought that a new saviour had been born as Castro cleverly presented himself as José Marti reborn.

Cuba's Communist Party had accepted posts in Batista's government but was opposed to the armed struggle and dismissed Castro as a wild romantic. When he took over Cuba, Castro needed an organisation, an army and a programme to consolidate his position which was to go through three stages: the first was a genuine coalition government. Castro had no post in the government although he was the commander in chief of the armed forces. One third of the government was from the 26 July Movement, but the Communist Party was absent. The second revolutionary stage: a sham coalition began in February 1959, with Fidel becoming prime minister. Castro's first visit to the US as leader, in April 1959, was not a success as the US government and business were suspicious of him and saw the revolution as communist. A National Agrarian Reform Institute was set up and rapidly sidelined the cabinet. It engaged in radical agrarian reform, expropriating estates and redistributing the land to poor peasants. The Castro family land was not spared.

Figure 6.2 Che Guevara, the iconic image of the Cuban Revolution and more famous
dead than alive

© Hemis/Alamy.

The 26 July Movement merged with the Communist Party in 1961 and became
known as the Integrated Revolutionary Organisation (IRO). Although Castro confessed to being a communist, he was wary of ex-communists turning this organisation
into a power base to remove him and dismissed most of them. In 1965, secure in
the knowledge that he was master, the IRO became the Communist Party of Cuba
(CPC) with Fidel as general secretary. After visiting the Soviet Union in 1963, Cuba
was officially recognised as a communist state by Moscow. This was the beginning
of the third revolutionary stage: the building of a people's democracy.

Cuba viewed the Cuban Missile Crisis as a Soviet climb down and capitulation. It drew various conclusions from the debacle. One was that the Soviet
Union had ceased to be a driver of revolution in the Third World, so Cuba
would now play this role. To begin with, the Cubans focused on Latin America
and the Caribbean and trained at least 1,500 guerrillas. However, as expected,
the Soviets advised caution with the Latin American Communist Parties all following the Moscow line. They took umbrage at Cuba's attempts to shake them
up and, in November 1964, they criticised Castro for interfering in their affairs.
So Cuba turned towards Africa. Helping the African liberation movement was
natural because, after all, one third of Cuba's population were descendants of
African slaves. Attacking colonialism in Africa would also strike at the US.

Che Guevara was in charge of aiding foreign revolutionary movements. He
was a doctor, but after the taking of power Castro asked: '¿Hay un economista

aquí?' ('Is there an economist here?'). But Che understood: '¿Hay un comunista aquí?' ('Is there a communist here?'). He put up his hand and was put in charge of the National Bank!

Guevara had been radicalised by his journeys around Latin America in his early years. He assisted in the reforms of President Arbenz of Guatemala until the president was removed in an American supported coup. Guevara concluded that the abysmal poverty he encountered was the product of monopoly capitalism and imperialism and so the only remedy was revolution. This was an orthodox Marxist analysis. The problem was that the Latin American population was predominantly peasant. Based on the success of the Cuban Revolution, he developed guerrilla war tactics which could be applied to other Latin American states. Cadres of fast-moving paramilitary groups could provide a *foco* or focus for popular discontent against the incumbent regime and spark a general insurrection.

One of his most fervent admirers was Jean-Paul Sartre, the French Marxist philosopher. After meeting him, Sartre commented that Che was 'not only an intellectual but the most complete human being of our age'. He was the 'era's perfect man'. Presumably it was the violence Guevara preached which so appealed to the French intellectual. He was equally effusive about Castro and other revolutionaries:

> Sleeping doesn't seem like a natural need, just a routine of which they had more or less freed themselves . . . They have excluded the routine alternation of lunch and dinner from their daily programme . . . Of all these night watchmen, Castro is the most wide awake. Of all these fasting people, Castro can eat the most and fast the longest . . . They exercise a veritable dictatorship over their own needs . . . They roll back the limits of the possible.

> (Andrew and Mitrokhin 2005: 29)

A sarcastic commentator remarked that Sartre had evidently indulged in self-administered brain surgery!

The Frente Sandinista de Liberación Nacional (Sandinista National Liberation Front or FSLN) guerrillas were easily routed by the Nicaraguan National Guard in 1963 and made another attempt to take power in 1967, but they were again routed; it did not help that the KGB had judged the move premature. In October 1966, Che flew to Moscow and the following month went to Bolivia where he stated that a 'guerrilla war is a people's war', and if it is not fought with the support of the people it will end in disaster. This proved very prescient as not a single peasant joined his guerrillas.

Che preached hatred in a message to the Tricontinental Conference, in April 1967 (Guevara Works Archive):

> Hatred is an element of the struggle; a relentless hatred of the enemy, impelling us over and beyond the natural limitations that man is heir to

and transforming him into an effective, violent, selective and cold killing machine. Our soldiers must be thus; a people without hatred cannot vanquish the brutal enemy.

Mao and Stalin, not to mention Pol Pot, could not have put it better. Castro's impatience with Moscow's conservative Marxism provoked him into staging a show trial of pro-Moscow members of the Cuban Communist Party.

The FSNL guerrillas were useful to Moscow, and a KGB sabotage and intelligence group was formed on the Mexican-US border to reconnoitre US military bases, missile sites, radar installations and the oil pipeline which ran from El Paso, Texas, to Costa Mesa, California. Mines, explosives, detonators and other sabotage materials were hidden in safe locations. Castro repaired relations with Moscow by condemning the Prague Spring and supporting the Warsaw Pact intervention. The reason for this volte-face was the economic crisis in Cuba which had been exacerbated by declining Soviet exports. Moscow, as a mark of its pleasure at Castro's U-turn, extended large credits. Control over the population was increased and Castro admitted that there were over 20,000 political prisoners in camps. Long-haired youths and mini-skirted girls were targeted, and Castro's dislike of gays resulted in their being excluded from positions where they could influence young people. Gays were refused tenancies in new housing blocks and often sent to work in forced labour units. The American New Left who came to Cuba to help the revolution contained many homosexuals and drug addicts. The Cuban security service even thought of using homosexuality to 'bring about the physical degeneration of American imperialism' (Andrew and Mitrokhin 2005: 53–5).

In 1965, Guevara, bored with life in Cuba, set off for Africa (Congo) with a group of advisers to fight with the rebels; after that failed, he returned to Cuba and then moved to Bolivia to put his guerrilla war tactics into practice. He was betrayed in Bolivia, arrested, murdered and buried under an airfield runway in October 1967. Castro declared 8 October, the day of his death, as the Day of the Heroic Guerrilla Fighter. In 1997, his remains were exhumed and given a state funeral in Havana.

Guevara, not surprisingly, had little time for the orthodox Communist Parties of Latin America, guided and funded as they were by the Soviet Union, and Castro also was scathing about their lack of revolutionary drive. In 1967, President Lyndon Johnson complained to Aleksei Kosygin, the Soviet prime minister, about Guevara's revolutionary activities in Bolivia. The Soviets wanted better relations with the Americans, so Guevara had to restrain himself. This did not go down well with Castro, but given the economic plight of Cuba, he had to accept Moscow's non-revolutionary policy in Latin America. Whether this had anything to do with Guevara's arrest is a moot point, and there were even rumours that Guevara was betrayed by a fellow communist. Whatever the truth he became more famous in death than in life. He has remained an anti-establishment icon in many countries ever since.

Vietnam

French colonial rule was broken by the military defeat at Dien Bien Phu, Vietnam, in May 1954. At an international conference in Geneva in 1954, it was agreed to partition Vietnam, and the communists reluctantly agreed to this. They were supported by the Chinese who provided war matériel, moral support and 100,000 Chinese logistical troops to work on communications and infrastructure (Kissinger 2012: 204). This left the US as the main backer of the South Vietnamese government. Perceptive Americans realised that the communist agenda was more attractive to the average Vietnamese than anything Saigon could offer. The Viet Cong (Vietnamese Communists or National Liberation Front), formed to fight against the South Vietnamese and Americans, were a much more effective force than their southern opponents. Their political wing concentrated on land confiscation and redistribution to poor peasants in areas they controlled, and this was a doubly effective weapon: it gained peasant support and reduced the number of well-to-do supporters of the Saigon government. Brutal South Vietnamese tactics, such as the shelling of villages which supported the Viet Cong, were counterproductive.

When the US escalated its involvement in Vietnam in February 1965, Leonid Brezhnev sent Aleksei Kosygin to Hanoi to sign a treaty which provided financial aid, military hardware and technical advisers. He then moved on to Beijing to propose a joint alliance, but Mao lectured him for several hours and refused to get involved as he was gearing up for the Cultural Revolution at home. Lin Biao, minister of defence, stated that China had no interest in helping revolutionary movements abroad and advised them to rely on their own resources.

American policy was in a quandary. The military wanted more troops, arguing that the communists could be defeated by the use of force while many ordinary Americans and politicians wanted out. Strategists feared the domino effect, believing that if Vietnam went communist so would other neighbouring countries. The Vietnam War became the first to be shown on TV, and this had a dramatic effect as the relentless violence upset the average viewer. The defoliation of forests by using chemicals enraged many.

The turning point was the Tet (New Year) Offensive in January 1968. Almost 70,000 Viet Cong troops attacked the major southern cities. The offensive was a suicide mission and failed militarily but succeeded politically. Even the US embassy in Saigon was occupied for a short time. The US could no longer sustain such military expenditure, and President Lyndon Johnson, visibly ageing by the day, said he would not seek a second term. The smiles in Hanoi were almost as wide as the Gulf of Tonkin.

Vietnamese communists did not wish to subordinate themselves to Moscow or Beijing but wanted aid from both. The Soviet aim during the 1950s was to

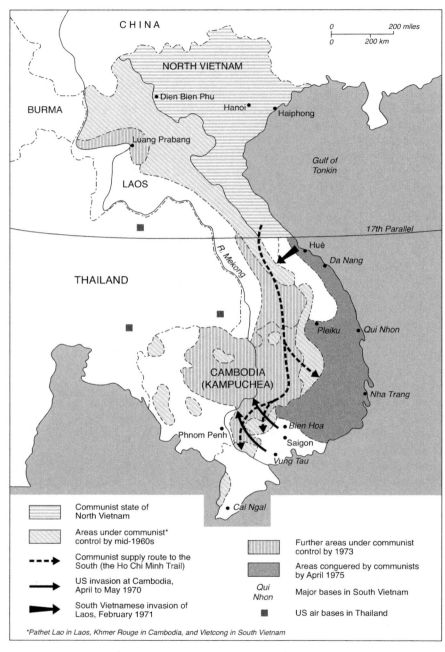

CHINA

NORTH VIETNAM

BURMA

Dien Bien Phu

Hanoi

Haiphong

Luang Prabang

Gulf of
Tonkin

LAOS

17th Parallel

R. Mekong

Hué

Da Nang

THAILAND

Pleiku

Qui Nhon

CAMBODIA
(KAMPUCHEA)

Nha Trang

Phnom Penh

Bien Hoa

Saigon

Vung Tau

Cai Ngal

	Communist state of North Vietnam
	Areas under communist* control by mid-1960s
	Communist supply route to the South (the Ho Chi Minh Trail)
	US invasion at Cambodia, April to May 1970
	South Vietnamese invasion of Laos, February 1971

	Further areas under communist control by 1973
	Areas conquered by communists by April 1975
Qui Nhon	Major bases in South Vietnam
■	US air bases in Thailand

*Pathet Lao in Laos, Khmer Rouge in Cambodia, and Vietcong in South Vietnam

Map 6.1 War and the advance of communism in Indo-China

build a viable socialist state in North Vietnam on the Soviet model. When it became politically, economically and militarily strong, it would be a magnet for the South. On the other hand, communists in the South were keen to organise attacks against the government as a way of radicalising the peasants and getting them to fight the regime. Moscow opposed this tactic, but Beijing was all in favour. During the 1950s, the Chinese insisted the communists in the North introduce collectivisation, but the results were unpromising. In 1960, Hanoi decided to endorse the armed struggle in the South and thereby set the country on the path to civil war. Needless to say, the Soviets opposed this new policy. Mao was also against it because of the weakness of the Chinese economy after the Great Leap Forward and the People's Commune Movement. He wanted to consolidate his position domestically and did not favour the possibility of the US intervening in the South to help Saigon. The Sino-Soviet split came at an unfortunate time for Hanoi as it needed military aid from both. Moscow concluded that it was only a matter of time before Hanoi sided with China. When the US intervened in the South in 1964, Moscow resignedly increased military aid to the North, but it held out little hope it could influence it ideologically. A North Vietnamese journalist estimated that the Soviet Union provided about 80 per cent of the military hardware but only 8 per cent of political influence. The KGB was only given limited access to US prisoners of war, and Moscow could not examine captured US military technology.

Indonesia

In the early 1960s, Indonesia puzzled not only Washington but also Beijing and Moscow. Sukarno was big on anti-Western rhetoric but small when it came to economic growth. The Indonesian Communist Party (PKI) was close to China, but the latter was concerned about the treatment of the ethnic Chinese, who dominated banking and commerce, in Indonesia. Covert US operations against the communists – sanctioned by Kennedy – were being stepped up. Sukarno resented the existence of Malaysia which had been set up to prevent the unification of all Malays in one Indonesian state. In 1963 and 1964, Indonesia came close to war with Malaysia and Britain.

Brian Tovey was the British Government Communications Headquarters (GCHQ) representative on the Joint Intelligence Committee Far East, responsible for the presentation of SIGINT (signal intelligence gathered by GCHQ) of MI5 and the Security Service (MI6) and military intelligence staffs in Singapore. SIGINT coverage was highly effective, and Tovey was able to plot the deployment of the Indonesian forces with a degree of accuracy that left Sukarno's naval, air and ground force commanders outmanoeuvred. As the economy faltered, Sukarno moved to the left, and he told Tito, at the Non-aligned Movement summit in Cairo in October 1964, that his aim was to move politics to the left to neutralise 'reactionary' elements in the army. He wanted to continue with the alliance of nationalists, Muslims and communists.

In September 1965, young officers assassinated six generals in an attempt to crush army opposition to Sukarno, and the revolution and the PKI supported them. Sukarno hedged his bets but some generals managed to escape, headed by Suharto. They, together with nationalist and Islamic supporters, massacred over half a million communists and left wingers. The killing lasted into 1966 with many of them being ethnic Chinese. Sukarno was now only a leader in name and stepped down in 1967, and General Suharto then assumed power.

The end of the Indonesian revolution shocked Moscow and Beijing. The Soviets blamed the Chinese and the inept tactics of the PKI. Moscow was in the bad books of the PKI which accused it of being part of neo-colonialist and imperialist forces which opposed Sukarno and the PKI. For the US, it was a dream come true as Sukarno and the PKI became yesterday's men. The move to the right in Indonesia changed the geopolitics of the region. It was a blow for the Soviets, but it meant they would concentrate more on ensuring that communism in Vietnam did not also collapse. If that happened they would be excluded from South East Asia. All in all, it was the greatest defeat suffered by communism in the Third World.

The military successes of the Viet Cong in South Vietnam led Washington to seek a peace settlement. It mistakenly thought that Moscow had considerable influence in Hanoi. The successes of the Vietnamese communists encouraged the left in Laos and Cambodia to launch their own offensives. In Laos, the Pathet Lao (Lao Nation) began a campaign against the government and gradually they received more and more help from the Vietnamese, and the latter increased their influence in Laos generally. In Cambodia, the Khmer Rouge appeared to have little chance of success. Prince Sihanouk had allowed Vietnamese supply bases in Cambodia and had broken off relations with the US in 1965. In 1969, the Khmer Rouge leader, Pol Pot, began receiving military aid from Vietnam to help fight the Americans and the Cambodian military that supported them.

Guerrillas in Malaysia were almost exclusively ethnic Chinese, and when China cut off support, they melted away. In Thailand, the US provided substantial aid to the Thai military, and this saw off the insurgents. In the Philippines, communist guerrillas numbered about 20,000 by the mid-1980s and were spread out over the archipelago, but they never fused into an effective fighting force capable of overthrowing the government in Manila.

During the student revolts of 1968 in Europe and the US, students lauded Guevara, Castro, Ho Chi Minh and Mao as inspirational leaders. Gone were the days of looking to Moscow for guidance about how to achieve revolution. The Soviet invasion of Czechoslovakia in 1968 also added to the disillusionment (Westad 2005: 185–94).

7   The war of cultures

The war of cultures centred, first and foremost, on Germany. The Soviet practice of males kissing one another on the lips as a greeting never really caught on. Words such as Kombinat (large enterprise), Kader (cadres), Nomenklatur (nomenklatura) and Plansoll (plan targets) found their way into the language in the German Democratic Republic (GDR). Subbotnik (working unpaid on a Saturday) was also adopted.

One of the greatest coups for GDR culture was the attraction of Bertolt Brecht (1898–1956) to East Berlin. As a Jew and a communist, he and his family had to leave Germany and go into exile under Hitler, eventually ending up in the US. His reputation was universal, and the GDR authorities milked it for all it was worth. Brecht did not join the Socialist Unity Party (SED), the GDR communist party, but his wife Helene Weigel did. When she died in May 1971, the GDR authorities tried to take control of the Brecht estate which had passed to Weigel's daughter, the formidable Barbara Brecht-Schall. She had joined the Berliner Ensemble in 1951 and conceded that she was not a 'big actress but a good one', appearing in several GDR films. She was summoned to appear before Politburo member Kurt Hager, the SED's top ideologist, who demanded she hand over the key to the bank vault where her father's manuscripts were stored. She refused point blank. 'Hager, that nasty piece of work, muttered that they did have other methods at their disposal too.' She later related, 'I knew he was bluffing. He would not have dared touch a Brecht relative.' Brecht-Schall maintained a running battle with the GDR Academy of Arts and also had great influence over the Berliner Ensemble, the theatre company which performed Brecht's plays in the GDR. She insisted on approving casts and directors and, in 1976, managed to oust the company's manager. 'It is always good to be a nuisance in a world full of so much feigned love,' she commented. She was a fierce defender of her father's rigorously Marxist plays and ended one production with the acid comment that her father had never intended the audience to see seven naked cardinals on stage. Her critics called her and her husband 'salon Bolsheviks' because they lived in East Germany, paying lip service to communism, but enjoyed a West German lifestyle. Others called her Cerberus (the multi-headed hell hound of classical mythology). An avid collector, she filled her home with antiques bought on trips all over the world. She regretted the fall of the Berlin Wall. 'Such a shame,' was her comment.

On reunification, Brecht's works were handed over to the state, but she earned royalties running into millions of marks. Her father, as far as she was concerned, was a 'Sunday papa' who lived for his work. He was very funny but did not wash often and smelled always of cigars. She gave all his mistresses short shrift. Brecht's violent temper was passed on to her, and she remained a dedicated communist to the end. Being obstructive gave her pleasure all the more so because 'some were furious that a woman could decide what could and what could not be done in plays' (*The Times*, 9 September 2015). GDR communism was dominated by males, and she was probably the only female who could tell Ulbricht, Honecker and company where to put their comments and get away with it. After the fall of the Wall, she insisted she had never been a communist, a phenomenon which I encountered among other SED members.

In West Germany, many Americanisms took hold such as job, comic, fan, hobby, beat and pop; *Bravo* appeared in 1956 and was an instant hit. Radio and television were enormously influential and contributed to the popularisation of American culture in East and West with pop music going ballistic. Concepts such as single, song, boogie-woogie, blues, beat, rock, pop and disco became common currency. The GDR did its best to repel the waves of Western pop but eventually, in 1965, produced a Beatles album under licence. To counter American dance music, the GDR came up with *Lipsi*, a party-approved dance, but it never caught on. The Vietnam War protest songs of Joan Baez, Pete Seeger and Bob Dylan were played in the GDR with the approval of the Communist Party. The American pop singer Dean Reed moved to the GDR and became an icon. He was called the 'red Elvis' and even toured the US as the GDR's musical ambassador. The GDR authorities could not resist the rising influence of Western pop, and it became acceptable for youths to wear jeans; Soviet culture, on the other hand, had little impact. In West Germany, the same phenomenon was present. American pop culture was modern and cool, and Bill Haley and Elvis Presley became idols. The American influence could also be observed in architecture and management, but Soviet developments evoked little interest.

Americanisation was criticised in East and West Germany. Ulbricht's comment that American culture, such as jazz, was akin to monkey culture was also taken up in West Germany. Right-wing West German parties railed against the Coca-Cola culture and warned about the pitfalls of consumerism. There was a view that Americanisation and Bolshevism were equally toxic for Western culture.

In 1960, Robert Zimmerman dropped out of university, renamed himself Bob Dylan, and became famous for the song, *A Hard Rain's a-Gonna Fall* (written in summer 1962), which articulated his generation's fear of nuclear fallout. The theme of *Blowin' in the Wind* (also written in summer 1962) is peace, war and freedom and became associated with the civil rights movements in the 1960s. The musical *Hair* (1967) introduced the Age of Aquarius and was hippie culture at its most exuberant. The Vietnam War was lighting the fires of protest across the nations. Cassius Clay became Muhammad Ali and took heavyweight boxing by storm. When he refused the draft – 'I ain't got no quarrel with those Viet Cong' – he was sentenced, in June 1967, to five years' imprisonment, fined $10,000, stripped of his world boxing title and banned from boxing in the US for three years. In 1971, the US Supreme Court overturned his conviction, and he became a potent symbol of protest against the Vietnam War.

The 1968 protest movement saw the left pillorying American attempts at global hegemony, and the vehemence of the criticism reflected the disillusionment felt that the American dream of emancipation and liberalism was being betrayed. To balance this, the Soviet Union was seen in a new light and its role in Eastern Europe and the Third World defended. The invasion of Czechoslovakia in 1968 was regarded as legitimate, but the US role in South East Asia was illegitimate. One can trace in the criticism of both superpowers the fear that one's national identity was under threat; this was particularly acute in Germany, which was dominated by the superpowers. Animosity towards Moscow was read by the Soviets as anti-communist and in Washington as anti-American.

America's involvement in Indochina produced some literary attacks, led by Graham Greene, a war correspondent there in the early 1950s. *The Quiet American* (1955) is an anti-war tale about the futility of what is happening in Vietnam and was turned into a movie in 1958. Greene followed this with *Our Man in Havana* (1958), which poked fun at how easily MI6 agents were duped in Cuba and was also quite prescient. The story includes secret missile installations and became a movie in 1959 with Alec Guinness in the title role. *The Ugly American*, by Eugene Burdick and William Lederer (1958), was a sensation and an instant bestseller. It relates the story of incompetent American diplomats who have no understanding of local culture or traditions which is in sharp contrast to skilful Soviet diplomats who effortlessly gain influence.

A good story becomes even better when there is a good guy versus bad guy conflict. The Cold War was a gift for Hollywood, and the extraordinary appeal of James Bond movies reflected this. Based on the novels of Ian Fleming (he had been in British naval intelligence during the Second World War), Bond (he introduces himself as: 'My name is Bond, James Bond') battles and always beats nefarious Soviet and Chinese attempts to take over the world, and other nasties (as in *Moonraker*) are also dealt with. His famous Aston Martin car was a stunner, and a constant diet of beautiful girls was also part of his appeal. Sean Connery and Roger Moore became household names by playing Bond.

The spy novels of John le Carré (né David Cornwall), a former member of MI6, also became extraordinarily popular. Many of his novels were turned into films, such as *The Spy Who Came in from the Cold* (1966), in which Richard

Burton plays an agent who reflects the double standards of the intelligence community. Le Carré's opus reflects his jaundiced view of the spy game. That said, his work is often a brilliant evocation of the immediate post-war world in Berlin, Moscow and Eastern Europe; his novels are more than thrillers and become literature. In other words, le Carré is a great novelist.

Adam Sisman (2015) provides the most detailed biography and reveals that le Carré's father was a brilliant con man with junior being used to help him fleece old ladies of their savings. His father was in and out of jail in various countries, and his scams provided a first-class training for a spy whose main skill is to tell lies with consummate skill.

Len Deighton's spy thrillers were also great successes, and several were turned into films such as *Funeral in Berlin* (1964) and *The Ipcress File* (1965). Michael Caine brilliantly plays Harry Palmer, the first working-class top agent. Alfred Hitchcock's gripping thriller *Topaz* (1968) uses as its background the Cuban Missile Crisis. Détente led to *Telephone* (1977), in which Charles Bronson plays a KGB officer sent to the US to neutralise sleepers who might engage in sabotage in a crisis.

Television also produced the *Avengers*, which ran from 1961 to 1969. Patrick Macnee played the dapper, bowler-hatted agent John Steed assisted by Emma Peel played by Diana Rigg. They made 99 episodes together, and it was a big hit in Britain and the US.

The catastrophic aftermath of a nuclear war is depicted in *Planet of the Apes* (1967), where the primates take over, and it was so successful that there were four follow-up films. *Fail Safe* (1963) concerns the implication of computer failure to respond to a nuclear attack. *The Day the Fish Came Out* (1967) is based on the (actual) collision of two US aircraft over southern Spain which resulted in four atomic bombs being dropped with one landing in the Mediterranean.

Billy Wilder's *One, Two, Three* (1961) is set in West Berlin and treats the East-West conflict as a huge joke. The plot includes a young American socialite who arrives in Berlin and announces that she is married to Otto Piffl, an ardent East German communist, and they are on their way to Moscow to live happily ever after. Lines such as 'They've assigned us a magnificent apartment, just a short walk from the bathroom' are typical. The black humour of *Dr Strangelove or: How I Learned to Stop Worrying and Love the Bomb* (1964) made it probably the most influential film of the Cold War genre, with the Cold War being treated as a male sexual neurosis. The main characters are borrowed from real life. General Jack D. Ripper reminds one of Curtis LeMay, first commander of the Strategic Air Command who sends B-52 nuclear bombers to wipe out the Soviet Union. Peter Sellers memorably plays the president and Dr Strangelove (one is irresistibly reminded of Henry Kissinger although the role owes more to Herman Kahn and Wernher von Braun) who has difficulty in keeping his right arm down (he always wants to make a Nazi salute). They aim to recall the bombers but to no avail. The film ends with nuclear explosions and Vera Lynn singing: 'We'll meet again.' Kissinger was also rumoured to be the model for the sinister Professor Groeteschele in *Fail Safe* (1964).

Irony and satire did not surface in communist bloc films. Their aim was pedagogical, and they were usually quite serious. An exciting GDR thriller, *For Eyes Only* (1963), tells the story of an East German (Stasi) agent, masquerading as a refugee, who penetrates American military intelligence in West Germany. Many spies and saboteurs are being infiltrated into the GDR, and an invasion is planned to overthrow the communist regime. The agent eventually smuggles the safe with all the information over the border, hotly pursued by the US military and police. The plot was based on fact, as in 1956 agents penetrated an American intelligence unit in West Germany and 140 agents were arrested in the GDR. The Soviet film, *A Night without Mercy* (1961), relates the story of a US soldier sent on a special mission in the Near East but comes to realise the 'true character' of what the West is up to. He pays for trying to contact the Soviets with his life. Stereotypes abound in communist films, and the message is that the West's intentions are always nefarious.

Psychological warfare was conducted on radio and television. Voice of America and Radio Free Europe/Radio Liberty broadcast in Russian and Eastern European languages. Although normally jammed, it reached its target audience with jazz programmes being wildly popular. Radio Moscow broadcast in many languages but had limited impact in the Western world. Television was a powerful propaganda medium. West German television was available to almost all GDR citizens and the same applied to GDR television in the West. Both countries put out regular programmes painting the other in black colours. Over half of GDR citizens polled in 1979 said they watched West German television on a regular basis. Gerhard Löwenthal's *ZDF-Magazin* went out weekly from 1969 and was hard-hitting and anti-communist, and about 40 per cent of GDR viewers tuned in. The NVA (East German military) radio programme aimed at the West German military gained popularity between 1956 and 1971. Even more popular was a youth radio programme which mixed sharp political commentary with Western hot music. Erich Honecker, the GDR communist leader, questioned the wisdom of playing Western hot music as it might be part of plan X to organise another uprising to destroy the GDR. He thought that beat rhythms could be used by the West to provoke GDR youth to commit 'excesses'. In West Germany, the programmes were regarded as a coup for the GDR as they could actually make East Germany interesting. Eventually, the hot music proved too hot for the GDR leadership, and they imposed stricter political censorship from 1965 onwards, and this resulted in a loss of listeners in East and West.

The GDR authorities fought a losing battle trying to counter the appeal of pop groups such as Led Zeppelin, AC/DC or Queen. Young East Germans wanted to be able to attend their concerts in the West. How were communists to counter 'American monopoly capitalism with its lack of culture, its criminal and psychopathic films, it empty sensation mongering and above all its war and destructive lust?' How indeed? The American authorities understood the value of Elvis Presley – the king of rock 'n' roll – who was doing his military service in West Germany. In 1969, the rumour spread that the Rolling Stones would give a live concert near the Berlin Wall on 7 October, the twentieth anniversary of the founding of the GDR. The Stasi and police arrested 383 youths who were trying to get near the Wall to hear the music. The rumour turned out to be just that, a rumour, and the disappointed fans took their ire out on the police by calling them 'pigs' and shouting support for Alexander Dubček, the leading light of the Prague Spring.

The popularity of Western pop crossed all boundaries, and the Beatles – *Sgt Pepper's Lonely Hearts Club Band* (1967) and *All You Need Is Love* (1969), to mention only two – and Rolling Stones even became icons in the Soviet Union. Paul McCartney eventually, in 1989, produced a long-playing disc for Soviet fans. In 1973, at the Tenth World Youth Festival in East Berlin, about 200 GDR bands played in open air concerts, but hippie culture was a headache for the Stasi. Ulrich Plenzdorf's 1972 play, *Die neuen Leiden des jungen W.* (*The new travails of the young W.* – a play on Goethe's *Die neuen Leiden des jungen Werthers*) relates the enthusiasm of GDR youth for this culture. A year later it appeared as a novel in West Germany and became a best seller. Our anti-hero has long hair, loves pop music and wears jeans; the influence of J. D. Salinger's *Catcher in the Rye* is unmistakable. Plenzdorf peppers his text with anglicisms.

Journalism, architecture and sport

Both sides strove to gain cultural influence and prestige by displaying their most talented artists, musicians and sportsmen and women throughout the world. Between 1950 and 1967, the Congress for Cultural Freedom (CCF), financed by the CIA, attracted many of the greats of culture such as George Orwell, Arthur Koestler, Manés Sperber, Bertrand Russell and Ignazio Silone. The US government sent Dizzy Gillespie and Louis Armstrong, even Broadway shows such as *Porgy and Bess* round the globe, and symphony orchestras also did the rounds. Huge congresses were organised to bring together the great and the good of the world. About 170 publications, most notably *Der Monat* for German speakers and *Encounter*, were published with the help of CIA money to win the information war for the West. *Encounter* lost its editor and many contributors in 1967 when it was revealed that it was financed by the CIA. The Soviets helped finance a French paper, and the GDR put money into the *Konkret* magazine.

Exhibitions were held by both sides in many parts of the world. Moscow regarded presenting a positive image very seriously, and up to 1955 there were 133 exhibitions covering many aspects of Soviet life throughout the world. The US even managed to hold the American National Exhibition in Moscow during the Berlin crisis of 1959. It followed a Soviet exhibition the year before in New York City. Vice President Nixon opened the July 1959 exhibition and then followed the famous 'kitchen debate' with Nikita Khrushchev. Nixon showed the kitchen to the Soviet leader as a typical American one, but Khrushchev, of course, with Soviet living standards way below American, could not accept this and labelled the kitchen a pure propaganda stunt.

Figure 7.1 Nikita Khrushchev and Richard Nixon at the American exhibit in Moscow in 1959

© World History Archive/Alamy.

In divided Korea, Vietnam and Germany, placards, slogans and loudspeakers were visible on both sides of the border. The erection of the Wall in Berlin – called the anti-fascist defence wall – closed off West Berlin for East Berliners and East Germans. West Berliners could visit East Berlin after an agreement in 1963, and in 1971 West German and other foreign citizens could visit East Berlin.

After the Bolshevik Revolution, architects were requested to design the socialist city. This was to be a new concept which would replace the capitalist city which separated rich and poor. It was to be 'communally owned, democratically run, consciously created, made by its inhabitants, dedicated to their own enjoyment and development' (Hatherley 2015: 532), but it has yet to appear. In the Soviet Union, after 1917, Modernist architecture dominated, either in dynamic Constructivism or block-like public buildings set in parkland. From the early 1930s to the mid-1950s, a reaction set in and Modernism was seen as inhuman, technocratic and tedious. The new wave harked back to tradition, history, ornament, hierarchy and beauty and would be later called Postmodernism, which had many similarities to what emerged in the West in the 1970s and 1980s. Practically the first thing Nikita Khrushchev did when he emerged as Stalin's successor was to turn this trend into reverse and to turn to functional mass housing. Prefabricated panels were churned out in vast quantities to build miles and miles of blocks of flats – up to five storeys with no lifts (derided as Khrushchevki) – around each

Soviet 'socialist' city in an effort to solve the desperate housing crisis. Soviet cities were dominated by two phenomena: huge magistrale (to permit vast military parades) and microraions (the housing for the workers on the periphery). Eastern Europe was expected to follow suit. Then in the late Brezhnev era, the clock went back again and classical details and traditional streets made an unexpected return. This revealed the country was turning its back on radicalism and embracing traditional conservative values (Hatherley 2015: 6).

Stalin was captivated by skyscrapers, and they began to appear in Moscow. This was strange given that land had been nationalised, and there was plenty of space. The reason was Manhattan, so Moscow had to build bigger and better skyscrapers which underlined the Soviet fixation with everything American. The Soviets were especially proud of the Moscow Metro. Completed in the 1930s, it served as a bomb shelter during the war and continued to be expanded afterwards. It was a stupendous achievement which, it should be stated, cost many workers their lives, but cost was of no concern. It had to be the most astonishing underground railway in the world and it was. It ushers the traveller into a world of amazing luxury and beauty or a glimpse of what communism over ground would look like.

In Berlin, the plan in 1945 was to develop it as a single city, but the Cold War resulted in each part going its separate way. East Berlin was heavily influenced initially by Stalin who invited East German architects to Moscow to inform them how to develop the city because Stalin saw himself as an architect manqué. The Stalinallee, which reached to the Brandenburg Gate, was called the 'first socialist street'. There were many apartments intended for workers but, in reality, they were occupied by party and government officials. Khrushchev moved away from Stalin's neo-classical, 'wedding style' architecture mainly because of its expense. West Berlin took on an American aspect, except the French sector which was visibly French. In 1957, foreign and German architects collaborated to design the Hansa-Viertel which was an anti-totalitarian counter to the Stalinallee. It was part of an international exhibition, Interbau, which aimed at demonstrating how different Western architecture was.

There were many architectural competitions, but one group of young GDR architects pushed its luck too far. They ended up in jail for proposing a 'watchtower' for a playground in Bersarinplatz from which the children could be 'shot' for trying to 'escape'!

The Soviet dictator's gift to Warsaw after the war was the monumental Stalinist style edifice, the Palace of Culture and Science. It was Soviet-designed and built by Soviet labour. It dominated the skyline, underlining the dominant, not to say domineering, presence of the Slav neighbour. Poles hated it, but nowadays it is a major tourist attraction. The Academy of Sciences in Riga, Latvia, built to the same design, had the same effect.

Sport was not only competition between East and West; it was also class warfare. The FIFA World Cup in Switzerland in 1954 permitted the Federal Republic of Germany once again to play football in front of a world audience; the Germans got to the final and played Hungary. As a communist state, Hungary represented the East and the Germans the West. The Hungarians were dubbed the 'maroon Magyar marvels' after becoming the first foreign team to beat England, in 1953, at Wembley on home soil (6–3). They were expected to win, especially as they had already beaten Germany 8–3 in an earlier round, but the Germans had fielded a weakened team and this was a tactical ploy. The Hungarians led 2–0 in the final, but the Germans fought back and won 3–2, and the whole of Germany wildly celebrated. Sport was politics, and Germany had won respect for the first time since the war. When the Hungarians returned to Budapest they were labelled traitors and rumours spread that they had been bribed with 2,000 Mercedes cars to lose. The police had to protect them from the furious fans, and the secret police investigated the bribery claims. Several players were demoted to lower league clubs, and others never played for Hungary again. Ferenc Puskas, the captain and one of the greatest footballers of all time, moved to Real Madrid after the Hungarian Revolution. He scored 514 goals in 529 matches in the Hungarian and Spanish leagues.

In 1974, in the FIFA World Cup, the two Germanies played one another in Hamburg. Both German states had joined the UN the year before, and it was class war. The Federal Republic was expected to win but, sensation of sensations, the GDR won 1–0. Very few GDR fans were allowed to travel to watch the game. However, there were many East German fans who supported West Germany and were annoyed, but the West Germans had the last laugh as they went on to become world champions by defeating the Netherlands in the final.

The Soviet invasion of Afghanistan in 1979 led to the US and some other Western states boycotting the Moscow Olympics in 1980. The Soviets returned the compliment in 1984 by staying away from Los Angeles, and only Romania, among communist countries, participated. Chess was also a Cold War game, and the American Bobby Fischer and the reigning Soviet world champion Boris Spassky met in Reykjavik in 1972. Fischer won and became world champion and thereby ended twenty-four years of Soviet domination of international chess.

Defections of artists and sportsmen and women were regarded as body blows to Soviet prestige. One of the most striking was that of the ballet dancer Rudolf Nureyev, who defected in Paris in 1961 and went on to form a very successful partnership with Margot Fonteyn. Mikhail Baryshnikov, regarded as one of the greatest ever ballet dancers, defected to Canada in 1974 to fulfil his potential.

Religion

John Foster Dulles, whose father was a Presbyterian minister, always regarded religion as a major factor in the war against the 'political religion' of communism. Various fundamentalist Christian groups, among them *Christian Voice* and *Moral Majority*, were active in domestic and foreign policy. The fight against communism was simply a struggle between good and evil. The liberation theology of left-wing Roman Catholic priests found great resonance in Latin America as it was a response to the poverty and social injustice of the continent. Some critics even bracketed the Catholic hierarchy with other privileged oppressors of the poor. This reflected the move away from theology to sociology after 1945 which was evident in Roman Catholicism and Protestantism. Religion could bring about revolution, and that revolution was anti-capitalist. Social justice signified the redistribution of wealth away from the wealthy to the poor, and the World Council of Churches embraced this creed. The gospel of poverty took hold, and the result was that the pews emptied. The Vatican reacted, in 1984, and condemned the lurch towards 'Christian Marxism', and as a result Rome lost influence afterwards. A reaction to the gospel of poverty was the remarkable rise of charismatic Protestant groups – especially the Pentecostals – in Brazil. The young and the poor flocked to hear the theology of hope and not the politics of poverty. The wanted to hear a message which told them they could escape from poverty themselves and not rely on others and took to the gospel of empowerment in droves. To ignore the envy of others and build one's own life resonated across Brazil and spread to other parts of Latin America.

The US sought a positive relationship with Islamic states which were pro-Western, such as Pakistan and Saudi Arabia, that had helped in the offensive against the Soviet Union and Iran after 1979. The support of Islamic groups against the Soviet Union in Afghanistan proved to be a double-edged sword. The Americans poured billions of dollars into Pakistan where the Taliban was trained and armed. In Indonesia, Islam was viewed with suspicion because of its alliance with the communists.

Buddhism was different as it was viewed as apolitical. However, some Buddhist monks had helped the communists in Vietnam during the conflict with the French. The division of Vietnam in 1954 led to huge numbers of Buddhists moving to the South. The French and Americans supported Ngo Dinh Diem, who headed the government in the South from 1954 to his assassination in 1963. He was from the small Christian minority, and this aroused opposition to Catholicism because the majority Buddhist population complained of discrimination. An example of this was in Hué where the Buddhists wanted to celebrate the birthday of the founder of their religion, Buddha. Buddhist flags were banned while Catholic flags flew, and Diem ordered soldiers to fire at Buddhist processions. Eventually over 11,000 monks, nuns and lay people were arrested, and a Buddhist monk engaged in self-immolation in June 1963.

The Soviets were confronted by four main religions: Christianity, Judaism, Islam and Buddhism. Regarding Islam, they appointed Muftis (about 90 per cent of Soviet Muslims were Sunnis) and this was referred to as official Islam, but unofficial Islam continued in secret. Chechens and other Muslims in the Caucasus were deported, in 1944, by Stalin to Central Asia for allegedly collaborating with the Germans. While there, they became more religious, and when they returned to their homeland in the 1950s they resisted Soviet anti-religious policies. The Russian Orthodox Church was rehabilitated in 1941 but was under close surveillance, and many priests and bishops became KGB informers. Khrushchev closed down many Protestant churches. Churches became focal points of protest against communism, especially in Lithuania and the GDR. The election of a Polish Pope, John Paul II, in 1978, gave an enormous fillip to Christians not only in Poland but elsewhere in Eastern Europe. He was a conservative and disciplined several Latin American clerics who belonged to the left wing of the church.

The rise of political Islam begins with the Algerian War of Independence between 1954 and 1962. It was a mobilising force against the French, and there were those who regarded the struggle as a holy war or jihad. The defeat of Egypt in the Six-Day War against Israel in 1967 had profound political implications as it discredited the vision of a pan-Arab socialist future for the Middle East. Nasser had forced the Muslim Brotherhood to dissolve in 1954, obliging many of their leaders to emigrate, and attempted to forge a secular state. Nasser's successor, Anwar el Sadat, brought many of the Muslim Brotherhood leaders back to help solve the problems the country was facing. His assassination, in 1981, revealed the existence of a huge Islamic conspiracy against him based on his rapprochement with Israel (Stöver 2011: 247–96).

8   The Prague Spring

Czechoslovakia, after Khrushchev's removal in 1964, began to show signs of independence and sought credits from West Germany. Czechs and Slovaks no longer needed to study Russian, and a majority in the party favoured recognising West Germany diplomatically. Brezhnev arrived in Prague in December 1967 to observe the removal of Antonin Novotny, who had reneged on Slovak autonomy. He had taken over from Klement Gottwald after the latter's death in 1953. Gottwald was a brutal leader and handed down 230 death sentences during his five years in power, and about 200,000 were sent to prison or forced labour camps. Novotny was not brutal but rather a conservative bureaucrat unable to cope with the rising ferment of the mid-1960s. The new top comrade was Alexander Dubček, a Slovak, but his proposals for change alarmed Moscow which began to suspect a Western plot to undermine the socialist commonwealth. Aleksei Kosygin, the Soviet prime minister, rejected this analysis and thought that the goal was social democracy, along the lines of Austria. This was sacrilege as it could lead to the loss of Soviet war gains. Dubček naively believed if he swore allegiance to Moscow, he could engage in building socialism with a human face at home. Marshal Andrei Grechko, the Soviet minister of defence, stated that action had to be taken even if it provoked a Third World War. Leonid Brezhnev was fed exaggerated reports of the dangers facing socialism by Yuri Andropov, the KGB chief, but some of his associates thought he was suffering from a 'Hungarian complex'. This referred to his time in Budapest during the Hungarian Revolution and led him to believe that any ideological deviation had to be nipped in the bud before it began to undermine socialism. Brezhnev accepted Andropov's analysis, but Kosygin did not.

Operation Dunai (Danube) was a brilliant Soviet military success. The invasion – which also included other Warsaw Pact armies – came as a tremendous shock, not only to the Czechs and Slovaks but also to the North Atlantic Treaty

Organization (NATO) and the West. It was carried out in complete secrecy and NATO gloomily concluded that it could not have carried out such an operation (Haslam 2011: 245–8). On the other hand, there was one person who was not surprised and had predicted the invasion: Brian Tovey, who was head of J Division at Government Communications Headquarters (GCHQ) and responsible for special SIGINT (signal intelligence) on the forces of the Warsaw Pact, was in receipt of satellite-acquired photographic intelligence from the CIA. This added a visual dimension to the signal intelligence on Warsaw Pact formation deployments in and out of their bases in the Soviet Union and Eastern Europe. Using the CIA's satellite intelligence as collateral, he plotted the moves of the Soviet and other Warsaw Pact divisions to the Czech border meticulously: only one Soviet tank division briefly escaped detection – it was transported at night by rail under radio silence. When his assessment of Warsaw Pact deployment around Czechoslovakia was presented to the Current Intelligence Group, the chair asked the Defence Intelligence Staff (DIS) representative if he thought that an invasion of Czechoslovakia was imminent. 'It will take only a hand on the shoulder of the commander of the [Soviet] Guards Tank Division at Altenberg [in Saxony, GDR] at midnight for his tanks to trundle into Prague at first light,' came the reply. 'You don't really think that they would be mad enough to invade, do you?' Forty eight hours later they did so. The subsequent inquiry found that the DIS, working on intelligence from Brian Tovey's J Division and the CIA, had been correct, whereas the Foreign Office and MI6 had based their conclusions on Western rather than Soviet logic (*The Times*, 2 January 2016). The intervention gave rise to the Brezhnev Doctrine, which required Soviet and other Warsaw Pact military intervention if communism were deemed to be in danger in a satellite.

How was it that the Czechs and Slovaks had so miscalculated what was permissible and what was not permissible? One can trace this back to Khrushchev's speech at the 20th Party Congress in 1956. Condemning Stalin, he proclaimed that socialism could now be built differently in each country. A remarkable change in Soviet policy occurred at the 22nd Party Congress in 1961, where Khrushchev declared that the common goal was the economic victory of the socialist world over the capitalist. There was a new motto – 'Catch up and surpass' the West – and this would be achieved by a socialist division of labour. Countries would specialise on what best suited them, and a new economic model would come into existence: the socialist management of the economy. Each country would become highly specialised, and Moscow would coordinate everything. As goals were expressed in economic terms, communists were now to aspire to Western standards and rationality took over from ideology. Whatever was more efficient was ideologically acceptable, and this led to countries such as Poland, Czechoslovakia, Hungary and Romania developing their own economic model. Moscow no longer claimed that its model fitted all, and this meant that the Soviet economic and social model began to lose legitimacy.

As a new generation of communist officials took over, national interests were placed ahead of international interests. Enormous diversity emerged among economists about the best way forward, but a major problem with Khrushchev's division of labour was that it fixed countries at their present level of development. Romania, for example, was an agrarian country with some industry and oil, and it rebelled against the idea that it should feed other countries. As a result, it launched an industrialisation drive and obtained technology from the West. As the last Soviet troops had left in 1958, there was not the constant threat that they might intervene in domestic politics.

Hungary was an agrarian country with few natural resources, but it had to become internationally competitive. By the early 1960s, the emphasis on heavy industry had petered out.

Poland, like Romania, was unhappy about the socialist division of labour. It was to concentrate on energy and electro-mechanical engineering, but it could not escape the Soviet embrace as it depended, to a far greater extent than Romania, on Soviet imports. Poland needed to develop other sectors which would allow it to export to the West. In the 1970s, it gambled on high-tech products and secured Western bank loans to import Western technology. It was called building a 'second Poland' and by 1975, trade with the West made up almost 50 per cent of Polish foreign trade.

Czechoslovakia set out to develop an economic model which was neither capitalist nor communist, with Marxism taking over from Leninism. This Marxist humanism promoted democratic socialism, which was to be pluralist with the party still retaining its leading position, but other groups would have access to decision making through the Popular Front. Oto Šik developed the concept of a socialist market economy with efficiency becoming the guiding principle of change. It was capitalism, if truth be told, but this could not be said openly. Dubček maintained that Czechoslovakia had taken very seriously Khrushchev's call to build socialism differently. No wonder he and other communists were stunned by Brezhnev's view that Czechoslovakia was undermining socialism, not developing it.

Normalisation with a human face now took over. Little by little, the reforms were whittled away, and citizens gradually became resigned to the end of the socialist experiment. In April 1969, Gustáv Husák took over as party leader, and the trigger for the change was the violent Czechoslovak rioting on the occasion of the meeting of the Czechoslovak and Soviet ice hockey teams in Stockholm, which resulted in two Czechoslovak victories.

The invasion had established the Brezhnev Doctrine, but the Soviet Union never again invaded another Eastern European country. The Brezhnev leadership had had their fingers burnt in Czechoslovakia and were wary of trying again to change politics by military means. They did invade Afghanistan, in December 1979, and the mess they made of that confirmed the wisdom of not using force in Eastern Europe.

Charter 77 emerged as a protest after the invasion, but it did not destabilise the country. A major reason for this was that there was no economic crisis. Czechs exacted some revenge on Russians who, on opening their tin of Czech sausages, sometimes found faeces as well.

The crushing of socialism with a human face did irreparable damage to Soviet communism worldwide.

9 Détente
1969–79

Détente was born out of American pessimism. The Vietnam debacle had led President Nixon and Henry Kissinger to the conclusion that the US could not transform its political and economic superiority into military superiority. The Soviets had the scientists, engineers and the willpower to match and, possibly, outstrip US military might. Washington could not win a war against its greatest foe because such a conflict would involve both in nuclear annihilation. A conventional war, without nuclear weapons, would almost certainly be won by the Soviets. So pessimism produced realism and a realist foreign policy which can be called *Realpolitik* (policy based on national interest without reference to ethics or morals). Another reason for realism was the fact that the Soviets had decided, after the Cuban crisis, to build a massive missile force and, by 1969, had 1,274 ICBMs and 204 SLBMs. On the other hand, the US had 1,000 Minuteman ICBMs, fifty Titan ICBMs, 656 Polaris SLBMs and over 7,000 tactical nuclear weapons in Europe. This amounted to mutual deterrence.

So how was the US to engage the Soviet Union in such a way as to benefit Washington more than Moscow? Détente should stabilise the arms race, contain American-Soviet rivalry and, if crises arose, resolve them. Washington also wanted Moscow to accept the existing world order by offering rewards for cooperation and penalties for non-cooperation. Détente was viewed by Kissinger and Nixon as a way of maintaining US primacy in the world at a time of rising Soviet and Chinese military and political influence. As such, it can be regarded as a new version of containment. Linkage was a key concept and involved deals with Moscow on strategic arms, the Middle East, Berlin, Germany and European security in return for Soviet help in securing a settlement in Vietnam. If Moscow did not cooperate, threats could be issued, and there was always the possibility of playing the China card – playing the Soviet Union off against China (Burr and Kimball

2015: 44, 85). Hence foreign policy was like a spider's web where every issue was linked to every other one.

The Vietnam War also put severe pressure on US finances and on its alliances, especially in Europe, where the left saw it as a crime and conservatives a needless distraction. The Vietnam War was lost at home as the moral dimension of US foreign policy emerged again and led to many people questioning and undermining the legitimacy of American political institutions. America was getting tired of foreign adventures.

President Nixon had assured Americans that the Vietnam War would be brought to an end as soon as possible. He favoured a 'decent interval' of between three and five years. This would allow the South Vietnamese to build up their armed forces to prevent a North Vietnamese takeover, but the North Vietnamese army would have to leave the South to ensure this. Kissinger, Nixon and Anatoly Dobrynin, the Soviet ambassador, agreed to set up private, backroom meetings when deemed necessary. Kissinger made clear to Dobrynin that he sought a solution to the Vietnam imbroglio which, on the face of it, did not appear to be an American defeat.

From the Soviet perspective, détente was the favoured policy since the mid-1950s. Peaceful coexistence meant better relations with the West but the recognition that the Soviet Union had the right to aid its allies – for example, Vietnam – in their struggles. President Johnson was obsessed with Vietnam, and it eventually proved his nemesis. The Soviet invasion of Czechoslovakia and the emergence of the Brezhnev Doctrine passed almost unnoticed. Johnson conceded that Czechoslovakia was within the Soviet sphere of influence and that was that. The Soviets, on the other hand, were obsessed with China. They needed to reduce defence expenditure in order to boost domestic living standards. President Nixon, who came to power in 1969 after eight years as vice president, had grasped the opportunity to travel the globe and obtain foreign policy expertise at first hand.

Nixon, in 1971, prior to going to Beijing and Moscow, viewed himself as the greatest master of foreign policy in the twentieth century – he actually meant in US history! In 1985, he viewed Khrushchev as the 'most brilliant world leader I have ever met . . . because he nurtured a reputation for rashness, bellicosity, and instability. He scared the hell out of people.' In the 1950s, Western leaders thought he would not hesitate to launch a nuclear war. This was a misreading of the Soviet leader, who had no intention of starting a nuclear war, but Nixon's point was that he had created a persona that was so unpredictable that it was unwise to put pressure on the Soviet Union. To Nixon, he played the madman brilliantly and had taken brinkmanship to a new level.

Nixon decided to adopt this approach and named it the Madman Theory. It involved threatening excessive force to the point where it risked nuclear war and gave the impression that he was irrational, impetuous, totally unpredictable and seemingly crazy. In order to carry off this act, he had to appear utterly Machiavellian and ruthless and was to become the Frankenstein of Western diplomacy.

The Vietnamese Politburo fell for his act and described him as 'rabid, frenzied, violently angry and crazed'. This message was also relayed to Moscow when Kissinger briefed Leonard Garment, a presidential counsel, to inform Georgy Arbatov and other members of the USA and Canada Institute, in Moscow, that Nixon was 'somewhat crazy – immensely intelligent, well organized and experienced . . . but at moments of stress or personal challenge unpredictable and capable of the bloodiest brutality'. The Soviets got the message that the president was capable of being a cold-hearted butcher (Burr and Kimball 2015: 52, 65, 198).

Nixon was not the first to advocate the madman approach to diplomacy. Henry Kissinger, in a lecture in Pakistan in February 1962, stated that

> what one has to do is prove in certain situations one is likely to go out of control, and that regardless of what sober calculation would show one is simply so nervous that a gun is going to go off. A madman who is holding a hand grenade in his hand has a very great bargaining advantage.

He went on to say that this policy could not be conducted in a democracy but was clearly an option for Khrushchev (Ferguson 2015: 525).

The North Vietnamese were not giving an inch in negotiations in Paris, and the timetable of getting out of Vietnam by the end of 1969 was slipping. As a result, in July 1969, naval plans (codename DUCK HOOK) for mining Haiphong and blockading North Vietnam and Cambodia began to be drafted. The aim was to oblige Hanoi and Moscow to cooperate on a Vietnam settlement. Nixon concluded there were only two options: negotiate a withdrawal or escalate the war: he chose the latter but added a bombing campaign.

On 13 September 1969, a 'concept of operations' paper developed DUCK HOOK further. It included ground troops crossing into North Vietnam and the use of tactical nuclear weapons. Possible Action point 4 stated: 'Clean nuclear interdiction of three NVN [North Vietnam]-Laos passes'. Point 5 read: 'Nuclear interdiction of two NVN-CPR [People's Republic of China] railroads'. Point 3 proposed: 'Conduct ground sweep through the DMZ [Demilitarised Zone] into NVN, employing reinforced ARVN [Army of the Republic of Vietnam or South Vietnamese army] division, supported by US air. Cross border operations (brigade size) into Laos and/or Cambodia. Complete breaching of the dike system'. Point 4 stated: 'Conduct major air strikes against high value targets (electric power, war supporting industry, transportation support facilities, military complexes, POL [petroleum, oil and lubricants] and air defense'.

Hence the decision to go nuclear had been taken by Kissinger and Nixon. The destruction of North Vietnamese dikes would have crippled the economy by flooding, drowning at least 200,000 people. In October, a worldwide Readiness Test was carried out which involved army, air force and naval forces and the deployment of nuclear weapons. It was intended to signal to the Soviet Union and North Vietnam that an imminent conventional and nuclear attack was possible and thereby force North Vietnam to make concessions in the Paris talks. DUCK HOOK was to be launched in early November.

Why did Kissinger and Nixon abort DUCK HOOK? The Moratorium to End the War in Vietnam gathered momentum in October. There was a huge candle-light march on the grounds of the Washington Monument, led by Coretta Scott King, on 15 October 1969. Demonstrations became larger and larger with the largest on the Mall on 15 November. The president had intended his speech to the nation on 3 November to announce the bombing and mining of North Vietnam; instead he had to turn it into a defence of his policies. He appealed to the silent majority to support the war until an honourable peace could be achieved as North Vietnam could not 'defeat or humiliate the United States . . . Only Americans can do that' (Burr and Kimball 2015: 171, 311). American public opinion was now firmly against escalation of the war and in favour of peace and the withdrawal of US forces. The North Vietnamese had won the political war and nullified the vast superiority of US arms – there were over 550,000 military personnel in June 1969 there. Kissinger and Nixon continued with threat diplomacy but Hanoi paid little attention. In July 1971, Kissinger made clear to Zhou Enlai that the US would withdraw all forces and allow the Vietnamese to determine their own future. Despite this, the US continued to bomb North Vietnam until 1973 and Laos and Cambodia in 1972 and 1973. North Vietnam launched an Easter offensive in 1972 and, in response, on 16 April 1972, President Nixon ordered the mining of Haiphong harbour and other harbours and inland water-ways. The following month, a naval blockade was imposed on the North Vietnamese coastline. The aim was to restrict the flow of weapons and other war matériel to North Vietnam and force it to make concessions in Paris. Nixon again thought of using nuclear weapons to destroy the enemy but had to accept that it was politically impossible to go ahead; conventional bombing continued but to little effect. A peace settlement was reached in Paris in January 1973 and envisioned the removal of all US forces from Indochina. The North Vietnamese ignored the settlement and launched one offensive after another, culminating in the taking of Saigon (renamed Ho Chi Minh City) on 30 April 1975. By then, Nixon was out of office, having resigned over the Watergate Affair.

The president was very concerned about building up a strong man image and thought bombing North Vietnam would burnish this; he wanted both to improve relations with the Soviet Union and win the Vietnam War. He won by a landslide in November 1972 and cited the mining of Haiphong Harbour in May, only a few weeks before the summit with Leonid Brezhnev in Moscow, as the single most important reason for his victory. The mining of Haiphong Harbour placed Brezhnev in a very difficult position and could have scuppered a planned meeting, but the Soviet leader placed improving relations with the US ahead of helping Vietnam.

In May 1972, a senior White House economist informed the president that the federal government was facing fiscal collapse within a year. The government, ever since the 1960s, had been overspending, and the war was bankrupting

America. The solution was drastic cuts in spending or a huge rise in taxation. Ending the war would result in large savings, so it had to be terminated as soon as possible but 'with honour'. During the presidential campaign Nixon lambasted George McGovern, his Democratic opponent, for promising to withdraw all US troops within ninety days of assuming office. This had discouraged Hanoi from negotiating seriously in Paris in anticipation of a Democratic victory and, thereby, prolonged the war (Renkama 2015: 98, 118–25).

The Middle East

Nixon did not regard the Third World as very important unless it involved conflicts with the other superpower over the flow of raw materials. He had little interest in nation building and fostering democracy there. Talking about Thailand, Iran and Mexico, he stated that they were not democracies but functioned well as states. Hence he did not believe that American democracy was necessarily the best form of government for Asia, Africa and Latin America. Events in the Third World were secondary to the contest with the Soviet Union.

Kissinger, on the other hand, favoured modernisation and pursuing the American mission throughout the world. Policy should be based on aid and political and economic pressure. He also believed that the fragmentation of power and the complicated nature of international relations made it more difficult for the superpowers to influence the actions of other governments. He thought that US non-governmental organisations, technical, commercial and cultural influence were increasing worldwide. However,

> Both Nixon and Kissinger agreed that reducing US military interventions in the Third World was necessary. What was needed was that others should take on the role of dealing with communists and communist insurgencies. It was up to the US's allies to shoulder the responsibility for this but, of course, they would receive American aid to do this. This was the Nixon Doctrine, enunciated on 25 February 1971. Israel would be supported as before because it was a bulwark against the rise of Soviet power in the Middle East. Japan would eventually need to rearm so as to gradually take on the role of countering Chinese influence in Asia. States should not become dependent on the US for their security and the American public was weary of foreign adventures and did not favour an activist foreign policy.
>
> (Westad 2005: 194–206)

The Soviet Union regarded the Middle East as its 'backyard'. By 1967, KGB and GRU codebreakers had been able to decrypt 152 cipher systems used by seventy-two states. Every day, an inner group in the Politburo received copies of the most important decrypts. These codebreakers penetrated Middle East cipher systems with relative ease and, as a result, these states were conducting open diplomacy. During the Suez crisis, Britain's Government Communications

Headquarters (GCHQ) produced volumes of decrypts for the British government. One of the reasons for the remarkable success of the Soviets was their successful break-ins of Middle East embassies in Moscow. The Syrian embassy, especially, provided a rich harvest of material. The Politburo possibly discovered President El Sadat's secret contacts with the Nixon administration by cracking the presidential cipher (Andrew and Mitrokhin 2005: 139–40). It can be assumed that US, British and other Western embassies in the Middle East were also targeted.

The Arab-Israeli wars of 1967 and 1973 tested the superpower relationship. In 1967, Soviet agents in Syria spread false rumours of an imminent Israeli attack with the result that Syria appealed to President Nasser for help. The latter demanded the removal of UN forces, which were separating his troops from the Israelis, and advanced towards the Gulf of Aqaba. The Soviets provided military support to Egypt and Syria, and President Nasser then provoked an Israeli attack. The US was aware of what was coming but did not intervene. The Six-Day War was a brilliant Israeli military success and revealed the incompetence of the Syrian, Jordanian and Egyptian armies. At one time Israeli tanks were outside Cairo and could have taken it as the Egyptian army had fled. Moscow intervened and Leonid Brezhnev phoned President Johnson and threatened to put strategic aviation in the air. The Israeli tanks retreated, and the Soviets replaced the lost equipment almost free of charge.

In March 1969, Nasser launched a war of attrition against Israel to recover the lost territories but by December, Israel had destroyed the Egyptian air defence systems and, in January 1970, penetrated deep into Egypt. On 22 January, Nasser secretly visited Moscow and asked for Soviet military aid. The Soviets had been very critical of the use of their hardware during the war and did not want to be sucked into a war in the Middle East while they were helping Vietnam. The Egyptian air force was no match for the Israelis, but Brezhnev could not countenance the complete defeat of an ally and provided artillery, air defence and air force units. Over 20,000 Soviet personnel served in Egypt, and Soviet air force pilots took on the Israeli air force which had been bombing Egyptian targets. As a consequence, Israel agreed to a ceasefire in August 1970. Nasser died a month later, and the new leader, Anwar el Sadat, asked the Soviets to help reconquer the land lost to the Israelis, but Moscow was more interested in reaching an agreement with Washington. El Sadat was aware that there was a plot to remove him and declare Egypt a socialist state. The plotters had asked for Soviet assistance but were arrested before they could attempt a coup. In July 1971, when army officers, supported by communists, overthrew the Sudanese President al Nimeiri, the Soviet ambassador proposed to El Sadat that he recognise the new government, but he informed the ambassador he had no intention of recognising a communist government on Egypt's borders.

Shortly after the Nixon-Brezhnev summit in Moscow, in May 1972, El Sadat suddenly expelled the Soviet military. In his memoirs, he commented that the Soviet Union 'began to feel that it enjoyed a privileged position in Egypt – so much so that the Soviet ambassador had assumed a position comparable to that of the British High Commissioner in the days of the British occupation of Egypt' (El Sadat 1978: 231). A high-ranking Egyptian officer commented later that one of the reasons for the decision was the Soviet claim that the bases were their territory and that Egyptians could not enter them without permission. But the key reason appears to have been the realisation that the US held the key to the Middle East. The Soviet Union would always place its relations with the US ahead of those with the Arabs. Despite this, the Soviet Union continued to provide Egypt with all the military matériel it needed.

On twenty-two occasions in 1972 and 1973, Egyptian forces were mobilised for war against Israel but always returned to bases. Then, on 6 October 1973, Arab armies struck suddenly on Yom Kippur, when all Israelis were observing their most important religious festival, and drove the Israelis back. It exploded the myth of Israeli military invincibility; the Soviets jumped in and resupplied their clients and also called on other Arab states to intervene. The Americans kept their distance for a week and then flew in vast amounts of supplies as the Israelis penetrated deep into Egypt. A ceasefire, proposed by Moscow and negotiated by Kissinger, ended the fighting. However, the Israelis broke the ceasefire, and Moscow countered by threatening to send in combat troops. Nixon placed US troops on nuclear alert (DEFCON [Defense Readiness Condition] 3 or two moves away from nuclear war), and the superpowers were back again at one another's throats.

An increasing number of Americans began arguing that the USSR had not honoured its obligations under détente. Afterwards, Kissinger, in never-ending diplomacy, tried to put together a Middle East settlement but conspicuously excluded the Soviets (Garthoff 1994: 404–33; Kissinger 1979: 569–99). When Moscow requested that Havana send tank crews to Syria after the Yom Kippur war, Castro agreed immediately, and Cuba was rewarded with increased Soviet aid.

The Soviets discovered that détente did not mean that the US would defer to the Soviet Union in the Middle East. Moscow then switched its support away from Egypt to Syria and Iraq. In 1974, Syria received over 300 Soviet fighter aircraft, including forty-five MiG23s with Cuban and North Korean pilots, over a thousand tanks, thirty Scud missiles (up to 300 km range), 100 shorter range Frog missiles and other equipment. Over 3,000 Soviet advisers also arrived (Andrew and Mitrokhin 2005: 204). They were viewed as progressive military regimes and were vehemently anti-Israeli and anti-American. The Palestinian Liberation Organization (PLO) also benefited from Soviet largesse. The only problem was that the Baath regimes in Syria and Iraq dealt brutally with the local communists. El Sadat's peace treaty with Israel, signed in Washington in March 1979, was the final straw.

In May 1972, on his way home from signing the SALT I treaty, Nixon and Kissinger dropped in on the Shah of Iran. They concluded a secret agreement whereby Iran was to encourage Iraq to break its close ties with Moscow. However, the Shah's headlong pursuit of modernisation was building up trouble for the future. Tehran became the largest recipient of US arms in the Third World.

In Latin America, Chile posed a problem in 1970 when the left-wing Salvador Allende was elected president. Washington immediately set about removing him. Allende appealed directly to Moscow for funds and was given $50,000. The Chilean Communist Party was the best funded in Latin America and was allocated $400,000 for 1970, and the party provided Allende with an extra $100,000. The KGB had also given a left-wing senator $18,000 not to stand against Allende. After Allende's election, KGB head Andropov advised providing him with another $30,000 if needed. He instructed KGB officers to make clear to Allende the need to reorganise the army and intelligence services and to establish a close relationship between the two countries' intelligence services. Allende agreed to this.

Immediately after Allende's election, President Nixon ordered the CIA to 'make the Chilean economy scream'. Chile depends on the export of copper to finance its budget, so the tactic chosen was to restrict the export of this commodity. Inflation and strikes undermined the economy. Cubans made up many of Allende's personal guard (*Grupo de Amigos Personales* or Group of Personal Friends), and the president's daughter married a Cuban intelligence officer called Luis 'Tiro Fijo' (quick on the trigger) Fernández Oña. The KGB was concerned about the amount of time Allende spent with his secretary and mistress, and he 'tries to surround himself with charming women. His relation with his wife has been harmed as a result.' In October 1971, Allende was given $30,000 to 'solidify the trusted relations' with the Soviet Union, and he also asked for and was provided with two icons for his private art collection. On 7 December, Andropov offered $60,000 to support his 'work' (bribing politicians, military officers and Members of Parliament). A KGB Chilean monthly was given $70,000 to expose 'local reactionaries and imperialist intrigues'. Nevertheless, Andropov was careful not to provoke President Nixon in Latin America.

> Latin America is a sphere of special US interests. The US had permitted us to act in Poland and Czechoslovakia. We must remember this. Our policy in Latin America must be cautious . . . Do not permit anything that would cause complaints about our activity in Chile and Peru. Do not force the establishment of liaison with the [intelligence] service in Chile. Arouse their interest by passing them intelligence of a topical nature.

When Allende visited Moscow in December 1972, he returned home with much less than he had hoped for. However, in February 1973 the Politburo agreed to $100,000 for KGB special measures in Chile and $400 to Allende for providing 'valuable information'.

The KGB complained that Allende paid little attention to their warnings of a coup, but the Communist Party, led by Luis Corvalán who was primed by the KGB, was much better prepared when General Augusto Pinochet launched his coup on 11 September 1973. Allende remained in his presidential offices in La Moneda, protected by about sixty Cuban guards. He sat on a sofa, placed the muzzle of an automatic rifle (a present from Castro) under his chin and blew his brains out. The CIA spent $425,000 helping to oust Allende (Andrew and Mitrokhin 2005: 71–85).

The Cultural Revolution in China meant that the Soviet Union had to take over the main burden of equipping the Vietnamese military. As trains had to pass through China to reach their destination, the Chinese helped themselves to whatever they fancied and allowed the rest to reach Vietnam. With Washington seeking to improve relations with Moscow and Beijing, pressure was put on the communists to reach a negotiated settlement. This inevitably meant that Vietnam would remain divided, but Beijing made it clear it opposed the unification of Vietnam as it assumed this would strengthen the Soviet position there.

So why did the most powerful state on the planet lose to a 'bunch of gooks'? The term is revealing. The Americans underestimated the Vietnamese, and they also fought the wrong type of war. The Viet Cong became the masters of irregular war or insurgency and were also in it for the long term. General Giap, the North Vietnamese commander, believed that the US did not 'possess the psychological and political means to fight a long drawn out war'. This led to short-term US solutions, poor strategy and tactics, and ill-disciplined troops. Henry Kissinger put this neatly in January 1966:

> Our military tend to expect to fight this war as they have studied war at Fort Leavenworth while the other side is not doing anything of the kind. The Viet Cong is using political and psychological criteria [based on Sun Tzu's *Art of War*] where we are applying some very traditional military criteria.
>
> (Ferguson 2015: 668)

The US was launching too many competing civil programmes; as a result, they failed, and Kissinger thought that America had manoeuvred itself into an untenable position. He also concluded that the South Vietnamese government's writ hardly extended beyond Saigon as local officials only implemented policies they agreed with.

Someone else who concluded that America was losing the war was Brian Stewart. He was MI6's representative in Hanoi and was used to being bombed regularly by the Americans. During the Tet Offensive, he dashed off several telegrams to MI6 headquarters in London underlining his fear that the US was heading for defeat. One of these was passed on to the CIA and was placed on President Johnson's desk. As a spy, Stewart had no diplomatic immunity and had to survive by his wits, and this provided him with valuable information about life on the ground which was denied diplomats and the top military.

Giap fought a David and Goliath war because the Vietnamese did not possess American firepower and concentrated on simple weapons and tactics. Their objective was not to confront the might of the US in battle but to nibble away at its sinews. As long as Hanoi did not lose, it was winning. As the stronger side became frustrated, it deployed even more violence. The US dropped more bombs on Vietnam than on Germany during the Second World War (6 million tons), but they chose not to obliterate Hanoi or the port of Haiphong or the Red River dikes whose destruction would have devastated the country. The asymmetry between the two sides widened, and this dynamic then led to the lowering of the threshold of what was acceptable in war. Destroying the enemy at any cost became legitimate and led to Lieutenant William Calley's slaughter of civilians at My Lai and My Khe. He was made a scapegoat by the politicians but received strong support within the military with the officer who had reported him being vilified.

The silent majority in the US had a slogan: 'Win or get out.' Only the second part was achievable. The moral dimension played a critical role as America could not retain the moral high ground and win militarily. So the Vietnamese gained moral supremacy as well because they were fighting to rid their country of foreign overlords. Nationalism proved a potent force, and discipline was such that endless numbers of soldiers were willing to die to achieve the liberation of their country. They gave the impression they would continue fighting even though the country resembled a graveyard. In contrast, the South Vietnamese army soon revealed it had no stomach for the fight.

Robert McNamara, US Defense Secretary, in brutally frank memoirs, concluded that the Vietnamese War was a colossal and catastrophic blunder. America failed abjectly to grasp that nationalism, not communism, was the driving force of Vietnamese resistance. The domino theory – if Vietnam fell to the communists, the whole of South East Asia would be lost – was nonsense.

McNamara conceded he committed six major blunders (McNamara 1999: 384–8):

- Failure to consult allies, despite the existence of the South East Asia Treaty Organization (SEATO);
- Failure to appreciate how an army with unsophisticated weapons could defeat the most sophisticated weaponry;
- Failure to see the limits of economic and military aid in attempting state building;
- Failure to promote democratic principles in South Vietnamese government;
- Failure to appreciate the complex relationship between the use of military force and the achievement of political objectives;
- Failure of the American decision making process itself.

The main failure was not to question policies and step back and reconsider the trajectory of the war. This was because everyone was caught up in a headlong rush to achieve military goals, so no one could halt the slide down the slope of greater and greater involvement. Most policymakers failed to appreciate that the war they were fighting was not military but psychological. Vietnam was a classic case where counter-insurgency failed because too much emphasis was placed on

Figure 9.1 Robert McNamara
© Everett Collection Historical/Alamy.

military might, but America had never been engaged in a Vietnam style conflict before. They failed to innovate and change tactics quickly enough to cope with new challenges posed by the Viet Cong, making the fatal mistake of underestimating the enemy. Besides they were still beholden to the domino theory: lose Vietnam and Asia is lost or even the whole Third World.

So what were the lessons for international communism? Vietnam proved that a guerrilla movement, backed by peasants, could take power and retain it. Start with a base, then set up more bases and win over the peasants by redistributing land. Introduce a new administration which responds to popular needs, and elements of the alienated middle class will always join a winning side. Propaganda should be simple and repetitive and identify the struggle as a mission to liberate the land and mould Leninism according to local needs. Refer to the number of communist states to demonstrate that Leninism is a winning ideology, and then find a patron and protector. Without these, winning will be even more difficult. States which bordered on the Soviet Union and China were in a favourable position because if military defeat looms, cross the border to safety. A charismatic leader is absolutely essential to success, and the preferred choice will combine political and military leadership: Mao – as did Castro – fitted this format and in Vietnam, Ho was the political leader and Giap the military leader. The military struggle leads to a militarised Communist Party, and the ruthless elimination of opponents – the enemy – is absolutely essential to success.

This is the good news. The bad news is that a guerrilla movement has no experience of developing an economy. Should the market economy continue to function? If it does, communism cannot be built. The only model available in the 1970s was a planned economy, but it was in terminal decline in the Soviet Union, so how would Vietnam escape from this trap?

Vietnam was a Soviet ally and had become an implacable enemy of China. Overconfidence led Hanoi, in May 1975, to invade Kampuchea and defeat the Chinese-backed Khmer Rouge.

By February 1976, China had suspended its aid programme, and a year later, it cut off all deliveries based on existing programmes. The Vietnamese Politburo, in June 1978, identified China as its main enemy. Vietnam joined Comecon and, in November 1978, the Soviet-Vietnamese Treaty of Friendship and Co-operation was signed, and it included military clauses (Kissinger 2012: 347). When Deng visited the US in January 1979 – diplomatic relations had been established on 1 January 1979 – he impressed on President Jimmy Carter that their common enemy was the Soviet Union. He also told Carter that China was going to attack Vietnam and asked for 'moral support'. Carter warned Deng it would be a serious mistake. Deng warned Carter that if China did not act resolutely against Vietnam, the Soviet Union would attempt to encircle militarily the People's Republic by invading Afghanistan (this actually occurred in December 1979).

In early 1978, Vietnam began nationalising ethnic Chinese property, and about 10 per cent of the 1.5 million Chinese in South Vietnam moved to Hong Kong and China. Supported by the Soviet Union, Vietnam attacked Kampuchea in December 1978 and took Phnom Penh, the capital, the following month. The Khmer Rouge retreated into the jungle and also crossed the border into Thailand. Deng visited Thailand in November 1978 and claimed that the recently signed Soviet-Vietnamese treaty threatened the peace and security of Asia, the Pacific and the whole world . . . 'it is not directed at China alone . . . It is a very important worldwide Soviet scheme. You may think the meaning of the treaty is to encircle China alone but it has a most important meaning for Asia and the Pacific' (Kissinger 2012: 358). In other words, what was needed was a new containment policy. The Chinese read Vietnam's invasion of Kampuchea as an attempt to establish an Indochinese Federation dominated by Vietnam, and after that Thailand would be added.

China attacked in February 1979, deploying between 200,000 and 400,000 troops and armour to teach Vietnam a 'lesson'. The Vietnamese side only counted around 100,000 soldiers. Brezhnev phoned Carter to discover whether the Chinese were acting with America's approval, and Carter told him he had tried to dissuade the Chinese. After twenty-nine days of ferocious fighting, the People's Liberation Army (PLA) withdrew in March 1979. The battle-hardened Vietnamese had shown themselves a match for the PLA. The Chinese may have lost about 25,000 men and the Vietnamese 10,000.

China attacked Vietnam about three months after a Soviet-Vietnamese Treaty of Friendship and Co-operation, which included military support, had been signed. According to the pact, the Soviet Union should have come to the military aid of Vietnam, but Moscow did nothing, and this underlined the limits of its strategic reach. Even though the Chinese military had suffered defeat, it was a victory for Beijing and can be judged as a turning point in the Cold War, but its significance was not realised at the time.

China then backed the Khmer Rouge in a guerrilla war against the Vietnamese. Defence spending – perhaps 20 per cent of gross domestic product (GDP) – was bleeding Vietnam dry. With the Soviet Union in rapid economic decline, there were only two choices: forge an alliance with Washington or make peace with Beijing. The Politburo reluctantly decided to choose the American way, but the Tiananmen Square massacre in June 1989 sowed panic in Hanoi. Would Vietnam fall to the capitalists? A policy volte-face took place and Hanoi made peace with Beijing. Vietnamese forces left Kampuchea, and 114 km^2 on the border with China, occupied by the PLA during the war, were ceded to Beijing.

The conflict again exploded the myth that communist states do not go to war with one another and the Sino-Soviet conflict was another example. Observers find it difficult to understand why Hanoi invaded Kampuchea in the first place. It is also puzzling why there were Vietnamese cross-border raids into the People's Republic to provoke the Chinese. One reason may have been the need to have a foreign war so as to mobilise the population shortly after the acquisition of South Vietnam. There is nothing like war to stir up nationalist support for a regime.

The US defeat in Vietnam led to optimistic prognoses by some analysts in Moscow. Foreign policymaking was shared by Andrei Gromyko's Foreign Ministry, the KGB and GRU, and Party Central Committee departments. Gromyko was fixated on relations with the US and détente and did not even regard West Germany as worth much attention. Africa and the rest of the Third World hardly entered his mind. The ability of the Soviet military to shift hardware in long-distance cargo planes opened up new vistas.

Ostpolitik

Egon Bahr made a speech in 1963 which was to change the face of West German attitudes to relations with the communist East. It became known as the *Wandel durch Annäherung* (change through closer contacts) oration. In essence, it conceded that a policy of force or ideological confrontation would not change attitudes in the East but rather harden them. He advocated dialogue which consisted of many small steps and stages, building trust and economic co-operation. Bahr knew East Berlin well and had worked there as a journalist before being sacked for being too bourgeois. He then moved to West Berlin and broadcasting and struck up a close relationship with the governing mayor, Willy Brandt, becoming his press secretary and then followed him to Bonn when he became foreign minister, and then chancellor in 1969. *Ostpolitik* (eastern policy) was immediately pursued with vigour which annoyed conservatives in Bonn and Henry Kissinger who felt that Bahr did not feel any emotional attachment to America. Bahr was given considerable room for manoeuvre by Brandt, and he considered an agreement with the Soviet Union as the starting point for better relations with Eastern Europe. Andrei Gromyko and Brandt negotiated the Treaty of Moscow which was signed on 12 August 1970. Force was renounced, and the post-war boundaries of Eastern Europe were recognised as was the division of Germany, but Bahr had to outfox Gromyko to achieve his goal. The Soviet foreign minister insisted that Bonn recognise the GDR before a treaty could be concluded, but Bahr demurred. Valentin Falin, a leading Soviet German specialist, was sent to ask him if that meant no treaty. Bahr told him it did and he also informed Gromyko that his plane was ready to depart if negotiations failed, but this was quite untrue. Gromyko gave in, and the treaty was agreed.

A treaty with Poland was signed on 7 December 1970, and after the signing ceremony Brandt knelt before the memorial to the victims of the Warsaw Uprising of August–October 1944. This was of enormous symbolic significance, and Poles were aware that Brandt was an exile in Norway and Sweden during the Nazi era. He was criticised by the liberal FDP party and by the press for his action. Diplomatic relations were established with the GDR by the Basic Treaty of 21 December 1972. Ambassadors were not to be exchanged but permanent representatives. A treaty with Czechoslovakia followed on 11 December 1973. In order to get the treaties with the East through the Bundestag – they were vigorously denounced by the German right – a clever trick was deployed. They were put together with the September 1971 Four Power Agreement on Berlin which was welcomed by the right, and so the opposition could not vote against the package. Bahr later commented that it was not possible to tell all the truth, but what was said had to be the truth. This was the way to build up trust with Brezhnev, Honecker and other leading communist politicians.

Disarmament

This process began with the 1972 Strategic Arms Limited Treaty (SALT I). Negotiations had begun in 1968, but the Soviet-led Warsaw Pact invasion of Czechoslovakia in August stalled this initiative. However, just before the invasion it had been possible to sign the Non-proliferation Treaty in July 1968. It became operative in 1970 and was not controversial because it intended to limit nuclear weapons to members of a small club. The original signatories – the Soviet Union, the US and the UK – attempted to convince all other states to sign, but China, France, India and Pakistan refused as they did not trust the superpowers. Israel regarded the possession of nuclear weapons as security against annihilation and so it also declined to sign. There were regular five-year conferences from 1975 onwards, but it was accepted that many states did not abide by the treaty and continued with nuclear research.

In May 1972, Nixon and Brezhnev, in Moscow, signed the Anti-Ballistic Missile Treaty which permitted each side two anti-ballistic missile complexes. The SALT I was also signed. The goal of the SALT I agreement was to halt the race in ICBMs and submarine-launched ballistic missiles (SLBMs) when the US was

Figure 9.2 Leonid Brezhnev, Richard Nixon, Andrei Gromyko and US Secretary of
State William P. Rogers, 19 June 1973

Courtesy of the Library of Congress Prints and Photographs Division, Washington, DC 20540
USA, *US News and World Report* Magazine Photograph Collection, LC-DIG-ds-07190.

way ahead in nuclear warheads. This would permit the Americans to develop
systems not covered by SALT I: the Trident submarine, the MX missile, the B-1
bomber, and the cruise missile (Garthoff 1994: 256–74). Funding was a problem
during the upheavals of the Vietnam War but they all went ahead. SALT II talks
began immediately and culminated in agreement in 1979, but the Soviet invasion
of Afghanistan resulted in the US declining to ratify it. The détente period up
to 1979 produced eleven bilateral and multilateral agreements on nuclear arms,
but attempts to limit the number of troops by the superpowers were unsuccessful. Kissinger admitted in his memoirs that the US was less interested in détente
initiatives in Europe than in nuclear disarmament negotiations.

The Helsinki Accord

The Brezhnev leadership pursued various objectives in Western Europe:

- It wished gradually to detach the region from the US and thereby weaken
  NATO.
- It needed the technology and know-how which increased trade would bring.
- It wanted the borders of 1945 to be recognised as inviolable, thus confirm-
  ing the fruits of Soviet victory in 1945.

The non-aggression pact with West Germany in 1970 paved the way for the intra-German agreements of 1972 and the recognition of the GDR by the Western world. These were European initiatives in which the Americans played a minor role. The first approach for a grand European conference was made in 1954, but the Soviet Union was never quite clear whether it would be better off with the Americans out of Europe or with them in Europe as a brake on the Germans.

In December 1971, the Atlantic Council accepted a proposal by the Warsaw Pact for a security conference on Europe. Preparatory talks got under way, and a conference convened in Helsinki in July 1973, attended by thirty-three states, including NATO, the Warsaw Pact, the Non-aligned Movement and neutral states. Only Albania boycotted the proceedings, and NATO participation meant that the US and Canada were present. The Helsinki Final Act was signed on 1 August 1975 by President Gerald Ford, Leonid Brezhnev (technically as party leader, he should not have signed; he only became Soviet president in 1977) and other leaders.

Moscow had achieved its goal: the status quo in Europe. In order to gain their objective, the Soviets had to concede, for the first time, that human rights were of universal character and that there was to be a free exchange of ideas and people across Europe. This was Basket III and Moscow had to accept it to get Basket I: the inviolability of the 1945 frontiers. Brezhnev lived to regret this concession as it led to the founding of Helsinki monitoring groups and human rights groups in the Soviet Union and Eastern Europe as he had conceded that human rights were the legitimate concern of other states. They could now use it to criticise the Soviet record on human rights. A conference on Security and Co-operation in Europe (CSCE) was to convene to monitor progress and promote further developments. The next meeting, in Belgrade in 1978, occurred at a time of rising East-West tension, and there was precious little goodwill on show, but the CSCE process was revived under Gorbachev.

Nixon and China

The wealth showered by China on the world brought a meagre reward, and Maoism, on the world stage, was a flop. About 7 per cent of GDP was being disbursed on Third World revolutionaries. Mao decided that the Soviet Union was a greater threat than the US, and Lin Biao's view was that the Soviet Union was as much an enemy as the US. What if China could play the US off against the Soviet Union? Mao wanted President Richard Nixon to come to Beijing but aimed to give the impression it was Nixon who had proposed the visit. The US president came up with his famous lines:

> We simply cannot afford to leave China forever outside the family of nations, there to nurture its fantasies, cherish its hates and threaten its neighbors. There is no place on this small planet for a billion of its potentially most able people to live in angry isolation.

> (Nixon 1967: 121)

To Nixon, the world would not be safe until China changed, and it was the task of the US to encourage it to do so. Kissinger's *Realpolitik* entailed judging a state by its actions and not by its ideology, and he told the Kremlin that an attack on China would be a threat to world peace.

It was one thing to want contact with China and another to secure it. Walter Stoessel, US ambassador in Warsaw, was instructed to contact the Chinese and say that the US favoured dialogue. During a fashion show put on by the Yugoslavs, when the Chinese diplomats espied the Americans approaching them, they fled. The Americans raced after them and shouted, in Polish, the only common language they had, that President Nixon wanted to resume dialogue. Two weeks later, in February 1970, Stoessel was invited to the Chinese embassy and met the ambassador, but what were the Americans and the Chinese to talk about? China wanted the US to leave Taiwan, and the US wanted Beijing to renounce the use of force towards the island. It turned out that both sides wanted dialogue, and the difference in negotiating style became important (Kissinger 2012: 221–2).

> Chinese negotiators use diplomacy to weave together political, military and psychological elements into an overall strategic design. Diplomacy to them is the elaboration of a strategic principle. They ascribe no particular significance to the process of negotiation as such: nor do they consider the opening of a particular negotiation a transformational event. They do not think that personal relations can affect their judgments, though they may invoke personal ties to facilitate their own efforts. They have no emotional difficulty with deadlocks; they consider them the inevitable mechanism of diplomacy. They prize gestures of goodwill only if the serve a definable objective or tactic. And they patiently take the long view against impatient interlocutors, making time their ally.
>
> The attitude of the American diplomat varies substantially. The prevalent view within the American body politic sees military force and diplomacy as distinct, in essence, separate, phases of action. Military action is viewed as occasionally creating the conditions for negotiations, but once negotiations begin, they are seen as being propelled by their own internal logic. This is why, at the start of negotiations, the United States reduced military operations in Korea and agreed to a bombing halt in Vietnam, in each case substituting reassurance for pressure and reducing material incentives on behalf of intangible ones. American diplomacy generally prefers the specific over the general, the practical over the abstract. It is urged to be 'flexible'; it feels an obligation to break deadlocks with new proposals. These tactics can often be used by adversaries in the service of procrastination.

Establishing contact proved a long and tortuous affair as, initially, the Americans could not believe that Mao wanted to re-establish relations with the US. One of the reasons for this was that Chinese subtlety often passed Washington by. Mao gave an interview to Edgar Snow telling him that he was ending the Cultural

Revolution and deplored the cult of personality which had developed around his person; he maintained that 'between Chinese and Americans there need be no prejudices. There could be mutual respect and equality.' Mao expected Snow to convey his thoughts to the White House, but this did not happen as Snow was regarded as an apologist for Maoist China. The Snow interview, when it came to light, was not taken seriously. Eventually, Zhou Enlai sent a handwritten message to Islamabad and requested the Pakistani ambassador in Washington to deliver it to the White House, and another message was sent to Bucharest but it arrived a month later.

The breakthrough came when Mao instructed the Foreign Ministry to invite an American table tennis team to play the Chinese in Beijing. On 14 April 1971, the young Americans found themselves in the Great Hall of the People meeting Zhou Enlai. He told them that they had opened a new chapter in relations between China and the US and that the 'beginning of our friendship will certainly find support with the majority of our peoples'. Glenn Cowan, a table tennis–playing hippie, had met Zhuang Zedong, a former world champion, at the world championships in Tokyo. The photo of their handshake circled the globe. The US team then toured China, capturing the imagination of the world and creating the political atmosphere for Nixon to travel to China to meet Mao. Table tennis, or ping-pong diplomacy, had changed the world.

Zhou sent another message inviting either Henry Kissinger, Secretary of State William Rogers, or 'even the president of the US himself'; on 10 May, Nixon accepted the invitation to Beijing but Henry Kissinger secretly to meet Zhou Enlai to prepare the agenda.

He found him compelling. 'Short, elegant, with an expressive face framing luminous eyes, he dominated by exceptional intelligence and capacity to intuit the intangibles of the psychology of his opposite number' (Kissinger 2012: 241).

When Henry Kissinger visited Beijing to prepare the visit, he brought with him an armful of gifts. One of these was that Washington would abandon Taiwan diplomatically and enter into full diplomatic relations with the People's Republic by 1975. The latter would be helped to enter the UN and take over the seat on the UN Security Council then occupied by the Republic of China (Taiwan). Kissinger then offered to inform Beijing about Washington's discussions with Moscow, but information about Sino-American conversations would not be passed on to the Soviets. He then stated that the US would withdraw its troops from Indochina and abandon its South Vietnamese ally and even mentioned that US troops would eventually leave South Korea. No attempt was made to extract a quid pro quo for these startling concessions (Chang and Halliday 2005: 603–5).

When Mao met Nixon on 21 February 1972, he gave anodyne answers to all questions, not wanting the Americans to have a record of China's position. To ensure that there was no record of his one and only official meeting with Nixon, Mao insisted that the US president be not accompanied by his own interpreter and Nixon, naively, gave in. As he did not speak foreign languages, he was unaware of the fact that one needs one's own interpreter to pick up nuances and

Figure 9.3 Mao and Nixon

© Keystone Pictures USA/Alamy.

check the official translation. Nixon was euphoric about his trip and regarded it as the high point of his presidency. The 'week that changed the world' was his modest comment. Mao was complimentary about Nixon to his doctor but disparaging about Kissinger. A 'funny little man . . . eaten up by nerves', was his dismissive comment.

Nixon, who had made his reputation as an anti-communist, was careful to excise the word 'communist' from the record of his deliberations with Mao. He was simply the Chairman, and Kissinger and other US officials did the same; in the official record prepared by Washington, the word 'communist' does not appear. This occurred at a time when the murderous Cultural Revolution was still under way.

So how does one explain Nixon's astonishing démarche? The president had served as a naval officer during the Second World War but never saw combat.

From a very modest background, he needed money and made a small fortune playing poker. Hence he was a gambler and also someone who could calculate the odds. He had travelled around Europe in the late 1940s and met many communists and was struck by their fanatical adherence to Moscow but also their ruthlessness. When his career went into freefall, in the 1960s, he roamed the world again and came to believe that he understood communists better than anyone in Washington.

He believed that trade in technology products would gradually make China dependent on the US, so Beijing would then think twice about engaging in any political or military adventure in future. The same thinking was behind détente. Neither policy was expected to reap any economic rewards for the US except for a few corporations which would become rich. He preferred the Chinese to the Soviets as the latter were often abrasive in negotiations whereas the Chinese were very intelligent, knowledgeable and cultured. Zhou Enlai was his favourite.

> Mao Zedong, of course, is the leader. There is no question about that . . . but in terms of the government of the PRC, Zhou Enlai is the man who makes the decisions. He has incidentally more power, he can make a decision on the spot, much more so than any Soviet leader. Brezhnev, for example, cannot move as Zhou Enlai can move. He is a brilliant man, totally dedicated, enormous stamina, and great subtlety . . . a long head and a long view, and a very, very formidable opponent, if we are going to be opponents.
>
> (Renkama 2015: 113)

Nixon established quite a rapport with Brezhnev whom he did not regard as being in the same league as Khrushchev but more politically pragmatic (meaning less ideological) and emotionally balanced. In 1972, Brezhnev sent him a personal message saying he looked very good and wishing him success in the presidential campaign.

Zhou Enlai repaired to Hanoi to report after Kissinger's visit but was given an ear-bashing by the North Vietnamese comrades who told him Vietnam belonged to the Vietnamese and the Chinese had no right to discuss its future with the Americans. Zhou went again after Nixon's visit and once more was subjected to a torrent of criticism, so Beijing tried to placate Hanoi by increasing aid. The Sino-Vietnamese relationship was misunderstood by the Americans as they assumed that Vietnam was a client state of China, but nothing could have been further from the truth. The Vietnamese had no intention of expelling the French and Americans only to subordinate themselves to the Chinese.

Another beneficiary of increased Chinese aid was Albania. Enver Hoxha pretended he was scandalised by the Sino-American rapprochement but it was merely a ploy to squeeze more money out of Beijing.

Kissinger was back in Beijing in February 1973 for talks with Zhou, and he also had two long interviews with Mao. The Great Helmsman's speech was in

Figure 9.4 Richard Nixon and Zhou Enlai

© World History Archive/Alamy.

direct contrast to that of Zhou, but he stressed that China and the US were friends and promised to wage 'ten thousand years of ideological struggle with the Soviets' and that the country was a 'bastard'. Washington should cultivate further the Japanese and strengthen its role in the Middle East. A coalition of the US, China, Japan and Europe was bound to prevail against the Soviet Union (Kissinger 2012: 278–85). Kissinger was told that the world would be a better place if the Soviet Union attacked the People's Republic and was defeated. The level of Sino-American trade was very low, but China had a surplus of women so ten million women could be sent who would flood America and create disaster and hold back the country's growth. What was Kissinger to make of this example of male chauvinism?

When Leonid Brezhnev visited Washington in June 1973, he warned Nixon and Kissinger that if the US and the People's Republic concluded a military agreement, the Soviet Union would take drastic action. Brezhnev also warned the Americans not to trust the Chinese and related the experiences of his brother who had been one of the Soviet specialists who had provided assistance in China. A Sino-American alliance was Moscow's worst nightmare. Of course, there were those in Washington who wanted to play the two communist powers off against one another. A war between them would not be a bad thing providing the Soviet Union did not defeat and occupy China. That would not be a good thing.

Kissinger was back in Beijing in November 1973 and began pressing Zhou Enlai for a military alliance, and Zhou indicated that this might be possible providing that 'no one feels we are allies.' Mao was furious and blamed Zhou for not rebutting Kissinger's advances more strongly. He informed the Politburo that Zhou had moved towards a military alliance with the US, agreeing that the Americans would provide China with a 'nuclear umbrella', but Mao thought China did not need one. This was a travesty of what Zhou had agreed, and he was savaged by all the top politicians. Jiang Qing even accused him of 'treason' and 'right opportunism' (Pantsov 2015: 279). Zhou's nerves were shattered, and the altercation hastened his death.

Kissinger's last two conversations with Mao took place in October and December 1975. Mao could only wheeze, but he still spewed out vitriol. 'Sarcastic and penetrating, taunting and cooperative', Mao for a final time poured out his revolutionary convictions. With Kissinger about to leave, the following exchange took place (Kissinger 2012: 310):

Mao: You don't know my temperament. I like people to curse me (raising his voice and hitting his chair with his hand). You must say that Chairman Mao is an old bureaucrat and in that case I will speed up and meet you. If you don't curse me, I won't see you and I will just sleep peacefully.

Kissinger: That is difficult for us to do, particularly to call you a bureaucrat.

Mao: I ratify that (slamming his chair with his hand). I will only be happy when all foreigners slam on tables and curse me.

In December 1975 Nixon's successor, Gerald Ford, visited China and talked to Mao. He wanted to normalise relations; would China be interested in an alliance which would stretch from Beijing to Pakistan, Iran, Turkey and NATO? No, it would not. The American refused to accept the draft communiqué as unhelpful if not provocative, and this revealed a split in the leadership and made clear that there were those who opposed the opening to the US. Deng countered by issuing a statement underlining the usefulness of the president's visit. He was a harder nut to crack and annoyed Kissinger. Deng used a spittoon. 'A nasty little man', was Kissinger's assessment. Nixon, on the other hand, was treated like royalty when he arrived for a private visit, in February 1976. The meeting with Mao was embarrassing as the Chairman could only manage a 'series of monosyllabic grunts and groans'.

Africa

The first wave of post-colonial leaders in Africa behaved, in many ways, like their former colonial masters and were paternalistic and did little for the ordinary people. The dominant tribe normally supplied the leader, so African politics was tribal politics. The second generation of aspiring African leaders needed a new ideology and one that was not based on tribal loyalties and, as a result, Marxism became immediately attractive. There was only one major disadvantage: it was a white man's ideology. In other words, the new Africa would still have to follow in Europe's footsteps. There was also the problem that Africans reading Marx can feel insulted at times. Marx and Engels's famous *Communist Manifesto* (1848) is Eurocentric. According to one commentator, their thinking follows Hegel, who viewed the Orient and Africa as 'static, despotic and irrelevant to world history'. This view was not unique to Marx and Engels and was shared by many Europeans in the nineteenth century.

Some Africans in the post-war era sought to develop a purely African ideology. One was Léopold Senghor, a poet who eventually became the first president of Senegal. He developed the concept of Negritude (Negroness), and its task was to define the characteristics, culture and ideas of Africans. It opposed assimilation by French or other colonial cultures. Senghor was not a Marxist but mapped out a version of African socialism which was not based on violence, and Senegal was one of the few African states to avoid a coup. Hence its non-Marxist socialism did not influence the ideology of the national liberation movement which was based on taking power by military means. The latter was strengthened by Khrushchev, in January 1961, declaring his support for 'national wars of liberation'. These proxy wars were, of course, against Western powers headed by the US, and Uncle Sam became the personification of imperialism. Washington's response was to engage in 'black' propaganda and covert operations on a vast scale to slow down the march of communism and psychological warfare techniques were constantly being refined.

South Africa took the Marxist lead. The African National Congress (ANC) included Europeans and Asians in its ranks and the leadership was a mixture but the rank and file was African. The ANC promoted the formation of trade unions, and the South African Communist Party (SACP) instructed its members to join the ANC. When the ANC was banned in 1960, a military wing, *Umkhonto we Sitwe* (Spear of the People), was formed in exile. Joe Slovo, a Lithuanian Jew, was its chief of staff and a member of the leadership of the SACP and became secretary general of the party in 1984.

When Nelson Mandela was arrested, in 1962, he was a member of the Central Committee of the SACP. The following quotes come from the manuscript he penned while in prison (*The Spectator*, 18 January 2014):

> I hate all forms of imperialism and I consider the US brand to be the most loathsome and contemptible . . . To a nationalist fighting oppression, dialectical materialism is like a rifle, bomb or missile. Once I understood the principle of dialectical materialism, I embraced it without hesitation . . . Unquestionably my sympathies lay with Cuba [during the 1962 missile crisis]. The ability of a small state to defend its independence demonstrates in no uncertain terms the superiority of socialism over capitalism.

ANC leaders, headed by Nelson Mandela, were imprisoned on Robben Island and turned their prison into a home university. They read Shakespeare and everyone was asked to sign his name against a striking passage. Mandela chose Julius Caesar:

> Cowards die many times before their deaths / The valiant never taste of death but once / Of all the wonders that I yet have heard / It seems to me most strange that men should fear / Seeing that death, a necessary end / Will come when it will come.

In South Africa, Shakespeare was first translated into an African language – Tswana – by Solomon Plastje, who was general secretary of the South African National Native Congress, which became the ANC, as an act of 'linguistic activism'. Plaastje was a committed Christian all his life and wrote the first African novel in English and, among other things, was a remarkable linguist.

Portugal had several African colonies (derived from the days when Portugal was a leading maritime power). It eventually acquired Formosa ('beautiful' in Portuguese), which is now Taiwan, and Macau on mainland China. The Portuguese arrived in Angola in 1483; Mozambique was colonised in 1505, and other Portuguese colonies were Guinea-Bissau and Cape Verde (now officially known by the UN as Republic of Cabo Verde). The Portuguese never colonised the interior of Africa. FRELIMO (Frente de Libertação de Moçambique, or Front for the Liberation of Mozambique) was the liberation movement and was supported by the US.

In Angola, it was a different story where three liberation movements emerged, based on ethnic and ideological grounds. The largest group was FNLA (Frente Nacional de Libertação de Angola, or National Front for the Liberation of Angola), led by Holden Roberto, which was anti-Soviet and received aid from the CIA and China and was based on the Bakongo tribe. It also had close links with Mobutu's Zaire, which provided it with safe bases.

The MPLA (Movimento Popular de Libertação de Angola, or Popular Movement for the Liberation of Angola) was led by Europeans, mestizos and Africans.

Its leader was Antonio Aghostinho Neto, a doctor and a mestizo, who was influenced by the Portuguese Communist Party and had become a Marxist by the mid-1960s. He provided the political leadership while others directed the military struggle in Angola and abroad.

The third national liberation movement was UNITA (União Nacional para a Independência Total de Angola, or National Union for the Total Independence of Angola), headed by Jonas Savimbi who was supported by China. He was critical of the MPLA for being dominated by Europeans and the FNLA for being almost exclusively run by the Bakongo. Savimbi's ethnic support came from the Ovimbundi, and he was pragmatic when seeking allies.

Another Marxist liberation movement was in Guinea-Bissau, the PAIGC (Partido Africano de Independência da Guine e Cabo Verde, or African Party of Independence of Guinea and Cape Verde) and headed by Amilcar Cabral. He was greatly in favour of African liberation movements allying themselves to the Soviet Union and was strongly critical of the US stating: 'We are with the blacks from America, we are with them in the streets of Los Angeles; and when they are denied any possibility of a decent life we suffer with them.' This reso- nated throughout Africa in the 1960s and afterwards.

President Nixon's response was to seek a closer relationship with South Africa in the 1970s but the US was not the only country looking for allies in Africa. Cuba began training MPLA guerrillas in 1965 and in 1967 the Cubans moved into Guinea-Bissau. Cabral had visited Havana and impressed Castro very much; Cuban weapons, instructors, doctors, teachers and technicians found their way there. The US paid little attention, thinking that a few cigar-smoking Cubans were not a threat, but the Americans changed their mind in the 1970s when it became clear that the Portuguese were being defeated. Cabral was assassinated in 1973, and the appearance of Soviet surface-to-air missiles alarmed Washington and made it impossible for the Portuguese to defeat the insurgents.

Marshal Dmitry Ustinov, minister of defence, supported Castro's activities in Angola and promoted Soviet military expansion in Africa. Marshal Ogarkov, the chief of staff, and General Varennikov, deputy chief of staff, did not favour increasing Soviet military commitments in southern Africa as they took the view that Angolans, after training, should fight their own battles. Ustinov, as a Polit- buro member, imposed his view, and Dos Santos only got aid after appealing directly to the Soviet Politburo. The KGB and the GRU were also keen on expanding their reach in Africa and elsewhere in the Third World and were acutely aware of the strategic significance of the Portuguese colonies. The international department of the Party Central Committee was responsible for political links and also came up with a Marxist-Leninist apologia for moving into the continent. China was also stepping up its interest in Africa and targeted, naturally, those states in which the Soviet Union had a presence.

The Soviets had close contact with the ANC in Zambia where it had its exile headquarters. Their relationship with Joe Slovo and the South African Communist Party was not as good, as Slovo, they thought, was too keen on independence and much taken by Euro-communism. To underline their displeasure, Moscow only transferred $100,000 to the SACP. (The largest dollop of cash went to the Communist Party of the USA which received $2.5 million.) Tanzania wanted to scale down the presence of ANC camps and, in 1969, 1,500 members were flown to Simferopol, Crimea. Many of them would spend years in the Soviet Union and receive most of their education and training there. The Soviets decided to back the MPLA but found it difficult to coordinate efforts, as by early 1974 the MPLA had split into three factions. Soviet advisers devoted much effort to bringing them together and attempting to forge an effective fighting force as tribalism was a constant problem. In late 1975, Soviet and Cuban leaders agreed to back the MPLA militarily.

In April 1974, military officers took power in Portugal and the country moved left. It appeared that it could go communist and the coup completely changed the situation in the Portuguese colonies. In January 1975, Angola was informed that Portuguese forces would leave the country. In March, the FNLA attacked the MPLA headquarters in Luanda, accusing Neto of planning to seize power himself, and this marked the beginning of the civil war. The US supported the FNLA and UNITA, and Moscow stepped up its support of the MPLA. The FNLA also received weapons and instructors from China. Mao's main aim was to prevent a MPLA victory in Angola because it would consolidate the Soviet position in southern Africa. There were about 300 Chinese instructors training the FNLA in Zaire and another fifty North Koreans and Romanians were recruited. The US and China cooperated and China pushed for greater US support for FNLA and UNITA and the Ford adminis-tration stepped up its support for these two movements; in July 1975, South Africa decided to intervene to prevent a MPLA victory.

The Cubans acted as a general staff for Neto and the MPLA, but Moscow decided against any direct Soviet military intervention. However, Moscow's surrogates, the Cubans, were not deterred, and 500 troops arrived and deployed in Angola. In November, Neto declared the independence of Angola, and Cuban forces helped the MPLA defeat the FNLA and turn on the South Africans. This had been possible because about 4,000 Cubans had been ferried to Luanda on Soviet aircraft. About 12,000 Cuban soldiers were transported, by sea and air, to Africa between November 1975 and mid-January 1976. Tanks, anti-tank missiles, MiG-21 fighters and other ordnance were also provided. When the US Senate voted against funding for covert operations in Angola, in December 1975, the South Africans regarded this as a betrayal and withdrew.

The Angolan civil war was over by March 1976 and by then there were 36,000 Cubans in the country. This revealed they had played the decisive role in southern Africa. It was a great victory for Castro, and he regarded it as payback time for the Cuban Missile Crisis and the murder of Che Guevara. The Cubans supported Neto and when Nito Alves, favoured by the Soviets, tried to overthrow him in May 1977, Cuban tanks stopped him. The Ford administration was devas-tated and in Mao's words, America was a paper tiger. The rising tide of anti-interventionist protesters in the US added to the gloom. What had détente brought Washington? Increased Soviet influence in the Third World.

Not surprisingly, the Soviet leadership was jubilant as Moscow saw itself as being in the vanguard of the march to socialism in Africa and the Third World. The US had been defeated in Vietnam and Angola, and the future was bright – the future was red (Westad 2005: 207–49).

Mozambique achieved independence in June 1975 and instead of choosing an African language as the official language, Portuguese was declared the only official language. Remarkably, Angola, Guinea-Bissau and Cape Verde followed suit. Education and the affairs of state were to be conducted in the former colonial language. I remember seeing a TV report on life in the bush during the independence struggle in Mozambique where a teacher was instructing small children under a few palm trees, in Portuguese! The same phenomenon can be observed in former British and French colonies (the exception is Algeria) where the colonial language remains the main or one of the main languages. In South Africa, the black elites, known as the black diamonds, insist their children are educated in English.

Some Soviets became cynical about the conversion of African leaders to Marxism-Leninism, prompted less by a desire to follow the Soviet path than by the hope of getting some money. Nikolai Leonov, a KGB officer, noted in his diary on 6 December 1974 (Andrew and Mitrokhin 2005: 428):

> The latest miracle of miracles has occurred. In far-away, impoverished Dahomey [now Benin] . . . President Kerekou has proclaimed himself a Marxist-Leninist . . . and his country as taking the path of the construction of socialism. He is asking for our help in organizing an army, special [intelligence] services, not to mention the economy. Our ambassador, to whom he set forth all this, broke into a sweat out of fear, and was incapable of answering yes or no . . . This action of the Dahomeyans looks absurd . . . 80 per cent of the population of three million are illiterate, power is in the hands of a military clique. There is neither industry, nor parties, nor classes.

Kerekou was blithely unaware that several members of his administration were KGB agents, one of whom was being primed to become the next president.

After the MPLA victory in Angola in 1975, the South West Africa People's Organisation (SWAPO) set up guerrilla bases in Angola and received Soviet arms and training. In 1976, the SWAPO leader, Sam Nujoma, travelled to Moscow on two occasions and the following year received a hero's welcome in Havana during his two visits. Nujoma became Namibia's first president. If this was encouraging for the Soviet Union, it suffered a setback in Zimbabwe, which became independent in 1980. It supported Joshua Nkomo's ZAPU but was defeated at the polls by Robert Mugabe's ZANU. Thereupon, Nkomo's intelligence chief wrote to Andropov requesting further assistance, and by this he meant both financial and security help (Andrew and Mitrokhin 2005: 462).

Ethiopia and Somalia

Emperor Haile Selassie, in power since 1930, was called the Lion of Judah and claimed descent from King Solomon and the Queen of Sheba, and most Ethiopians were Coptic Christians. The emperor tried, with American help, to modernise the country by promoting industry and developing a competent civil service and professional military. Student numbers rose dramatically and hundreds studied in the US and elsewhere. In the heady 1960s, they eagerly imbibed Marxism which was all the rage on campuses in the Western world. The obverse of Marxism was, of course, anti-Americanism, and everything American was hated, from the miniskirt to Third World interventions, especially in Vietnam.

In short, young Ethiopians were ashamed of their country's backwardness. The University of Addis Ababa, in the capital, called for land redistribution and an end to 'feudal' practices. The famine of 1973–4, hidden from the world, and the rapid rise in oil prices triggered revolution. During the summer of 1974, a group of radical young officers, the Derg (Committee), took power, and the emperor was deposed in September and imprisoned. In November 1974, sixty former high officials, including nobles and two prime ministers, were murdered without trial and the Patriarch was also killed. Haile Selassie died in September 1975. Christianity was mocked and Ethiopian children were taught a new version of the Lord's Prayer.

> Our party which rulest in the Soviet Union,
> Hallowed be thy name,
> Thy Kingdom come,
> Thy will be done in Ethiopia
> and in the whole world.
> Give us this day our daily bread,
> and don't forget the trespasses
> of the Imperialists and we will not
> forgive them.
> And may we resist the temptation
> to abandon the fight,
> And deliver us from the evils of
> Capitalism. Amen

Major Mengistu Haile Mariam quickly established himself as the leader by assassinating most of his rivals in the Derg in February 1977. The Soviets immediately began delivering military hardware, and Mengistu asked for Soviet and Cuban advisers, and the transfer of Cuban regiments from Angola and US organisations were expelled.

Mengistu was from the south, not one of the ruling Amharas and was darker-skinned than the northerners. His lowly ethnic status proved an advantage as he thought and acted as an outsider. He was a good orator and soon had quite a following. He adopted Leninism and wanted a highly centralised power structure which would modernise the country from the top down, and, like Lenin, terror was the chosen weapon to enforce change. Land was nationalised, in 1975, and handed over to the peasants. Young radical urban students descended on the countryside to enlighten it and drag it into the twentieth century. One of the problems the campaign threw up was that ethnic minorities were happy to see their landlords go but then asked for autonomy. Violence was used to keep Ethiopia a unitary state, and the peasants responded in kind. On one occasion they locked the students in the building and set it alight.

There were two left-wing parties, one dominated by southerners (the All-Ethiopian Socialist Movement [MEISON]) and the other by northerners (the Ethiopian People's Revolutionary Party [EPRP]). The former was more Soviet and the latter Chinese. Mengistu lined up with the northerners. In early 1977, a vicious civil war broke out and rivers of blood flowed. The crackdown on the EPRP was called the Red Terror and the attacks on the student wing of MEISON the White Terror.

Ethiopia had over time acquired an empire, and its periphery was populated by ethnic groups which wanted independence. Eritrea, which borders on the Red Sea, was run by the Eritrean People's Liberation Front, a Marxist grouping which had received substantial aid from South Yemen, the GDR, Cuba and the Soviet Union; the Tigreans, in the south, were mainly Maoists. Mengistu encountered increasing opposition within the Derg because of his deployment of violence.

Mengistu pretended to be an assimilated Amharan, and coercion was used to keep other ethnic groups in their traditional subordinate role. Not surprisingly, he adopted some of the trappings of the former emperor such as sitting on a gilded throne.

The Americans withdrew funding. Somalia judged that Addis Ababa was weakening and invaded the Ethiopian Ogaden which the Ethiopians had acquired through conquest, but this was a misjudgement as war strengthened the Derg. Mengistu presented himself as the protector of the fatherland and engaged in a rapprochement with the Coptic Church – all strikingly reminiscent of Stalin during the Great Fatherland War.

In November 1977, President Siad Barre of Somalia announced that he was going to break with Cuba, expel all Soviet and Cuban military personnel and close Soviet air and naval stations at Berbera and Mogadishu. This permitted the Soviets to switch sides, and a huge airlift of military equipment followed. Two armoured battalions from the People's Democratic Republic of (South) Yemen – established in 1970 – arrived to help the Ethiopians. Castro sent 11,600 Cuban soldiers and more than 6,000 advisers as he thought that Africa could be freed from the influence of the US and China. Over a thousand Soviet military personnel also arrived. General Vasily Petrov, deputy commander of Soviet ground forces, became head of Ethiopian military planning and it became the most important Soviet military involvement, outside the Warsaw Pact, since the Korean War. One estimate is that between March 1977 and May 1978 the Soviets delivered weapons to the value of about $1 billion, but the Cuban and Soviet military never took orders from Ethiopians.

The Ethiopian army, composed of southerners, and its allies won the Ogaden war, and the separatists and Mengistu's opponents had been crushed. He then launched an ambitious agricultural and industrial modernisation drive, and collectivisation of agriculture was part of this. I remember hearing the Ethiopian Minister of Agriculture extolling the virtues of Soviet collective farming, but he appeared blithely unaware that socialist agriculture could not feed the Soviet population and that Moscow was spending billions of dollars importing grain and other foodstuffs from the West. The result of Ethiopian collectivisation was peasant passive resistance and a devastating famine in 1984. Mengistu's solution was to forcibly relocate the peasants and settle them in new villages. This only fuelled resentment and added support for the guerrilla movements fighting the government. The Soviet ambassador bemoaned the fact that Mengistu had 'no concept of cooperation with advisers' on party building. Ethiopian revolutionaries, on the other hand, wanted to build a Soviet-style state, and this was very exciting news for Moscow (Westad 2005: 250–87). The educated elite got the message and two-thirds fled between 1974 and 1980.

In March 1988, government forces suffered a humiliating defeat at the hands of the Eritrean People's Liberation Front, losing 15,000 dead or captured. Almost a year later, an even heavier defeat resulted in 20,000 soldiers dying or taken prisoner. A coup was launched in May 1989 but Mengistu crushed it. In May 1991, the Ethiopian People's Revolutionary Democratic Front advanced on Addis Ababa and Mengistu fled to Zimbabwe. He still lives there in luxury as an advisor to President Mugabe. In May 2008, he was sentenced to death in absentia by an Ethiopian court, and the charge was genocide. Mengistu blames the demise of communism in Ethiopia on Mikhail Gorbachev because the collapsing Soviet Union cut off military aid.

As early as April 1988, the Soviets had concluded that Ethiopia was a lost cause. General Varennikov, deputy minister of defence, personally took a letter to Mengistu urging him to enter into talks with the Popular Front for the Liberation of Eritrea but the Ethiopian gave this advice short shrift. Cuban forces were being withdrawn from Ethiopia and the Soviets ended their material assistance. The Soviets also ended arms supplies to Angola, Mozambique, Vietnam, Iraq, Libya, Yugoslavia, Cambodia, North Korea and Mongolia but financial aid was still possible. On 11 December 1989, the Soviet Politburo approved the disbursement of $22 million to 'seventy three communist, workers' and revolutionary parties and organisations'. Another way of subsidising them was to buy large quantities of communist newspapers. Cuba escaped the cull. Mindful of its relationship with Mrs Thatcher, the Kremlin turned down a request, in January 1989, by Sean Garland of the Workers' Party of Ireland to train five activists, presumably to aid the Irish Republican Army (IRA) in Northern Ireland (Service 2015: 391–7).

There were over 7,000 Soviet and Eastern European military and civilian advisers in Ethiopia by 1979. The Ethiopian ministries dealing with public utilities

were run by Soviets, Cubans, East Germans (secret police) and Bulgarians (agriculture), and Ethiopian specialists were being trained in the Soviet Union and
Eastern Europe. The Soviets found the Ethiopians very frustrating and regarded
them as overconfident and unwilling to listen to advice. In fact, this was the pattern throughout Africa as locals simply ignored the proffered advice extended by
the Moscow comrades. Moscow made clear that it would not intervene domestically to keep the Ethiopian communists in power and they had to put their own
house in order. In private, the Soviets and Cubans expressed bewilderment at the
extent of the bloodletting as it resembled the worst excesses of the Soviet Purges
of 1936–8 and was utterly self-defeating. The Soviets bemoaned the fact that
Mengistu had little interest in setting up a ruling Communist Party as he preferred
to rely on the military to keep power.

In 1979, Mengistu eventually agreed to set up a Communist Party. There
was only one problem: most of the Marxists in the Derg had either been murdered or driven into exile. The Workers' Party of Ethiopia came into existence
in 1984 – it had taken five years to organise it.

Ethiopia qualifies as the most brutal communist regime in Africa. The Soviets
and Cubans trained the military, and the GDR trained its secret police, even
providing some of the jailers. Indigenous Ethiopian traditions were trampled
on in a wild rush towards communism. Where was the capital for modernisation
to come from? The rural sector and, needless to say, the private farmers resisted
this. Hence terror was the chosen instrument to achieve the state's objectives
but famine inevitably followed. However, modernisation, meaning a successful
industrialised economy, cannot be produced by terror. Like Mao, Mengistu was
frustrated by slow growth, so he chose Mao's methods to speed up the march
towards communism. Another way of looking at Mengistu is to see him as
taking revenge on his ethnic superiors. Leninism was the ideal vehicle for the
physical elimination of the former ruling elite because they belonged to the past
and were holding up progress, so they deserved to die.

The end of détente

The Brezhnev leadership believed it had the right to intervene to help national
liberation movements and other radicals in the Third World. If the US could
get involved in Chile, why should the Soviet Union not be able to do the same
in Africa and elsewhere? Brezhnev assumed that this would not impinge on his
cherished aim, détente with the US, but Washington began to be alarmed by
Soviet and Cuban military involvement in Africa. It was shifting the balance of
world power towards Moscow, and hawks began to express doubts about détente.
One of them, Zbigniew Brzezinski, said that détente 'lies buried in the sands
of Ogaden'.

Things were not going as well as hoped for Moscow. Doubts were expressed
about the way regimes supported by the Soviet Union were developing. They
were not devoting much effort to forming Communist Parties which could guide

the working class towards socialism. Revolution had come about due to military force, and civilian institutions were weak. The oft repeated complaint was that the new African regimes would not accept Soviet advice, but there was no attempt by communist specialists to analyse why their proposals fell on deaf ears. Advice was held to be irrelevant at best and destructive at worst, and the Soviets were discovering what the British and Americans had found in post-colonial Africa. Money and weapons were welcome, but foreigners should stay out of local politics.

In 1979, Saddam Hussein began to wipe out the Iraqi Communist Party. Thousands of Iraqi communists were either executed or died in prison, and Baghdad ceased to be a Soviet ally.

Laos

Laos, or the Land of a Million Elephants (only a few hundred now remain), borders China in the north, Myanmar and Thailand in the west, Cambodia to the south and Vietnam to the east. It is the only landlocked country in South East Asia, and the northern part consists of a mountainous chain and dense forests. The 2005 census identified forty-nine ethnic groups and 240 minor ethnic groups, and the Lao accounted for 55 per cent of the 6.8 million population in 2014.

Until the declaration of Lao independence in 1945, Laos remained the least developed and least important part of French Indochina (Laos, Cambodia and Vietnam).

During the Japanese occupation, Laos was treated as an independent state and when Japan surrendered, King Sisavangvong proclaimed the independence of Laos on 8 April 1945. Lao forces proved weak, and French and Vietnamese forces reoccupied Laos in 1946. Lao nationalist forces linked up with the Viet Minh (League for the Independence of Vietnam) in northern Vietnam and did not return to Laos until 1949. France ceased regarding Laos as an appendage of Vietnam and began to defend its independence. This is the reason for establishing their military base at Dien Bien Phu, north west of Hanoi. In July 1949, a Lao-French agreement recognised Laos as independent within the French Union (Stuart-Fox 2002: 12–22).

From the declaration of independence to the proclamation of the Lao People's Democratic Republic, on 1 December 1975, the leading political actor Suvanna Phuma was prime minister several times over twenty years. After the communists took over, he became an adviser to the government until his death on 10 January 1984. Regarded as the greatest Lao politician, he nevertheless failed in his endeavours to guide Laos towards a middle way and neutrality.

The Viet Minh invaded Laos in April and December 1953 and handed over the occupied territories to the Pathet Lao (Lao Nation) Resistance government, headed by Suphanuvong. In Geneva, two provinces were allocated to the Pathet Lao, but the matter was complicated by the fact that Suvanna and Suphanuvong were half-brothers, and it took Suvanna a long time to realise that his half-brother was a communist and not a nationalist. The shattering defeat of the French by the Viet Minh at Dien Bien Phu, in north west Vietnam, in May 1954, paved the way for the Pathet Lao to acquire more territory. The Viet Minh marched triumphantly into Hanoi and the Democratic Republic of Vietnam was declared by Ho Chi Minh. This defeat ended the First Indochina War (1946–54). The Geneva Accords divided Vietnam along the 17th parallel, with a demilitarised zone between North and South. The Geneva agreement stipulated elections in 1956 to unify the country but Ngo Dinh Diem, a Roman Catholic and prime minister of South Vietnam, refused to permit elections as required by the Geneva Accords. This resulted in Viet Cong (Vietnamese Communists) guerrilla forces in South Vietnam, aided by regular North Vietnamese Army troops, attacking South Vietnamese forces. All this was very bad news for Laos as it was tied closely to Vietnam, and it was inevitable that it would be drawn into the Second Indochina War (1955–75).

So what tactics did the Viet Cong deploy in fighting a guerrilla war and how did they differ from conventional warfare? Here are Henry Kissinger's answers (Kissinger 1969: 213):

> Guerrillas seldom seek to hold real estate; their tactic is to use terror and intimidation to discourage cooperation with constituted authority . . . Saigon controlled much of the country in the daytime . . . the Viet Cong dominated a large part of the population at night . . . The guerrillas' aim was largely negative: to prevent the consolidation of governmental authority . . . We fought a military war; our opponents fought a political one. We sought physical attrition: our opponent aimed for our physiological exhaustion. In the process, we lost sight of one of the cardinal maxims of guerrilla war: the guerrilla wins if he does not lose. The conventional army loses if it does not win. The North Vietnamese used their main forces the way a bullfighter uses his cape – to keep us lunging in areas of marginal political importance.

John Foster Dulles was strongly opposed to any agreement between the government and the Pathet Lao which he regarded as communists. The US embassy in Viang Chan (Vientiane) repeatedly emphasised the need to resist the communists, including the use of military force. The US would have liked military bases in Laos but no Lao government ever acceded to this request but accepted military advisers. In 1957, a coalition government was formed with the Pathet Lao despite all the efforts of the US ambassador to abort negotiations. The Lao Patriotic Front, a communist front organisation, was recognised as a legal party.

When John F. Kennedy became president he immediately supported Laos's neutrality and the Soviet Union did the same. In May 1961, fourteen nations confirmed Lao neutrality in Geneva. Suvanna again became prime minister and remained in office for the next thirteen years (Stuart-Fox 2002: 51–61).

The assassination of President Ngo Dinh Diem of South Vietnam in November 1963 encouraged the Viet Cong to step up their attacks on government forces. His assassination, and that of his brother, in the course of a military coup was initiated by Washington; Henry Cabot Lodge, ambassador in Saigon, held President Kennedy responsible for it. The removal of the corrupt Diem, far from strengthening South Vietnam, had the opposite effect and made it more dependent on the US.

President Lyndon B. Johnson took the fateful decision to deploy US combat troops in South Vietnam in March 1965 (there were already 23,000 US military advisers there), and this led to an intensification of the conflict. Laos became involved unwillingly as almost all troops and matériel passed through the Ho Chi Minh trail. The main task of the Pathet Lao was now to protect the Ho Chi Minh trail and in so doing defend the Vietnamese revolution. One of the American responses was to use Agent Orange and other defoliants – about 80 million litres were sprayed over Vietnam and Laos between 1961 and 1971. Britain had used the tactic during the Malayan insurgency of 1948–60. The chemicals were to kill vegetation around military bases, reveal communist supply lines and remove cover for potential ambushers. Dioxin was also added; it is one of the most potent toxic chemicals ever made and has a devastating effect on humans who come in contact with it. Deformed children were still being born long after 1971 (Hayton 2010: 196). As a result, between 1964 and 1973, Laos sustained the most brutal bombing in history when more bombs were dropped on it than on Germany during the Second World War. This worked out to about 2,500 kg per capita. Today bomb craters and tons of unexploded ordnance bear testimony to one of the great strategic misjudgements of the twentieth century, and mines are still causing horrific injuries to civilians.

When it became clear that the North Vietnamese had no intention of respecting Lao neutrality, the US followed suit. It began training and arming a secret force of mainly non-ethnic Lao in the north (Hmong and Mien) and bombing the Ho Chi Minh trail. Suvanna strongly opposed US and South Vietnamese troops entering Laos to destroy the trail. When they did this, in 1971, he immediately called for their withdrawal. In 1971, Suvanna praised China's 'non-aggressive attitude' and looked to China to prevent Laos falling under Vietnamese control.

On 21 February 1973, the Pathet Lao and pro-government forces agreed on a ceasefire. The halt to bombing demanded by Congress in mid-1973 ensured that there would be no further US bombing. As the US prepared to withdraw its ground forces in Vietnam, it was clear that there would be no US military support for Laos or Cambodia.

The collapse of the governments in Cambodia and South Vietnam, in April 1975, meant the barriers to the communists taking power in Laos had been removed. The Lao People's Democratic Republic was proclaimed on 2 December 1975. The generals and leading politicians made for Thailand, soon to be followed by the middle class. Kaison Phomvihan, secretary general of the Lao People's Revolutionary Party (LPRP), became prime minister. Suphanuvong was given the ceremonial role of president.

Figure 9.5 President Lyndon B. Johnson

Courtesy of the Library of Congress Prints and Photographs Division, Washington, DC 20540 USA, LC-USZ62–13036.

The government adopted a hard line from the beginning, calling for solidarity and basing its power on the almost non-existent proletariat and peasant alliance. Peasants made up about 85 per cent of the population, and Kaison mentioned that collectivisation would be the means for increasing agricultural output. North Vietnam was the model to be followed, and Marxism-Leninism would make it possible for Laos to jump over capitalism into socialism. Party cadres, often from non-Buddhist ethnic minorities in the mountainous north, began condemning dancing, singing and festivals which form an integral part of Lao culture. As a result, many peasants, the middle class and technical personnel crossed the Mekong into Thailand en route to the US, Canada and Australia. China even offered to take 10,000 Lao and Hmong refugees. About 100,000 Hmong, Mien and other minorities, who had sided with the Americans, had emigrated by 1980; many Hmong were resettled in the US and some of those who remained are Christians. This has led to persecution (Stuart-Fox 2002: 73–89).

In February 1978, a high-level Soviet delegation visited Laos and established a Lao-Soviet Commission for Economic, Scientific and Technical Co-operation. This was the pattern of Soviet relations where economics dominated and politics was left to Vietnam.

Vietnam decided to intervene militarily against the Pol Pot regime in 1978 and was aware that this would exacerbate relations with China. As a result, the Vietnamese sought a closer relationship with the Soviet Union, and a Treaty of Friendship was signed in November 1978. Hanoi pressed the Lao to follow their anti-Beijing line, call the Chinese international reactionaries and expel them from northern Laos. They had been building roads and other installations there, but Viang Chan feared the Chinese would train and arm the hill tribes in the north and set out to 'liberate' Laos from Vietnamese influence. Laos would then find itself in a proxy war between China and Vietnam.

Laos had attempted to pursue a policy of neutrality with Cambodia under Pol Pot, but the invasion by over 100,000 Vietnamese troops on Christmas Day 1978 resulted in the collapse of the regime a fortnight later. Viang Chan immediately recognised the Heng Samrin regime, and the Lao followed the Vietnamese line by denouncing the crimes of the Pol Pot regime.

In March 1979, Laos joined the Soviet Union and Vietnam in virulent, verbal attacks on China, but the Lao tried to sugar the pill by hinting to Beijing that they were not altogether happy with the course of events. The result was that the Chinese media reserved its most savage criticism for Vietnam and comments on Laos were mild.

By the mid-1980s, it was clear that China no longer regarded the destabilisation of Laos as a priority. Chinese foreign policy during that period concentrated on improving economic relations with the capitalist world. As a consequence, Lao relations with the Soviet Union improved and reached their zenith under Mikhail Gorbachev. Vietnamese economic aid to Laos between 1975 and 1985 was about $13 million annually and Soviet economic aid about $50 million annually. Soviet military aid, on the other hand, was running at about $100 million annually. This included MiG jets, Antonov 24 and 26 military transport planes and Mi-8 helicopters. The Soviets supplied the aircraft technicians and trained the pilots. Whereas the air force was dominated by the Soviets, ground forces were the preserve of the Vietnamese. More Lao students studied in the Soviet Union than Vietnam, and Soviet teachers staffed the Soviet-built Viang Chan

Polytechnic (Stuart-Fox 2002: 282–5). Some of the communist and government officials had been trained in the GDR, and the command of German of some officials is quite impressive. Unfortunately, some of them studied economics in the GDR and hence have little understanding of a market economy. The Laotian secret police are even called the Stasi! China is the new destination for Lao students especially in medicine and technical subjects.

Vietnamese forces withdrew from Laos and Cambodia as part of the deal to improve Sino-Vietnamese relations in the 1980s. In January 1991, three new economic agreements were concluded but remained only on paper as the Soviet Union headed towards the abyss.

Late in 1986, at the prompting of the Soviet Union, the Lao People's Revolutionary Party welcomed the first high-level Chinese diplomatic delegation in almost a decade; about a year later, a Lao delegation paid a return visit to Beijing. The Chinese promised not to support armed insurgent groups in northern Laos and ambassadors were exchanged six months later. Vietnamese troops leaving Laos was given as the reason by Viang Chan for the re-establishment of normal relations. Li Peng, the Chinese prime minister, dropped in and a border agreement was signed. Direct flights to China began, Laos purchased Chinese aircraft and aid began to flow. China now had replaced the Soviet Union as Big Brother, and this only irked the Vietnamese (Stuart-Fox 2002: 285–7).

Laos was always a sideshow for the Americans. They failed to transform the Lao into a military force to fight the Vietnamese, and it became a lost cause as more and more of the country fell under the Pathet Lao. Washington would have preferred a neutral Laos, but President Eisenhower had spoken of the 'domino effect', and Presidents Kennedy and Johnson always had this at the back of their minds. The worldwide revolts in 1968 appeared to point to the victory of radicalism.

What about US policy in Laos? One Lao commented that it was always easy to divine American intentions, but the Chinese were masters at masking their intentions. The Pathet Lao were the insurgents, and counter-insurgency measures had to be devised. The Lao government preferred to pursue a policy of negotiations with the Pathet Lao and formed several coalition governments with them, but the Americans always opposed this strategy, seeing the Lao elite as foolish to enter into any agreement with communists. The Pathet Lao set out to capture hearts and minds, but the Americans chose money as their source of influence, and this inevitably corrupted top officials who took to infighting to secure a larger slice of the pie for themselves. The best tactic in dealing with communists, from Washington's perspective, was to deploy military force. The problem with US bombing of the Ho Chi Minh trail was that it undermined support for the government in Viang Chan and helped the Pathet Lao. Hence counter-insurgency measures ended up strengthening the insurgency. The Pathet Lao had little understanding of Marxism-Leninism and the population even less. The story is told of a meeting being addressed by a communist who praised Lenin to the skies. When he asked for questions at the end of the lecture, a woman stood up and, full of enthusiasm, asked where she could get some of those wonder plants called Lenin! The Lao word for the plant and Lenin was almost the same!

The fact that Laos is run today as it was in pre-communist times (with a different elite in power) testifies to the fact that culture and tradition are stronger than imported ideologies. American and Soviet worldviews have met the same fate: they have been consigned to the rubbish bin of history.

North Korea

Relations with Moscow became frosty and, in 1960, all Korean students in the Soviet Union and Eastern Europe were recalled; they only restarted two decades later and on a smaller scale. Mention of the Soviet Union almost ceased in the official media, and Soviet advisers were sent packing. Korean husbands were ordered to divorce their Soviet and Eastern European wives who were then expelled, and *Pravda* was pilloried by the Korean press. The Soviet Union was accused of exploiting Korean weakness, but the North Korean ambassador wrote a critical letter to Kim and asked Moscow for political asylum, and it was granted. Relations improved after the Cultural Revolution convulsed China and Kim commented to Brezhnev that it was 'idiocy on a monumental scale'. From 1970 until the collapse of the Soviet Union, North Korea sided with neither the Soviet Union nor China as it desperately needed aid from both countries.

The decline of the economy led to North Korea working the black market. In 1976, Norwegian police caught diplomats selling thousands of smuggled bottles of liquor and millions of cigarettes on the black market. The Norwegians estimated that smuggling was bringing in about a million dollars. The operation in Sweden was even more ambitious and Finland was also a lucrative market. In 1976, Egyptian police found hashish in the bags of North Korean diplomats, and there were rumours that the North Koreans were trying to launder huge quantities of high-value US dollar notes.

Another practice was to abduct Japanese and South Koreans. Presumably, the aim was to use their language skills and knowledge of the way of life to train spies. In 2002, Kim Jong-il admitted the abductions and promised to repatriate all the survivors (Lankov 2013: 185–8).

The challenge of Poland

The ferment in Czechoslovakia had originated within the Communist Party and had been spearheaded by intellectuals, and workers had then joined the calls for greater democracy. In Poland, in contrast, workers were in the vanguard of change, and intellectuals then joined later. In Czechoslovakia, the party was swept along by a wave of enthusiasm for socialism with a human face. In Poland, on the other hand, the Polish United Workers' Party (PUWP) had only a limited desire to reform. The party's task was to hold the fort and make as few concessions as possible. By August 1968, the Czechoslovak Party had ceased to be

Leninist, as Dubček would not countenance the use of force against opponents; in Poland, the party remained Leninist and was thus willing to shed the blood of workers.

The events in Czechoslovakia in 1968 stirred the blood of many students and intellectuals. Gomułka targeted Jewish intellectuals for the unrest and did not regard them as patriots. Many leading Jewish scholars were dismissed from academic posts, and the minister of the interior, General Mieczysław Moczar, grasped the opportunity to remove 'Zionists' (Jews) from high positions and 'revisionists' from national life. About 20,000 Jews left the country.

Living standards hardly improved during the 1970s, but in early December 1970 Gomułka agreed to price increases for food and consumer goods. This ham-fisted move came just before the Christmas festivities in an overwhelmingly Roman Catholic country. There were worker protests in Warsaw and elsewhere, notably in the Baltic ports of Gdańsk and Szczecin. Faced with this defiance, Gomułka revealed himself a Leninist and ordered the military and police to shoot. Forty-five workers died and many others were injured at the appropriately named Lenin Shipyard in Gdańsk. The deaths sealed Gomułka's fate, and he was replaced by Edward Gierek.

Gierek was an astute tactician; he sought a rapprochement with the Roman Catholic Church, and churches could be built in new housing estates. He even had an audience with Pope Paul VI in the Vatican in 1977. The Church was not keen on worker confrontation as this could lead to loss of life.

It went from bad to worse for the communists when the Archbishop of Kraków, Karol Wojtyła, was elected pope in October 1978; God was now on the side of the activists. This moral sense of superiority was enhanced by the triumphal nine-day visit Pope John Paul II paid to his native land in June 1979. The pope had no intention of becoming head of the opposition. Instead his message was: 'Don't be afraid.'

On 1 July 1980, the government decided to increase the price of consumer goods, and meat prices almost doubled. The inevitable strikes followed, and in August the Lenin Shipyard in Gdańsk was paralysed; one of the demands was the reinstatement of two workers who had been dismissed. One of them was Lech Wałęsa. Factories in Szczecin and elsewhere also came out, and an Inter-Factory Strike Committee (MKS) was formed, led by Wałęsa. The strike bulletin of the Lenin Shipyard, *Solidarność* (Solidarity), appeared in late August. The prime minister and others were dismissed, and the new prime minister promised to implement an agreement with the MKS. The pope weighed in and instructed the Polish Church to 'help the nation in its struggle for daily bread'.

The PUWP conceded defeat and agreed to free trade unions. Solidarity became legal and adopted the slogan: 'There is no freedom without bread.' Gierek was made the scapegoat and Stanisław Kania the party leader. The new independent trade union, Solidarity, was set up on 17 September, and by December it counted over eight million members. The leader was Lech Wałęsa, and he attracted about a third of the members of the PUWP.

Figure 9.6 Lech Walesa and Pope John Paul II
© epa european pressphoto agency b.v./Alamy.

Solidarity included within its ranks Roman Catholics, party members, dissidents, political prisoners, nationalists and even Marxists. Its programme was essentially syndicalist, aiming for a self-managing republic (Hatherley 2015: 500). This state of affairs lasted until December 1981 when martial law was declared.

Solidarity gained strength from its Catholic roots. All previous Polish revolts (1956, 1968, 1970 and 1976) had been secular. A cross hung on the gates of the Lenin Shipyard. In 1980 new imageries were adopted: the cross, the rosary and the famous Black Madonna of Częstochowa. Wałęsa began his day with Mass at 7.30 a.m. and often prayed to the Virgin Mary. In January 1981, Wałęsa went to Rome and obtained the pope's blessing.

A striking fact about the rise of Solidarity was that Cardinal Wyszyński refused to back the movement publicly and instead he called for calm during the 1980 strikes. There was also the point that those Solidarity activists who could get a church reference were allowed to apply for asylum and receive aid. Those who could not – Trotskyists and anarchists – felt the full force of the repression (Hatherley 2015: 192). So the Church was a loyal opposition, and the party was happy with that.

The Soviets had two options: intervene themselves or get the Polish military to do it for them. Contingency plans were drawn up with several divisions ready to move into Poland. Defence Minister Ustinov envisaged the calling up of 100,000 reservists and 15,000 vehicles would have to be requisitioned. Commander in Chief of the Warsaw Pact Forces, Marshal Viktor Kulikov, arranged for allied 'exercises' in Poland and the troops arrived in December 1980, but at the end of the exercise the troops did not leave as Kulikov called for more exercises. They stayed and stayed but eventually were withdrawn in April 1981. The Poles had not been intimidated.

In February 1981, General Wojciech Jaruzelski, defence minister since 1968, took over as prime minister. He immediately drafted plans for martial law and presented them to the Soviet leadership. Jaruzelski's preferred option was an understanding with Wałęsa which would permit the PUWP to rule and Solidarity to govern. 'We don't want to overthrow the PUWP. We only want to remove the people who are holding back Poland's revival,' Lech told the general on numerous occasions.

On 18 October 1981, Jaruzelski became party leader as well as prime minister. The Soviet leadership was resolutely opposed to military intervention. Jaruzelski told the Soviets Poland needed a new military dictatorship similar to that under Piłsudski and Poland needed an immediate $1.5 billion in aid. The Soviet Politburo had to give in to the blackmail. Dejected, Andropov muttered that if Solidarity took over Poland, 'that's the way it will be.' Despite all this, Jaruzelski still asked for Soviet military intervention. Rebuffed, he tried on two more occasions to get the Soviets to send in their tanks. Revealingly, Mikhail Suslov, number two in the party and chair of the Politburo group on Poland, expressed the view that military intervention would provoke a catastrophe.

Because the Soviets would not intervene, martial law was declared on Sunday, 13 December 1981, and Lech Wałęsa was placed under house arrest in various locations. Seventy thousand Solidarity activists were taken into detention and the official death toll was seventeen. Over 80,000 Polish troops and police swept through Poland and snuffed out Solidarity, and this revealed that Solidarity had not penetrated the security services. Solidarity activists did call for a general strike, but there was a weak response even though the movement had ten million members, or one in four Poles. However, the communists had the willpower and loyalty of the instruments of coercion to re-establish their rule. This underlined the fact that Solidarity could not bring down communism. The PUWP lost about a quarter of its members (down to 2.5 million), but it was not a meltdown.

The wily Jaruzelski always argued that if he had not imposed martial law, Soviet troops would have entered Poland. He was fully aware that this was not so and even allowed the pope to visit again, in June 1983. The pope travelled to a cabin in the Tatra Mountains to commune with Wałęsa.

In February 1982, CIA agents were sent to Poland, with a helping hand from the Israelis, to cooperate with Solidarity members in hiding. Equipment was smuggled in to Gdańsk from Sweden, in tractor parts, and within months Solidarity had received $8 million. Jacek Kuroń sent President Reagan a letter from prison saying that an insurrection could be organised, and the president always kept it on his desk. The US embassy in Warsaw had a four-man electronics team which could pick up most Polish traffic, and there was also an underground co-ordinating committee which could communicate with the Americans. Under

Reagan, the CIA's disinformation budget was $3.5 billion annually and Radio Free Europe received $1 billion a year. The US Information Agency, headed by Charles Wick, a Hollywood film director, got upwards of $1 billion a year to attack communism.

Martial law was lifted on 31 December 1982 and those imprisoned were gradually released. In 1983, Wałęsa was awarded the Nobel Peace Prize to the utter embarrassment of the PUWP.

10 The Islamic challenge
Iran and Afghanistan

The Iranian revolution of 1979 was an Islamic revolution and, as such, it rejected the models of modernisation offered by Washington, Moscow and Beijing. In fact, it turned away from the whole concept of modernisation. Its aim was to return Iran to the world which had been destroyed by Western imperialism in the nineteenth and twentieth centuries and to recreate a theocratic state ruled by Sharia or Islamic law. Why had Iran, viewed as the main ally of the US, suddenly turned into its greatest enemy – the Great Satan?

Mohammad Reza Shah Pahlavi, ruler of Iran from 1941, adopted the title of Shahanshah (King of Kings) in 1967 and, as such, exercised supreme power. He initiated a White Revolution, in 1963, the aim of which was to modernise the country – in the Western sense of the word – rapidly. The Shah's revolution collided with the ordinary Iranian's belief that the clergy, the ayatollahs, should frame policy. Ayatollah Ruhollah Khomeini told the Shah he was a wretched, miserable man. A secular state for Muslims was sacrilege and could lead to jihad – a holy war.

It was clear that by 1976, the Shah's White Revolution was running into serious trouble. The government collapsed in December 1978 when around a million marched in Tehran calling for the removal of the Shah and the return of Ayatollah Khomeini. The Shah left Iran the following month. On 1 February 1979, the Ayatollah landed at Tehran airport and was welcomed by an adoring crowd as they regarded him as the imam who would redeem his people. Khomeini rejected Western society but not the technology and science it had produced because these were to be used to develop the new Islamic state.

President Jimmy Carter, a Baptist, thought that a line of communication could be established with the Ayatollah. Iranian students stormed the US embassy in Tehran, on 4 November 1979, and held fifty-two US diplomats and citizens

Figure 10.1 President Jimmy Carter

Courtesy of the Library of Congress Prints and Photographs Division, Washington, DC 20540 USA, *US News and World Report* Magazine Photograph Collection, LC-DIG-ppmsca-09783.

hostage for 444 days. The president tried to resolve the crisis peacefully but made the fundamental mistake of trying to negotiate with the Iranian government rather than with the person who actually held power, the Ayatollah, and was contemptuously rebuffed. A botched American attempt to rescue the diplomats amounted to the greatest humiliation the US ever suffered in the Middle East. A small victory emerged from the wreckage of US-Iranian affairs. Six US diplomats had managed to escape and found refuge with the Canadian ambassador. They knew it was only a matter of time before they were discovered and tried as spies and executed. Tony Mendez, a CIA officer, came up with a daring plan to get the diplomats out of Iran. He set up a film production company, Studio 6, in Hollywood and promoted it so well that Steven Spielberg sent a script to it! The diplomats were to become production staff involved in the making of a film in Iran. They learnt their roles and managed to fly out of Tehran with the rest of the film crew in a Swissair jet. They were welcomed as heroes by President Jimmy Carter, but Tony Mendez stayed in the background, and his key role was only made public in 1997. The 2012 film, *Argo*, tells this gripping story with a touch of Hollywood exaggeration.

Moscow was not sure how to react to the events in Tehran. On the one hand, the Tudeh or communist party had a great opportunity to expand its influence and told Moscow it was backing Khomeini. The Soviets were aware that Iran was promoting political Islam in Afghanistan and further afield. In 1983, the Tudeh party was smashed and hundreds were executed, but others reconverted to Islam in order to be released from prison. From a Marxist perspective, Islamism was a throwback, a rejection of the modern world. For a Marxist it was unbelievable that religion could form the basis of a viable political philosophy. Because it was reactionary, it would naturally gravitate to the imperialist camp, led by the US.

Afghanistan

Afghanistan is a huge, underdeveloped country of thirty million people. The dominant ethnic group are the Pashtuns, and they dominate Kabul, the capital, the centre and the south. Tajiks, Uzbeks and Turkmen are the majority in the north so the country has never really been unified. It is dominated by tribes and clans that are fiercely independent. Britain detached part of eastern Afghanistan and added it to present-day Pakistan, and those inhabiting the North West Frontier, the Federally Administered Tribal Areas and Waziristan, have traditionally been ignored by the Pakistani government in Islamabad. The feeling of being cut off and different is the natural response. Hence ethnically much of eastern Afghanistan and western Pakistan is similar.

How was the country to modernise? There were two main models: the Western and the communist. The first step was to make the country a republic, and the king was deposed in July 1973 by his prime minister and cousin, General Mohammad Daoud, but no outside power was involved. Daoud identified communists and Islamists as the greatest threat to stability and came down on them hard.

The People's Democratic Party of Afghanistan was founded in 1965 and consisted of two Marxist factions which mirrored the divisions in the country. Nur Mohammad Taraki and Hafizullah Amin, headed the Khalq (or the masses), the more radical, mainly rural Pushtun speaking wing. The Parcham (or flag) were the other, predominantly urban Farsi speaking, group, led by Babrak Karmal. The main ideological difference between the two was the Parcham took the view that the country had to be industrialised before it could move towards communism. Khalq, on the other hand, wanted to seize power and then industrialise and modernise. Khalq was dominated by Pushtuns from non-elite clans. Parcham supported Daoud's attempts at agrarian reform, and Moscow favoured them.

Moscow was taken by surprise when, on 27 April 1978, Daoud and other ministers were assassinated by the Khalq. Nur Muhammad Taraki became president and Hafizullah Amin prime minister, and it became clear very quickly that the Khalq were in a hurry so most of the Parcham group was imprisoned or killed. Babrak Karmal was sent to Prague as ambassador. Khalq was dependent on the Soviet Union for aid and arms and Taraki, especially, was frustrated by the fact that Moscow would not provide the amount of arms and helicopters he wanted.

Amin, wisely, had sworn loyalty to the Soviet Union, but it soon became quite clear that he did not listen to a word the Soviets said. He engaged in a series of radical reforms which alienated more and more people. Particularly unpopular were agrarian reforms and moves to curtail the influence of the mullahs.

On 17 March 1979, Leonid Brezhnev placed Afghanistan on the Politburo agenda. The situation in Herat, near the border with Iran, was causing concern. Andrei Gromyko informed the meeting that the Afghan army division sent to restore order there had disintegrated and other army units had defected to the insurgents' side. Gromyko, the minister of defence, Dmitry Ustinov, and Yuri Andropov, the KGB chief, all argued that Soviet troops be sent to crush the insurgency, but Aleksei Kosygin, the prime minister, argued strongly against intervention and won the day.

Hafizullah Amin was invited, in September 1979, to Taraki's residence to discuss policy. Taraki's guards opened fire and killed two of Amin's assistants, but Amin escaped. Now it was a straight contest: who would kill the other first? Amin was more cunning, and Taraki was arrested, tied to a bed and suffocated with a pillow.

Andropov forwarded a letter to Brezhnev on 1 December 1979 which accused Amin of secret contacts with an American agent, attacks on Soviet policy and a move towards neutrality. It is now known that the US had broken Soviet codes and was able to infiltrate Soviet communications. The Americans spread disinformation about Amin having contacts with them, and Moscow took the bait.

On 10 December, Marshal Ustinov, minister of defence, summoned Marshal Nikolai Ogarkov, chief of the general staff, and informed him that the Politburo had decided to intervene militarily. About 80,000 soldiers or eight divisions would subdue the country, but Ogarkov disagreed and stated that thirty to thirty-five divisions would be needed. Ustinov cut him off and told him: 'We make policy here. Your task is to carry out the military tasks assigned to you.' On 12 December, Leonid Brezhnev, in no fit state to resist, signed an order to prepare the invasion.

A battalion of Special Forces (Spetsnaz), consisting of Central Asians, had been formed in May 1979, and the 500 men were flown to Bagram, in Afghan uniforms, and moved to Kabul on 21 December. Two KGB units joined them. At 3 p.m. on 25 December, almost 8,000 Soviet troops crossed the border into Afghanistan, most of them by air. The primary target for the KGB units was the Tadj-Bek Palace in Kabul where Amin was hiding; he naively thought the Soviets were coming to protect him. He and his personal guard, up to 150 men, were all to be killed and relatives and aides were also to die. At a dinner on 26 December, Amin was very careful what he ate and drank but trusted his own cooks who were Soviet Uzbeks but soon everyone was writhing in pain. Amin was given an injection and a drip feed by a Soviet doctor who was not privy to the fact that Amin was to be assassinated. The Soviet troops then attacked, and Amin rushed from his sick bed to see what was happening, but he was mown down along with his five-year-old son who was clutching his leg. The KGB lost about a hundred men killed or wounded. Babrak Karmal, a long-standing KGB agent, was installed as the new leader.

According to one of the Soviet commanders, the operation was poorly planned, causing chaos with some units unaware of the existence of other units. A paratroop division fired on the commander's company, killing some of his men.

On 27 December 1979, Karmal announced that he was president, prime minister and also general secretary of the People's Democratic Party of Afghanistan. The Soviets, to justify their assassination of Amin, revealed that since September he had liquidated over 600 communists. The government was filled with exiles who had returned with him.

The Soviets thought that they would be in and out of Afghanistan quickly. The objective was to stabilise the situation and withdraw after about six months, leaving behind only political advisers and intelligence agents. Lieutenant General Ruslan Aushev, an Afghan war hero who spent five years there, commented in 2009:

> We were there for 10 years and we lost more than 14,000 soldiers, but what was the result? Nothing. We wanted to bring peace and stability to Afghanistan, but in fact everything got worse.
>
> (*BBC News*, 14 February 2009)

A vicious civil war ensued with the mujahidin (strugglers for freedom) receiving arms and funding from the US and even China. When the Soviets invaded, Zbigniew Brzezinski, President Jimmy Carter's National Security Advisor, punched the air and exclaimed: 'They have taken the bait!' In a note to the president, he crowed: 'We now have the opportunity to give the USSR its Vietnam War' (Haslam 2011: 326). In February 1980, Andropov travelled to Kabul and met

Karmal and submitted an optimistic report to the Politburo as the new leader understood what he had to do to stabilise the situation. Ustinov was less optimistic and thought it would take up to a year and a half to stabilise Afghanistan.

The Soviet Union was blithely unaware of the hole it was digging itself into. On 23 June 1980, at a Party Central Committee plenum, Andrei Gromyko, the foreign minister, spoke eloquently about the rising power of the Soviet Union (Wilson Center Digital Archive [Russian text]):

> The most important factor in international affairs [is] the constant strengthening of the position of socialism on the international stage. The world map bears eloquent testimony to this. In the eastern hemisphere there is glorious Cuba; in South East Asia, Vietnam is building a new life; the large family of fraternal parties has welcomed Laos and the Republic of Kampuchea; a form of socialist development is evident in different countries on various continents: Angola, Ethiopia, South Yemen, and a short time ago, Afghanistan.

By 1982, Gromyko had regretted his support for the invasion, and Anatoly Kovalev, when asked by him to take over the Near and Middle East desks at the ministry, flatly refused as he wanted nothing to do with the war. Evgeny Primakov told Soviet diplomats that it was futile to bring 'revolutionary change' to Afghanistan, and Gromyko muttered his support. Andropov, now Soviet leader, in March 1983, conceded that there had never been the prospect of a swift victory over the mujahidin.

The turning point in the war came in the summer of 1986, when the US began to supply Stinger lightweight ground-to-air missiles to bring down Soviet helicopters which hitherto had given the Soviets control of the air. The US military and CIA opposed the move but George Shultz, the secretary of state, sided with the radicals. US aid to the mujahidin was channelled through the Pakistani Directorate for Inter-services Intelligence (ISI), and billions of dollars and equipment flowed through their hands and they used it to arm the fundamentalist groups. By 1986, they believed the Soviets would be defeated, and the battle for the future of Afghanistan got under way. The Islamists made clear that they opposed both Great Satans: the Soviet Union and the US (Westad 2005: 353–7).

At the height of the conflict there were over 120,000 Soviet troops in the country (wholly inadequate for a country the size of Western Europe). The Soviet Army was not defeated as it held the cities but lost control of the countryside and found it could occupy territory but when it retreated, the mujahidin simply returned to take control. It lost about 14,000 dead and thousands more wounded during the conflict. Gorbachev conceded defeat and withdrew from Afghanistan on 15 February 1989. The Saudis were pleased and immediately handed the Soviet leader a $4 billion loan. Secretly, 200 military and KGB advisers remained in Kabul and when President Yeltsin discovered this subterfuge, he withdrew them.

The Afghan invasion was one of the worst mistakes ever made by a Soviet leader. Not only did it unite Islam against Moscow, it also led to the US supporting the 'God fearing mujahidin' against the 'godless communists'. President Jimmy Carter, in so doing, also committed one of the worst mistakes of an American leader. How did this come about? The CIA, in 1981, could choose which Afghan opposition group to support: either the moderate Islamic, nationalist, pro-monarchical Afghan parties or a group of three fundamentalist Islamic factions. The latter promised, after expelling the Soviets from Afghanistan, to then move into Tajikistan and begin undermining communist rule there and in the rest of Central Asia. Unfortunately, the Americans went for the short-term gain and ignored the long-term consequences of supporting Islamic fundamentalists and were to pay a heavy price for their short-sightedness.

11 Cambodia-Kampuchea

The excesses of the Khmer Rouge communists in Cambodia-Kampuchea did more to discredit Leninism than anything else. The Khmer Rouge's thirst for blood was unquenchable, and eventually 1.7 million died in four years from starvation, overwork, restrictions on the supply of medicines and executions. Religion and education were banned. The leader, Pol Pot, was a xenophobe who wanted to eliminate all foreign influence in his country and harboured a special hatred for the Vietnamese. His Leninism idealised the peasantry, and like Mao he saw them as the springboard to power. Rural bases could gradually take over the countryside before the assault on the towns became possible. The Buddhist monks, regarded as lazy because they could not grow rice, were another target. One devotee remarked that it was preferable to have a thinly populated Cambodia than a country of incompetents.

Pol Pot was as economically illiterate as Mao, Castro and Gorbachev, but for him willpower conquered all. His route to communist glory began with the 'pastorialisation' of the country, and this meant turning everyone into a peasant. The quickest way to achieve this was to empty the cities and force everyone to do manual labour. Anyone who was educated or spoke French was an enemy and could be killed, but this should have also applied to Pol Pot. I was astonished to hear him speak French during an interview with a foreign journalist.

Pol Pot admired Mao's Great Leap Forward and People's Commune Movement and concluded it had failed because Mao was not radical enough. From his point of view, Mao should have pressed on until he had killed all those standing in the way of its success. He launched his own Great Leap Forward which was, predictably, a dismal failure. He abolished money – one of the elements of full communism – and expected his country to leap over capitalism into full communism.

When Pol Pot visited Hanoi in 1965, he was told not to attack the government of Norodom Sihanouk as the latter had abandoned the US and sided with North Vietnam and China. This démarche was a ploy to stay out of the Vietnam War. He found Beijing more receptive and visited again in 1970 during the Cultural Revolution. He was excited by what he saw and then changed the name of the party to the Communist Party of Kampuchea, as Cambodia had become the Republic of Kampuchea.

In March 1969, the US began bombing Vietnamese bases in Kampuchea, and this caused anti-Americanism to rise. Sihanouk was removed as prime minister, and the American-backed Lon Nol took over. In 1973, Washington managed to get the Vietnamese to agree to withdraw from Kampuchea. The Khmer Rouge were now left alone to fight the government and were strong enough to occupy Phnom Penh in April 1975.

The Khmer Rouge disguised the fact that it was communist. Even in government it was secretive, and leading officials were Brother no. 1, Brother no. 2 and so on. In the elections of April 1976, Pol Pot was described as a 'rubber plantation worker'!

The cities were emptied with over two million trudging to the countryside to be re-educated. The peasantry were the repository of moral virtue; cities were decadent, and the existing urban culture was nothing more than 'filth'. Children were told to call their parents 'comrade father' and 'comrade mother'. There were three classes in society: the urban expellees, the reliable and the unreliable peasants.

Pol Pot, for some reason, began engaging in cross border raids into Vietnam, and a four-year plan was launched in 1976. Kampuchea aspired to be Communist State no. 1 on the planet. Like Stalin, he blamed economic failure on internal enemies, especially within the party, and it was virtuous to seek them out and kill them.

The Democratic Republic of Kampuchea collapsed in late 1979 when the Vietnamese invaded. The Khmer Rouge went back to the hills on the Thai-Cambodian border and fought a guerrilla campaign during the 1980s against the pro-Vietnamese government. Kampuchea became Cambodia again. When the Vietnamese withdrew in 1989, the communists faced obliteration, and Cambodia ceased to be a communist state in 1991. This is the only case in Asia of a communist state collapsing under the weight of its own contradictions.

12 Post-détente
1979–85

One of the American, and indeed the British, fallacies about the Soviet Union was that as it became a superpower, its revolutionary zeal would decline. This analysis was based on rational decision making as it would not put its increasing power at risk by falling out with the West. In a world of nuclear parity, the risk of war would decline. The West now saw the world through rose-tinted spectacles.

The Soviet Union, on the other hand, also had its rose-tinted spectacles on. It saw its version of socialism spreading not only in the Third World but also in France and Italy. As far as Moscow was concerned, the West had simply to accept that the correlation of forces was moving inexorably in the Soviet direction. It assumed that the travails of capitalism in the early 1970s presaged terminal decline.

True, Washington conceded, in 1977, that the chances of repelling a Warsaw Pact attack in Central Europe were remote. What irritated Western Europeans was that the US assumed it was the best judge of Western European security and a deal between the superpowers was all that was needed. Henry Kissinger's penchant for secret diplomacy added to the frustration. France was anti-American, but it had nuclear weapons, but West Germany had abjured nuclear weapons in 1969. Would Washington come to its defence if the Soviets applied pressure?

Brezhnev's health was a cause of concern, and there were many cruel Soviet jokes about his incompetence. By the mid-1970s, he was only able to work for short periods, and a troika took over: Yuri Andropov, head of the KGB; Andrei Gromyko, foreign minister; and Marshal Dmitry Ustinov, the minister of defence. Andropov was a fundamentalist and Gromyko excessively cautious, but Ustinov was robust and tough. No one spoke for the economy as Kosygin, the very able prime minister and therefore responsible for the economy, was sidelined. Another was that arms control was in the hands of the KGB and military, and this meant that Gromyko and the foreign ministry had to carry out military policy. The military was against making concessions to the US as it was aware that technically the Americans were improving their nuclear arsenal faster than it was.

The decision to deploy the SS-20 in the western USSR and Eastern Europe was, therefore, not taken in the Politburo but by the troika. Ustinov was very proud of the deployment, but it was a military decision which failed to take into consideration the political fallout. The SS-20 was an intermediate range ballistic missile with a nuclear warhead and it had a range of up to 5,500 km; some were mobile. It was deployed in 1976 and it changed the balance of power in Europe as it permitted the removal of ICBMs to other theatres. NATO's response was a dual-track policy: if the Soviets removed the SS-20s, NATO would not deploy Pershing II and cruise missiles to counter them, but more SS-20s were put in place. The US then developed a neutron bomb, which was first conceived in 1958 as an 'enhanced radiation' weapon. The release of fusion-produced neutrons would kill humans in the vicinity of its detonation, but the smaller thermal and blast effects would mean that buildings and infrastructure would suffer less damage than from a hydrogen bomb. It was intended to counter a massed Soviet armour attack on Western Europe while causing little damage to the local infrastructure. Opposition at home and effective Soviet propaganda prevented its deployment. The Soviets tested their own version in 1978, and President Reagan restarted the programme in 1981, but it transpired that the neutron bomb was not very effective.

Helmut Schmidt, the West German chancellor, was alarmed by the increased number of SS-20s and lobbied Moscow and Washington to halt this process but he failed. The Soviets thought they could hold Europe hostage and would not give way. Schmidt was afraid that the US would sacrifice cruise missiles in order to get a SALT II agreement. The supremely confident German chancellor had served as a Wehrmacht officer on the Eastern Front during the war and was acutely aware of the dangers to Western European security. He was irritated by Jimmy Carter, whom he did not regard as being up to his own intellectual and political level. On occasion, Schmidt, a fluent English speaker, would repeat slowly what he had proposed. Andropov, head of the KGB, thought that the anti-war demonstrations in Western Europe and the US would prevent the deployment of counter missiles. He was mistaken, and the decision to move the Pershing II and cruise missiles to Western Europe was taken in December 1979. As more SS-20s were deployed, the foundations of détente began to give way.

The Ministry of Defence, GRU, KGB (with an estimated 480,000 agents) and the Central Committee (CC) international department (providing the Marxist-Leninist analysis) were active in expanding Soviet power in the Third World. On the other hand, the Ministry of Foreign Affairs, headed by Andrei Gromyko, was more concerned with relations with the US. Nuclear parity, the ability of the Soviets to move forces great distances (the Antonov An-225 transport plane was the game changer) and the development of a blue water navy provided the USSR with a global presence. Angola was the first focal point, followed by Ethiopia and Nicaragua. Soviet military aid between 1955 and 1984 was put at $85 billion, half of which was disbursed between 1978 and 1984. The number of countries with more than 100 Soviet military advisers doubled. There were thirteen countries dependent on Soviet military equipment (Syria, for example, imported arms costing over $3 billion from the Soviet bloc in 1980) and of these Vietnam, Cuba, Ethiopia, South Yemen, Syria and Angola provided facilities for naval, military aircraft and signals intelligence.

The Reagan administration claimed to have discovered a window of vulnerability through which a Soviet first strike would devastate the US. This highly dubious claim was used to justify the extraordinary expansion of the military-industrial complex in the early 1980s [**Doc. 12**]. Although 1981 was a poor year economically, defence expenditure in 1982 was to increase 13 per cent, and over 8 per cent in succeeding years. The CIA budget went up even more steeply, and the American military began to think it could launch a nuclear war. One option was to prepare for a six-month nuclear conflict with the Soviet Union as the new weapons were more accurate and could take out Soviet military and political targets with surgical strikes. Communications were being developed to function in the US after a Soviet nuclear strike.

Despite his military's thoughts of starting and winning a nuclear war, President Reagan had a horror of such weapons. His major objective was to ensure that no Soviet first strike was ever launched against the US. Later he was to concur with Gorbachev's goal of eliminating all nuclear weapons.

The Soviets were alarmed by the deployment of Pershing II and cruise missiles, whose accuracy and speed made them extremely difficult to counter. In Geneva, the Americans began discussing an intermediate range missile (INF) agreement, and the SALT talks were renamed the Strategic Arms Reduction Talks (START). Given the attitude of the Reagan administration to the Soviet Union, these talks promised to be long-drawn-out. Casper Weinberger, secretary of defense, and Richard Perle, assistant secretary of defense, strongly opposed entering into serious negotiations with the Soviet Union and advocated increasing pressure on Moscow. Perle was dubbed a 'destructive son of a bitch' by Henry Kissinger and the 'prince of darkness' by others. The CIA normally supported Weinberger. George Shultz, secretary of state, favoured negotiations but faced an uphill task to convince Reagan.

There was another issue on which the US's European allies did not see eye to eye with Washington. When martial law was proclaimed in Poland in 1981, the US imposed sanctions on both Poland and the Soviet Union and asked the Europeans to follow suit. One sensitive issue was the natural gas pipeline to carry Soviet gas to Western Europe. Washington wanted Western Europe to cease supplying pipes and equipment, but such was the resistance that the US backed off and the pipeline went ahead (Halliday 1983: 203–33).

The chief American and Soviet negotiators, against all the odds, while walking in the woods near Geneva, arrived at a compromise on intermediate range weapons, but the White House was not pleased as it wanted talks but no agreement. In the end, Washington was spared acute embarrassment when Moscow turned down the deal, in September 1982. The Brezhnev leadership thought Reagan was a president with whom they could do business. They had disliked Jimmy Carter for his zigzag policies, inability to meet commitments and his obsession with human rights, and there was also his violent rhetoric when it came to Afghanistan. With the US economy not doing well, they assumed that Reagan would do a deal in order to cut defence expenditure.

In July 1979, the Frente Sandinista de Liberaciòn Nacional (FSLN; the Sandinista Front for National Liberation), headed by Daniel Ortega, deposed President Somoza. The Sandinistas moved from their base in Costa Rica, and arms were provided by Cuba and Nicaragua, thus becoming the second communist state in Latin America. More arms flooded in from El Salvador, Honduras and Guatemala, and Cuba poured in military and civil advisers. The Soviets allowed Cuba to take the lead but, besides being a loyal Soviet ally, Havana had its own revolutionary agenda.

Everything seemed to be going against the Americans. Nevertheless there was one bright spot. Advances in computer technology permitted the US government from 1979 to read Soviet political, diplomatic and military traffic. This ended in early 1980 when Geoffrey Prime, working in the British code-breaking centre, Government Communications Headquarters (GCHQ), at Cheltenham, informed the Soviets (Haslam 2011: 295–319). As a communist he had been passing information to his KGB handlers since 1968. Among the information he had passed on was the Anglo-American system for tracking Soviet submarines. Prime retained 500 documents on leaving GCHQ and handed them over to the KGB in two batches in May 1980 and November 1981.

Secret wars

In 2000, the Institute of Military History of the Russian Ministry of Defence published a book titled *Russia (USSR) in Local Wars in the Second Half of the 20th Century*. These are known as 'black ops'. The publication listed forty-six wars and conflicts that involved Soviet or Russian personnel from 1945 to 2000, but only a few of these had ever been officially recognised as having taken place. Tens of thousands of Soviet or Russian soldiers had participated; hundreds or even thousands had died. However, at the time, this was officially denied. These secret wars took place in Africa, Asia, Latin America and the Pacific. An example was the conflict in West Papua (Irian Jaya), in 1961 and 1962, when thousands of Soviet soldiers, ships, submarines and military aircraft were secretly deployed to Indonesia. At that time, Indonesia was a Soviet ally, and the Soviets were there to confront Dutch forces. After a few skirmishes the Dutch withdrew and West Papua was taken over by Indonesia. At least three Soviet soldiers were killed and over 200 decorated for the mission. Soviet advisers, pilots and soldiers also fought in the Arab-Israeli wars, the Algerian war of independence, Korea,

Vietnam, Ethiopia, Nicaragua, Mozambique and in Angola together with Cuban forces (Militera.lib.ru 2000).

Soviet youth culture

Sergei Zhuk (2010) examines youth culture in Dniepropetrovsk, Ukraine, from 1960 to 1985. It was called the rocket city, as rockets and nuclear weapons were manufactured there. As such, it was a closed city (between 1959 and 1987) and had probably the leading engineering faculty in the country as large grants attracted the most gifted from across the Soviet Union.

Jazz came in during the 1950s. The transistor radio changed everything, and tape recorders and cassettes made it possible to record illicit music and sell it. Rock 'n' roll took off in the mid-1960s. The Beatles were a sensation, but the Soviet authorities saw them as subversive as the miniskirt or Vladimir Nabokov and regarded them as purveyors of 'bourgeois false art'. The satirical journal *Krokodil* maintained in 1964 that the Fab Four had no talent, but Krokodil soon changed its tune. The following year, it was raving about the Beatles 'playing jolly songs fervently and enthusiastically'. They were making an 'indelible impression' on young American minds and hearts. To avoid being seen as square, *Pravda* in 1966 viewed them as fine lads with progressive views. Between 1967 and 1970, the Soviet record company Melodiya issued twenty-six Soviet and foreign disc versions of twelve Beatles' songs. The first was John Lennon's *Girl*, billed as an English folk song, and it was followed, in 1968, by a *Hard Day's Night* sung in Russian by Emile Gorovets. *Lady Madonna* came next, also in Russian. In July 1969, a youth journal published 550,000 copies of the Russian text of Gorvets's vocal, but there were many mistakes in the translation as it had been written down by ear. One estimate is that 2.25 million copies of ten Beatles' songs – with Russian and English lyrics – were published in 1970. During the last three years of the Beatles (1967–70), over three million copies of their songs were made available to Soviet audiences. A Soviet group, copying the songs, sold nearly sixteen million recordings between 1969 and 1991. Twenty-two Soviet films incorporated Beatles songs (Tony Cash, *East-West Review*, Vol. 13, no. 3, Winter 2014: 13–16). John, Paul, George and Ringo did not bring down the Soviet Union, but traditional Soviet culture never recovered from the shock administered by the Liverpool lads.

One needed excellent contacts to get hold of a copy of George Orwell's *1984* or see *Midnight Cowboy*. However, rock was democratic as it was freely available on Radio Luxembourg or the BBC. As one aficionado said, paraphrasing Mayakovsky: 'I'd learn Russian just because it was spoken by Lenin' to read 'I'd learn English just because it was spoken by Lennon.' Rock, to him, was a breath of freedom.

Zhuk sees young people identifying with Western rock music as a way of cultivating an identity, and they idealised the West. The Beatles opened the door to other forms of Western pop music to penetrate Dniepropetrovsk. These young cultural consumers rejected efforts by the Soviet authorities to force acceptance of Soviet imitations of Western pop music. The palaces of culture had to turn in a profit, and Soviet TV, in the 1970s, was showing Western films and drawing audiences away. So rock music was promoted and was a huge success with alcohol and food being served. Large official and unofficial (private) profits were made. Discos took off in a big way, but there had to be an hour's political lecture to qualify as a socialist educational programme, followed by three hours of dancing. Discos appeared all over the Soviet Union, and Riga, Latvia, was a major centre. Defence plants played a leading role as they possessed the technical and financial resources. The defence industry, far from being reactionary, was in reality promoting the westernisation of Soviet youth culture.

Western movies had an electrifying impact. During the Brezhnev era only two original Western films were released: *My Darling Clementine* (Wyatt Earp in Tombstone) and *Mackenna's Gold*. Westerns were praised by the critics at a time when they were regarded as expressions of American imperialism. Needless to say, John Wayne did not make it past the censors. *Mackenna's Gold* (1977) was an overnight sensation and became a cult Western movie for millions of young people. The Komsomol organised special meetings to make clear the 'ideological danger of such movies'. The KGB was perplexed to find that young males began imitating the criminal behaviour of their heroes: cowboys and juvenile delinquents. *The Magnificent Seven* was, predictably, a huge hit. Another cult movie was the French trilogy *Fantomas*, about a mysterious criminal mastermind who commits crimes disguised as others, baffles the police and always escapes miraculously. On one occasion, he got away on an intercontinental ballistic missile and a bicycle! Soviet youth began copying his crimes or inventing some of their own and sometimes thieves left a note: 'Fantomas did it.' Another cult movie was the Japanese *A Judo Genius*, and young people began to set up karate and Japanese wrestling groups. The results were predictable, and the police linked them to brutal, violent crime and, as a result, all karate groups were banned. The Danish comedy *Strike First, Freddy* was a sensation. It is about a travelling salesman who becomes involved with gangsters and spies. The censors rated it anti-Western, but its popularity was probably due to the supermarkets stacked high with exotic products, naked girls and trendy clothes. *The Magnificent Men in Their Flying Machines* was, of course, a huge hit. Many of the nomenklatura loved Western pop, and some took to wearing jeans!

Another extraordinary success was *Jesus Christ Superstar* (1972), and it provoked a renewed interest in the Bible and the wearing of crosses. Such was the impact that some Komsomol members converted to Christianity, and some even became Orthodox priests and Baptist pastors. Official estimates are that about 2 per cent of the city's population were Christian, but this probably considerably underestimates the number.

As a former head of the KGB, Andropov was fully aware of the level of corruption, or put another way, how deep capitalist thinking had penetrated the economy. He hit youth culture hard as he was appalled by the popularity of bands with 'repertoires of a dubious nature'. By 1984, over half the discos in Dniepro-petrovsk had been shut down because of 'ideological unreliability'. Huge numbers of videocassettes and other material were seized by the KGB. One suspects that much of this found its way back on to the black market! Sound engineers and disco activists, who were providing the thriving black market with material, could be prosecuted for entrepreneurial activity and illegally engaging in trade. In October 1984, the USSR Ministry of Culture published a list of sixty-eight Western rock bands and thirty-eight Soviet 'unofficial' rock bands whose music was not to be played within the city limits of Moscow. Among the Western bands were the hugely popular KISS, AC/DC, Black Sabbath, Alice Cooper and Pink Floyd. Some of those arrested began complaining that their human rights were being violated and quoted the Helsinki Final Act.

A major reason for the spread of discos was that Komsomol activists and others could make serious money and the black market was an integral part of their world. Gradually networks of party, Komsomol, KGB and Soviet officials emerged, and these became the foundation of the shadow capitalist economy under Gorbachev. Zhuk estimates that nine out of ten of the top business people in Dniepropetrovsk in the 1990s emerged from the Komsomol disco network. Top of the list was Yuliya Tymoshenko who was to become prime minister and the richest girl in Ukraine.

Zhuk's analysis overturns the traditional view that Soviet society was apathetic and passive; at least as far as youth were concerned, it was vibrant and dynamic. Young people wanted their own identity and disliked being herded together into a mass.

The Third World

Ronald Reagan's arrival as president marked a radical change in American attitudes to the pro-communist Third World, but the term itself was fragmenting. Third World countries such as South Korea, Taiwan, Singapore, Hong Kong, Brazil and Mexico registered annual economic growth of about 7.5 per cent during the 1970s, and this presented a challenge to the centrally planned economic development model being followed by Marxist-Leninist regimes. In countries such as Angola, Ethiopia, South Yemen and Nicaragua, about 90 per cent of exports were raw materials and energy, but prices of these commodities fell by almost a half between 1979 and 1983. The drop in oil prices also hit the Soviet Union hard. Soviet defence expenditure was rising as well as requests for more aid by its allies, but this occurred at a time when the Soviet economy was slow-ing. The Western ban on sales of the most advanced computers to Moscow led to intensive espionage by the KGB. One agent, Lieutenant General Vladimir Vetrov, committed a murder in France and was found guilty. Until then, he had been handing over to French intelligence thousands of pages of documents, includ-ing the names of 450 intelligence officers and seventy-eight traitors in OECD countries, and President François Mitterrand then passed on this information to the US. As a result, in January 1982 US intelligence began slipping false data into the Soviet collection system, which caused so much chaos that Moscow began to doubt its own sources.

What was Reagan to do about Nicaragua? Reports came in stating that arms were arriving and Sandinistas were being trained in Cuba and Bulgaria. The number of Cubans in Nicaragua was put at 6,000 with a third of them military or security personnel. The numbers kept on rising, and credits were made available by the GDR and the Soviet Union. In El Salvador, the insurgency was also under way with arms being provided by Cuba and Nicaragua. Congress opposed the US getting sucked into another conflict, but, by legal and illegal means, a counter-revolutionary army (the Contras) of 15,000 was trained and equipped in Honduras which operated along the borders and inside Nicaragua.

The Iran-Contra affair

On 3 November 1986, a Lebanese magazine stated that the US was secretly shipping weapons to Iran in order to free American hostages in Lebanon. This became known as the Iran-Contra affair and would rock the Reagan administration to its foundations. It all began in 1984 shortly after Reagan's triumphal march into the White House when an Iranian intermediary hinted that Tehran had concluded it had nothing to gain from international isolation. Then, in May 1985, the Israelis asked for the green light to complete a deal involving selling large quantities of TOW (Tube launched, Optically tracked, Wire guided) anti-tank and Hawk (Honing All the Way Killer) medium range surface-to-air missiles to Iran. The money received from the Iranians would be transferred to the US but, in return, Washington had to agree to restock Israel's arsenal with the same weapons. The president, recuperating from an operation for colon cancer, gave his approval, but George Shultz, secretary of state, and Casper Weinberger, secretary of defense, were strongly opposed. The whole operation had to remain secret as it contravened official US policy.

On 20 August 1985, the first delivery of 100 TOW anti-tank missiles arrived in Iran and 400 more followed. In November, eighteen Hawk surface-to-air missiles were delivered, but the Iranians did not regard them as the missiles they needed so the arms for hostages deal was off. In comes Lieutenant Colonel Oliver North, a marine specialising in anti-subversive activities in the National Security Council. It occurred to him that the Iranian money could fund the Contras, the anti-communist guerrillas fighting the Sandinistas in Nicaragua, and the CIA came on board. This would be a neat way of circumventing Congress's ban on funding the Contras. To warn the Americans that the weapon deliveries had to continue, the USS *President Taylor* was boarded and searched by the Revolutionary Guards in the Strait of Hormuz. The CIA immediately chartered aircraft to airlift deliveries of spare parts for Hawk surface-to-air missiles, but the Iranians played hard ball and, angered by the delays, refused to release more hostages. Tehran wanted more missiles, the freeing of Shiite prisoners in Kuwait and Hezbollah fighters held by Israel, as well as US intelligence on Iraq's forces. Matters became more complicated after the US attack on Libya, Iran's ally, on 15 April 1986, as retaliation for the bombing of a West Berlin discothèque which killed some US personnel. Two days later, an American and a British hostage were executed in Lebanon. Vice President George H.W. Bush travelled to Kuwait to press the Kuwaitis not to execute the Shiite prisoners, but this did not assuage the Iranians. The Americans, as a desperate measure, delivered 500 TOW missiles to Iran, and this resulted in Tehran accepting a small group of Americans, on 25 May 1986, to negotiate the release of the hostages; they were the first US representatives to arrive in Iran because diplomatic relations had been suspended. The Iranian negotiators adopted the time-worn tactic of referring all decisions higher up so as to frustrate the Americans. The latter then went for broke: in order to show goodwill, the Iranians were immediately to release a hostage or the US delegation would leave, but the Iranians could not effect the release of a hostage in such a short time, and the Americans returned to Washington. Despite this failure, dialogue continued, and an American hostage was released on 26 July and, a week later, the US sent more spare parts, followed by an Iranian delegation travelling to Washington in September. In October, another 500 TOW missiles were sent to Tehran, and the following month another US hostage was free, and proved to be the last American released during the Iran-Iraq war. Then the Iran-Contra scandal broke and ended deliveries. In total, the Americans had only secured the release of three out of five hostages in return for 2,500 TOW missiles and 300 Hawk missiles. It turned out that the leak to the Lebanese magazine came from those in Tehran who had opposed the whole deal. Israel was also in a difficult position because it had often acted as intermediary and had itself sold the Iranians over a thousand TOW missiles. In response, another six Americans were kidnapped in Beirut, and now there were eight being held. The president decided that Iran would be confronted head on, even if it meant war.

Someone who was beside himself with rage when he found out that the Americans had been sending weapons to Tehran as well as satellite images of the deployment of Iraqi armed forces was Saddam Hussein. The US appeased him by providing more arms and satellite intelligence of Iranian forces as well as turning a blind eye to Iraq's use of chemical weapons.

President Reagan survived but many of those involved in the scandal had to go with the highest casualty being Caspar Weinberger, secretary of defense. National Security Adviser Robert MacFarlane, the originator of the scheme, attempted suicide and was given two years' probation for abuse of authority. His successor, Admiral John Poindexter, was also forced to resign, but on assuming office, President George H.W. Bush pardoned all three and rehired Admiral Poindexter. Lieutenant Colonel Oliver North was found guilty of lying to Congress and was given a three-year suspended sentence, but two years later the charges against him were dropped and he went on to become a best-selling author.

The US hostages in Lebanon were only released in 1991 after all the Shiite prisoners involved in terrorist attacks in Kuwait and Europe, the Lebanese civil war had ended and the Shah's assets returned (Razoux 2015: 379–87). It was a matter of game, set and match to the Iranians.

The main weakness of the Sandinistas was their chronic economic mismanagement. They fought on until the mid-1980s, but the country paid a terrible price: over 30,000 dead and 100,000 refugees. In El Salvador the losses were even greater (over 70,000 dead). All this meant that Cuba was again the only communist state in Latin America.

The US did intervene directly in Latin America: in Grenada, a Caribbean island which was part of the British Commonwealth. The New Jewel Movement, headed by Maurice Bishop, took power in March 1979 and formed the People's Revolutionary Government. Fifty Cuban military advisers arrived by ship and large amounts of arms and ammunition and, in September, 400 Cuban troops came to train a Grenadian army. The KGB arranged for huge military assistance to be sent to the island. In October 1983, Bishop was ousted and fighting broke out, and US marines were sent in and the communists overthrown. Margaret Thatcher was livid as she had not been informed by her friend, Ronald Reagan, about the invasion. Soviet television showed marines going ashore to take over the island. The map they used was of Granada, in Spain. It is landlocked!

The Reagan administration turned to finance as a more effective tool to wean countries off communism. The Washington consensus – move towards a US-style market economy and democracy – was enforced by a combination of the International Monetary Fund (IMF), World Bank and the US government. This involved balancing the budget, cutting back on international loans and removing subsidies to local industries and social programmes, but this increased inequality and poverty in many countries. Used to being preached at and chastised for not implementing Marxist-Leninist-Mao Zedong Thought, the Third World was now gazing at the fruits of unbridled capitalism in the Middle Kingdom.

Countries such as Ghana, Mali and the People's Republic of the Congo began studying the Chinese model, but Beijing had no money to disburse as its main objective was to grow its own economy, not gain influence abroad. The pro-Moscow Third World thought that the US rapprochement with China was only tactical and was aimed at hurting the Soviet Union, but it quickly became clear that China had ditched the Soviet economic model.

The main source of loans were now the IMF and World Bank. The loans were available but only if these countries gave up central planning and an attempt to build a socialist state and society. A case in point was Mozambique, where President Samora Machel faced huge economic problems, but he found his communist friends were unable to help. So in 1982, he began trying to improve relations with the US. Two years later, he signed an agreement with South Africa to stop helping opposition groups in each country, so the ANC had to go.

The Soviet Union and its satellites were unable and China unwilling to extend substantive loans to communist Third World states. This led many of them to begin moving back to the market economy before 1985. Washington had now found a model which was more successful than military intervention in undermining communist states: money.

Reagan escaped assassination in March 1981 when a bullet ricocheted and stopped about an inch from his heart. He was bundled into a car, and Special Agent Jerry Parr told the driver to take him to the White House. On the way, he complained of chest pain and Parr immediately ordered the driver to take him to hospital as quickly as possible, and this saved his life. A practising Christian, the president saw this as Providence sparing him for a special purpose which, he divined, was to save the world from nuclear catastrophe. In December 1981, he had a meeting with the National Security Council and Admiral James Nance provided a chilling report which concluded that, in the event of a Soviet nuclear attack, the US would lose 150 million people, about half of its population at that time. It stated that the Soviets could hold their losses down to less than were killed in the Second World War. As there was no alternative to mutually assured sestruction, abolishing nuclear weapons became Reagan's goal.

Andropov and Reagan: missed opportunities

Brezhnev passed away in November 1982 and was succeeded by Yuri Andropov. As a former head of the KGB, he was well versed in the weaknesses of the Soviet system and was aware that the Soviet economy was not doing well. He could never understand why other men were so enamoured of girls and booze. This led to gross indiscipline and alcoholism so he identified labour discipline as a major problem and those caught moonlighting were to be punished. One of his officials was unwise enough to go home on the Moscow Metro, the underground, and was kidnapped, tortured and murdered by Mafiosi. Andropov's furious response was to launch a campaign against corruption but he discovered to his horror that many police were mafia bosses.

It was soon discovered that he was terminally ill, dying of kidney failure. The Soviets were aware that the expansion of their nuclear arsenal had provoked the US's more belligerent stance. Moscow, like Washington, was trying to achieve superiority, and as long as this continued a slowing down of the arms race was unlikely.

In the early 1980s, the Soviets perceived that the burden of empire was becoming too heavy. Subsidies to countries such as Vietnam, Cuba, Afghanistan and Ethiopia, to name only a few, were growing by the day. The war in Afghanistan was unpopular at home and eroding the status of the military and it was also promoting drug addiction, trafficking and corruption in the military.

On 8 March 1983, President Reagan delivered a speech to the National Association of Evangelicals in Orlando and characterised the Soviet Union as the 'evil empire' and its political system as the 'focus of evil'. On 23 March, he announced a startling initiative, the Strategic Defense Initiative (SDI) or 'Star Wars' programme. He had been fascinated for a long time about the concept of protecting the US from missile attacks by erecting a shield in space and it was consistent with his horror of nuclear war. The concept was born during a 1979 visit to the North American Aerospace Defense Command, buried in Cheyenne Mountain, Colorado. He was shown how the US could track incoming missiles but not destroy them and was shocked to find that although enormous sums of money had been expended 'there is nothing we can do to prevent a nuclear missile hitting us.' SDI, despite being called defensive, could provide the shield behind which the US military could launch a nuclear first strike. Few US scientists, and fewer Soviet scientists, took it seriously, but the Soviet military could not ignore it. The Soviets were alarmed by the research and development implications of SDI: it might lead to a technological breakthrough in a related defence field.

Marshal Ogarkov took SDI seriously at first, and in an off-the-record interview with the *New York Times*, he stated:

> We cannot equal the quality of US arms for a generation or two. Modern military power is based upon technology, and technology is based on computers . . . We don't even have computers in every office of the Defence Ministry. We will never be able to catch up with you in modern arms until we have an economic revolution. And the question is whether we can have an economic revolution without a political revolution.
>
> (Haslam 2011: 341)

Someone else who was horrified by SDI was Margaret Thatcher. The idea that the US would erect a shield to protect itself was appalling as that would leave Western Europe exposed to a Soviet attack.

US negotiators now had a bargaining chip. Moscow launched violent propaganda attacks on SDI, thereby convincing many observers that the Americans had something the Soviets feared. It was illogical to claim simultaneously that SDI was science fiction and then claim it was a threat to world peace. SDI was thus at the centre of arms talks during the whole Reagan administration.

The low point in the Reagan-Andropov era was the shooting down by Soviet fighters, in September 1983, of Korean Airlines flight KA007 en route from Alaska to Seoul. Two hundred and sixty-nine passengers and crew, including some American citizens, died. It had strayed into Soviet airspace and was taken for a spy plane. The Soviets first of all denied shooting it down and then insisted that it was a spy plane. Reagan mirrored American and international outrage and the Soviet Union was belaboured in the United Nations. Andrei Gromyko, lost for words, simply turned his back on some film evidence presented by the Americans. The situation was compounded by the choice of Marshal Nikolai Ogarkov, the highly competent chief of staff, as the Soviet spokesman. A poor diplomat, he made no attempt to regret or apologise for the incident, merely stating it would be repeated if another spy plane penetrated Soviet airspace. His performance was technically brilliant but sent shivers down Western spines. Ogarkov had stood in for Yuri Andropov, the commander in chief of the armed forces, who was terminally ill. In Geneva, in December 1983, talks on reducing conventional forces ended without agreement or when to meet again.

The appointment of George Shultz as secretary of state in June 1982 heralded a more pragmatic approach to the Soviet Union. The US was becoming more self-confident, and things were not going very well economically in the USSR. Reagan, despite his reference to the Soviet Union as the 'evil empire' and calls for a crusade of freedom, was keen to visit the country and China. Shultz explained that an improvement in relations was necessary before a visit could take place.

Reagan had a secret meeting with Anatoly Dobrynin, the Soviet ambassador, in February 1983, during which he talked of constructive dialogue and reducing tension between the superpowers. Nothing happened because the Moscow establishment was, understandably, very suspicious of Reagan and, furthermore, Andropov was dying. In January 1984, Reagan delivered an uncharacteristically hopeful speech about improving relations and George Shultz impressed on Andrei Gromyko that Reagan meant what he said. Andropov sent a letter to the president informing him of his interest in promoting contact between them. Again nothing came of it, as Andropov died soon afterwards and was succeeded by the emphysemic Konstantin Chernenko. The Party Central Committee was appalled by the choice but voted dutifully for his appointment. Prime Minister Nikolai Tikhonov tried to block Gorbachev's appointment as his deputy by saying that that he was occupied with agrarian matters in the Politburo and this 'can express itself negatively in the activity of the Secretariat and engender an agrarian deviation in its work'. In other words, he was saying an agricultural type should not be deputy leader, but Gorbachev had more fans than detractors and was appointed. Chernenko was only permitted to work three days a week and a few hours daily during the others. One of the reasons for choosing Chernenko was that he immediately halted Andropov's campaign against high-level corruption. Gorbachev proposed the withdrawal of Soviet forces from Afghanistan; the General Staff applauded and General Varennikov thought he was a 'fine fellow'. Ustinov sacked Ogarkov in September 1984, and he was succeeded by his deputy Sergei Akhromeev who liked to call himself the 'last of the Mohicans' due to his length of service. The best way to improve US-Soviet relations was for the leaders to meet face-to-face, but the likelihood of this happening was slim given that Chernenko was more concerned about breathing than meeting the president.

On 26 September 1984, Reagan met Andrei Gromyko for the first time while the latter was attending the UN. It was a grand occasion, and the foreign minister surprised the guests with his bonhomie. He turned on the charm with Nancy Reagan and when she assured him that her husband favoured peace, he counselled her to whisper 'peace' in his ear every night. Quick as a flash, she responded: 'Of course, I will and I'll also whisper it in yours too.' The barriers gradually came down and Reagan was re-elected in November 1984. He and Shultz set out to improve relations with Moscow, but Weinberger was against

Figure 12.1 Andrei Gromyko

Courtesy of the Library of Congress Prints and Photographs Division, Washington, DC 20540
USA, *US News and World Report* Magazine Photograph Collection, LC-DIG-ds-07436.

and Shultz in favour, and the president sided with Shultz. In November, it was announced that Gromyko and Shultz would meet in January 1985 to discuss arms control. In Geneva, they agreed on three sets of talks: START, INF and defensive systems, including those based in space. Konstantin Chernenko died in March 1985, and Mikhail Sergeevich Gorbachev, the youngest member in the Politburo, took over. He desired to improve relations to an extent undreamed of by Reagan or Shultz (Cohen 1993: 219–30; Garthoff 1994: 1125–46; Kissinger 1982: 286–320; Oberdorfer 1992: 18–75; Service 2015: 104, 109).

Oleg Gordievsky

Oleg Gordievsky will go down in history as one of the most important, if not the most important, spies ever recruited by Britain's MI6. A KGB officer, he was posted to Copenhagen in 1966 and the cultural shock of Danish life turned him against Soviet communism. There

> I started to learn the truth about the world, about Europe, about the Soviet Union – I realised that life in my country was not a normal life. We had been told all the time that we lived in the best society, but the poverty, the ignorance was enormous . . . I became very idealistic, very philosophical.

The suppression of the Prague Spring in 1968 was the turning point. 'I had become increasingly alienated from the communist system and now this brutal attack on innocent people made me hate it.'

In 1972, he was posted back to Copenhagen and Danish intelligence indicated to MI6 that he might be a candidate for recruitment. In November 1973, MI6 contacted him. In 1971, a Czech intelligence officer had defected and reported that while studying in Moscow he had been friends with an outspoken fellow student called Gordievsky, so he was sent to Copenhagen to re-establish contact with him. Gordievsky was on side and offered his services 'out of ideological conviction'. Over the next three years he provided a stash of valuable information including Soviet agents in Scandinavia. Gordievsky's tour of duty in Copenhagen ended in 1978, and he agreed with his MI6 minder to suspend operations while in Moscow. However, if he needed urgently to pass on some important information and if he had to escape, there would be contact. In June 1982, Gordievsky was posted to London. Once a week he handed over papers and film to MI6 in a Bayswater flat; his intelligence was of enormous value and provided information on the recruiting and running of Soviet agents, the work of illegals and orders from Moscow Centre.

During the early 1980s, the Soviet leadership had become convinced that the West was planning a nuclear first strike, and President Reagan's aggressive rhetoric about the 'evil empire' nourished this belief. The KGB response was Operation Ryan, which instructed all Soviet intelligence gatherers to report any movement of troops, lights burning all night in defence establishment and the stockpiling of blood supplies. NATO's exercise Able Archer in 1983 was read by Moscow as preparation for a nuclear first strike. The information from Gordievsky was fed to the Americans (the source disguised, of course), and they toned down the fierce anti-Soviet rhetoric and the scale of military exercises. Robert Gates, deputy head of the CIA, commented that the information helped to 'reinforce Reagan's conviction that a great effort had to be made not just to reduce tension but to end the Cold War'. The NSA described Able Archer as the 'most dangerous Soviet-American confrontation since the Cuban missile crisis'. MI6 provided Gordievsky with impressive looking analyses of British policy.

In June 1983, a document was pushed through the KGB *rezidentura*'s letter box, and it listed all the suspected Soviet intelligence officers in London and proposed a meeting. The letter was signed Koba, one of Stalin's aliases. The KGB *rezident* thought that British intelligence was playing games but MI5 realised that it had a traitor in its midst, and he was unmasked as Michael Bettaney. Gordievsky became the *rezident* in early 1985 and thus the USSR's top spy in Britain.

The CIA wanted to know who MI5's Soviet contact was, and the task of discovering his identity was given to Aldrich Ames, head of counterintelligence in the CIA's Soviet division. By March 1985, Ames had identified London and Gordievsky as one of the most probable sources. Ames was short of money, and the KGB gave him $50,000 as a down payment, part of the $4.6 million they paid him before he was unmasked in 1994 and, in return, he gave the KGB the names of the US's Soviet spies.

In May 1985, Gordievsky received a message to return to Moscow immediately. He decided to return and was immediately arrested. 'I realised I was going towards death's embrace. But I still decided to go to show I was not scared.' He took with him an escape plan written by John Scarlett, who later became head of MI6. He was given cognac laced with a drug, and a KGB general interrogated him for hours, but he did not crack and was then released. Why? Probably the KGB had not interrogated the other suspects or had not broken them. Had they eliminated the others, Gordievsky would have been doomed so he had to get out before he was rearrested. The emergency escape plan was hidden in invisible ink in a book of Shakespeare's sonnets. Covering his head with bed sheets to avoid surveillance cameras, Gordievsky soaked the book cover in water, revealing a set of instructions and he memorised them.

The plan, Operation Pimlico, was that he should appear in Kutuzovsky *prospekt* with a Safeway bag and the British contact would be eating a Mars bar. The first meeting was botched, but the second was in St Basil's Cathedral, where he was to pass a note to a British spy on the narrow staircase leading up to the second floor of the cathedral. However, after walking for three hours to throw off his KGB tail, he discovered that it was all in vain – Red Square had been closed for repairs. The third meeting was successful.

At 5 p.m. on Friday, 19 July 1985, a short thick-set man in an old jacket and corduroy trousers slipped out of a west Moscow apartment. He stayed close to bushes to avoid the surveillance cameras and crossed to an adjacent street. He took the overnight train to Leningrad and then on to Zelenogorsk by electric train; from there he boarded a bus going to Vyborg, near the Finnish frontier. But where exactly was he to meet his contacts? Feigning nausea, he asked the driver to let him off the bus when he guessed the agreed layby. 'I was surrounded by woodland and I lay down waiting for the diplomatic car. I lay there three hours waiting for the moment when the car was supposed to come.' Two cars from the British embassy had made for the Finnish border, and Gordievsky was to be smuggled over the border in the boot of one of them (diplomatic cars were not to be searched at the frontier). However, several KGB cars were following the British vehicles. How were they to shake them off so as to get Gordievsky on board? They accelerated and then cut into a layby, and the KGB tail sped past. It was 2.20 a.m. 'I dived into the trunk of one of the cars. The whole operation took no longer than a minute.' Luckily, a slow goods train chugging through a level crossing separated the British diplomats from the KGB tail and put considerable distance between them.

Our pursuers, having reached a traffic police post, asked the police: 'Where are the English cars?' 'What cars? No one has passed.' Then our cars appeared and they surrounded us. 'Right, that's it, now we are going to be arrested,' they thought.

But the KGB were also tired as it was 5.30 a.m. on Saturday morning and they had been on duty since 7 a.m. on Friday. They were let through without being checked. With their prize on board the British cars set off again but they outsped the Soviet cars very quickly. Gordievsky had been covered with a thermal blanket which neutered heat-detecting sensors at the border. When the car was stopped the wife of one of the British agents had a brilliant idea: she placed her baby on the boot and started changing its nappy. She dropped the dirty nappy in front of the sniffer dogs, and they lost interest. Gordievsky heard the strains of Sibelius's *Finlandia* on the car's radio: he was in Finland and free. The car was met by another British agent who called MI6. 'The luggage has arrived. It's all in order' (*The Times Magazine*, 5 July 2015; RFE/RL 20 July 2015). The episode resembles scenes from a James Bond movie, but this time it was for real.

The Czech intelligence officer was not the only communist defector in 1971; an even bigger fish was Oleg Lyalin, the most senior member of Department Five, the KGB's sabotage section responsible for drawing up contingency plans in the event of a war with the West. Among the information he revealed were plans to flood the London Underground, assassinate key British figures and land a sabotage unit at Hayburn Wyke on the Yorkshire coast. Operation Foot was launched, in September 1971, and 105 Soviet intelligence officers, working under diplomatic cover, were expelled from Britain. MI5 regarded it as a 'turning point in counter-espionage operations during the Cold War' (*The Times*, 22 January 2016).

China

Zbigniew Brzezinski travelled to Beijing in May 1978, and Deng and Hua Guofeng, the prime minister, impressed on him that the 'polar bear' (the Soviet Union) was their common enemy and the most dangerous source of war. World hegemony was the fixed strategic goal of Soviet 'socialist imperialism'. Vietnam was attempting to establish an Indochinese Federation and 'behind that lies the Soviet Union.' Hua argued that it was imperative to

> try to upset the strategic deployment of Soviet aggression because in order to achieve hegemony in the world, the Soviet Union has first to obtain air and naval bases throughout the world, so that it can engage in strategic deployment. And we must try to upset its plans for global deployment.
>
> (Kissinger 2012: 350–6)

China was proposing a joint attempt to force the 'polar bear' to retreat. Negotiations got under way, and the US agreed to withdraw its military personnel from Taiwan and end diplomatic relations with Taipei, but the Americans were to continue supplying arms. A joint statement on 15 December 1978 by President Carter and Hua Guofeng revealed that diplomatic relations would be established on 1 January 1979. The way was now clear for Deng to visit the US, and Sino-American relations entered a new phase.

Mao liked the adage 'learn truth from facts,' and Deng Xiaoping was to use this deftly but to change the priorities of the party. Whereas Mao had concentrated on class struggle and campaigns – politics – Deng shifted to economics. Several years in a poor province working in a tractor factory during the Cultural Revolution led Deng to conclude that poverty and destitution were the greatest threats to socialism. Hence as regards priorities, they were as far apart as the Isle of Man is from the Virgin Islands. Mao tried on more than one occasion to get the better of Deng but failed. Deng was to get the better of Mao but in politics they had a shared belief: the party was to have a monopoly of political power. Economic reform could only be forced through if the party remained united.

Coase (2012: 159–61, 164–5) traces four marginal revolutions which were critically important in the march to a market economy.

- The first was the decision by starving peasants to cultivate some land privately. The yields were much higher than those on communal land and party bosses at the local level took notice. Such was its success that the party was forced to acknowledge that private farming was more productive than socialist farming. Needless to say the term 'private' could not be used officially, so the euphemism used was the 'household contract responsibility system'.
- The second was self-employment in cities before 1980. The party was obliged to legalise this due to the lack of jobs for those who returned to the cities from exile during the Cultural Revolution.

- The third was self-employment in cities after 1980 which led to the formation of town and village enterprises (TVEs). This was a pseudonym for family businesses. Various campaigns were launched to restrict or even eliminate them, but Deng ensured that they survived.
- The fourth was the establishment of Special Economic Zones (SEZs), but the party leadership was very sceptical of them and they only operated on the fringes; this was to ensure that if they failed they would not have a disastrous effect on the rest of the economy.

So reform in China was bottom-up and not top-down which is the norm in any communist state. Starving peasants turned to private farming at considerable risk to themselves. Underemployed peasants took to making things to sell, and jobless urban workers became entrepreneurs out of necessity. Most of the economic advance of the 1980s was driven by these sections of the population.

Communism in China can be divided into two parts: the Mao period and the post-Mao period which began in 1978. How was the party to evaluate the Mao period? In 1981, a party plenum passed a revised party history. In a nutshell, it concluded that the late 1950s to 1966 were full of dreadful mistakes and the Cultural Revolution was a disaster. How was Mao to be evaluated? His virtues were primary and his excesses secondary because China was too fragile after his death to dump him. No one wanted to go down in history as China's Khrushchev so denigrating him was taboo. Simply put, Mao Zedong Thought was to be further developed. Hence Deng had to present his policies as a continuation of Mao's, so he talked about the four modernisations:

- Agriculture (at least 20 per cent of the population at Mao's death suffered from chronic malnutrition [Dikötter 2016: 266]);
- Industry;
- Defence;
- Science and technology.

There was a fifth modernisation – democracy – but Deng had no interest in it.

Deng transformed China and without consciously attempting to replace the centrally planned economy with capitalism, he brought about the greatest economic boom in recorded history.

In July 1977, Deng made his first public appearance at a football match (one of his loves) between a local Beijing team and West Bromwich Albion. A spontaneous roar of approval greeted him as he took his seat. He was the people's champion.

In 1978, China broke out of its self-imposed isolation. Delegations of deputy ministers, central and local government officials and enterprise managers visited over fifty countries including Japan, the US, West Germany and France. The country also played host to delegations from around thirty countries. Japan was of particular interest and a trade agreement was signed in February 1978. Hua and a delegation went to Yugoslavia to study worker self-management, and this led to the conviction that a Stalinist model – rejected by Belgrade – did not make use of all the potential of socialism. The Chinese also visited Poland, Czechoslovakia and other Eastern European countries. Ota Šik, one of the fathers of the Czechoslovak move towards a socialist market economy, visited China to give lectures.

Deng travelled to Japan in October 1978, on the occasion of the normalisation of diplomatic relations with China; to Thailand, Malaysia and Singapore in November 1978; and to the US in January 1979. Japan was a revelation; he was stunned by the Nissan plant and commented that he now knew what modernisation meant. In Singapore he sought Lee Kuan Yew's advice on how to modernise the Chinese economy. He was particularly interested in the role of foreign direct investment, and Yew pointed out that the Chinese in Singapore were the descendants of illiterate and landless peasants from Guangdong and Fujian. 'Look what they have achieved. China could do even better.' Needless to say he mentioned that Singapore was willing to help. Deng took up the challenge and told his officials to do better than the Singaporeans. Deng adopted a totally different approach to the outside world. Whereas Mao gave the impression China had nothing to learn from foreigners, Deng stressed that the Middle Kingdom was a poor country and needed to acquire technology and know-how from advanced countries.

There was another problem. In Singapore, Lee Kwan Yew pointed out that China wanted South East Asian countries to confront the 'Russian bear' but, in fact, they wanted to unite and isolate the 'Chinese dragon'. There were no Russians in South East Asia leading communist insurgencies, whereas 'overseas Chinese', supported by China, posed a threat to Thailand, Malaysia, the Philippines and Indonesia. Beijing claimed a special relationship with overseas Chinese because of blood ties and appealed for support over the heads of their governments.

The third plenum of the Central Committee, in December 1978, was a watershed and marked the beginning of the astonishing rise of modern China. It was a triumph for Deng and he announced an era of reform which was to consist of three steps:

- The first step was to double China's gross domestic product (GDP) over the period 1981–90 and ensure food and housing for all.
- The second step was to double GDP again in the 1990s so as to ensure that people enjoyed a moderately prosperous lifestyle.
- The third step was to achieve modernisation by 2050 by raising per capita income to the level of a medium-level developed country.

By 2010, the first two stages had been achieved. In 2015, according to the IMF, nominal per capita income was $8,280 or seventy-fourth in the world.

There was no blueprint on how these steps were to be achieved. Out went revolutionary zeal as the main motivating force of workers and in came material incentives, but the term 'market' or 'market economy' does not appear. Over-centralisation was a major weakness, and the solution was to enhance the power of local government but also of enterprises. Mao Zedong Thought was praised even though it was being undermined. The party regained its authority as the energy of the people was moved from class struggle to socialist modernisation, and practice was to be the key criterion for testing truth.

Eventually, private farming was accepted across the rest of China but only in January 1982 after intense debate. Mao had vehemently opposed it as it under-mined socialist values such as sharing and common labour. The strong party opposition was finally overcome by the clear fact that private farming was more productive than collective farming. Supporters of private farming pointed to the maxim that practice was to be the main criterion of truth. There was no con-testing the fact that private enterprise was vastly superior.

The breakthrough began in eastern Anhui province where Wan Li became party secretary in 1977. He was shocked by the poverty he countered. 'Can this be considered socialism? What's really the problem with people's communes? Why don't farmers show initiative anymore?,' he asked during months of visits. In Xiaogang, eighteen farmers entered into a secret agreement to divide up land and tools in return for delivering a fixed output quota. Families could eat the remainder or sell it in private markets. Wan took a considerable risk in support-ing such an initiative, given the strong party opposition to abandoning Maoist methods. 'What was criticised in the past isn't necessarily wrong, but must be tested in practice,' he maintained. 'What was promoted before is not necessarily right.' By 1982, the 'household contract responsibility system', also promoted in Sichuan province by Zhao Ziyang, became national policy. By 1983, over 90 per cent of rural households were working individual plots and output soared (*The Times*, 21 July 2015).

When Deng made the first visit by a Chinese leader to the US in January 1979, the press competed to find adjectives to describe the diminutive Deng – he was less than five feet tall, but he was a great success. At a private dinner, the host, National Security Adviser Zbigniew Brzezinski, explained that there had been considerable political opposition to the normalisation of relations with China in the US. Had there been any opposition in China? Quick as a flash, Deng replied: 'Of course, there was a great deal of opposition – in the province of Taiwan!' President Carter asked about human rights and the ability of Chinese to leave. 'Sure,' said Deng, 'How many do you want: 40 or 50 million Chinese?' In Texas, Deng put on a ten-gallon hat and rode in a stage coach. The message was clear: it was acceptable to borrow from the Americans. Chinese men began wearing high heels!

Deng took umbrage at Reagan's support for Taiwan during the presidential campaign in 1980, and Reagan sent George H.W. Bush, his vice presidential nominee, to placate him. He handed over a letter from Reagan, but Deng crumpled it in his fist and spat into his spittoon every time Bush mentioned Reagan's name.

In July 1981, the Pentagon intimated willingness to consider selling 'non-lethal' military technology, and the administration proposed cooperation in developing nuclear energy for peaceful purposes. It also provided intelligence about Soviet capabilities. The US set up reconnaissance stations in China, replacing those lost after the revolution in Iran. Washington thought that if China expanded its influence around the world, it would put pressure on Moscow to be more cooperative in nuclear arms talks. In July 1983, the president recognised China as a 'friendly, non-allied country'.

Agricultural output had increased substantially by the mid-1980s, and Guangdong, bordering on Hong Kong, set the pace. Special Economic Zones (SEZs), copied from Taiwan and elsewhere, were set up in four cities in Guangdong and Fujian provinces. The zones attracted foreign investment and new technology and were exclusively for export. The yuan was steadily devalued in order to keep Chinese goods competitive.

A major problem facing Deng was that the closing of schools had left China with an unqualified workforce. In 1982, 34 per cent had only a primary education, 28 per cent were classified as illiterate or semi-literate and only 0.9 per cent had university degrees (Spence 1999: 654–5).

Modernisation had its drawbacks. Party and government officials began asking for bribes and going into business on their own account. How should the new foreign ideas be assimilated? Deng came up with a famous formulation in September 1982: China had to develop its own societal model and 'build socialism with Chinese characteristics'; 'Chinese characteristics' meant whatever brought greater prosperity to China. This was splendidly vague and allowed creative minds to flourish.

One of President Reagan's wishes was to visit China. His visit began on 26 April 1984 and lasted six days. He met Prime Minister Zhao Ziyang and informed him that the US was not seeking an alliance with China and was quite satisfied that the Middle Kingdom retained its non-aligned status in world affairs. Four documents were signed, and one of them concerned American assistance for China's nuclear power programme. The subject of Taiwan was avoided, and it would remain independent as the Republic of China. Reagan came up with a few sentences in Mandarin such as *tong li he zuo* (connect strength, work together) and *hu jing hu hui* (mutual respect, mutual benefit) to describe the Sino-American relationship. In a speech, Reagan criticised a 'major power' for massing troops on China's borders, but this sentiment was omitted from the Chinese broadcast.

The president found economics and strategic theory, disciplines which required a long concentration span, boring. He had a sense of what the ordinary person wanted to hear and was extremely skilled at delivering a message and was dubbed the Great Communicator. Only he could present a change in policy towards the Soviet Union as something absolutely natural. Those advisers who proved most adept at gaining his ear promised to be most influential, and Shultz turned out to be one of them. As the champion of the right, Reagan was always surrounded by those who were close to Chiang Kai-shek, who dreamed one day of returning to

Beijing to take power, and Shultz knew this was nonsense – perhaps dangerous nonsense.

The Iran-Iraq War

In December 1971, the British government withdrew from the Gulf region and left Oman, the United Arab Emirates, Qatar and Bahrain to join Saudi Arabia, Kuwait and Iraq to contain Iran's regional ambitions. Iran, which had concluded major arms deals with Britain, immediately seized three small islands which controlled access to the Strait of Hormuz, through which two-thirds of Middle East oil passed. The islands belonged to the United Arab Emirates but London, conscious of the fact that it could not defend them, preferred they fell under the control of Iran, a British ally. In exchange, the Shah gave up Tehran's claim to Bahrain. The US also sent huge quantities of military hardware to Iran in order to boost the country which Henry Kissinger regarded as the West's bulwark against Soviet advances in the Middle East; thereby Iran became the best-armed country in the Middle East. Thousands of young Iranians were trained in the US, including all its pilots.

Saddam Hussein eagerly cooperated with Moscow in the latter's attempt to contain US influence in the region and a treaty of friendship and cooperation was signed between Iraq and the Soviet Union on 9 April 1972. In exchange, the Baathist regime agreed to stop persecuting members of the Iraqi Communist Party. The Soviet request for military bases was turned down. Saddam burnished his reputation as an Arab nationalist by sending troops to the Golan Heights to fight the Israelis during the Yom Kippur War of October 1973. Saddam's greatest rival remained the Baathist regime in Syria. Iraq nationalised the oil industry on its territory and, with the assistance of France, became a major player in OPEC and a serious rival to Iran in energy. Saddam Hussein harboured a deep hatred of Jews and broke off diplomatic relations with the US after the Six-Day War in 1967.

The ousting of the Shah and the coming to power of Ayatollah Khomeini in February 1979 completely changed the balance of power in the Middle East. The seizure of US hostages in November 1979 and the inability of diplomacy to secure their release led to the formulation of the Carter Doctrine on 23 January 1980. This new containment doctrine stated that any attempt by an outside power to take over the Gulf region would be tantamount to an attack on the vital interests of the US and, as such, would be met by military force. A Rapid Deployment Force to protect American interests in the region was set up. This was a clear warning to the Soviet Union, which had armed Iraq and Iran, not to take advantage of the volatile situation. The Carter administration was split between taking a firm line and appeasement and, as a result, the president committed himself to neither. Diplomatic relations with Iran were broken off on 7 April 1980. When he did decide to use force to free the hostages, the mission failed miserably. The debacle led the Iranians to conclude that they could exclude US military intervention in the near term (Razoux 2015: 52–5; 69–80).

On 22 September 1980, the Iran-Iraq war got under way. Saddam reasoned that the convulsions in Iran afforded him the best opportunity to defeat the eternal enemy – the Persians (Shias) and the Ottomans (Sunnis) had vied for control of the Middle East for centuries – and make himself the leader of the Arab world, displacing President Hafez al Assad of Syria.

In early October, in a desperate bid to resolve the hostage crisis before the presidential election the following month, Washington offered to deliver spare parts and lift the freeze on Iranian assets but Tehran turned the deal down, banking on Ronald Reagan to win the election. On 20 January 1981, the day when Reagan was sworn in as president, the US hostages were released as a result of an agreement signed in Algiers the day before. In exchange for the hostages, the US released $8 billion frozen Iranian assets and promised to deliver spare parts for the Iranian military and air force to the value of $480 million – despite a congressional embargo. These deliveries were channelled through South Korea, Taiwan, Greece and Turkey – to spare American blushes – with the Pentagon compensating these countries with the supplies they had delivered to Iran. Henry Kissinger realised that there could be long-term benefits for the US in the weakening of two major Israeli enemies, thus permitting Washington to engage with Syria, a Soviet ally. He commented ruefully: 'Pity there can only be one loser!' in the Iran-Iraq war.

Saddam Hussein had omitted to inform Moscow of his planned attack on Iran and had intimated to the Soviet ambassador in Baghdad that he had no intention of going to war a few days before the attack! Saddam was in the Kremlin's bad books because he had strongly criticised the Soviet intervention in Afghanistan and had been persecuting local communists despite promising to take a soft line towards them. Moscow feared that his conflict with Iran would strengthen the US position in the Middle East. There was also the concern that if things went pear-shaped, Baghdad would ask for Soviet military assistance to save it from defeat. Iran was much more important than Iraq and there were still hopes that a rapprochement with the Islamists was possible. Eventually, Brezhnev decided to steer a middle course and sided with Iraq but halted all further arms shipments – a severe blow to Baghdad. He appealed for an end to the war which could only benefit the bourgeois imperialists (the West). Moscow then offered to provide military assistance to Iran but the Ayatollah said no. Nevertheless, in early 1981, Tehran informed Moscow it was willing to accept military assistance but it had to remain secret and there were to be no political conditions. This was a logical move as the Iranians had captured large quantities of Soviet manufactured equipment and they needed spare parts and ammunition to integrate them into their own units. During 1981, Iran received tanks, light weapons and munitions from Bulgaria and SAM-7 surface-to-air missiles which permitted Iranians to bring down several Iraqi jet fighters, and about 300 military advisers were sent to repair and maintain Soviet-built tanks. The Iranians paid in dollars but also sent a Tomcat fighter, the most sophisticated US fighter, for the Soviets to study and copy. To ensure Iraq was not defeated, Romania, Czechoslovakia, Poland and Hungary supplied many tanks and a huge quantity of light weapons from Warsaw Pact reserves, and in this way, the Soviet Union could claim that it had not supplied any war matériel directly to Iraq.

The war was a potential disaster for China which feared that it would increase Soviet and American influence in the region. The Middle Kingdom had maintained very good relations with the Shah and presumed that Iran's hostility to the US would lead to a rapprochement with Moscow. Beijing was also wary of events in Iran radicalising the Uyghur Muslim population in Xinjiang autonomous republic. Deng Xiaoping, ever the pragmatist, regarded Baghdad's cooling of its relation with Moscow as an opportunity for China to come to Iraq's aid. With the US in retreat in the region, a defeat of Iraq could only benefit the Soviet Union. A deal was done and Chinese equipment – inferior copies of Soviet tanks, Kalashnikovs and much other equipment – began arriving in early 1981. During the war, China turned out to be Iraq's third main source of weaponry, after the Soviet Union and France (Razoux 2015: 81–7).

Israel immediately supported Iran after fighting began even though Ayatollah Khomeini called Israel the Little Satan and called on all Muslims to liberate Jerusalem. As an Iraqi victory would be a nightmare, it was natural to lean towards Tehran as the Israeli goal was to prolong the war as long as possible. Because Jews feared for their safety under the Ayatollah, Israel looked for a way to help them move out and decided military aid was the ticket, and so 55,000 Iranian Jews moved to Israel. Over the years 1980–6, Israel earned $1–2 billion from arms sales and thereby became Iran's fourth-largest weapons supplier. Equipment was sourced through an Argentinian company and made its way to Iran by various routes so as to keep the deal secret, and Israel was paid in Iranian oil. Among the hardware supplied were missiles, radar equipment, jeeps, howitzers and masses of ammunition.

On 7 June 1981, Israeli fighter bombers took off from the Sinai, and their target was Iraq's nuclear facility at Osirak which was due to begin operating in November. The Israelis knew from French technicians that nuclear fuel had not yet been put in the reactor, so there was no risk of radioactive fallout. The bombs destroyed the facility, and surface-to-air missiles had no time to react as the whole mission had only taken two minutes. Gone was Saddam's hope of nuclear power and atomic bombs forcing Iran to end the war and his cherished dream of leading the Arab world. The destruction of Iraq's nuclear capability meant that there would be no proliferation in the Middle East, and both the US and the USSR intimated that closer relations were possible. Moscow began delivering forty MiG-25s which could intercept Iranian Tomcats.

In late spring 1982, US Secretary of State George Shultz attempted to improve the standing of the US in the Middle East, as Washington did not want Iraq or Iran to win and was fearful that Iraq was facing defeat. The Soviet Union had also to revise its goals in the region as the days when a closer relationship with Iran were gone and the Iranians were arming the mujahidin in Afghanistan. Saddam was doing badly but could not be permitted to lose, so Marshal Ustinov, minister of defence and a staunch supporter of Saddam, was able to get the ageing Politburo to agree to supply tanks, surface-to-air missiles, MiG-21s and missile boats.

On 10 November 1982, Leonid Brezhnev died and was succeeded by Yuri Andropov, former chairman of the KGB and a strong advocate of Soviet expansionism. Moscow's ties with Baghdad were strengthened to counter Iran's increasingly hostile stance towards the Soviet Union. The Tudeh party had given up hope of collaboration with the theocratic regime and, in February 1983, forty-five members were accused of spying for the US and executed. The Iranians obtained an unsolicited gift from the CIA which had received the names of Soviet agents and their informants in Iran from MI6. A GRU officer in Baghdad had defected and provided the information. The Soviet agents were expelled and aid to the mujahidin increased and one can assume that their contacts met a swift end. The Kremlin reacted by ending all military aid via Bulgaria and Syria to Tehran. Iraq was flooded with MiGs, helicopters, tanks, self-propelled guns and transport planes at a time when Moscow was protesting that it was neutral.

The Soviets departing Iran opened the door for the Chinese. Tehran, isolated as it was, welcomed Chinese advances and paid top dollar for civilian and military goods. Technically, North Korea delivered the Chinese goods as Beijing wanted to keep up the pretence that it was neutral. Tanks, cannons, rocket launchers, mortars, surface-to-air missiles and motorboats which permitted the Pasadaran e-Enqelab (Revolutionary Guards which had been founded as an alternative army) to begin building a naval force. In return, Iran permitted China to inspect and copy modern Soviet weapons which had been captured. At the same time, China delivered copies of MiG-21s to Iraq because Beijing and Pyongyang wanted the war to last as long as possible, so they carefully balanced deliveries to both sides (Razoux 2015: 165–9; 207–8; 239–42).

Yuri Andropov was replaced as Soviet leader by Konstantin Chernenko, but he was in no condition to take weighty decisions in foreign affairs, and this mantle passed to Andrei Gromyko, the foreign minister. He tried to convince President Hafez al Assad to make a gesture of support for Saddam Hussein but without success. Tariq Aziz, the Iraqi foreign minister, travelled to Moscow to inform the Soviets that Saddam Hussein was going to restore diplomatic relations with the US. Baghdad would desist if Moscow provided military hardware and write off part of the Soviet debt. Gromyko assured Aziz that arms shipments would continue and a $2 billion loan was guaranteed, but Saddam was not impressed and restored relations with Washington.

The reason for America's volte-face towards Iraq was the kidnapping on 16 March 1984 of the CIA station chief by the Lebanese Hezbollah, who passed him on to Tehran where he died either under torture or of a heart attack. Donald Rumsfeld went to Baghdad and promised $2 billion in loans but no weapons, and diplomatic relations were restored on 26 November 1984. The US provided Iraq with invaluable intelligence information on Iranian deployments and capabilities and, in addition, sold civil aircraft. The Hughes company supplied eighty-six civil helicopters which could be easily modified to became attack helicopters. Iraqi pilots went to the US for training on Jordanian passports and President Reagan authorised the transfer of fragmentation bombs.

The Iranian reaction was swift and their Hezbollah allies kidnapped several American citizens in Beirut. Tehran claimed it had not been involved in the kidnappings but offered to negotiate their release if a long list of conditions was met. Washington flatly refused the offer and warned that it would sanction a military intervention to prevent an Iranian victory and a Shiite takeover of the government in Baghdad. On 24 September 1984, a car bomb exploded at the US embassy in Beirut and killed and wounded many; this meant that as far as the US was concerned, it was at war with Iran. Around thirty Western hostages were taken in Beirut, and Tehran could hold them to ransom. Germany was willing to pay, but Britain refused and three of its nationals were executed.

With the oil price high, Iraq had no difficulty replacing equipment, as thirty countries were willing to sell it hardware, but the USSR, China and France accounted for 85 per cent of deliveries. Iran was not in such an advantageous situation as the US embargoed all military supplies; Syria, China and North Korea provided about a third of Iranian needs because they did not fear US sanctions. Where were the other two-thirds to come from? Tehran was very creative and managed to get twenty-five other countries to deliver hardware, but this meant paying much higher prices on the black market and being cheated into the bargain. Low-level cheating was ignored, but egregious cheating resulted in the Iranian secret service hunting down the perpetrators and liquidating them. London was the centre of the Iranian arms trade as there was a branch of the National Iranian Oil Corporation there, and the commercial attaché at the Iranian embassy was a key middleman known as Mister 10 Per Cent. Neutral European countries such as Austria, Sweden and Switzerland would sell Iran anything if the price was right, with Sweden even providing a munitions factory. Gunpowder and explosives were also supplied, enabling Iran to produce vast quantities of munitions. In Athens, a factory producing munitions for Iran was blown up, probably by Iraqi special forces. The Yugoslavs shipped over a billion dollars' worth of frigates, minesweepers, and millions of shells and other hardware to Iran. Altogether about forty states sold war matériel to Iran and Iraq, with half of them supplying both sides; apparently only Ireland did not engage in this lucrative trade.

On 30 March 1984, the US and the Soviet Union vetoed a UN Security Council resolution denouncing Iraq for using poison gas on the Iranian front. Washington wanted to improve relations with Baghdad at the time, and the Soviet Union did not want a precedent to be established as it was secretly using chemical weapons in Afghanistan. It turned out that US companies had provided Iraq with components which helped develop chemical weapons, and a West German company was exporting 'pesticides' to Iraqi factories making chemical weapons. Bonn banned these sales, but Baghdad then turned to the GDR for the necessary materials. Iran had some chemical munitions, inherited from the Shah, but stated that it was against the Qur'an to deploy them. Iran bought gas masks from Western companies, and by 1985 most front units had them.

In 1983, CIA director William Casey floated the idea of suffocating Iran and, by extension, the Soviet Union, by flooding the oil market with more Saudi oil, but Riyadh turned it down. Two years later it resurfaced and this time the Saudis agreed. Some in the US administration thought that a collapse in the oil price would bring the Soviet system to its knees. The Americans began to devalue the dollar and it was to lose 37 per cent of its value over the next eighteen months; this dented the value of oil further. The Saudis were producing over six million barrels a day by late summer, nine million by autumn, then ten million in January 1986; as a result a barrel of oil dropped below $10. In early 1986, President Bush and Saudi King Fahd agreed to stabilise it at about $15 a barrel.

The collapse of oil prices caused consternation in Iran, Iraq and the Soviet Union, but Saddam was promised more loans to continue fighting the war. The incoming Gorbachev administration could hardly have faced a more uphill struggle as the Soviet economy slowed and gold had to be sold to buy vitally necessary high-tech products for the military and civilian economies. The Gorbachev team wanted to place national interest ahead of ideological imperatives and set out to improve relations with Middle East states, especially the oil rich Saudi Arabia and the Gulf states. An encouragement was the visit of an Iranian delegation in 1984, which proposed economic ties be promoted. Tariq Aziz told Gorbachev that Iraq needed the newest military technology, and to underline the need, Saddam arrived in December 1985 on an official visit, his first trip there since 1978. The two leaders could not find common ground as Gorbachev was offended by the Iraqi leader's bumptious behaviour. He made clear that the Soviet Union could no longer extend credit, and there was a contradiction between Baghdad's good relations with Washington and its attempts to come closer to the Soviet Union. Saddam was told that he was nowhere near the top of the USSR's priorities. Despite this, Iraq was to continue receiving Soviet advanced technology, such as the Su-25 which was very effective in Afghanistan.

The Iranian used an indirect approach to catch Gorbachev's attention, and four Soviet diplomats were kidnapped in Beirut by a Hezbollah faction run by Tehran. A week later, the mutilated body of one of the Soviet diplomats surfaced, and the message was abundantly clear: Tehran wanted to negotiate but had no fear of Moscow. A Spetsnaz team arrived in Beirut once the KGB and GRU had located the imprisoned Soviet diplomats. Several Hezbollah officials were assassinated and, as the story goes, the severed head of one was delivered to the Iranian embassy. The three surviving diplomats were soon released. Georgy Kornienko, deputy foreign minister, travelled to Tehran to inform the Iranians that Gorbachev wished to restore cordial relations, and the two countries agreed to build a railway linking them and restart flights between the two capitals, and the Soviet Union would become Iran's advocate in the UN Security Council, but it would no longer deliver weapons to Iran as the war was inimical to Soviet interests. As soon as hostilities ended, Moscow would provide high-tech weapons and help with nuclear research. Ayatollah Khomeini turned the alluring offer down as he wanted to punish Saddam and, in a personal note, suggested the Soviet leader convert to Islam (Razoux 2015: 277–81; 290–301; 332–40).

The Iraqis desperately needed advanced Soviet equipment but knew that Moscow was making efforts to improve relations with Tehran but this was hindered by Iranian support of the Afghan mujahidin. Tariq Aziz was aware that Moscow was in great need of Western currency so a deal might be struck and MiGs, Su-25s and SAM surface-to-air missiles as well as anti-tank missiles were to be sent. The Soviet-Iraqi Treaty of Friendship and Cooperation of 1972 was extended. China weighed in and supplied long-range bombers (copies of Soviet bombers), missiles and sixty F-1 fighters (based on the MiG-21) and surface-to-air missiles with all this hardware being sent through North Korea. The Chinese, with an eye for business, agreed to supply Saudi Arabia with ballistic missiles which could reach Tehran – in return for guaranteed supplies of oil.

On 13 March 1988, the Iranians captured Halabja, populated by Kurds, in an effort to cut electricity supplies after vainly trying for years to reduce Iraqi oil exports. Saddam was furious and accused the Kurds of colluding with the Iranians to enable them to take the city. On 16 March, ten MiGs dropped napalm which surrounded the city with a wall of fire, and other aircraft dropped chemical agents containing mustard gas, phosgene, tabun and sarin nerve gases. An artillery barrage further devastated the city. The searing pictures of the carnage went round the globe, and Iraq was placed beyond the pale of civilised states. The Iraqis claimed that the Iranians had also fired chemical shells at the city, and this has led to controversy about who was to blame for the massacre.

There were regular firefights between the Iranian and US navies during the conflict due to attempts by the Iranians to restrict the flow of oil to international markets; even the Iraqis got in on the act. On 17 May 1987, the USS *Stark* was hit by two Exocet missiles from an Iraqi Mirage F-1 (it turned out later to have been a Falcon 50 which had been modified) which killed thirty-eight crew and seriously wounded twenty-one. The Iraqis apologised and claimed the attack had been an unfortunate error on the part of the pilot.

On 18 April 1988, during an air and sea battle in the Gulf, the US navy sank several Iranian ships and destroyed two offshore platforms. On 3 July 1988, the USS *Vincennes*, a state-of-the-art guided missile cruiser, was sailing near the Strait of Hormuz when it detected an aircraft which had taken off from Bandar Abbas, a civil and military airport fifty miles away. It was Iran Air flight 655, an Airbus A300, with 274 passengers and 16 crew on board, for the half-hour flight to Dubai. Commercial flights were consulted, and there was none at that time but what the naval officer failed to realise was there was a 30-minute time difference between Bahrain (used by US ships) and Iran. The Airbus did not respond to a request to identify itself, and a final warning was given that it would be shot down if it came within twenty nautical miles of the cruiser (it was now eight nautical miles from the ship). One minute later, two SM-2 Standard missiles at three and a half times the speed of sound hurtled towards the aircraft and smashed it to smithereens. Two accompanying US ships had identified the aircraft as civilian but had not been consulted by the captain of USS *Vincennes*. It was a tragic mistake, brought about from a succession of human errors, which the Iranians immediately classified as a war crime. Five months later, on 21 December 1988, Pan Am flight 103 exploded over Lockerbie, Scotland, killing 270 people. The Boeing 747 was brought down, in the judgement of the investigators, on the orders of President Gaddafi who was presumably seeking revenge for the US attack on Libya, in 1986, after the West Berlin discothèque bombing. In 2003, Gaddafi accepted responsibility and paid the victims' families compensation. After his removal, a high-ranking Libyan intelligence officer stated that Gaddafi had indeed intended to bring down an American airliner but at the request of Iran which wanted revenge for the destruction of the Airbus. A US Defense Intelligence Agency report, in February 1991, concluded that Gaddafi had been paid $10 million to bring down the airliner. On 10 March 1989, Captain William Rogers's wife survived after a car bomb exploded near the US naval base in San Diego while her husband was still in command of the USS *Vincennes*. The US immediately began negotiating with the Iranians and agreed to pay $131.8 million compensation in return for Iran withdrawing its case before the International Court of Justice.

On 15 July 1988, Iran announced it was withdrawing its forces from Iraq as it had concluded that the country could no longer continue the war because it had no more money and the losses had been too high. Tehran informed the UN Secretary-General that it accepted Resolution 598, adopted a year earlier, which stipulated a ceasefire a month later. Iraq did not feel bound by this statement, and a few hours later MiGs and Phantoms attacked and downed Iranian fighters. On 20 July, the Ayatollah bitterly conceded defeat by accepting the ceasefire, despite swearing to fight to the death, and it became effective on 20 August 1988.

The war, Baghdad claimed, had cost 350,000 soldiers and the Iranians 600,000, but this was later amended to 125,000 Iraqi dead. In all, 680,000 died (180,000 Iraqis and 500,000 Iranians) and over 1.5 million were wounded which made the Iran-Iraq war the deadliest ever fought in the Middle East. The number of civilians killed by bombing amounted to 15 per cent of the total. Per capita losses during the First World War came to 4 per cent of the total population of the main belligerents over four years, whereas Iran and Iraq only lost 1.3 per cent of their people over eight years. Military losses came to the combined losses of the Israeli and Arab armies during the Six-Day and Yom Kippur Wars combined. The war cost $1.1 trillion (in 1988 dollars), with Iraq spending 40 per cent and Iran 60 per cent of the total. The only positive thing one can say about Saddam is that he attempted to spare as many military lives as possible whereas Tehran used child soldiers, each provided with a golden plastic key to paradise; some of the child soldiers also became suicide bombers by hurling themselves under Iraqi tanks. Saddam could be ruthless, with civilians such as the minister of health who, during a 1982 meeting, wanted the war to end. Saddam invited him outside, shot him dead and returned to the meeting.

The Soviets earned about $40 billion from arms sales to Iraq, but Saddam no longer trusted Moscow and thereby the USSR lost a valuable ally in the Middle East. Sales to Iran only came to $1.5 billion (China and North Korea earned $3 billion each), but relations flourished after an Iranian delegation visited Moscow from 20 to 23 June 1989. Mikhail Gorbachev and President Akbar Hashemi Rafsanjani hit it off and a huge arms deal was agreed, with the Soviet Union supplying state-of-the-art technology. The USSR was to take over the construction of the Bushehr nuclear power plant but Iran did not become an ally. Moscow also established a rapport with Kuwait, Saudi Arabia, Qatar and the United Arab Emirates (UAE) with Kuwait, the UAE and Oman establishing diplomatic relations (Razoux 2015: 443–73).

13 Gorbachev and the end of the Cold War

Margaret Thatcher was keen to learn more about the Soviet leadership, so she invited several top politicians to London in December 1984, but only Mikhail Gorbachev would come. The British prime minister was very impressed by Gorbachev's willingness to engage in debate. She commented (BBC, 16 December 1984):

> I like Mr Gorbachev. We can do business together. We both believe in our own political systems. I firmly believe in mine. He firmly believes in his. We are never going to change one another. So that is not in doubt, but we have two great interests in common: that we should do everything we can to see that war never starts again, and therefore we go into the disarmament talks determined to make them succeed.

Mrs Thatcher immediately made for Camp David to brief her friend President Reagan on her new acquaintance. She persuaded Reagan that the West could do business with Gorbachev.

Konstantin Chernenko died on 10 March 1985. Gromyko had struck a deal with Gorbachev which was that he would vote for him, and Gromyko was aware, as someone whose career was in government, that he would never head the party. A quick vote was called for because the Americans might use the impasse to their advantage, but two members did not make it to Moscow on time: the Ukrainian and Kazakh First Secretaries. Had they been present, it is possible that Viktor Grishin, the Moscow Party boss, might have been elected leader. Egor Ligachev became the new leader's no. 2; Nikolai Ryzhkov, an engineer, became prime minister in September 1985; Viktor Chebrikov stayed as KGB chief.

Gromyko expected Georgy Kornienko, an Americanist, to succeed him. This would allow President Gromyko – he became Soviet president in June 1985 – to

Figure 13.1 Margaret Thatcher
Courtesy of the Library of Congress Prints and Photographs Division, Washington, DC 20540
USA, *US News and World Report* Magazine Photograph Collection, LC-DIG-ppmsca-09786.

exert a huge influence on foreign affairs. Gorbachev, on the other hand, did not want a Gromyko clone as foreign minister and instead chose Eduard Shevardnadze, the Georgian First Secretary, who was a charming comrade but with imperfect Russian and even less knowledge of foreign affairs. Anatoly Dobrynin, the suave Soviet ambassador in Washington, was not pleased and commented to George Shultz that an 'agricultural type' (i.e. a stupid peasant) had taken over. It was plain that Gorbachev planned to run the show himself. The link between foreign and domestic policy was crucial as better relations with the West would allow less spending on defence. Shevardnadze shared Gorbachev's concern for change and on Afghanistan they saw eye to eye: it had been a disaster from the very start. The most influential adviser was Aleksandr Yakovlev. Squat – the British ambassador Rodric Braithwaite labelled him a 'dyspeptic frog' – a war veteran, he had been an exchange student at Columbia University and had met Gorbachev when, as Soviet ambassador in Ottawa, he had accompanied him round Canada. Yakovlev was no friend of the US but regarded Stalin as a Russian fascist. On the other hand, during his years in Canada, he never developed an understanding of how a market economy worked.

When Vice President George H.W. Bush attended Chernenko's funeral, he handed Gorbachev a letter from the president proposing a meeting in the US.

Two weeks later, Gorbachev agreed in principle but suggested they meet in Moscow. In June, they agreed their first meeting would take place in Geneva, in November 1985. During the spring and summer Gorbachev and Reagan exchanged letters quite frequently, and this permitted both sides to float proposals to discover if there was any common ground. In October, Gorbachev introduced the concept of 'reasonable sufficiency' in assessing the size of the armed forces.

When Donald Regan became chief of staff, in February 1985, he was shocked to discover that Nancy Reagan regularly consulted an astrologer, Joan Quigley, and that, following the failed assassination attempt, her husband had become a devotee. In modern times, the Reagans were almost certainly the only Western leaders to seek guidance which was neither Christian nor scientific. Regan later wrote:

> Virtually every major move and decision the Reagans made during my time as White House chief of staff [February 1985–February 1987] was cleared in advance with a woman in San Francisco who drew up horoscopes to make certain that the planets were in favourable alignment for the enterprise.

Some church leaders demanded that the Reagans abandon their 'ungodly' reliance on Quigley. The Reagans issued a statement that, unlike Caesar's wife, they believed in predestination. No decisions or policies had been based on horoscopes as astrology was merely a hobby (*The Times*, 3 November 2014).

The Geneva summit, on 19 and 20 November 1985, was a watershed in relations. Gorbachev's attitude to Reagan was that he was more than a conservative: he was a political dinosaur. The US president reciprocated by viewing the Soviet Union as Upper Volta with rockets but potentially a threat to the free world, and he despised communism. His dislike of the Soviet Union and its people was abstract because he had never visited the country, but the few Russians he had encountered – Dobrynin and Gromyko – he liked.

Gorbachev sided with the military in thinking SDI could be countered. He told Shultz beforehand that he believed the aim of the US was to force the Soviet Union into a corner and, anyway, SDI would bankrupt the US. The Soviet Union would engage in a build-up which would pierce the US's shield, but this was bluff. A party document, in late summer 1989, concluded that the USSR was 'increasingly out of touch with the latest technologies'.

Gorbachev proposed that the superpowers issue a statement that neither would be the first to launch a nuclear war. Reagan rejected this as it precluded a nuclear response to a conventional Soviet invasion of Western Europe. The compromise reached was to agree to prevent any war between them, whether nuclear or conventional. They also pledged not to seek military superiority. Gorbachev wanted American help to secure a settlement in Afghanistan. Reagan was irritated by Gorbachev's harping on SDI as offensive and countered by claiming that the early warning system at Krasnoyarsk contravened the ABM treaty. (It did.) Reagan read out a statement proposing a 50 per cent cut in offensive nuclear arms and other weapons reductions. Gorbachev agreed but said he was disappointed they had not made more progress but, overall, they hit it off and one of the reasons for this was a fireside chat.

In May 1986, the new political thinking in foreign policy was formally launched. The main components were:

- Confrontation between the superpowers is counterproductive because any tangible gain by one side stimulates the other to match and improve on it.
- Military power does not guarantee security; it can only be achieved by political means and the search for common solutions.
- The security of one state is not enhanced if it is achieved at the expense of another state.
- The conflict between the superpowers in the Third World has brought Moscow little tangible gain, indeed it has exacerbated tension between them; the Soviet Union and the US should combine their efforts to solve Third World problems together.
- All states are interdependent; hence their security depends on interaction with others.
- Common universal values, such as human rights, the non-use of force to solve political problems, democracy and freedom of conscience, should inform foreign policymaking.
- The class approach to foreign policy formation should therefore be dropped in favour of the common interests of humankind.
- The Soviet Union is a normal state which is not seeking world hegemony; it wishes to work closely with all other states.

Gennady Gerasimov, renowned for his suave performance and one liners, such as the Sinatra doctrine 'we'll do it our way,' became the foreign ministry press spokesman.

In the months following the summit, the Soviets launched proposal after proposal to end the arms race. Everything now appeared to be negotiable, and Moscow's flexibility caught Washington off guard. In January 1986, Gorbachev dramatically proposed the phasing out of nuclear weapons by 2000 and on intermediate range missiles, the Soviet position was almost the same as the American. Moscow was willing to accept limits on ICBMs, and the balance of conventional forces in Europe and Soviet troops, perceived as a threat by NATO, would be redeployed but the Soviet military bridled at cuts in conventional forces. In February 1986, Gorbachev referred to Afghanistan as a 'bleeding wound' and signalled that the USSR wanted out in order to improve relations with Washington. Gorbachev, when it came to arms reductions, always encountered opposition from Marshal Sergei Akhromeev, the chief of staff, who confessed he did not believe in the elimination of all nuclear weapons by 2000. The military wanted to keep their SS-20s in place but Gorbachev received strong support from Eduard Shevardnadze and Anatoly Adamishin, deputy minister of foreign affairs.

Gorbachev was still not in a position to overrule the military whom he conceded had primacy in security matters.

On 15 April 1986, the Americans bombed Tripoli, after a bomb attack which had killed three people and injured 229 in a West Berlin discothèque on 5 April. Two of the dead and seventy-nine of the injured were US servicemen. It was a clear warning to the Libyan leader, Muammar Gaddafi, to cease such acts or face severe reprisals. The CIA began to supply the mujahidin with Stinger missiles which were promptly used to bring down Soviet helicopters. In May, Reagan declared that the US would no longer observe the unratified SALT II agreement.

The shock of the Chernobyl explosion in April 1986 led the Soviet leadership, on 29 May, to drop their demand that SDI should be scrapped. Laboratory testing was now acceptable but external deployment and testing would not be countenanced. This was an opportunity for Washington to make progress in arms negotiations, as they all concluded that SDI had rattled Moscow, and Washington was aware that Gorbachev had provided funding to build a comparable system.

The first direct conflict between the two leaders occurred in August 1986, when the Americans arrested Gennady Zakharov, a Soviet UN employee, when he was on the point of purchasing classified documents, and the KGB responded by arresting Nicholas Daniloff, the Moscow correspondent of *US News and World Report*. Reagan wrote a personal letter to Gorbachev confirming that Daniloff was not a spy. However, Shultz and the editor of *US News and World Report* were aware that Daniloff had acquired secret Soviet documents and photographs and had passed them on to the State Department. Shultz was furious when he discovered that the CIA had used Daniloff as a contact with a Soviet source and had discussed him on an open telephone line. He regarded the whole episode as a CIA ploy to stymie his efforts to improve relations with the Soviet Union.

During the three weeks Gorbachev took to respond to a Reagan letter, the US ordered twenty-five Soviet UN employees, whom they deemed to be engaged in intelligence gathering, out of the country. Moscow was warned that if it retaliated, more would go. The Americans also demanded that Yury Orlov, a prominent human rights campaigner, be released and permitted to move to the US, along with his wife (they eventually left). Shultz's excellent personal relations with Shevardnadze, which included taking the foreign minister on a boating trip down the Potomac, serenading Shevardnadze with the song 'Georgia on My Mind'. He arranged for three diplomats from the US embassy to sing it in Russian. The comment was: 'Thank you, George. That shows respect.' Daniloff was released. Zakharov was expelled, and Reagan then announced the Reykjavik summit, in October 1986, but this was not the end of the affair. After the summit, Moscow ordered out five US diplomats and Washington retaliated by sending fifty-five Soviet diplomats packing.

In the run up to the Reykjavik summit, Gorbachev offered more and more concessions. ICBMs could be eliminated over ten years and US and Soviet tactical nuclear weapons could be removed from Europe. The sticking point, as before, was SDI. Initially, Gorbachev gained the upper hand. Noting that

Reagan's answers were vague, the Soviet leader then posed specific questions. The president then shuffled his cards to find the right answer but some of them fell on the floor. When he had gathered them up, they were out of order. Reagan accepted Gorbachev's goal of the elimination of nuclear weapons but refused to agree that testing SDI should be restricted to the laboratory. The president could have agreed to laboratory testing without slowing down research, but he was unaware of this. He offered to share SDI technology once the system was in place. SDI, from Reagan's point of view, was to make nuclear war impossible, but Gorbachev did not accept this and wanted to eliminate all nuclear weapons, which would make SDI irrelevant.

Marshal Akhromeev, at Reykjavik, was unhappy with Gorbachev's proposed concessions but afterwards proposed to the General Staff Academy that both superpowers move to defensive strategic planning. This implied that the Soviet doctrine of automatic massive retaliation after an American attack would be revised. The new policy would be to engage in defensive operations which might last several weeks and, if that failed, a massive counter-attack would be launched (Service 2015: 227). This was subjected to severe criticism by officers, but it did reveal that Akhromeev was thinking creatively about how to avoid nuclear Armageddon.

Margaret Thatcher's reaction to President Reagan's proposal to abandon nuclear deterrence was as 'if there had been an earthquake beneath my feet'. Another who was in despair was Kenneth Adelman, director of the US arms control and disarmament agency, who failed to dissuade the president. 'He'd hear the arguments, respond to bits, and then reiterate his goal of a nuclear free world.' Adelman, in his memoirs, recounted that he once attended a New York soirée at which a celebrated anti-nuclear writer, Jonathan Schell, outlined a utopian proposal for nuclear disarmament. 'I was dumbfounded', recalled Adelman, 'and said that I had heard such notions from only one other person in my life, the President of the United States' (*The Times*, 11 November 2014).

The two leaders came tantalisingly close to an official statement, but unofficially they had agreed on more issues than ever before. The Soviets now accepted on-site inspection and human rights as subjects for negotiation. When he returned to Moscow, Gorbachev gave vent to his frustration at a Politburo meeting, using insulting, demeaning language to describe Reagan but, when he had calmed down, he confessed that the two leaders were 'doomed to co-operate'. Formal failure at Reykjavik resulted in a better INF agreement in 1987, when all missiles were eliminated. Britain and France would have resisted giving up their nuclear deterrent if Reagan's acceptance of the elimination of all nuclear weapons had remained.

A stroke of luck for Gorbachev was the flight on 28 May 1987 of Mathias Rust, a young West German adventurer. From Finland he flew his small Cessna plane to Moscow, circled the Kremlin and landed in Red Square. Gorbachev was attending a Warsaw Pact meeting in East Berlin and felt humiliated when he heard the news. Hitherto, he had hesitated to do battle with the General

Staff and the Ministry of Defence which had resisted arms concessions, but now he had the chance to establish his authority. The minister of defence was sacked and replaced by a general who had spent much of his career on personnel matters. About 150 generals and officers were put on trial or demoted. Gorbachev and Shevardnadze now concluded that no disarmament treaty could be agreed unless the Soviet Union conceded that it had more medium range nuclear missiles in Europe than NATO, and this meant that the Kremlin was now willing to negotiate a separate treaty on intermediate- and short-range nuclear forces. Gorbachev had abandoned his insistence on an agreement on SDI before progress on other weapons systems.

Reagan pursued four objectives in his relations with Gorbachev:

- Arms reduction;
- Withdrawing from military confrontation in third countries;
- Building respect for human rights;
- Raising the Iron Curtain.

Gradually the Soviet side came to realise that progress on these issues could be of mutual benefit. If progress were made on one issue, it would not be that the Soviets had lost out to the Americans as zero-sum diplomacy came to an end. The breakthrough came in November 1987, when Shultz and Shevardnadze reached agreement on verification.

In December 1987, Gorbachev travelled to Washington, and he and Reagan signed the epoch-making INF agreement. It eliminated a whole class of nuclear weapons, those carried by intermediate range ballistic missiles – over 2,500 in all. It was the first arms agreement signed by the superpowers since 1979. The verification procedures were so intrusive that American officials began to worry that the Soviets might learn too much about US defence. On the last day of his visit, on 10 December, en route to the White House, Gorbachev suddenly instructed his driver to stop, and he got out and started working the crowd. He was enthusiastically received and was exhilarated by the warmth and emotion he encountered. Gorbymania was born. Over lunch, he confided that his reception had made a deep impression on him. Then everyone went out to the South Lawn of the White House to address the public. A shower of rain interrupted them, and President Reagan put up his umbrella for Nancy to shelter under. This struck the Russians as odd as back home it was the task of the wife to look after her husband, not the other way round. The Soviet delegation stayed at the Madison Hotel where the minibar was replete with wines and spirits. They imbibed so heartily that the head of mission had to ask the hotel to replace the alcohol with soft drinks! Outside, they gorged on Big Macs and Cola.

Gorbachev's wife Raisa was not so impressed by America and on a trip around Washington declined to get out of the car to view the Lincoln Memorial. Her comments were normally negative, and she had the habit, after shaking hands with a row of guests, of opening her handbag and taking out a wet wipe to clean her hands. This became known as the Pontius Pilate syndrome! The relationship between Raisa and Nancy Reagan was frosty as they were always trying to upstage one another.

Shevardnadze and Shultz established quite a close relationship and the latter was well aware that the Georgian did not like jokes about national stereotypes, but this was in sharp contrast to Reagan, who was always telling Irish jokes to break the ice with Gorbachev. Someone should have explained to him that the Irish love to tell jokes which ridicule the national character.

Paddy goes to the doctor in Dublin and complains about bad feet. He is advised to walk a mile a day. Some time later he phones and says: Doc, I'm in Cork, what do I do now? Paddy goes to see the doctor and says his feet are killing him. The doctor advises him to put on a clean pair of socks every day. Later he phones and says: 'Doc. I took your advice but I can't get my shoes on now!

Reagan asked US embassy staff in Moscow to collect Russian jokes but Bush put an end to such practice.

Shultz negotiated hard with Gorbachev but usually with tact. However, in April 1988, he informed the Soviet leader the only thing that was stopping America treating the USSR as another Panama was that it had nuclear weapons. The previous December, Gorbachev had told Bush that the Soviet Union was building a supercomputer and giant computers for industry. Bush realised later that this was pure fiction (Service 2015: 255, 257, 275). The Soviet leader had great faith in Soviet electronics, but one of the puzzles about Soviet industry was its weakness in electronics. Brilliant in physics, chemistry and other sciences, the USSR was a laggard in electronics and imported many GDR electronic components for its machines.

Psychologically, the visit came at a vital moment for Gorbachev. At home, he was finding it harder and harder to counter the populist appeal of Boris Yeltsin and opposition to perestroika from the party and the people. As things became more complex domestically, they flourished internationally. Doubters abroad were being silenced while domestically they were becoming more strident. The Washington summit cemented a partnership with the US and the end of the Cold War was in sight. Things began to change also in the Soviet Union and a softer line on human rights was taken and Jews who wished to emigrate were freed from detention and permitted to leave. The Russian Orthodox Church, with the support of the regime, marked the millennium of Christianity in Russia and the Soviet Union and churches were refurbished and reconsecrated.

In February 1988, Gorbachev announced that Soviet forces would be withdrawn from Afghanistan and an agreement on this was signed in April. In May, Soviet troops began to leave Mongolia and it was hinted that they would soon be departing Eastern Europe. Reagan travelled to Moscow for the last summit with Gorbachev, and on 1 June they exchanged the instruments of ratification which implemented the INF treaty. Reagan strolled in Red Square with Gorbachev and when asked by journalists if he still regarded the Soviet Union as the evil empire, answered in the negative. He had changed his mind, as had many Americans, with only about 30 per cent now regarding the Soviet Union as evil and threatening.

At the UN in December 1988, Gorbachev announced that Soviet armed forces would be reduced unilaterally by half a million within two years. Soviet troops, stationed in the GDR, Czechoslovakia and Hungary, would be gradually withdrawn. Astonishingly, he did not expect the US to reciprocate. The remarkable thing about this speech at the New York summit was that neither Gorbachev nor Shevardnadze had consulted the defence ministry before announcing the cuts. In protest, Marshal Sergei Akhromeev, chief of the General Staff, announced his resignation the same day, but another source states that he resigned for health reasons. He had gone along with strategic arms reductions but drew the line at conventional cuts if the US did not reciprocate. It was clear that the Soviet leader was engaged in a high-wire act with his own military. Gorbachev asked Akhromeev to stay as his adviser.

Gorbachev used the UN forum to elucidate his view of universal human values and stressed that freedom of choice was a universal principle. Many wondered if this extended to Eastern Europe. Afterwards he met President Reagan and President-Elect George H.W. Bush on Governors Island. The Armenian earthquake disaster intervened and the Soviet leader had to cut short his visit and cancel a visit to Cuba.

In 2010, Gorbachev, reflecting on the extraordinary relationship with Reagan, commented (*The Times*, 24 January 2011):

> I think it was stroke of luck that history brought two such like-minded people together . . . I am proud of what we did together because it brought us closer to abolishing nuclear weapons. And it opened the door to a new kind of co-operation in the world . . . We must pay tribute to Ronald Reagan. He was a great man.

Gorbachev and Bush

The impetus in Soviet-American relations was now lost as President Bush, after assuming office in January 1989, took his time to elaborate his foreign policy priorities. Bush felt that Reagan had been too quick to deal with Moscow and had been too accommodating. This revealed that the new president was having difficulty in comprehending the sea change in Soviet foreign policy. The conservative Bush administration did not want to believe that many of its cherished beliefs about the Soviet Union were dissolving before their eyes. In May 1989, Marlon Fitzwater, the White House spokesman, dismissed Gorbachev as a 'drugstore cowboy'. But George H.W. Bush changed his mind during his extensive tour of Eastern and Western Europe in July 1989. Everyone pressed on him the need to meet Mikhail Gorbachev as momentous events were taking place. Gorbachev was disappointed that Bush's first stop was Warsaw, not Moscow. The relationship eventually became very close and Gorbachev remarked, on one occasion, that it

Figure 13.2 President George H. W. Bush

Courtesy of the Library of Congress Prints and Photographs Division Washington, D.C. 20540 USA, LC-USZ62-98302.

was not in the interests of the Soviet Union to diminish the role of the US in the world. On some occasions, he excluded his own interpreter from meetings with Bush, relying entirely on the American interpreter. This behaviour was puzzling, but one explanation would be that Gorbachev's foreign policy agenda could only be carried out if the US shared it and continued to be the dominant world power. As one of his Soviet communist critics pointed out, this was a strange policy for a Soviet leader to be pursuing.

The turning point in the relationship between James Baker, who had succeeded George Shultz as secretary of state, and Eduard Shevardnadze occurred in September 1989. The latter accepted Baker's invitation to his ranch at Jackson

Hole, Wyoming. Before leaving Moscow, Shevardnadze had given vent to his frustration at the tardiness of Washington's response to Soviet arms proposals. The Soviet foreign minister stayed two weeks and developed as close a relationship with Baker as he had had with Shultz. On arrival he was presented with a ten-gallon Stetson, but enquiries at the Soviet embassy in Washington had failed to elicit information on the size of Shevardnadze's head. So the Americans worked it out for themselves. The dashing Georgian cut quite a figure in his ten-gallon hat, cowboy boots and three-piece suit.

To underline the economic crisis back home, Shevardnadze had brought along Nikolai Shmelev, a pro-market economist, who had published some devastating analyses of the Soviet economy. The minister was desperate for a partnership with the US, whatever the cost. Without gaining anything in return, he intimated that Moscow was prepared to sign a START treaty. He confirmed that the giant Krasnoyarsk radar station contravened the ABM treaty but had hinted at this during a speech to the UN in 1986. Gorbachev was later to inform Bush that he had decommissioned Krasnoyarsk in order to 'make things easier for the president'. The facility was not a satellite tracking station, as the Soviets had been maintaining for years, but a sophisticated battle management radar in a potentially anti-ballistic missile system. On his return to Moscow, Shevardnadze made other concessions. He accepted Washington's demand that it be permitted 880 submarine-launched cruise missiles, but Marshal Akhromeev and others berated him for not having gained reciprocity on this issue.

A Conference on Security and Co-operation in Europe (CSCE) document was signed on 17 January 1989, and one of the provisions was that talks would begin on reducing conventional forces in Europe. This resulted in the Conventional Armed Forces in Europe Treaty, signed in Paris by sixteen NATO states and six Warsaw Pact states on 19 November 1990.

Gorbachev faced another embarrassment when, on 25 April 1989, the British ambassador reported to the Ministry of Foreign Affairs that London did not believe that the Soviet Union only possessed 50,000 tonnes of poison gas. The British government had information, from a Soviet defector, that an illegal biological weapons programme was operating. The Soviets did have a germ warfare facility at Sverdlovsk (Ekaterinburg), but Gorbachev hoped their research could be classified as defensive. The Soviet Union had been caught in breach of its obligations. On 14 May 1990, the British and US ambassadors pressed Deputy Foreign Minister Aleksandr Bessmertnykh to end the Soviet Union's illegal production of biological weapons. Moscow conceded that the programme had been under way in breach of the 1972 Biological Weapons Convention but this was because, it contended, NATO countries had moved production to third countries. The Soviet Union agreed to end the manufacture of biological and chemical weapons, and Soviet and US stockpiles were to be destroyed by 2002 (Service 2015: 372–3, 428–9).

Shevardnadze advised Gorbachev, in November 1989, that it was very important to get Bush's 'public commitment for the reform programme' and warned him that Bush was an 'indecisive leader' (Dobrynin 1995: 634). Bush made up his mind about perestroika before he arrived in Malta on 1 December: it was a good idea, and he had a raft of proposals about economic co-operation. The Americans had warned Gorbachev against trying to outsmart Bush at his first meeting by launching a series of new initiatives. Reykjavik obviously still rankled.

The Soviet leader understood that Bush was offering him an economic partnership, although he soon demonstrated that he had a woolly understanding of a market economy. There were informal agreements on Eastern Europe, Germany and the Baltic republics. Eastern Europe did not present a problem because Gorbachev and Shevardnadze had reiterated, on several occasions, that the Soviets would not use military force to prevent the peoples there deciding their own fate. Gorbachev said he hoped the Warsaw Pact would continue. Bush countered by saying that as long as force was not used the US would not seek to embarrass the Soviet Union in the region.

On Germany, Gorbachev counselled caution because no one in the Soviet Union favoured reunification in the short term. On the Baltic republics, he said he was willing to consider any form of association but not separation. Bush made it clear that the use of force there would be disastrous for their relationship, and the US again promised not to make life difficult there for Moscow. He also told Gorbachev that he did not accept Mrs Thatcher's views on Germany.

> She thinks history is unjust. Germany is so rich and Great Britain is struggling. They won the war but lost an empire and their economy. She does the wrong thing. She should try to bind the Germans into the European Community.
>
> (Service 2015: 423)

On arms, it was agreed to work towards the signing of a conventional forces in Europe (CFE) treaty, in 1990. A START treaty might be ready for signing at the next proposed summit, in Washington in mid-1990, but there were also sharp disagreements. Bush was critical of Soviet arms deliveries to Latin America and the behaviour of Moscow's ally, Cuba. Gorbachev retorted that he had kept his promise not to supply arms to Nicaragua. On Cuba, the Soviet president thought the best solution was for President Bush to meet Fidel Castro face-to-face and offered to arrange a meeting. Bush brushed this aside contemptuously and advised Gorbachev to stop wasting his money on the island. Gorbachev took umbrage at Bush's assertion that Western values were prevailing. This implied, countered Gorbachev, that the USSR was caving in to Western norms. He preferred the term 'universal, democratic values'. Eventually, they agreed to say 'democratic values'. Malta was a watershed in Soviet-American relations. Gorbachev assured Bush that he, as other Soviet citizens, did not consider the US the enemy anymore. Shevardnadze put it graphically. The superpowers had 'buried the Cold War at the bottom of the Mediterranean' (Beschloss and Talbott 1993: 165). There was another bonus in 1990, when Shevardnadze transferred the Barents Sea shelf to the US.

Gorbachev and Europe: our common home

Gorbachev came up with the expression 'Europe is our common home' (the concept was elastic: it also included the US and Canada) in Paris in February 1986, during his first visit to Western Europe after taking office. He chose France because it was a nuclear power and it would be a feather in his cap if he could interest the French in a nuclear-free world, but President Mitterrand proved quite unresponsive. When Mitterrand visited Moscow, in July 1986, he confided to Gorbachev that he opposed the whole idea of SDI and viewed it as accelerating the arms race instead of slowing it down. After the Reykjavik summit, however, the French repeated their commitment to nuclear deterrence, disappointing Gorbachev.

Figure 13.3 President Ronald Reagan and President Mikhail Gorbachev

Courtesy of the Library of Congress Prints and Photographs Division, Washington, DC 20540 USA, LC-USZ62–117700.

Figure 13.4 Mikhail Gorbachev, Raisa Gorbacheva and the author
© Martin McCauley.

In April 1987 in Prague, the Soviet president floated his pan-European idea but found little response from the leaders of Western Europe who preferred to take their lead from the Americans. When British Prime Minister Margaret Thatcher visited Moscow in March 1987, she forcefully reiterated her commitment to nuclear deterrence ('nuclear weapons have been invented, you cannot de-invent them,' she said). She also believed the goal of the Soviet Union was to promote communism worldwide. Nevertheless, the two leaders got on extremely well as Mrs Thatcher enjoyed a good argument. As she had the ear of President Reagan, it was important for Gorbachev to attempt to win her over to his way of thinking. She was enthusiastic about something else: perestroika.

A joke circulated after the meeting.

> *The two leaders are having tea at Gorbachev's dacha. A dog appears. 'Come, come, Geoffrey Howe, come and say hello to the nice lady,' the Soviet leader says. 'Why do you call him Geoffrey Howe?,' enquires Mrs Thatcher. 'Oh, that's because he always does what I say!'*

Shevardnadze cracked another joke about Mrs Thatcher:

> *She goes up to Heaven and God welcomes her. 'How are you? How are things down there, my daughter?' 'First of all, I'm not your daughter and, secondly, you are sitting in my seat!'*

Gorbachev told a story about a man who decided to change jobs and chose work in a toy factory. After all the pieces had been assembled, he found he had a machine gun. This was a subtle way of pointing out to the US president that in the Soviet Union appearance is not always reality.

Mrs Thatcher was famous for her dress sense, from her colourful power suits to the formidable handbags and pristine strings of pearls. On one occasion, visiting the Kremlin in winter, in felt boots, her Special Branch bodyguard was observed by KGB security to have bulging pockets which they assumed was 'impressive weaponry'. The bodyguard waited until Mrs Thatcher had moved into the warm and then pulled out a pair of high heels for her to change into.

Although President Mitterrand regarded Reagan's belief in SDI as bordering on the mystical, he maintained a hard line on France's nuclear deterrent: it was non-negotiable, and the French Parliament even voted to upgrade their armed forces. In Moscow in April 1987, Mrs Thatcher also confirmed her belief in nuclear deterrent. In December 1987, Gorbachev dropped in on Mrs Thatcher en route to the Washington summit to sign the INF treaty. Geoffrey Howe, the British foreign secretary, was very impressed by their work rate and compared them to two star Stakhanovites (exemplary Soviet shock workers). Gorbachev's first extended official visit to Britain, in April 1989, found Mrs Thatcher passionately interested in the development of perestroika. When Gorbachev commented that many in the West were having doubts about it, she brushed this aside and assured him that all in the West were enthusiastic about it. (This was pure fiction!)

After visiting France and Britain, the two Western European nuclear states, it was time for the Soviet leader to visit West Germany in June 1989. The Germans had been feeling left out of Gorbachev's diplomacy. When Chancellor Kohl saw Gorbachev at Chernenko's funeral, the new Soviet leader enquired where the Federal Republic was drifting. He used the verb *driftovat*, to drift, which is not to be found in any Russian dictionary. Kohl was probably the first Western leader to be treated to such neologisms – Gorbachev loved to pepper his remarks with newly mastered English expressions. Kohl found the Soviet president's communicative skills brilliant and attempted to pay him a compliment. Unfortunately, he likened him to Joseph Goebbels, the silver-tongued Nazi propaganda chief, which soured relations for a while. This led Helmut Schmidt, the ex-chancellor, to offer this comment about the monoglot Rhinelander: 'I think there are still two or three fields in which he still needs a lot of education: international affairs, arms control and military strategy, and economics and finance.' In July in Paris, Gorbachev told the French the post-war era was over, and at the Sorbonne, he underlined that pure intellect without morality constituted a terrible danger. He was in Helsinki in October and then he went to Italy. The reception he received in Milan was the most emotional of his career and was feted everywhere as if he had arrived from Mars. On 1 December, he was the first Soviet leader to enter the Vatican and informed the Polish Pope John Paul II that democracy was not enough: morality was also essential. The pope spoke Russian with him for a while and assured him that he would not do anything to undermine perestroika. When

Gorbachev thanked him in Polish, the pope corrected his Polish and was then invited to visit the Soviet Union.

The home front

> You know, I changed things in Stavropol krai and that pleased me a lot. I thought I knew how to do it, so when I arrived in Moscow I thought I'd do the same but on a bigger stage. Then I realised, as regards appointments and personnel, you cannot even move one single person because the system (*sistema*) is so tightly knit and inter-dependent. I was really in despair.
>
> —Gorbachev

> The oblast Party leader was a king; the republican Party leader was a tsar; and the general secretary was practically God's equal.
>
> —Gorbachev

The main priority for Gorbachev was raising living standards. One of the reasons for the ousting of Khrushchev in 1964 had been food shortages. The share of the budget accorded agriculture increased from 16 per cent to 18 per cent and then to 25 per cent in 1985, and food was heavily subsidised. Andropov cancelled increases in bread and other food products at the last moment, in January 1983, because he feared social unrest. Billions of dollars were spent annually on importing grain and other foodstuffs.

Andropov lamented this and told the Central Committee on 22 November 1982 that the country had become accustomed to such purchases.

> It became an automatic sort of procedure: we start to buy grain abroad every year; and we got butter from somewhere else, milk from somewhere else again. Of course, you will understand that they haven't given us all this because they thought we had beautiful eyes. Money is demanded. I don't want to scare anyone but I will say over recent years we've wasted billions of gold roubles on such an expensive thing.

What solution did Andropov offer? None. This analysis was so bleak it was not published. Unfortunately, the world prices of gold and diamonds began to fall as did Soviet oil output. Nonetheless, by the mid-1980s, the South African company De Beers was paying the Soviet Union about a billion dollars a year for high-quality diamonds. On the other hand, Soviet propaganda hammered any businessman who traded with South Africa under apartheid!

On 18 January 1983, Nikolai Ryzhkov, CC secretary for the economy, was scathing about the fulfilment of national plans to fellow CC secretaries:

> Of course, it's said that the plan had been fulfilled but that won't be the truth because it is the corrected plan that has been fulfilled whereas the plan

envisaged by the national economic plan has not been fulfilled. This is how we get a situation here where we ourselves create disinformation.

(Service 2015: 55–6, 58)

The concept of a socialist market economy surfaced in 1984. There was talk of promoting co-operatives and individual labour activity. Gorbachev took part in many discussion groups, but his contributions were marked by a lack of clarity and understanding of economics. This was his Achilles's heel and like Mao, he could not comprehend the dismal science.

Everyone agreed that economic reform was necessary and even Marshal Ogarkov had reached that conclusion, but the problem was how to implement it. The gulf between labour productivity in the Soviet Union and the US had been narrowing until 1973 but afterwards it began to widen. This was due to the information revolution in the US (computers, etc.) which the USSR was slow to emulate. The Soviet economy began to slow down in the mid-1970s. Growth between 1981 and 1985 was zero, according to Abel Aganbegyan, one of Gorbachev's leading economic advisers, but he only reached this conclusion in 1989.

The first reform was *uskorenie* (acceleration), the brain child of Abel Aganbegyan. Only about 15 per cent of the capital stock was up to world standards. A mere 5 per cent of exports went to capitalist countries so retooling industry became the goal. However, the investment required cut investment to consumer goods industries. The results were meagre. The next move was to combat alcoholism. This noble goal had two main drawbacks: one was the hole in the budget which would result as booze was the main source of revenue for the state, and the other was that the male population liked its vodka. My own experience revealed that one cannot separate a Russian from the bottle. Psychologically it turned males against Gorbachev and his reforms, but the female population applauded but that had little impact in such a male-dominated society.

The name given to the new economic policy was perestroika or restructuring. The goal was to rethink, reorganise and restructure the way things were done, and it was to apply to all aspects of activity. Because the economy was not taking off, Gorbachev concluded that party and government officials were holding it back. They were preventing the creative potential of workers bearing fruit. So glasnost was launched and it permitted ordinary people to criticise their bosses. This would kick-start progress, but this was a complete misreading of the reasons for the failure of perestroika to produce quick results. The main reason was that enterprises did not regard perestroika as beneficial.

Chernobyl

The explosion at reactor number four of the Chernobyl atomic power station at 1.26 a.m. on Saturday, 26 April 1986, exposed the limits of glasnost. Gorbachev was told at 5 a.m. and a special commission of top scientists were sent to the site but forwarded no information for two days. (The first nuclear power plant to register the explosion was the facility at Forsmark, in Sweden. At first, the personnel thought that the source was their own plant, so high was the reading!) All 47,000 inhabitants were evacuated from Pripyat, 3 km from the plant, on the afternoon of 27 April, but by then they had been exposed to radiation for forty hours. A short item appeared on the evening of 28 April on Soviet television but it gave no indication of the seriousness of the catastrophe, and the May Day parades in Kiev and other cities went ahead – all within the zone of contamination. On 2 May, everyone was evacuated from the village of Chernobyl, 7 km from the plant.

Another explosion in reactor number two was possible as radioactive magma was seeping through the cracked concrete floor. If it came into contact with the water table underneath, an explosion at least ten times as powerful as Hiroshima would occur. On 13 May, thousands of miners were ordered to dig a tunnel in the sand under the reactor in order to pour in concrete to prevent seepage. Finally, on 14 May, Gorbachev appeared on television to tell his fellow citizens what had happened, but his delivery was hesitant. The fact that it had taken him eighteen days to decide to inform the public angered many. Untold thousands of people had been unnecessarily exposed to radiation due to the refusal of the Gorbachev team to act immediately. Chernobyl demonstrated to some citizens that Gorbachev was a bumbling leader who was unlikely to lead the country forward. Politburo minutes even revealed that plans to cover up the nuclear accident had been discussed. This tactic had worked when an explosion at the Mayak nuclear facility in the Urals in 1957 caused a nuclear catastrophe almost as serious as Chernobyl.

Thousands of troops were drafted in to 'liquidate' the problem of Chernobyl. In September, radioactive graphite had to be removed by hand from the roof of the reactor, but a man could only work forty-five seconds due to the radiation. By November, the reactor had been sealed in a huge concrete and steel sarcophagus. Chernobyl had cost seventeen billion roubles but also thousands of lives. The heroes were the firefighters and soldiers who gave their lives to save their country and Europe from an unimaginable nuclear catastrophe.

Chernobyl dashed hopes about socio-economic acceleration. It was a watershed, and the culture of secrecy and lack of personal responsibility had to be tackled. Gorbachev made clear that politicians and scientists at lower levels had been incompetent and mendacious. Glasnost expanded rapidly, and Gorbachev used terms such as 'socialist pluralism' and the 'pluralism of opinion'. It was beginning to take on aspects of the Prague Spring.

Chernobyl added urgency to the need to reach agreement on nuclear weapons. Gorbachev, in a conversation with George H.W. Bush on 10 December 1987, mentioned that if nuclear power stations in France or elsewhere were destroyed, it could lead to nuclear war. The idea that one could do something after the beginning of a nuclear conflict was nonsense. If foreign ministers could not reach agreement in arms control negotiations, they should be fired (Service 2015: 189).

There was no coherent pattern to the economic reforms which were introduced. One instance was the law on co-operatives and individual labour activity, in 1986. It was followed by legislation which criminalised money grubbing, unearned income (letting a room in one's flat, for example) and living above one's means. Often legislation would afford enterprises greater autonomy in production and distribution of goods, but the second part of the same legislation restricted these concessions. Ministries were downgraded but they had arranged intersectoral transfers, financed research and development, trained personnel and lobbied the centre on behalf of their enterprises.

The most radical reform so far was the law on the state enterprise of July 1987. It promoted self-financing and self-management. Workers could elect the director and other personnel, including foremen. If they disagreed with management, they could dismiss it and elect new management. Government and party officials could no longer give orders to enterprises. Of all the economic reforms this was the most disruptive. Self-financing did not make a lot of sense without a comprehensive price reform. As a consequence, perestroika began to run out of steam by the end of 1987.

The 19th Party Conference

The conference, in June 1988, was a great leap forward towards democratisation. The USSR Congress of People's Deputies (CPD), extinct since Lenin's day, was resurrected. Fifteen hundred deputies were to be directly elected in multi-candidate elections and 750 nominated by social organisations, such as the party and Komsomol. The CPD would elect from its members a Supreme Soviet of 400 members. They would be full-time law makers. This move transformed the role of the chair of the USSR Supreme Soviet, which hitherto had been a more or less decorative post. The present holder was Andrei Gromyko but Gorbachev, wanting the post for himself, pushed Gromyko into retirement. A Belarusian, Gromyko spoke beautiful Russian and had a keen sense of humour but never displayed this in public. He followed the Russian tradition that if someone smiled all the time, he was regarded as an idiot. One has to remember that he had a hard taskmaster, Josef Stalin, who believed that a Soviet diplomat should be feared and not loved. 'Grim Grom' (foreign minister from 1957 to 1985) will go down in history as Mr Nyet (Mr No). He would have achieved much more had he been more flexible but, after all, Russians do not bargain but negotiate. He was to rue the fact that he had helped make Gorbachev party leader.

The conference highlighted the fact that the party had split into various factions. Those who wanted to proceed slowly were probably in the majority, and one of the critics was the writer Yury Bondarev. He did not like what had happened over the previous three years and likened perestroika to a plane which took off and had no idea where it was going to land.

Yeltsin was also quite a performer. He proposed that those members of the Politburo who had been there under Brezhnev resign because they were

responsible for the mess the country was in. He attacked the party nomenklatura's privileges: their special polyclinics, special shops and the like. There 'can
be no special communists in the Party', he thundered, and the little people
loved it. He called for multi-candidate elections to all party posts and then he
turned cheeky. Would the delegates rehabilitate him by removing the charges
made against him at the October 1987 plenum? He would prefer it now rather
than fifty years after he was dead. He was showered with abuse.

He also proposed the privatisation of public property. But who could buy
this property? Party bureaucrats, enterprise managers, those who had done well
from the shadow capitalist economy, the black market rich, the KGB – these
groups stood to do very nicely from the rise of Yeltsin. Boris presented himself
as the champion of the Russian Federation as it did not have its own Communist
Party, Academy of Sciences and so on and this amounted to discrimination.
Russian nationalists flocked to his colours.

An even more radical reform was the decision to remove the party from the
industrial economy (agriculture remained a party responsibility until the collapse
of the Soviet Union). Party secretaries had been the glue which kept the planned
economy together. Party First Secretaries, almost always engineers – except in
oil regions where they were geologists – were recruited from successful enterprise
managers. He had four main functions:

- Manage his region's activity in order to fulfil national plans;
- Promote intersectoral co-operation;
- Help obtain scarce resources for his enterprise;
- Resolve conflicts between and among enterprises.

Who was to take on these responsibilities? The local Soviet, but it had no department of industry and therefore had no expertise in such matters. So a vacuum
began appearing at the local level. Enterprises gradually paid less attention to the
centre and began forming trusts and associations, and this had an important side
effect in non-Russian republics: the growth of nationalism.

A popular ditty made the rounds:

> Sausage prices twice as high
> Where's the vodka for us to buy?
> All we do is sit at home
> Watching Gorby drone and drone

Another caustic comment was: 'How do you translate perestroika into English?'
'Easy. Science fiction.' A cartoon depicts an enterprise director dictating a telegram to Moscow. 'Have successfully implemented perestroika. Await further
instructions.'

The Soviet Union became more and more dependent on international markets
for grain and food imports. The first large grain imports were in 1963, and

in 1984, they had risen to forty-six million tonnes, costing $25 billion in 2000 prices, and in 1985 they were 45.6 million tonnes, costing $22.5 billion. Gold was also sold to raise the money to pay for these huge imports. The grain was for human, cattle and poultry consumption. Cattle were raised in huge complexes (following the US example) but Soviet farmers could not supply enough feed grain and the same applied to poultry production. The Soviet Union began to run up a hard currency debt in 1974, and it rose inexorably afterwards. By 1985, Soviet debt was $22.5 billion but, if Eastern Europe is added, it became $115.7 billion. (According to Gaidar [2007] in 1988, Soviet debt had risen to $41.5 billion and all socialist countries to $205.7 billion.)

A law on cooperatives was passed in May 1988 but most of them were set up in state enterprises. They mushroomed and by mid-1989, the number of workers in cooperatives had risen to 4.9 million. Wages in cooperatives were at least double those in state enterprises and in early 1991, six million were working in cooperatives. They often raised the ire of the general public as enterprise goods were simply sold at a handsome profit. They were also used as a cover for drinking, as tea cups were distributed but then filled with vodka. Cooperatives were useful channels for laundering currency acquired through bribery and corruption.

Legislation in July–August 1988 permitted the Komsomol to engage in foreign economic activity. In other words, the Komsomol elite could set up scientific and technical centres and undertake research for domestic and foreign firms. Legislation in November 1989 permitted an enterprise to purchase, wholly or partially, property it was renting. This, in effect, privatised property and allowed management to acquire valuable assets at low prices.

China

In 1985, the six military members of the Politburo retired and, among the new talent promoted was Deputy Prime Minister Li Peng, who had studied hydraulic engineering in the Soviet Union. Hainan Island, off the south east coast, became an SEZ to produce, among other things, rice and sugar cane. Guangdong province became, in effect, an SEZ; other coastal cities followed and Shanghai itself could attract foreign investment. Two Chinese economies emerged: the SEZs based on foreign capital and expertise and becoming enormously prosperous, and the rest of the economy where living standards lagged far behind. Zhao Ziyang, the prime minister, became enamoured of the scientific technical revolution and after a visit to the US became even more excited by the potential of technology to change the world.

Huge state projects, such as the Shengli oil refinery, were launched but local officials expected a cut to turn a blind eye to irregularities. It was in their interests to promote business in their region and tax evasion became the norm. Deng said on American TV: 'To get rich is glorious. To get rich is not a sin.' (He is also credited with another aphorism: 'It doesn't matter if a cat is black or white as long as it catches mice.' What he actually said was: 'It doesn't matter if a cat is black or yellow.')

Because unemployment was not permitted to exist under socialism, surplus labour, mostly young people, was sent to the countryside from the 1950s onwards. This ended with Mao's death and they then returned to the cities. There were over twenty million of them, and they accounted for about 10 per cent of the urban population. Few of them could find work and they began blocking railway lines, surrounding government buildings and the like. In November 1979, the government was forced to legalise individual economic activity and a person could now become an entrepreneur. Pressure from below – fear of mass protests – had again won the day. Two years later, the party and government declared that private entrepreneurship was a 'necessary complement' to the socialist economy. This opened the floodgates to capitalism in cities and towns. During the 1980s, the authorities discriminated against TVEs and individual activity, and it was only in 1992, when capitalism was officially recognised as part and parcel of socialism, that discrimination ended.

Students wanted more democracy, which Deng was determined to deny them. In January 1987, Hu Yaobang resigned as secretary general of the party. He had favoured dialogue and some movement towards democracy but he refused to stand and fight for his convictions. Zhao Ziyang took over the top party post, and a battle developed between hardliners and reformers over who should become prime minister. Eventually Li Peng got the nod. A conservative, dour comrade, he was an uninspiring choice.

In April 1989, Hu Yaobang suffered a heart attack at a Politburo meeting and died a week later. Hu was extremely popular with intellectuals and students, and he was revered as that rara avis, an honest communist. During student demonstrations in 1986, he had sided with the students. A list of political demands was handed to the country's parliament, and they included calls for freedom and democracy. At another demonstration there were shouts of 'Down with the Communist Party!' Deng declined to visit Hu in hospital and he became a target for the demonstrators.

Student protests were normal but this time it was different, as the public joined them, and the leaders were stunned by the number of Beijingers who joined the protests. The railways allowed masses of students to travel free to Beijing. Deng became exasperated at the extent of the protests which spanned 130 cities.

On some days, there were about a million protesters on Tiananmen Square. A policeman, told by an old lady not to touch the students because they were 'our' children, told her: 'If it weren't for this uniform I would join them.' Li Peng, the prime minister, told Deng that the protesters wanted to overthrow the regime. One of the golden oldies, the Party Elders, called the students 'bastards'.

In the midst of this crisis, the Soviet leader Mikhail Gorbachev arrived. This was not his first attempt to improve relations with the Middle Kingdom. When Li Peng was in Moscow for Chernenko's funeral, he had rejected the olive branch extended by the new Soviet leader and stressed that China would never accept subordinate status to the Soviet Union but did not rule out an improvement in relations. He returned in June 1985 to sign an agreement on scientific and technical cooperation. When he visited again in December 1985, Gorbachev stressed they had a common interest in opposing SDI. He wondered why China supported America's policy in Afghanistan and assured Li that Moscow had no interest in causing trouble for China in Vietnam. Li made it clear to him that China would not accept the 'little brother' status and there would be no normalisation of relations until the USSR changed its policies in Afghanistan and Cambodia. Moreover, he was sharply critical of Moscow endorsing Vietnam's military presence in Cambodia. On a more positive note, a visit by Deputy Prime Minister Yao Yilin in December 1985 saw negotiations on arms control and the signing of a bilateral trade and economic co-operation.

Gorbachev's visit had been prepared by Shevardnadze who had visited Beijing and Shanghai in February 1989. In the Chinese capital, Shevardnadze proposed the normalisation of relations and therefore a visit from Gorbachev would be welcome. He met Deng in Shanghai who advocated better relations and assured Deng that there were no Soviet troops in Afghanistan in false uniforms. Deng made clear there could be no peace in Cambodia until all Vietnamese troops had been withdrawn. Shevardnadze even hinted the Soviets might stop providing aid to Hanoi. What made Deng angry were the machinations of the Vietnamese to set up an Indochinese Federation, dominated by Vietnam. He even brought up the territories lost to Imperial Russia during the nineteenth century: 'There will come a time when China will perhaps restore them to itself.' Stung by this, Shevardnadze even asked the Politburo on 16 February to consider returning some territory around Vladivostok (it had been taken as recently as 1860).

The depth of Chinese feeling about the unequal relationship with Tsarist Russia and the Soviet Union was brought home to me in an interview, in August 1988, with a member of the Central Committee of the CPC who had studied in the Soviet Union. He delivered the first two sentences in Russian and then reverted to Mandarin. He proceeded to launch a violent tirade against the Russians for the way they had demeaned, insulted and taken advantage of the Chinese, beginning with the Treaty of Nerchinsk in 1689, the first treaty signed by the two countries. He went through all the subsequent treaties, ending with the one which Stalin had imposed on the People's Republic in 1950. I was warned never to trust Russians (not Soviets) as they were cheats, thieves, dishonourable and disreputable people.

To put it mildly, Gorbachev was not impressed by China's reforms and on 29 September 1986 informed his aides:

> The Chinese have developed agriculture on a private basis. They have achieved stunning success but there should not be euphoria as if China had resolved everything. But what next? They don't have fertilizers, technology or intensive methods. We have all of these but we have to unite these with personal interest. This is our problem. This is where we can insure a burst forward. Ilich (Lenin) tormented himself about how to unite the personal interest with socialism, and this is what we have to think and think about.

Gorbachev failed to appreciate that socialist agriculture had failed in China and that was the reason why private or capitalist agriculture had re-emerged.

He told Anatoly Chernyaev, in August 1988:

> I don't understand all the fuss about China . . . Yes, there is everything on the shelves in the shops but nobody is buying. It is a capitalist market. And the law of that market operates in such a fashion that prices are inflated to the point that everything lies around on shelves and when the goods go stale they sell them off cheaply.
>
> (Service 2015: 380–5)

What an extraordinary analysis! If anyone needs evidence that Gorbachev did not understand economics, this is it. I spent two months in China in the summer of 1988, mostly in Beijing, and can testify that goods moved off the shelves. There were two currencies: the hard and soft yuan, and one could buy choice goods with the former. There was a Friendship Store for foreigners but only hard currency was accepted. It is true the quality of the goods was not very high and this extended to the construction industry. I stayed with a middle-class family in a new flat and one can only say the quality of workmanship was very low. On the other hand, one had to be at a bakery at 6 a.m. to get the bread one wanted in Liaoyang, in central China. It did a roaring trade in wedding, birthday and other cakes which were as delicious as anything one could buy in London. I asked what the secret was: all the flour was imported.

Students were enthusiastic about Gorbachev's reforms and many wanted their own Gorbachev. Some were fasting in Tiananmen Square in the hope he would intercede on their behalf and they and their supporters cursed Deng. The Soviet leader was keen to repair relations with the Middle Kingdom, and some of Deng's speeches were published in Russian and favourably reviewed in *Pravda*.

On 16 May, Gorbachev arrived in Beijing and was met by Deng – the welcoming ceremony had to be held at Beijing airport because Tiananmen Square was full of students – who had warned him there was to be no hugging and kissing. He then proceeded to give him a lecture on Russian imperialism: 1.5 million km² had been stolen from China, no one would forget this, and there was no point in speeding up the normalisation of relations between the two Communist parties. When he met Li Peng, the prime minister showed no interest in more trade but concentrated on issues which divided the two countries. He regretted the depredations Japan had wrought in China during their occupation from 1937 to 1945 but said that pragmatism dictated economic relations as Japan was an advanced industrial country. It was high time that the Soviet Union and China agreed on their frontier. Gorbachev responded by saying he would like to demilitarise the frontier. He then met Zhao Ziyang, party general secretary; the discussion was very open, and it was clear that the Chinese Party boss wanted to go down the same route as the Soviet Union. But Deng did not, and hence Gorbachev was an unwelcome guest. However, he was able to make a speech in the Great Hall, on Tiananmen Square, in which he highlighted the fact that 436 short- and medium-range nuclear weapons would be destroyed in the Soviet East. He proposed that the Soviet railway network could form a new Silk Road by transporting Chinese goods to Europe, and he ridiculed Western commentators who saw Soviet and Chinese reforms as leading to the restoration of capitalism. Gorbachev asked China to provide desperately needed consumer goods and would be paid in raw materials, and he also requested a loan which was agreed.

Shevardnadze held talks with Jiang Zemin, Shanghai Party boss and Politburo Standing Committee member, who informed him China was willing to act as intermediaries to resolve the conflicts in South East Asia. Gorbachev was taken around a modern factory in Shanghai but was not impressed. It became clear that Deng and Li had little interest in expanding trade with the Soviet Union now that capitalist countries were investing in China. Gorbachev's inability to recognise that China was modernising rapidly was reflected in his comment to James Baker, in late May 1989, when he informed the American that China's scientific and technical capacity would soon hit the buffers (Service 2015: 387–8). Gorbachev held to the Western capitalist view that successful modernisation had to be accompanied by democratisation. What he had not realised was that China was undergoing economic democratisation but not political and that was the secret of its success.

Annoyed at Zhao's comments to the Soviet leader, Deng called a meeting on the morning of 17 May. He informed the leadership that the students' goal was to set up a 'bourgeois republic on the Western model'. Multi-party elections would cause chaos like the 'all-out civil war' the country had experienced during the Cultural Revolution. 'You don't need guns and cannons to have a civil war; fists and clubs will do just fine' (*New York Times*, 6 January 2001). National stability came before democracy, and the party thought that if it retreated any further it was finished. Deng informed them that the People's Liberation Army (PLA) would be brought in to restore order and martial law. Zhao Ziyang disagreed and asked Deng to rescind the martial law decision whereupon Deng reminded him that the minority submits to the majority. Rumours spread about the imminent declaration of martial law and over a million appeared on the streets. They supported the hunger strikers and called for Deng to go. Zhao and Li Peng went out to meet the students but Zhao conceded tearfully they had come too late. Deng was furious at Zhao's tears and words, and martial law was declared on 20 May.

Troops began moving into the city, but about two million Beijingers set up road blocks with buses and lorries and prevented them reaching their destinations; some units went over to the demonstrators. The troops retreated to their bases, and it looked as if China was sliding into anarchy.

On the night of 3–4 June, troops moved forward, encountering the usual road blocks. This time they opened fire and killed many ordinary citizens in the western parts of the city. In the bloodletting that night, most deaths occurred outside Tiananmen Square. The crowd's anger was vented on the soldiers and some of them were lynched. The Goddess of Democracy, a huge statute erected by the

Figure 13.5 Deng Xiaoping

Courtesy of the Library of Congress Prints and Photographs Division, Washington, DC 20540 USA, *US News and World Report* Magazine Photograph Collection, LC-DIG-ppmsca-09796.

students, which had stood facing Mao in Tiananmen Square, was flattened by tanks. This symbolised the squashing of hopes for democracy for decades to come. Demonstrators in sixty-three cities across China protested against the slaughter of the demonstrators in Beijing.

The official death toll was put at 200 but the most realistic was 775. Anatoly Lukyanov informed the Soviet Politburo, at its meeting on 4 October 1989, that the real number of casualties was 3,000. Gorbachev commented: 'We must be realists. Like us, they have to defend themselves. Three thousand – so what?' Deng Xiaoping's comment was as chilling: 'You call this a slaughter? This is a petty matter compared to what China saw not so many years ago.' It is difficult not to conclude that Deng was also taking revenge for the humiliation which he and his family had suffered during the Cultural Revolution.

The crackdown was a disaster for the demonstrators but even more for Deng as foreign investors could not get out of China fast enough. President Bush announced a cessation of weapons sales to Beijing, worth $600 million, as did the European Union, and the World Bank said it would end lending to the Middle Kingdom.

Jiang Zemin took over as party leader and reverted to pre-reform language. The entrepreneurs, who had benefited from reform, had sided with the students so they had to be closed down. Private companies were not to be permitted to compete with SOEs. Farmers were encouraged to go back into communes. Party secretaries reappeared in factories and farms and claimed precedence. Red had taken over from expert and profit was a dirty word again.

Deng took a back seat but was still acknowledged as the paramount leader. The period after Tiananmen Square was characterised by a fierce struggle between the conservatives and those who wanted to continue with market reforms. The execution of the Romanian dictator Nicolae Ceauşescu and his wife in December 1989 underlined the importance of military support as Ceauşescu had fallen after the army deserted him. The PLA cleansed its ranks of those regarded as unreliable with some being court-martialled, and the military budget was cranked up 15 per cent.

The increasing chaos in the Soviet Union was another warning of the consequences of not keeping a tight rein on political reform, and Jiang Zemin even called Gorbachev another Trotsky. He had studied in the Soviet Union and was as near to a technocrat as the party had. He surprised Richard Nixon on a private visit in 1989 by reciting the Gettysburg Address in English and was well-versed in Western classical music. He realised that the only course for China was to improve relations with developed countries as only they could provide the technology the country needed. This would permit the Middle Kingdom to become deeply embedded in the world economy and play a role in key international institutions. In foreign affairs, he was well served by the astute Qian Qichen, and in economic policy by Zhu Rongji, who later became prime minister.

Deng met military leaders and won them over so the PLA would now protect his reforms. In January 1992 he set off, accompanied by his daughter, on a southern tour which he disguised as a family holiday. He made for the Shenzhen, one of the SEZs, and was given a hero's welcome, and also went to Zhuhai and Shanghai. Deng said that without economic progress, the events of 3–4 June would have resulted in civil war. China had to move forward boldly and assimilate all the fruits of civilisation, including those of advanced capitalist countries.

In 1992, the constitution was amended to stipulate that the head of the party and the prime minister could only serve two five-year terms in office as no one wanted another Mao. At the 14th Party Congress, in October 1992, Deng underlined the fact that the party could not be challenged and that China would not adopt a real multi-party system. There are eight other political parties, but they are dubbed 'flower pot parties' as they perform merely a decorative function.

The battle between those who wanted to retain a centrally planned economy and those who favoured moving to a market economy lasted from 1978 to 1992, when the country moved to a market economy with Chinese characteristics.

An important factor was that the US opened its doors to Chinese goods, and China had an advantage over the Soviet Union in that overseas Chinese began to invest and added their know-how. Taiwan also joined in. Suzhou, near Shanghai, is a modern city and was built in collaboration with Singapore. Deng's attitude to foreign affairs was succinct: 'Bide our time and conceal our capabilities.' Hence Chinese foreign policy consisted of not interfering in the domestic politics of any country. China, instead, concentrated on trade as a way of expanding its influence. For instance, China signed 1,395 bilateral treaties between 1973 and 1982. Almost all of them were commercial, and the Middle Kingdom did not enter into any military alliances. Instead, it concentrated on building up the strength of the armed forces, and almost all the modern hardware came from the Soviet Union. The Chinese tactic was to order, say fifteen MiG fighters, but only take delivery of one. Then they copied it – reverse engineering – and cancelled the order for the other fourteen. They also did this with trade in civilian goods. A German company delivered a state-of-the-art printing press, and when the representative visited again he was shown a replica of his press. SEZs naturally involved technology transfer as did joint ventures with foreign firms. Thousands of Chinese students went to the US and Europe to study. The main subjects were science, engineering and computing. At Imperial College, University of London, the only arts subject Chinese study is the Russian language.

Eastern Europe

Only two communist regimes in Europe were endogenous: Yugoslavia and Albania. All the others – in Poland, the GDR, Hungary, Romania and Bulgaria – were exogenous. Without the Red Army, the communists would not have acquired and retained power. Czechoslovakia was in between. It was an endogenous revolution in February 1948 but an exogenous force – the Soviet Army – kept it in power.

Had it not been for Big Brother in Moscow, the communist regimes would have been swept away. Experience was to show that once communism collapsed in other states, Yugoslavia and Albania would go the same way.

So what would the new comrade in Moscow do? Having visited Czechoslovakia after the suppression of the Prague Spring, Gorbachev was well aware of the depth of hatred felt by most Czechs and Slovaks towards the Soviet Union. One of his university fiends, Zdeněk Mlynář, was able to report to him on the temperature of relations. Gorbachev took it for granted that Eastern Europe, once it had chosen communism, would remain communist. The debate was about the type of communism which could evolve.

Eastern Europe was secure behind the shields of the Soviet Army. The US and its NATO allies did not contemplate starting the Third World War over Bratislava or Sofia, and the Warsaw Pact had troops everywhere except in Romania and Bulgaria.

Gorbachev, in March 1985, told Eastern European leaders that the Soviet Army would no longer be used to resolve political conflicts on their patches. What were they to make of this? They were used to communist speak: the boss said one thing and meant another. All this talk of communist states being equal and responsible for their own affairs was probably eyewash. Anyway, it was important that the population of Eastern Europe continued to believe that if they stepped out of line, Ivan would come marching in. Then at the June 1988

Party Conference, Gorbachev reiterated this view: 'to reject freedom of choice is to oppose the objective movement of history itself. That is why the policy of force in all its forms has historically outlived itself.' At the United Nations in December 1988, he talked about the universal right of choice and claimed there were no exceptions.

Erich Honecker did not like what he saw in the Soviet Union. He was known as Erich 'Don't Tell Me Any Bad News' Honecker. Erich informed Gorby there was no need for perestroika in the GDR and it should be dropped in the Soviet Union. Alarmed at the contagious effect of information about the political and economic changes in the Soviet Union, the GDR leader took the unprecedented step of banning *Sputnik* which was a popular Soviet magazine. The Soviet ambassador responded by distributing it from the embassy!

Gorbachev was aware of the fragility of the Eastern European economies. On 23 October 1986, Nikolai Ryzhkov presented a bleak report to the Politburo. Poland was knee deep in debt and Hungary was looking into the abyss. No economist there thought the solution was integration with the Soviet economy – they were all looking westwards for salvation. Another analyst concluded that Warsaw Pact countries would collapse in 1989–90. Gorbachev waxed eloquent about the desire of the region to undertake perestroika, but this was a myth. In January 1989, Gorbachev even wondered what would happen if Hungary applied for membership of the European Economic Community (the European Union after 1993). He conceded that the Soviet Union could not provide any more aid, but Eastern Europe needed new technology, and inevitably it would look westwards. The Soviet military was also feeling the pinch, and its budget did not increase in 1989, the first time this had happened since the 1920s (Service 2015: 316, 367). So by 1989, the Soviet Union had accepted that the region could decide its own future.

There were two main reasons why Gorbachev did not want to intervene militarily in Eastern Europe. The first was that if he did, it would provide a precedent for the use of military force in the Soviet Union. Because most of the political establishment, the KGB and the military wanted force to be used at home, it would be impossible to resist. The other reason was economic. Military intervention in Eastern Europe would be followed by Western economic sanctions, and vital imports of grain, foodstuffs, fodder and technology would be embargoed. In 1989, the Soviet Union depended more on the Western world than vice versa, and so sanctions would weaken the Soviet economy. Under such a scenario it is difficult to imagine Gorbachev surviving.

Had Eastern Europeans known that Gorbachev would remain in office and that the Soviet military would not intervene, they would have blown the communists away before 1989. They were delighted by perestroika and the reforms it brought in. Taking the party out of the industrial economy, having multi-candidate elections to parliament, the laws on cooperatives and individual farming and the setting up of new banks were all Eastern European aspirations. They all wanted their own Gorby.

Poland

The rise of Solidarity in 1980–1 held out hopes for radical reform in Poland, but the fact that the Polish military remained loyal to the Polish United Workers' Party meant that the movement was suppressed and driven underground. Wojciech Jaruzelski knew that if the military remained loyal, he was secure in office. That was his first priority, and his second priority was to effect gradual change. In April 1984, Gromyko delivered a dismal report on Poland and concluded that the country was looking to the West for economic salvation. He criticised Jaruzelski for promoting the emergence of a kulak class in the countryside; Ustinov thought that the Polish military was too passive and, anyway, they were all sons of Solidarity. One solution was to give Jaruzelski a stiff talking-to!

Hungary was an obvious role model for Poland and the Hungarians had their New Economic Mechanism, but there was nothing similar in Poland. Reform economists worked with the Hungarian government, but this was not the case in Poland as all reformist economic thinking took place outside the party. In 1988, price rises afforded Solidarity activists the opportunity to lead strikes, and after a strike by coal miners – the elite of the working class – the government managed to lose a vote of confidence in the unreformed Polish Parliament or Sejm. Mieczysław Rakowski, a more open-minded communist, became prime minister.

Round table discussions with social organisations, headed by Lech Wałęsa and Solidarity, got under way in February 1989 and they proved a model for other communist states. It provided a forum whereby communist governments gradually surrendered more and more of their power.

In April 1989, Solidarity was again legal. The Roman Catholic Church was afforded full legal rights, although this had not hindered it in the past, and its new Primate, Cardinal Glemp, was a conservative. There were to be parliamentary elections, and 35 per cent of the seats could be freely contested. Wałęsa flew to Rome and thanked those at the Gemelli Clinic who had cared for the pope after the assassination attempt of May 1981. 'It's hard to imagine Solidarity would have survived without him,' he told them. The pope received him as a head of state.

On 4 June, Solidarity won all but one of the 100 seats in the upper house and just over a third of seats in the Sejm. President Jaruzelski made General Czesław Kiszczak – who had a reputation for suppressing dissent and was dubbed the 'thinking man's thug' – prime minister in August 1989.

President George H.W. Bush dropped by in July 1989, but the crowds in Warsaw were nothing like those that had welcomed President Nixon in 1972. Jaruzelski told Bush he was reluctant to run for president as Solidarity would oppose him, but Bush pressed him to run because a dangerous political vacuum would ensue if he stepped down. Bush thought Jaruzelski 'very special, particularly complex and yet clearheaded'. Bush found Wałęsa's aspirations 'unrealistic', especially the idea that Americans would buy up Polish farms. However, they did agree that German reunification was coming and because of this Poland wanted Bonn to agree on the country's western frontier.

Some Poles regarded this humiliation of the PUWP as the collapse of communism. The fact that the party accepted its defeat and did not attempt to use the military to defend its power signalled that it was dying a slow death.

The new prime minister was Tadeusz Mazowiecki, from Solidarity. Jacek Kuron, one of the Solidarity leaders, on seeing a government car draw up outside his apartment, assumed that he was going to be arrested once again, but he discovered that he was the new minister of labour and the limousine and chauffeur were part of the perks! Rakowski had made a last-ditch attempt to prevent Mazowiecki becoming prime minister, but Gorbachev phoned him and told him to concede. There was someone else who was trying to turn the tide back: President Ceauşescu of Romania. He wrote to the Warsaw Pact leaders and advocated military intervention in Poland – it was ironic that a Romanian should resurrect the Brezhnev doctrine. Rakowski also received the message and leaked it to the press. Gorbachev rebuked Ceauşescu and Vladimir Kryuchkov, the KGB chief, dropped in and wished the new Polish government well.

By the end of 1989, the communist system had been dismantled. The clause in the constitution which afforded primacy to the PUWP was removed, and the country changed its name from the People's Republic of Poland to the Republic of Poland. Leszek Balcerowicz became minister of finance and began moving to a capitalist economy but he was less radical than some other pro-market economists.

As a consultant in Eastern Europe in the late 1980s, I had the task of finding economic advisers to help with foreign investment. As an academic I had access to economists in the Academy of Sciences (except in East Berlin). In Budapest, I asked who I should consult in Warsaw and was told: 'Leszek Balcerowicz'. 'And in Prague?' 'Vaclav Klaus'. 'In Moscow?' 'Egor Gaidar'. It transpired that they had all been collaborating in drafting proposals for the transition from a planned to a market economy.

When Jaruzelski resigned as president, in December 1990, Lech Wałęsa took over as president of Poland. In October 1991, the first fully democratic elections in Poland since 1945 saw the Solidarity coalition parties sweep the board.

Hungary

János Kádár, put in power by Moscow in 1956, surprised many sceptics by becoming the most moderate communist ruler in the region. In the beginning he was known as a quisling and the 'iron fist in a velvet glove' but later he became the 'reformer'. His lugubrious appearance and lack of personal vanity made him appear a transitional figure, but it masked the fact that he was the master of the possible. That is, he knew the outer limits of Soviet tolerance and the population did as well. Hungary had the most reformed economy and intellectual life in the communist region. The searing experience of 1956 conditioned the country to accept the fact that it was a vassal state of the Soviet Union. Marxism-Leninism, if taken seriously, could get you into trouble and so ideology played a minor role in national life. So relaxed were the Americans about Kádár that they returned the symbol of Hungarian nationhood, the Crown of St Stephen, in 1978, from its repository in Fort Knox. Even Mrs Margaret Thatcher was pleasantly impressed by the modest Kádár.

In 1981, 5.5 million Hungarians travelled abroad including almost half a million to capitalist countries. This meant that about half the population left the country and the vast majority went back. Two million Western foreigners visited Hungary which revealed that there were no disaffected political groups. Pope John Paul II wanted the Roman Catholic Church to take a more aggressive stance against the regime, but Catholics politely declined as they had 'goulash communism' and it tasted fine.

In June 1989 in Budapest, US Secretary of State James Baker was told that when perestroika began in the Soviet Union, Hungary was implementing measures more radical than those envisaged in Moscow. When the first private restaurant opened in Moscow in 1986, Hungary had about 35,000 private businesses. The state fixed a thousand prices, but the market fixed another million and cooperatives and private plots flourished. Hungary was the only country in Eastern Europe which was self-sufficient in food. Until 1983, the Soviet Union had to subsidise Hungary, but when the money ran out in Moscow, Kádár switched to the West and obtained large loans. By 1987, Western debts had risen to $18 billion, and domestic prices and inflation were getting out of hand.

When Kádár died, in July 1989, hundreds of thousands lined the streets to bid him passage to a better world. Nowadays, he is regarded as one of the greatest Hungarians of the twentieth century, but that list, to be truthful, is not very long!

Kádár was ill-suited to the challenges of the Gorbachev era with its plethora of political and economic reforms, and foreign policy was also offering opportunities which he could not respond to. He was removed from power in May 1988 and replaced by Károly Grósz who had been prime minister and was a careful, uncharismatic apparatchik in the Kádár mould. The radicals in the leadership were Imre Poszgay and Rezsö Nyers, the leading economic reformer. They created the beginnings of a stock market, reduced business taxes and permitted full foreign ownership of Hungarian companies. Later in the year Forum and the Alliance of Free Democrats emerged as a result of dialogue with the HSWP.

Poszgay set the pace of change although there was no popular pressure to do so. In January 1989, he announced that the events of 1956 should be viewed as a 'popular uprising'. This was sensational as the standard communist view was that 1956 was a 'counter-revolution'. The Politburo set up committees to review the previous three decades.

Another Poszgay sensation was that the HSWP should prepare for life in a multi-party system, and legislation was passed which permitted this in February 1989. The same month the HSWP abandoned its claim to a monopoly of political power. In April, Moscow agreed to withdraw Soviet troops from Hungary by June 1991, but on Gorbachev's insistence, this was kept secret.

In May, the party accepted that the government should be responsible to parliament and not to it. Round table discussions between the HSWP and the democratic opposition led to further dramatic changes. Imre Nagy and four others, executed in the wake of the 1956 Revolution, were reburied with state honours. Symbolically, all the other victims were also reburied.

In October, most members of the HSWP split off and formed the Hungarian Socialist Party and adopted social democracy as their guiding principle. Some old parties were resurrected such as the Smallholders' Party and the Social Democrats. In late October, parliament decreed parliamentary elections and the direct election of a president. On 23 October 1989, the anniversary of the outbreak of the 1956 Revolution, the People's Republic of Hungary became the Republic of Hungary and the communist era was over. The transition of power from communism to post-communism in Hungary was the most peaceful in the Soviet bloc.

The German Democratic Republic

The GDR was the Soviet Union's stepchild. Egon Bahr concluded that Walter Ulbricht was a 'politically talented snake' and Edward Ochab, the Polish leader in 1956, thought that he was a 'good communist' but 'his brains were a bit defective' (Toranska 1987: 70). (Was Ochab implying that only someone with a defective brain could be a good communist?)

The hard winter of 1969–70 scuttled him. Potatoes were in short supply and Egypt sent some, and electricity spluttered on and off. Ulbricht was pushed aside in 1971, and Erich Honecker became Moscow's comrade in East Berlin. Willi Stoph, the prime minister, read a litany of complaints about the 'old goat's' mismanagement of the GDR: botched automation of production, motorways through cities with no traffic and so on. Ulbricht died in 1973 but no flags flew at half-mast and the old GDR died with him.

Honecker turned out to be just as troublesome and irked Brezhnev by claiming that the GDR was farther along the road to communism than the Soviet Union; this was hard for the Soviets to swallow as the GDR was economically dependent on Moscow. Gorbachev found Honecker very trying as Erich talked in mechanical phrases and could not be drawn into a real discussion. Everything was fine in the GDR, and Gorbachev should give up perestroika and glasnost at home. The two had crossed swords before when Chernenko had summoned the SED leader to Moscow in the summer of 1984 to account for his relations with Chancellor Helmut Kohl. The whole Politburo was of the mind that Honecker was becoming dependent on West German loans and this had to stop. As Chernenko was too ill to receive Honecker, Gorbachev stepped in and savaged the GDR leader. Ustinov informed the Politburo that the behaviour of the other Eastern European leaders was just as suspect.

President Ronald Reagan set the cat among the pigeons on 12 June 1987. Standing in front of the Brandenburg Gate, he had a message for the Soviet leader. 'If you seek peace, if you seek prosperity for the Soviet Union and Eastern Europe, if you seek liberalization: come here to this Gate. Mr Gorbachev,

Figure 13.6 President Ronald Reagan

Courtesy of the Library of Congress Prints and Photographs Division, Washington, DC 20540 USA, LC-USZ62–13040.

Mr Gorbachev, tear down this wall'. Actually it was not Gorbachev's wall to pull down, but that was beside the point. Honecker, in response, vented his fury on television and thought it would last another 100 years.

Erich was the type of comrade who thought if one had three square meals a day and a bed at night, what else did one need? His wife Margot was the minister of education and a hard-line communist. After the collapse of communism, the Honeckers lived in Santiago, Chile, as there was a special bond between them and Chilean communists. After General Augusto Pinochet's coup in 1973, communists sought to escape and with borders closed, some communists were smuggled aboard GDR ships in jute sacks with the cargo of fruit and canned fruit.

GDR planners did not wish to draw any positive lessons from the *Wirtschafts-wunder* (economic miracle) in the Federal Republic. An East German told me, in the late 1970s, that the *Wirtschaftswunder* in West Germany was nothing. 'Just look at the *Wirtschaftswunder* in the GDR!' This was an example of the level of debate one enjoyed (if that is the word) with East German officials.

I had many discussions with East Germans in the 1960s and 1970s. The best place was on a train passing through Poland or in Poland! On one occasion, in Warsaw, an East German official concluded our discussion by saying that he wished he could speak Polish as well as I spoke German! Had he realised I was British the conversation would have lapsed into *Parteichi-nesisch* (Party Chinese or communist-speak). However, one could have interesting conversations with some East German academics at conferences. In 1986, I asked one what he could do to improve the situation in the GDR, and he informed me he had no intention of doing anything until Honecker departed the scene. In other words, the price of being a critic was too high. This attitude paralysed the country and led to people living two lives: the official and the private.

The secret police, the Stasi, were very active. There were more Stasi officers per head of the GDR population than Gestapo per head of the population in Germany before 1945. As I had had regular conversations with Stasi officers in London, there was a Stasi file on me in East Berlin, but I decided not to read it because I knew from friends that I would encounter some nasty revelations. The Stasi had informers everywhere in Britain and abroad, but it did not do them much good. I was careful to make the point in my conversations with Stasi officers that the planned economy was a failure and only market-linked reforms could revive the GDR economy. One officer did not bother to hide the fact that he was Stasi, and he came to my office in the University of London on a regular basis. He greeted me with 'Good morning' then switched to German. He wanted to know my opinion about the Thatcher government, foreign policy and a host of other questions. Finally, he stood up and said in English: 'Thank you. See you again.'

My wife's family had relatives in East Berlin and East Germany. I visited a cousin regularly who was a professor of Greek mythology at the Humboldt University in East Berlin and he was a mine of information. A convinced communist and member of the SED, he waxed eloquently about life and said that many students arrived at university giving the impression they were schizophrenics. They knew what they had to say but did not believe it. His job was to explain that the ideology reflected real life, but in the 1980s he changed. He related that he usually went into the university library on Saturday mornings to do research. He was hauled in by the Stasi who told him that they had been studying him closely but could not work out what he was doing. He informed them that he was engaged in research, but they simply refused to believe that anyone would work on Saturday mornings without being paid! Eventually they had to let him go because they had nothing on him.

The only area of life where there was anything akin to dissent was in the churches. The Lutheran Church in Germany traditionally supports the state. Protestants concentrated on opposing the arms race and the stationing of NATO missiles in Europe, and they were also unhappy about the militarisation of East German society. Someone had a brainwave and came up with a brilliant biblical slogan: Swords into Ploughshares. 'They shall beat their swords into ploughshares and their spears into pruning hooks. Nation shall not lift up sword against nation. And never again shall they learn war.' Young East Germans sewed an embroidered badge on their jeans, and it depicted a man bending a sword with a hammer. The original was a statue in New York which was a gift from the Soviet Union, and it became a symbol of passive resistance laced with the delicious irony that the original had been a present from Big Brother.

There was a lot of dialogue with foreign churches. One of those who engaged in debate was Paul Oestreicher, an Anglican priest who told me that he and his interlocutors chose venues where they thought the Stasi could not overhear them. They were amazed to learn after 1990 that the Stasi had recorded every word of their conversations. It also transpired that some of the Protestant pastors were Stasi officers and others were Stasi agents.

No one in the GDR thought that communism could be overthrown, and what they desired was the reform of the existing system. Gorbachev kept on saying that each country had the right to decide its own future. He repeated this twice in July 1989 – at the summit of the Warsaw Pact in Bucharest and at the Council of Europe meeting in Strasbourg – that the Brezhnev Doctrine was dead.

Honecker knew that the old days of subsidised oil and cheap loans had gone and the fact that Moscow had caved in to the Poles in 1980–1 revealed that it was in no position militarily or economically to help out the Eastern Europeans. Erich ruefully conceded that the GDR would have to look after itself, but the problem was that the country did not have the raw material or resource base to sustain a modern economy.

Erich is at his wits' end. In desperation he calls in the country's bishops. 'Look, I'm no believer but I need advice. The Party does not listen to me anymore; the economy has gone to the dogs and Gorbachev is worse than useless. What can I do to turn things round?' 'Well, our Lord when facing a problem performed a miracle.' 'Could I perform a miracle?' 'Well . . .' 'Jesus walked on water. Could I do that?' 'Well . . .' 'Let's try.' The next day Honecker appears at one of the Berlin lakes and then proceeds to walk across the water. 'Look,' says a Berliner to his neighbour, 'he can't swim!'

At first Gorbachev was reluctant to attend the fortieth anniversary celebrations of the founding of the GDR on 7 October 1989. He had to go because it would have been a devastating blow to the SED had he boycotted the event, but talking to Honecker was like talking to a brick wall. In private, Gorbachev called him an 'arsehole'. During the celebrations the crowds greeted Gorbachev enthusiastically, and 'We want our own Gorby' was one chant. Another chant was *'Wir sind das Volk'* ('we are the people'). In other words, power rested with the people. Gorbachev later told his listeners: 'History punishes those who are left behind.'

On Monday evenings, for months, a weekly prayer meeting had been transforming itself into a peaceful demonstration in the Lutheran Frauenkirche, in Leipzig. On 9 October, there were 70,000 massed outside the church after prayers had finished, and they refused to disperse. As the police could not cope with such a crowd, heavily armed soldiers and tanks were brought out to meet them. Would there be bloodshed? The GDR leadership had welcomed the massacre on Tiananmen Square in June. One of those who helped ensure that there was no violence was Kurt Masur, chief conductor of the Leipzig Gewandhaus Orchestra, and the demonstrators were permitted to march on. Another was Vyacheslav Kochemasov, the Soviet ambassador in East Berlin, who ordered Soviet troops to stay in barracks without consulting Moscow. He asked for confirmation the following day and it was granted. Masur and Kochemasov were the heroes of the hour. The communists had lost their nerve, and those who wanted to bring down the communist regime knew that the GDR was living on borrowed time.

A coup removed Erich Honecker from power on 18 October, but his successor was the lugubrious, uninspiring Egon Krenz, a member of the Sorb Slav minority in the GDR. On 24 October, Krenz called for a candid report on the state of the GDR economy, but it made dismal reading as labour productivity in the GDR was at least 40 per cent below that of the Federal Republic. The GDR was facing financial collapse.

To make matters worse for East Berlin, Gennady Gerasimov, the witty Soviet foreign ministry spokesman, delivered his famous Sinatra quip on *Good Morning America* on 25 October. 'We now have the Sinatra Doctrine. He has a song: "I Did It My Way." So every country decides on its own which road to take.'

So could Krenz make a difference? When he talked to Gorbachev on the phone, on 1 November, the latter made clear he was quite aware of the mess the GDR economy was in and it was all Honecker's fault. Krenz said that if the country did not receive help, living standards would drop 30 per cent and such an event would be politically unacceptable, but the Soviet Union could provide little aid.

Krenz then wanted to know what space Gorbachev had allocated the GDR and the Federal Republic in his 'common European home'. He pathetically pointed out that the GDR was the child of the Soviet Union and that 'paternity for the child has to be accepted'. Gorbachev explained to Krenz that the Soviet Union was developing closer relations with the Federal Republic so East Berlin should ask Bonn for money. According to Krenz, Gorbachev assured him that the Yalta and Potsdam agreements would not be revised, and he believed that Gorbachev thought the GDR would continue as a state. He still thinks the Soviet leader deceived him.

At 6.53 p.m. on 9 November, East German TV carried a press conference chaired by Günter Schabowski, a Politburo member and a former editor of the party newspaper, *Neues Deutschland*. Surely he would know how to respond to journalists. The press conference was a shambles as Schabowski tried to articulate the new policy on travel. GDR citizens were to be allowed to visit West Berlin but had to obtain a visa in order to do so. 'When are these regulations going into effect?,' asked a Western journalist. Schabowski shuffled his papers and responded: 'As far as I know, this takes place immediately, without delay.' The Associated Press, at 7 p.m., carried the sensational news: 'According to information supplied by SED Politburo member Günter Schabowski, the GDR is opening its borders.' Hundreds of thousands of East Berliners converged on the border crossings and demanded to be permitted to pass through.

Eventually, at 11.30 p.m., Lt Colonel Harald Jäger ordered forty-six armed guards to open the barrier and stand aside, and the other border crossings followed suit. The GDR was trampled to death in the stampede to get to West Berlin.

Speaking twenty-five years later, Jäger commented:

My world was collapsing and I felt abandoned by my Party and military commanders. I was on the one hand hugely disappointed but also relieved that it had ended peacefully. There could have been a different outcome . . . When I saw Schabowski on TV, I thought, 'What a load of crap! He should have known that East Germans would head for the exits when they heard that. But they didn't inform us at all. We were kept in the dark.'

Jäger made a series of desperate phone calls to his superiors asking what to do. One told him to let those with the necessary documents through and send the rest home. When he called again and said he had to do something, he was told to let a few through in the hope it would calm the situation, but he could see the crowd was getting restive. 'There were fears they could get their hands on our weapons.' His border guards were urging him to do something, but they didn't know what it should be. 'I was only a lieutenant colonel and didn't have the authority. But when no one from above would give any orders, I was practically forced to take action.' At 11.30 p.m. he let everyone through, including future German chancellor Angela Merkel. 'It wasn't me who opened the Wall. It was the East German citizens who gathered that evening. The only thing I can be credited with is that it happened without any blood being spilt' (*The Times*, 7 November 2014).

I was in Berlin on that historic day attending a conference on Forty Years of Divided Germany in the Reichstag which backed on to the Wall at the Brandenburg Gate. On the morning of 10 November, young GDR conscripts were perched on the Wall and they were delighted but their officers looked as if their world had collapsed, which it had. The mood was euphoric, and about 3.5 million GDR citizens poured into West Berlin which had a population of about a million. Each received 100 marks (about £35) to spend. The ill, the halt, the lame and the crippled came, carried along by their families. One enterprising fellow

Figure 13.7 Fall of the Berlin Wall on the night of 9–10 November 1989
© imageBROKER/Alamy.

crossed and recrossed seven times before he was rumbled, and the most sought after products were bananas and pornography. A group of Japanese tourists asked me for a piece of the Wall, but a West Berlin police officer told me not to touch the Wall. 'It is the property of the German Democratic Republic', he stated. As soon as he had gone, I used a pick to knock a hole in the Wall. On the other side were two young Vopos, or police, swinging their Kalashnikovs. They looked at me and I looked at them. The day before they would have trained their guns on me. That day they just looked and continued on their way.

Chancellor Helmut Kohl launched a ten-point plan for German reunification without consulting anyone abroad; this caused great annoyance in Moscow, Paris, London and Washington and everyone hoped Gorbachev would veto the plan. When Hans Modrow, the GDR prime minister, visited Moscow on 30 January 1990, he informed Gorbachev that a majority of GDR citizens no longer supported the concept of two German states, and so it was impossible to preserve the republic.

The Alliance for Germany, backed by Kohl's Christian Democratic Union, won the elections in April 1990. I was in Leipzig during an election rally addressed by Kohl. What anthem should be sung beforehand? Eventually, it was decided the pre-1933 anthem would be appropriate, and music and words were handed out as no one knew either.

The West German Social Democratic Party (SPD) opposed a united Germany, favouring a democratic GDR as did most churchmen in the East. Willy Brandt, a pre-1933 social democrat, was strongly in favour of unification. It is striking that the older generation wanted Germany to be one but the younger generation of socialists preferred two Germanies.

When James Baker met Gorbachev in February 1990, he was at pains to stress that the US was not seeking any advantage from these developments. The Soviet leader then saw Kohl and said that it was up to the Germans to decide things for themselves. Gorbachev hoped for a neutral, united Germany but Kohl, now full of self-confidence, rejected this and proposed that a united Germany join NATO. In March, the Alliance for Germany, backed by Kohl's own party, the CDU, won the East German elections and, in April, the new government proposed that unification be achieved according to the federal constitution. The GDR would simply be integrated into West Germany and thereby disappear. In May, the GDR signed the state treaty with the Federal Republic on economic, monetary and social unity, and the Deutsche Mark (DM) became the common currency on 1 July. Kohl committed a grave error in agreeing that East German marks would be converted into DM at a rate of one to one, and this made almost all East German goods uncompetitive in West Germany.

The reunification of Germany, on 3 October 1990, resulted from the coming together of three factors: the Gorbachev revolution in the Soviet Union; the collapse of the GDR economy which led to large numbers of its citizens making for West Germany; and George H. W. Bush's determination to make German unity one of the crowning achievements of his presidency. The Soviet leader simply conceded everything the man in the White House wanted. On the important point of whether a united Germany would become a member of NATO, pressure from Bush and Baker led eventually to Gorbachev giving in, orally, to the consternation of his officials. In his memoirs, Gorbachev claims that the decision to allow Germans to decide their own security arrangements – it was a foregone conclusion that they would vote for NATO – originated with him and not Bush. The White House sees it the other way round. One of the reasons for the acceptance of Germany in NATO was Kohl's close personal relationship with the Soviet leader.

One striking example of this took place at Arkhyz, in the north Caucasus, in July 1990. Here, in formal and informal meetings, the two leaders agreed many of the details of reunification. Without consulting Shevardnadze, who had done all the spadework on Soviet-German relations, Gorbachev abandoned all claims as an occupying power and any restriction on German sovereignty, including a united Germany joining NATO. He agreed to the withdrawal of Soviet forces, with the German promising to build accommodation in the Soviet Union for the returning personnel and the Germans also paid for the troops to leave. Had Gorbachev not been so desperate for German financial aid, he could have struck a much more advantageous bargain. German reunification, and the Soviet terms for it, were not discussed in the Politburo. Shevardnadze was unhappy as he was aware that the ire of the military and the conservatives would descend on him for 'losing' the GDR.

The Soviet garrison of about 350,000 soldiers was to be withdrawn. Bonn paid a handsome sum to build accommodation for the returning soldiers, but it was never built as the money was embezzled by various officials. There was never any risk of the East German population attacking Soviet soldiers as relations between the two were not hostile, as I observed on numerous occasions. Only officers were allowed to visit towns when off-duty and ordinary soldiers were locked in their barracks where discipline was harsh.

A determined opponent of unification was Margaret Thatcher. In September 1989, in Moscow, she told Gorbachev that the 'reunification of Germany is not in the interests of Britain and Western Europe . . . We don't want a united Germany.' It would lead to post-war European borders being changed. 'We cannot allow that because such a development would undermine the stability of the whole international situation and could endanger our security' (*The Times*, 11 September 2009). She was also against the dissolution of the Warsaw Pact, and Chernyaev records that she asked for the following remarks not to be minuted as she was resolutely opposed to the unification of Germany and wanted to tell Gorbachev things that she could not say in public (Service 2015: 408).

France's President Mitterrand was also horrified at the prospect of a united Germany in the near term and wanted it to happen over a ten-year period. François Mauriac quipped that he loved Germany so much he preferred two of them. The Italian prime minister, Giulio Andreotti, went one better. 'We love the Germans so much that the more Germanies there are the better'. The French could not understand why Gorbachev had not vetoed the whole idea. Jacques Attali, an adviser, even said he would go and live on Mars if this happened, but he later moved to London as head of the European Bank for Reconstruction and Development.

The GDR needed Western currency. Alexander Schalck-Golodhowski, a Stasi colonel, acted as the GDR fixer. One estimate is that he earned the GDR DM25 billion (£8 billion) between 1964 and 1989. He procured consumer goods for the leadership – including soft porn – negotiated loans and business deals, and sold arms to Third World countries (when the Ethiopian dictator Mengistu needed weapons and bread, 'it was my phone that would ring,' he said). Schalck-Golodhowski also sold political prisoners and their relatives to West Germany (33,755 political prisoners and 250,000 of their relatives were sold for a sum of DM3.5 billion), and works of art were removed from their East German owners and sold to West German dealers. The art ranged from antique furniture to Picasso, and the owners had to hand it over or face a huge tax bill. Toxic West German nuclear waste was imported and disposed of. There were investments in Spanish holiday resorts and luxury Austrian hotels and secret accounts in Switzerland and Liechtenstein, and some bankers in West Berlin and Zürich were more than willing to do business with Schalck-Golodhowski. One of his biggest coups was, in 1983, to obtain a DM1 billion (£300 million) credit from Franz Josef Strauss, the top Bavarian politician, who was anti-communist on paper. A Bavarian sausage magnate was keen to gain access to cheap GDR pork and this facilitated the deal. One

West German contact commented: 'He gave the impression that the whole of the GDR was up for sale' (*The Times*, 1 July 2015).

Czechoslovakia

Czechs and Slovaks learnt a hard lesson in 1968: 'Don't bait the Russian bear.' Sullenly, they gradually accepted their lot, but a small group of active dissidents came together in 1977 to form what was known as Charter 77. The Chartists were a disparate bunch as they included expelled communists, academics, the religious and idealists, the most famous of whom was playwright Václav Havel. They were very serious people and studied classical Greek philosophy, Shakespeare and European literature; they kept burning the torch of independent thought as they were preparing for post-communist Czechoslovakia. The Chartists invited Western academics to come and address their seminars. They were smuggled in and were inevitably discovered, and that meant no more visas and prison terms for the Chartists. Havel was used to going to prison but stressed that he and the others needed to maintain moral superiority over the regime and had to cultivate their 'own garden'. The ranks of the Chartists provided many of the top state officials after the collapse of communism.

Gustáv Husák, a Slovak, was a sea of contradictions. He spent the years 1954 to 1960 in jail, but he, not Dubček, was the first to call for democratisation in 1968. After the August 1968 invasion, he was initially opposed to the Soviets but was accepted by Moscow as Dubček's successor.

Gorbachev's perestroika lit a fuse under communism in the region, but reform-minded communists were as rare as hen's teeth and new ideas came from outside the party. Gustav Husák resigned as party boss in December 1987 but carried on as president. He was succeeded by the uninspiring Miloš Jakeš who had welcomed the Soviet invasion of 1968. The Roman Catholic Church, even though it was a minority faith in the Czech lands (Bohemia and Moravia), was the dominant religion in Slovakia, and it began to demand greater religious freedom. In 1989, Prague stopped jamming Radio Free Europe and everyone could then listen to Václav Havel.

The fall of the Berlin Wall was the death knell of communism in Czechoslovakia. If the previously submissive East Germans could topple a communist regime, why not the Czechs and Slovaks? The crisis in the GDR was fuelled by economic decline but this was not the case in Czechoslovakia. A student demonstration in Prague, on 17 November 1989, was brutally dispersed and a student was 'shot dead'. He was filmed walking away after his 'death' had been recorded. In other words, the whole episode had been a put-up job by the secret police to discredit the old leadership and introduce a new team acceptable to the West.

On 18 November, the Civic Forum, headed by Havel and consisting of actors and students, came into being. Its membership became much wider than Charter 77 and included such figures as Alexander Dubček who was the hero of the hour. On 24 November, the party sacked Jakeš and replaced him with a nonentity.

Havel and Prime Minister Adamec then struck a deal: the government would agree to free speech, free elections and foreign travel if Havel would join a coalition government.

The coup de grâce to the communist regime was administered in Moscow. A Warsaw Pact meeting declared that the invasion of 1968 had been misguided and illegal and because all those in official positions owed their roles to the invasion, they were forced to resign. The prime minister stepped down on 7 December and Husák as president on 9 December, and leading Chartists joined the government. The most dramatic promotion was that of Jiři Dienstbier who was working as a stoker. When the foreman phoned his wife demanding to know why he had not turned up for work, she informed him: 'Jiři will not be coming in today. He has just become the Foreign Minister of our country'. On 28 December, Dubček was made speaker of parliament and the following day, parliament elected Václav Havel president of the Republic of Czechoslovakia.

The country had passed from being an orthodox communist state to a democracy within a span of just over a month. The catalyst was the brutal suppression of the student demonstration on 17 November. Havel coined the expression 'velvet revolution' to describe the peaceful collapse of communism, but none of this would have been possible without the revolution in the Soviet Union. The fall of the Berlin Wall was another powerful stimulus. I did an interview on BBC television about the situation in Czechoslovakia after the fall of the Wall. I said that communism in Czechoslovakia was doomed and could not survive, but the presenter looked at me in amazement and clearly did not believe his ears. He and others had got used to the idea that communism was impregnable.

Bulgaria

A young Bulgarian lady, looking as if she had just stepped out of a Parisian salon, came to see me in the University of London in early 1988. She informed me that Bulgaria wished to move away from the Soviet Union and towards Europe and Sofia wanted democracy and a capitalist economy. I did not believe a word she said, but my scepticism turned out to be ill-founded. Things were changing in Bulgaria which was regarded as the most supine pro-Soviet regime in the region; cynics described Bulgaria as the 'sixteenth republic of the Soviet Union'. A Bulgarian joke was: 'How would you describe Bulgarian-Soviet relations? Simple. They are like a cow which grazes in Bulgaria but is milked in the Soviet Union.'

Todor Zhivkov, nicknamed Uncle Tosho, based his power on tight security and between 1985 and 1989, 105 people were shot for trying to cross the border without a visa. Loans and technological aid from the Soviet Union kept the country going and the Soviets even built a nuclear power plant. There were no Soviet troops in Bulgaria but Moscow did not rank Bulgaria very highly, and it was easier for a Soviet citizen to visit there than Poland or Hungary. The main problem concerned the Turkish minority. Nine hundred thousand ethnic Turks were obliged to adopt Bulgarian names between December 1984 and March

1985, and perhaps a hundred Turks died violently. The Turkish language and books in Turkish were banned as was circumcision, and Zhivkov suggested that those who did not agree could leave for Turkey. Over 300,000 crossed the border before Ankara closed it.

There was nothing comparable in Bulgaria to Charter 77 or Solidarity. Hence change would have to come from within. A Club for the Support of Perestroika, headed by Zhelyu Zhelev, was formed in November 1988 and a free trade union appeared in February 1989. The creeping coup against Zhivkov began in the summer of 1989, and one of the leaders was Petur Mladenov, the foreign minister, and the minister of defence came on board. Things speeded up at a meeting of the Warsaw Pact in Bucharest in July. Gorbachev took the unprecedented step of walking down the hall to speak to Mladenov, but protocol demanded that he ask Zhivkov's permission first before moving on to the foreign minister. Mladenov informed the Soviet leader that Zhivkov would be removed in November, and Gorbachev simply commented that it was an internal Bulgarian affair. On 10 November 1989, Todor Zhivkov, First Secretary of the Bulgarian Communist Party since March 1954, was voted out of office but he would get a pension and a villa. The fall of the Berlin Wall ensured that the coup was bloodless and unchallenged. Mladenov succeeded Zhivkov as president a week later but the Bulgarian opposition had played no part in Zhivkov's removal. On 14 November, sixteen different organisations formed the Union of Democratic Forces (UDF), headed by Zhelev, and almost all of them were party members.

Mladenov headed off a revolution by promising free elections but was forced to resign in July 1990 after a video was shown in which he had advocated the use of tanks against demonstrations in December 1989. In June 1990, Zhelev won a seat in the Grand National Assembly to draft a new constitution, and, in August, the assembly elected him president of Bulgaria by a two-thirds majority.

Romania

Nicolae Ceauşescu had some grand nicknames such as 'The Genius of the Carpathians' and 'The Titan of Titans', but locals also called him 'Our Dracula'. Gorbachev referred to him as the 'Romanian Führer' intent on building 'dynastic socialism'. The secret police, the Securitate, were, by quite a distance, the most brutal in Eastern Europe, and at least a thousand dissidents were murdered. An estimated 617,000 were imprisoned, and 120,000 are thought to have died behind bars during his twenty-five-year reign. He took nepotism to an elevated level and about sixty family members were in top positions in the state. Elena, the dictator's wife, sat on every important committee in the country. In a bid to beautify Bucharest, whole districts were flattened in order to build huge, soulless blocks, and peasants were forcibly moved to 'agrotowns'.

He managed to convince the Soviets to withdraw their troops from Romania in 1958. The invasion of Czechoslovakia was perceived as a threat to Romania and was condemned, as was the Soviet invasion of Afghanistan. When the Soviet

Union and its allies boycotted the Los Angeles Olympic Games in 1984, Romania sent a full complement and won many medals.

Ceauşescu's independent line in foreign affairs won him many accolades and invitations to the West, and Romania was the first communist country visited by President Richard Nixon. Romania became a member of the International Monetary Fund and received large loans; Queen Elizabeth II made him a knight of the realm but the honour was revoked on 24 December 1989. On a state visit to France in 1980, Ceauşescu's entourage pocketed many antique clocks and other artefacts. George H. W. Bush called him a 'good communist'. He did have one secure source of hard currency as Chancellor Kohl paid him DM25,000 (about £8,000) for each of the 5,000 ethnic Germans who were allowed to move to West Germany.

Romania was hit hard by the economic crisis of late 1970s, and Ceauşescu decided to pay back all international debt as quickly as possible. This led to blackouts, food shortages and a rapid increase in poverty, but vast building projects in Bucharest, in a Postmodernist style, were still going ahead. One of the results was the House of the People, the largest building in Europe and the second largest in the world. It is now called the Parliament of the People and is Bucharest's main tourist attraction.

Where did the revolution begin? It began in a town with a considerable Hungarian minority, Timişoara; the pastor of the local Calvinist church, László Tőkés, was their spokesman. The position of the Hungarian minority in Romania was always a sensitive issue. When the Romanian authorities began a campaign to evict him, Budapest took up his case. The eviction order was dated 7 December, and on 15 December, Tőkés asked his congregation to assemble outside the church. A huge crowd gathered that day, and the same occurred the following day. The crowd then began to loot stores and attack the party headquarters but the Securitate dispersed them. On 17 December, protesters clashed with police and shouted: 'freedom, democracy and free elections'. Fighting ensued and protestors took control of the centre of the town. The police responded, killing over sixty civilians and arresting over 700. Ceauşescu ordered the military to shoot demonstrators and blamed Washington, Moscow and Budapest for the trouble. On 18 December, Ceauşescu departed for Tehran to sign a deal involving the exchange of Iranian oil and gas for Romanian arms. Leaving the country was a fatal mistake because rumours spread that he had fled taking with him gold worth billions of dollars.

On 19 December, the dead were brought to Bucharest, cremated and the ashes thrown to the wind. It was all secretive but fuelled the rumour mill and almost seventy dead grew into thousands. On 20 December, clashes occurred again in Timişoara and the prime minister arrived to negotiate. Ceauşescu was back on 20 December and dispatched 20,000 club-wielding workers by train to impose proletarian order, but most of them refused to leave their carriages when they arrived. Communists contacted Gorbachev but he insisted it had to be resolved by Romanians.

Just after midday on 21 December, Ceauşescu decided to address a huge rally in front of the Central Committee building and it was carried live by TV. There was a commotion and Ceauşescu looked alarmed. What caused the incident? A taxi driver, Adrian Donea, had heckled the dictator. Ceauşescu promised higher wages and pensions and some applauded but the meeting gradually descended into chaos. Donea later remarked: 'We could see he was scared. At that moment we realised our power.' Nicolae and Elena Ceauşescu deemed it wise to remain in the building that afternoon. Barricades appeared in the city and the police opened fire. Forty-nine bodies were counted on 21 December.

On 22 December, the rioters were out again. News filtered through that the minister of defence had committed suicide. He could be blamed for collaborating with foreign enemies as he had prevented the dictator's order to massacre the population being carried out. The army went over to the revolution and, in so doing, sealed the fate of the Ceauşescus. Soldiers handed out Kalashnikovs to civilians, and one skirmish led to another and almost total confusion reigned. A helicopter took off from the Central Committee building with the leaders on board and a new leader, Ion Iliescu, appeared on television. He had once been seen as Ceauşescu's successor but, like almost everyone else, had fallen out with him. At about 5 p.m., Iliescu had formed his revolutionary government from members of the National Salvation Front (NSF). Almost a thousand civilians were to die in the next few days as communism entered its death throes. Loyalists would not concede defeat and so the blood flowed.

The helicopter landed in the suburbs. Elena packed and threw in two loaves just in case they needed food; the helicopter took off again and headed north west. Apparently, a Boeing 707 was always ready there to fly them into exile and Libya appeared the most likely destination. The helicopter touched down and a car was commandeered, but it soon ran out of petrol and police took them to an army barracks on the evening of 22 December.

On the evening of 24 December, the National Salvation Front leaders decided to put the Ceauşescus on trial. A major reason for this was that the NSF leaders were all former party and government officials and wanted no embarrassing revelations about their past conduct to become public. The next day a revolutionary tribunal and a firing squad of three paratroopers arrived by helicopter. Elena was defiant. Nicolae refused to recognise the court; after a couple of hours the couple were sentenced to death, but the proceedings were a mockery of justice. Elena asked to die with her husband. As the firing squad took aim, they held hands. Nicolae shouted: 'Long live free, independent and socialist Romania! Death to the traitors! History will avenge us!' 'There were tears in his eyes,, remembered one of the firing squad. Nicolae puffed out his chest and began singing the Internationale. 'Arise, wretched of the earth! Arise prisoners of hunger!' He never got to the fourth verse. The soldiers had been told to fire 30 rounds into them – from the hip at a distance of about a metre. One soldier fired seven rounds at Elena and then his gun jammed. He changed the magazine and fired another 30 rounds, mainly to the head, and she flew backwards and her blood splattered his uniform but she did not die easily and moved in spasms. Nicolae died immediately from the bullets of the other paratroopers. 'His body jumped a metre in the air from the force of the bullets', remembered another soldier (*The Times*, 19 December 2009).

The Romanian revolution was a palace coup as one group replaced another. Power never rested with the people, but it was not a KGB plot or one planned by the generals and party apparatchiks who took over. The upsurge of popular anger which toppled the dictator could not have been pre-arranged. Nevertheless, without Gorbachev and the fall of the Berlin Wall, popular fury would not have brought about the Romanian revolution. Iliescu was as brutal as Ceaușescu, and in 1990, confronted by student protesters, he deployed the same tactics as the dead leader. He sent in workers with clubs to disperse them.

Albania

Albania remained the most Stalinist of the Eastern European communist dictatorship until the late 1980s. Tirana left the Soviet orbit in 1961 and moved into the Chinese orbit, but it did not copy Deng Xiaoping's pro-market reforms in and after 1978. With Mao gone, it looked inward and relied on 'muscular socialism' to keep it afloat. Albania did not even join the Helsinki process in 1975. Enver Hoxha died in 1985 from Parkinson's disease and was succeeded by Ramiz Alia. There was an attempt at economic reform in late 1989, but this opened the floodgates as protestors demanded even more change. As in the GDR, the young and ambitious wanted to leave, and the obvious destinations were Greece and Italy. A popular way of getting to Italy was to commandeer a boat and set sail. Albania was the poorest country in Europe and only counted about three million citizens. The state collapsed and chaos reigned. Albanians have a great facility for foreign languages. An aide to the president came to the University of London, in 1991, and articulated policy in excellent English. I asked him a question in Italian and he replied fluently; this indicated there was a small educated elite.

On 12 December 1991, the Democratic Party of Albania (DPA) was founded by former communists and others. Elections were held in March 1991, and the Socialist Party of Albania (the communists under a new guise) won two-thirds of the vote and the DPA 30 per cent. The ex-communists proved quite incapable of effecting a transition to a market economy and were removed from office the following year. The DPA took over, but the collapse of communism and law and order led to waves of crime and corruption. A major factor in fomenting a violent civil war was the credulity of Albanians in believing they could become rich quickly. A massive Ponzi scheme attracted almost half the population and defrauded them of about $1.5 billion. Its collapse in 1997 precipitated the fighting, but the country became a parliamentary republic in 1998.

Yugoslavia

The Yugoslavs pioneered worker self-management, and Milovan Djilas views it as a form of Marx's free association of producers. The factories would run themselves, but they had to pay a tax for military and other state needs; this would presage the 'withering away of the state'. The system was based on workers' councils, where delegates of workers as workers and workers as consumers would run the economy. Self-management (workers' councils) was extended outside the factory right up to the federal and republican levels, and this led to republics acquiring a high level of independence. Cities were run by self-managed communes. From the mid-1960s, a consumer economy with large amounts of Western capital and a largely free press got under way. The self-managed economy recorded some of the highest growth rates in the world, and this appeared to prove that worker-self management and decentralisation could produce a modern, industrial state. In 1965, further decentralisation was decreed. Enterprises were to be autonomous and to compete with one another. Foreign direct investment was promoted, and a foreign company could buy up to 49 per cent of a Yugoslav enterprise. This was called market socialism but the problem was that the north, Slovenia and Croatia, part of the Habsburg Empire until 1918, had a head start on the poor southern republics. Income differentials widened from 4:1 to 8:1. There was a tendency to seek foreign loans instead of generating capital inside the country. In the south, workers' council placed great emphasis on toilets and canteen and working conditions, whereas in the north it was about prices and enterprise development, and there was also a tendency for each republic to try to become an industrialised mini-state – all funded on foreign capital.

The oil price shocks of the 1970s resulted in Yugoslavia not being able to service its foreign debts. The IMF structural adjustment programmes required a reduction in social spending in order to balance the state budget, but hyperinflation and mass unemployment followed and this fuelled angry nationalism. As one commentator said, 'it is ironic that it was the West and not the East which dealt the final blow to worker self-management' and mass strikes and violence spread like wildfire (Hatherley 2015: 399–402).

No charismatic leader appeared after Tito's death in 1980. What was to bind the federation together? Communism had no appeal and the party had fragmented. Into this vacuum stepped Slobodan Milošević who became leader of the Serbian League of Communists in 1987 and played the most potent card he had: nationalism. His goal was the creation of Greater Serbia, and this involved expanding Serbia's frontiers.

Slovenia decided it was better off as an independent republic, and Slovene communists withdrew from the League of Communists of Yugoslavia in early 1990. It was an easy decision to take as there was huge inequality in Yugoslavia. Per capita income in Slovenia was about $14,000, which ranked it above Portugal in the First World. By contrast, in Kosovo per capita income was under $2,000. Needless to say Slovenes resented their taxes being diverted to the backward south. Croatia came second in the wealth league in Yugoslavia followed by Serbia.

Slovenia made an almost seamless transition to democracy but it was different in other republics. Milošević was elected president of Serbia in December 1989 in a fair election. The communists and some socialist allies merged and formed the Socialist Party of Serbia in July 1990. Civil war broke out in 1991 and eventually NATO bombed Yugoslavia in 1999. Milošević was indicted for war crimes; his trial began in The Hague in 2001 and he died there in 2006.

In Slovenia and Croatia, elections in April and May 1990 saw non-communist parties successful. The new leader of Croatia was Franjo Tudjman, a former communist whom Tito had jailed for nationalism. Tudjman's authoritarian style was reminiscent of Milošević. Serbs in the enclave of Krajina were 'ethnically cleansed', and crimes were committed. When Tudjman died in 1999, Croatia could then begin moving to democracy. All six Yugoslavia republics – Serbia, Slovenia, Croatia, Bosnia, Montenegro and Macedonia – had held competitive elections by the end of 1991. The federal president resigned as the Federal Republic of Yugoslavia had passed away. So too had the Communist Party, but it lived on under the guise of socialism in Serbia. Serbia and Montenegro called themselves the Federal Republic of Yugoslavia between 1992 and 2003 when Montenegro (Italian for Crna Gora or Black Mountain) declared independence on 3 June 2006.

Vietnam

The war with China in February–March 1979 made abundantly clear that Vietnam would not accept domination by any power, communist or not. Deng Xiaoping's market-oriented reforms after 1978 gradually transformed the relationship, and Vietnam and China have now reached agreement to integrate economically northern Vietnam and the adjoining southern Chinese provinces. A factor in this decision was that Vietnam began introducing capitalist economic reforms in 1986. In early 1989, Vietnam asked the Soviet Union for a loan of $400 million, but Moscow declined as its hard currency reserves were dwindling. The Vietnamese leadership took drastic action and abolished rationing, liberalised prices, cut food subsidies to zero, reduced the budget deficit significantly, devalued the currency by 450 per cent and disbanded collective farms. This did not have a negative impact on gross domestic product (GDP). In 1990, 71 per cent of the labour force was still employed in agriculture, and Vietnam reaped the same benefits as China when peasants became artisans and entrepreneurs (Hayton 2010: passim).

The Paracel and Spratly Islands continue to be a bone of contention between Vietnam and China. Perceiving South Vietnam to be losing the struggle with the Viet Cong, China seized the Paracel islands from Vietnam, and the new communist government was presented with a fait accompli. The two sides eventually fought a brief naval battle in the South China Sea, in 1988, over the ownership of the Paracel and Spratly islands. China won.

Gorbachev faces more challenges

Gorbachev told a joke in America about a man who got fed up with queuing for vodka.

> *'I'm going to shoot Gorbachev,' he announced. After a while he returned. 'Well, did you shoot him?' 'No.' 'Why not?' 'The queue was longer than the vodka queue!'*

In January 1989, Gorbachev announced a plan to reduce military spending by 14 per cent and arms manufacture by 19 per cent. He told the CPD on 30 May 1989:

> The state continues to live beyond its means. Budget expenditure in the five year plan is growing faster than revenue. The result is a growing budget deficit . . . the main culprit for this state of affairs is the Ministry of Finance.

What an extraordinary claim. The Ministry of Finance implemented Politburo decisions – even when they knew them to be ill-judged.

In November 1989, Gorbachev penned an article in *Pravda*. He made it clear he had changed his mind about a lot of things:

> Whereas, at first, we thought it was basically a question of correcting individual deformations in our social organism, of perfecting the system which had been developed, we are now saying that we must radically remodel our entire social system, from the economic foundation to the superstructure . . . reform of property relations, the economic mechanism and the political system.

In other words, he admitted that all his previous reforms had been misconceived and this was the key reason why perestroika had not transformed the country as planned. Attempting to graft market reforms onto a faltering planned economy could only end in failure.

> *Ivan hears that the local departmental store is going to sell sausages. He arrives home and finds his wife in bed with his best friend. He says to her: 'You can't do that. You need to get some sleep because you have to get up early tomorrow morning to queue for sausages.'*

In January 1991, the Russian Supreme Soviet legalised private property in land, capital and the means of production. Private enterprises could be established and hire as many workers as they liked. The Russian Federation began acquiring all-Union enterprises and property on its territory, and oil, gas and mining were gradually taken over. The goal was to suck the lifeblood out of the Soviet Union and re-establish the Russian Federation as the dominant republic, and attempts were undertaken to take over party property. The 'war of laws' proceeded apace as each republic sought to widen its autonomy and restrict Moscow's power; the result was that the Soviet economy gradually disintegrated.

One of the reasons for Gorbachev's lack of faith in private agriculture was his visit to Canada in 1983. He concluded that Canadian farmers relied on subsidies to survive and this turned him against capitalist agriculture. Between 1986 and 2010, annual subsidies to Canadian farmers ranged from US$6 billion to US$8 billion, and one of the reasons for this was that Conservative governments rely on rural votes. In OECD countries, subsidies averaged 19 per cent of gross farm income and in Japan, South Korea, Norway and Switzerland it was as high as 50 per cent. On a visit to a Soviet agricultural research institute, I was asked to explain how milk prices were arrived at in Britain. I said there was a state guaranteed price and a market price and if the market price was lower than the former, farmers received a subsidy to make up the difference. The problem with milk production was that it was too high and the government wished to reduce it. As the Soviet Union was a shortage economy, I am not sure they believed me.

The Gulf War

Saddam Hussein invaded Kuwait on 1 August 1990 in an attempt to recoup some of the losses suffered during the war with Iran. It was incorporated in Iraq, and this posed a severe test for the evolving Soviet-American relationship. Gorbachev faced a dilemma: Iraq was an ally and there were thousands of Soviet troops in the country. James Baker and Eduard Shevardnadze met at Vnukovo 2 airport, in Moscow, and agreed on a statement condemning the Iraqi aggression – the precursor of joint votes in the UN. On 9 September, Gorbachev and Bush met in Helsinki and talked most of the day. The Soviet leader wanted assurances on two points: that military pressure would be used against Saddam Hussein, without it escalating into war; and that US forces would leave Kuwait after it had been liberated. Gorbachev again brought up the subject of US financial aid for the Soviet Union and was thus obliquely hinting that Kuwait and credits were linked. A rift developed between Gorbachev and Shevardnadze when the former chose Evgeny Primakov to be his envoy to Saddam. Primakov spoke Arabic and was a specialist on the Middle East, and he put together a peace deal which involved two islands and an oil field in return for Saddam's withdrawal from Kuwait. James Baker regarded Primakov's proposals as more 'capitulation than compromise'.

Shevardnadze felt slighted and passed on his suspicions of Primakov to Baker. He informed Primakov, in Gorbachev's presence, that his proposals would be disastrous for the Middle East and Soviet foreign policy. Primakov lost his temper and denigrated the foreign minister's knowledge of the Middle East. 'How dare you, a graduate of a correspondence course from a teachers' college in Kutaisi, lecture me on the Middle East, the region I've studied since my student days!' (Primakov 2004: 51). It was not the first time Shevardnadze had felt aggrieved at

Gorbachev's behaviour. He had offered to resign, in December 1989, after coming in for fierce criticism in the USSR Supreme Soviet and not being permitted to defend himself. Gorbachev appealed for him to come back, and he withdrew his resignation. The military was very unhappy about the decision to side with the Americans against Saddam Hussein and even went so far as to send a very critical letter to Gorbachev.

On 23 October 1990, Anatoly Chernyaev and Evgeny Primakov forwarded a memorandum to Gorbachev:

> It would be expedient to share the data we have on Iraq's military preparations with the US government, in strictest confidence. The data includes information about Iraq's preparedness to use chemical and bacteriological weapons in case it is militarily attacked.

Gorbachev disagreed. The following month, Margaret Thatcher brought up the subject and said that Britain was aware that Saddam had chemical and biological weapons but she did not believe that Iraq had nuclear weapons. Gorbachev replied: 'We have no information to suggest that Iraq has nuclear or biological weapons. It does have chemical weapons' (*The Spectator*, 26 March 2011). In fact, Gorbachev was well aware that Iraq would use biological weapons under certain circumstances.

Several months after Saddam's attack on Kuwait, the American public was shying away from military intervention. Then a 15-year-old girl spoke at the United Nations and catalogued the brutality of Saddam's troops. Delegates were in tears as she related horror stories and one stood out. She said she had witnessed Iraqi soldiers plundering Kuwait's hospitals: 'They took the babies out of the incubators, took the incubators and left the infants to die on the cold floor.' Public opinion changed immediately, and the US went to war but it turned out later that the girl was the royal daughter of the Kuwaiti ambassador to Washington and had never been to the hospital and the incubator story was pure fiction. Why were Americans duped? The story played on their emotions as many, if not most, decisions are based on emotion.

Israel 'considered' using atomic weapons in response to the Scud missile attacks launched by Saddam Hussein during the Gulf War. Right-wing ministers, including Yuval Ne'eman (he was working on Israel's nuclear programme), Rafael Eitan and Rehavam Ze'evi, urged Yitzhak Shamir's government to respond forcefully. They meant a nuclear response. Shamir rejected Israeli military action out of hand.

Syria

In 1979, the KGB in Damascus provided the Syrian Communist Party with $275,000 and $329,000 the following year. Far greater sums flowed into the party's coffers through Soviet commercial contracts with companies controlled by it, and the party was also secretly supplied with arms.

In June 1982, during the unsuccessful Israeli attack on Lebanon to destroy the Palestinian Liberation Organisation (PLO), Israel and Syria fought one of the largest air battles of the twentieth century over the Biqa valley. The Israelis destroyed all of Syria's SAM-6 missile sites, shot down twenty-three Syrian MiGs without losing a single plane, and when new SAM sites were built, the Israelis took them out as well. When President Hafez al Assad visited Moscow for Brezhnev's funeral in November 1982, Andropov agreed to supply advanced weapons systems, some of them operated by Soviet personnel. Andrei Gromyko and Marshal Ustinov opposed this decision (Andrew and Mitrokhin 2005: 209–13).

In 1984, there were over 9,000 Soviet service personnel in Syria, mostly anti-aircraft combat units. While fighting in Syria and Lebanon in the early 1980s, dozens of Soviet officers, including three generals, were killed and hundreds wounded (Militera.lib.ru 2000).

Gorbachev developed a remarkable rapport with President Hafez al Assad of Syria. Despite ill-treating communists, the Syrian dictator was viewed positively because of his resolutely anti-Western policies. In a conversation with al Assad, in April 1987, Gorbachev floated the idea of Soviet support for Arab unification and made clear that Moscow would back al Assad as the leader of the Arab world. When al Assad came to the Soviet Union for medical treatment in 1988, Gorbachev visited him in hospital, and he was to get the best care as 'our friend, brother and comrade'. Al Assad was informed that his friends in the Soviet leadership: 'are always ready to help you in any circumstances. You can be sure that we shall never let any harm come to friendly Syria. We shall always think together, act together and constantly keep in touch' (*The Spectator*, 26 March 2011). Al Assad's comment after the demise of the Soviet Union was plaintive: 'We regret the Soviet collapse more than the Russians.'

Russia undermines the Union

Elections to the Russian Congress of People's Deputies led to the formation of Democratic Russia, and this grouping dominated Moscow and St Petersburg. Eighty-six per cent of the deputies were communists but this meant little as the party had split into many factions. Many deputies were heads of enterprises and the military and KGB were well represented, but workers and peasants only accounted for 6 per cent.

May Day demonstrations revealed the level of frustration and anger as thousands of people marched behind banners proclaiming: 'The Politburo should retire'; 'Down with the CPSU'; 'Down with Marxism-Leninism'; and 'Pension off Gorbachev.' The Russian tricolour, banned since 1917, made an appearance. Gorbachev did his best to prevent Yeltsin becoming speaker of the Russian Parliament in May 1990 but his comrade, Aleksandr Vlasov, a former head of the USSR Ministry of Internal Affairs, was a poor speaker and hence no match for Yeltsin.

The declaration of the sovereignty of the Russian Federation, passed by parliament on 12 June 1990, was a devastating blow for the Union and Gorbachev.

Russian law was now to take precedence over Soviet law, and Russia would now only acknowledge Soviet legislation that was deemed beneficial.

Russia was not the first republic to declare itself sovereign. Estonia, Lithuania and Georgia had declared themselves sovereign in March; Latvia in May; Uzbekistan and Moldova joined Russia in June; and Ukraine and Belarus in July. Republics were now claiming precedence over Moscow.

There was no mechanism for resolving these disputes and aspirations. The 1977 Soviet constitution permitted republics to leave the Union, but how was this to be done? The constitution was silent about this, and autonomous republics (mainly inhabited by non-Russians) wanted to become full republics. How?

What was Moscow to do about the Baltics? According to Vladimir Kryuchkov, Gorbachev had agreed to use force against 'extremists in Latvia and Lithuania'. Another source states that a document had been drafted to introduce presidential rule but Gorbachev never signed it. The party in Lithuania was clamouring for Moscow to 'restore order'. On 10 January 1991, Gorbachev forwarded an ultimatum to the Lithuanian Parliament to implement fully the Soviet constitution there. In other words, reject the demand for independence. The same day, he instructed the Ministry of Defence, the Ministry of Internal Affairs and the head of the KGB to prepare to use force in Vilnius, and an Alpha special unit was sent to Vilnius. On 11 January, Alpha and other security forces together with local worker volunteers from the committee of national salvation occupied the House of the Press. During the night of 12–13 January, army and KGB units advanced to seize the television centre in Vilnius, and in the resulting conflict fourteen people died. Citizens began building barricades around parliament.

Gorbachev had only given verbal orders to attack, but afterwards he refused to confirm this. Two days before the attack he had assured President Bush that force would not be used unless Soviet power was attacked.

Gorbachev's lack of openness offended the military as they had carried out an order and were now being accused of acting without authority. The conclusion they reached was that, in future, they would not use force unless they had a written order from the president. This was to prove crucial during the attempted coup in August 1991 when they were ordered to attack the White House which they would only do after receiving a written order; none ever came, so there was no military assault on the White House.

These events provoked a furious response throughout the Soviet Union. Donetsk miners demanded the resignation of Gorbachev and a democratic and economic transformation of the country, and Yeltsin called on Russian troops not to obey orders to suppress dissent in the republics.

The Vilnius tragedy revealed that the Soviet government was willing to use force to keep the Union intact, and force might now be deployed to resolve the political crisis in Russia. The most important lesson drawn by Yeltsin and his supporters was the need to establish a Russian army to defend Russia. After returning from Tallinn, Estonia, on 14 January, Yeltsin stated that the leaders of Russia, Ukraine, Belarus and Kazakhstan had decided to form a quadripartite pact. They were not willing to wait for the signing of a Union Treaty. Yeltsin had travelled by car to St Petersburg and then flew to Moscow. A friendly KGB officer had advised him not to fly from Tallinn to Moscow.

On 23 February 1991, the Warsaw Pact was dissolved at a meeting in Bucharest of foreign, and defence ministers from the Soviet Union, Czechoslovakia, Poland and Romania, and Comecon met the same fate on 27 June 1991. These were the last rites of the Soviet Empire in Eastern Europe.

How was Gorbachev to keep the Union together? He began planning a referendum, to be held on 17 March 1991, to find out. Voters were asked if they 'deemed it necessary to retain the USSR as a renewed federation of equal sovereign republics?' The leaders of the republics of Estonia, Latvia, Lithuania, Armenia, Moldova and Georgia declared they did not wish to sign a new Union Treaty. Yeltsin seized the opportunity to add another question. Were voters in favour of a directly elected president of the Russian Federation? Over 70 per cent voted for the Union, and Yeltsin got his yes vote.

The election of the president of Russia took place on 12 June 1991 with Democratic Russia and a host of other parties supporting Boris Yeltsin. A vice president, following the American precedent, would also be needed. Who would be Yeltsin's running mate? In the end Boris chose Colonel Aleksandr Rutskoi, an Afghan veteran, believing he would bring in the military vote and some communists. The winner needed to obtain a majority of registered voters, not a majority of those who voted. Yeltsin obtained 57.3 per cent and was sworn in as president in the Palace of Congresses in the Kremlin on 10 July. A new national anthem (without words, as no one could agree on them) was based on the music of Glinka. For the first time since 1917, the Patriarch of All Russia blessed the incoming ruler. Russia had been resurrected.

Gorbachev pressed the US ambassador for credits every time they met. A credit line of $1.5 billion was arranged in June, and the Soviet leader pointed out that the Gulf War had cost $100 billion and the money had been immediately found. Was it not worth raising the same to save perestroika? After all, the latter was ten or a hundred times more important than the Gulf War. The rich man's club was the Group of Seven (G7). Could the Soviet Union possibly join? In order to get an invitation, Gorbachev needed a financial plan.

The ideal person to draw up such a plan was Grigory Yavlinsky, so he went off to Harvard to work with Graham Allison. Yavlinsky called the joint effort the 'window of opportunity' and Allison described it as the 'great design'. Gorbachev pulled out all the stops and invited Mrs Thatcher to his Moscow dacha. She was completely won over and instructed the US ambassador to send a message to the president: he was to lead the Western initiative to save Gorbachev. When the ambassador pointed out that this would be difficult because the Soviet Union had still to adopt market reforms, she brushed aside his remarks and told him to think like a statesman, not as a diplomat, trying to avoid doing anything.

On 17 June, Kryuchkov spoke at a secret meeting of the USSR Supreme Soviet. He laid out the case for Gorbachev's removal and demanded that extraordinary measures be taken to cope with the gathering crisis, but the deputies did not side with him.

Negotiations on a new Union Treaty concluded on 17 June at Novo-Ogarevo, a splendid residence just outside Moscow and the draft was then forwarded to the Union republics. There was a closed session of the USSR Supreme Soviet on the same day where Gorbachev was subjected to withering criticism. Marshal Dmitry Yazov reported on the withdrawal of Soviet forces from Germany, Hungary and Poland. Gorbachev had cut the armed forces by half a million, including 100,000 officers, and many of them had no pensions because they had not served long enough. Boris Pugo, the minister of internal affairs, said that criminality and inter-ethnic conflicts were getting out of control. Since August 1990, the militia had confiscated about 50,000 firearms and tonnes of explosives. Kryuchkov wondered why Gorbachev was so popular in the West. Valentin Pavlov, the prime minister, asked for and was granted extra powers which placed him on a par with the president. Furious, Gorbachev turned up the next day, attacked Pavlov and demanded a vote of confidence which he got. Pavlov boasted about how much money he was making on the currency black market and, presumably, he was using the Ministry of Finance as a piggy bank. Gorbachev confronted him: 'Comrade Pavlov, you are a thief.' He countered, 'Yes, I am but I am a socialist thief!'

Gorbachev's bid for G7 money was doomed from the start. A programme was drawn up by the government but was not deemed viable. At the G7 meeting in London from 15 to 17 July, everyone listened politely to the Soviet leader. There was little reaction when he invited business leaders to invest in the Soviet Union. He asked for and was granted membership of the IMF.

On 23 July, republican and Soviet leaders assembled at Novo-Ogarevo, but Gorbachev sensed danger. Russia, Ukraine, Belarus, Azerbaijan, Kazakhstan, Uzbekistan, Tajikistan and Turkmenistan were to sign the Union Treaty on 20 August. Significantly, no parliament, not even the Soviet, was to be a party to ratification. Gorbachev knew that it would have been voted down.

The last Party Central Committee plenum took place on 25–26 July. A new party programme and preparations for the next Party Congress were on the agenda. Delegates insulted Gorbachev and the level of noise precluded rational debate. The draft programme was a remarkable document because it was a social democratic programme, not a communist one. It was to be debated at the Congress, which was to take place in November–December 1991.

Mikhail Gorbachev, Boris Yeltsin and Nursultan Nazarbaev convened, in Novo-Ogarevo, on 29 July, and decided to sack Vice President Yanaev, Vladimir Kryuchkov, head of the KGB, Boris Pugo, minister of the interior, and the head of the State Radio and Television Committee. The president of the new Union would be Gorbachev and the new prime minister would be Nazarbaev. Because the KGB bugged Novo-Ogarevo, Kryuchkov and the others learnt that they were to go. Parliament could not dismiss Gorbachev as he had been elected for five years, unless he had become mentally and physically incapable of performing his presidential functions. An attempt to introduce a state of emergency failed in March 1991, and in April the Security Council began drafting a state of emergency decree. Gorbachev, after all, had mentioned on several occasions the need for 'emergency measures'. On 3 August, the day before he left for his Foros holiday home in Crimea, he said that the situation was 'exceptional'. It was necessary to take 'emergency measures'. Then Gorbachev added: 'People will understand this.'

The last summit

George H.W. Bush arrived in Moscow in late July 1991 for his first Moscow summit as president. It was to be the fourth and last Gorbachev-Bush meeting. Ironically, it was the most rewarding for both leaders, on a purely personal basis. The START treaty was ready for signature, after ten years of hard negotiations; the CFE treaty was with the Senate for ratification; a bill was before Congress conferring on the Soviet Union most favoured nation status; and there was a tentative agreement on a Middle East peace conference, but the realities of the domestic situation impinged on the meeting. A note was passed to Bush, informing him that six Lithuanian customs officials had been killed during the night. Gorbachev was embarrassed as this was the first he had heard of the incident. It appeared that it had been staged by the minister of internal affairs to disrupt the summit, and it also revealed that Bush was better informed about Soviet domestic events than the Soviet president. It was clear that Gorbachev was not in full control of the police.

The growing influence of the republics was marked by Gorbachev's invitation to Boris Yeltsin and Nursultan Nazarbaev, the leader of Kazakhstan, to join him in a working lunch and to participate in some of the sessions. Yeltsin replied that he preferred to meet Bush face-to-face, president to president, in his office. He kept Bush waiting ten minutes and the encounter overran. At the official dinner, Yeltsin tried to upstage Gorbachev. When First Lady Barbara Bush entered, he attempted to escort her to the top table, as if he were the host.

In planning his itinerary, Bush had been advised by American diplomats to visit Kiev, the capital of Ukraine. Initially, the Soviet Ministry of Foreign Affairs raised no objections, but then it changed its mind and advised Bush against travelling to Kiev, given the tense situation there. Instead, he could spend some time with Gorbachev in Stavropol *krai*. Evidently, the Soviet leader was piqued by Bush's wish to visit Ukraine at a time when the Ukrainians were proving difficult during negotiations for a new Union treaty. It could boost the nationalist cause there. In Kiev, Bush was to meet the constitutional head of the republic, Leonid Kravchuk; all toasts were to be in Ukrainian and English, and no Russian was to be used. Bush countered by saying that he would cancel the visit but due to the advanced level of preparation, it would be embarrassing. On an open line, the US ambassador spelled out the negative consequences for Moscow as it would be blamed for the change of plan. Gorbachev changed his mind and agreed that the visit should go ahead. It underlined the changed nature of Soviet politics as it would be the first visit by a US president to a Soviet republic without the Soviet leader at his side. So, on 1 August 1991, President Bush and his entourage made for Kiev. Gennady Yanaev, the Soviet vice president, went along as well, at Gorbachev's request, and some thought he was there to keep an eye on Bush.

In Kiev, Bush was careful to stress that he was on Ukrainian soil. Nixon, in 1972, had spoken of Soviet soil and Kiev as the mother of all Russian cities. He declined to meet representatives of the opposition alone but met them with Kravchuk and other officials. His speech to parliament attacked naked nationalism (Plokhy 2014: 64):

> Freedom is not the same as independence. Americans will not support those who seek independence in order to replace a far off tyranny with a local despotism. They will not aid those who promote a suicidal nationalism based upon ethnic hatred.

Ukrainian Americans were furious, and it was dubbed the 'chicken Kiev' speech, a derogatory sobriquet. For them, it revealed that Bush was Gorbachev's man and Ukrainian nationalists were of the same opinion.

At Babii Yar, on the outskirts of Kiev, in September 1941, German Sonderkommandos had shot 34,000 Kievan Jews in two days. Bush's speech there was emotional and well received by nationalists and others. Kravchuk, as an eight-year-old boy, had witnessed the mass execution of Jews by German troops. Two members of the group looked out of place: Yanaev and the Soviet ambassador to Washington. The former did not understand Ukrainian and knew little English. An American official commented that Ukrainians treated him as if he were the chairman of the All-Union Leprosy Association!

The attempted coup

In order to succeed, a coup has to have the support of the KGB and military. The brain behind the attempted coup was Vladimir Kryuchkov, the head of the KGB. On 20 July, the KGB leaders convened a meeting with KGB republican chiefs, and they discussed measures to be taken if executive organs 'were paralysed'.

Gorbachev was warned about the impending coup. Gavriil Popov gave the US ambassador, Jack Matlock, the names of the plotters and the information was passed on to Boris Yeltsin, then in the US, and to Aleksandr Bessmertnykh, the minister of foreign affairs. In a telephone conversation with Gorbachev, President Bush warned him about an impending coup but he unwisely gave Gavriil Popov as his source. The next time that Gorbachev encountered Popov, he wagged his finger at him and asked, 'Why are you telling Americans fairy tales?'

On 6 August, Kryuchkov instructed two KGB officers to undertake a feasibility study on the introduction of a state of emergency but the conclusions were not very positive. On 14 August, Kryuchkov stated that Gorbachev was mentally confused and was unable to work, but this was a total fabrication. The following day, documents introducing a state of emergency were ready. All parties and social organisations – except the CPSU – were to be closed down and party rule reintroduced. These proposals were to be presented to Gorbachev in the interests of saving the motherland (Kryuchkov 1996: Vol. 1 passim). Gorbachev was informed by the KGB that the state was becoming ungovernable.

At 8 a.m. on 18 August, Minister of Defence Yazov ordered troops to be ready to move into Moscow and KGB troops were to be dispatched to Estonia, Latvia and Lithuania. Seventy politicians were to be arrested including the leaders of the Russian government and Eduard Shevardnadze, who had resigned in dramatic fashion as minister of foreign affairs on 20 December 1990.

> Reformers have run for cover. A dictatorship is coming – I declare this with a full sense of responsibility. Nobody knows what kind of dictatorship it will be, who will come to power, what kind of dictator or what kind of order will be installed.
>
> (*Pravda*, 21 December 1990)

Kryuchkov phoned Gorbachev four times to reassure him that everything was normal. Gorbachev also talked to Vice President Gennady Yanaev, Oleg Shenin, the party secretary responsible for party organisations, and Prime Minister Valentin Pavlov. They were all among the plotters. At 4.50 p.m. Foros security alerted Gorbachev to the fact that some visitors wished to see him, but this was strange as he has no appointments scheduled. General Yury Plekhanov, head of the KGB's ninth directorate responsible for the security of the leadership, was accompanied by Oleg Shenin, Oleg Baklanov, deputy chair of the Defence Council, General Valentin Varennikov, commander in chief of ground forces, and Valery Boldin, his chief of staff; it dawned on Gorbachev that the KGB, military and party had betrayed him.

The most aggressive stance was adopted by General Varennikov, who had commanded the troops in Vilnius in January. In response, Gorbachev told Varennikov exactly where he could go in the most obscene Russian he could muster. Gorbachev was advised that a state of emergency was needed immediately but he declined to sign the documents placed before him. Instead, he said it would be better to attain the stated objectives by 'democratic means'. Baklanov said Russian President Boris Yeltsin would be arrested on his return from Almaty, Kazakhstan, and Vice President Gennady Yanaev would assume the president's functions. 'Relax,' said Baklanov. 'We'll carry out the "dirty work" and then you can return' (Gorbachev 1996: 631–2; O'Clery 2011: 197–212). Two hundred thousand pairs of handcuffs had been ordered from a factory in Pskov. Finally, Gorbachev shook hands with each as they left, and his final words were 'Damn you all, go ahead!' Vladimir Medvedev, his chief of personal security, then reported that all communications had been cut. Gorbachev, Raisa, his daughter, son-in-law and two granddaughters were now under house arrest.

The composition of the State Committee for the State of Emergency revealed how incompetent Gorbachev was in choosing his team. Anatoly Lukyanov, the speaker of the USSR Parliament, had been a friend since university days; Yazov had been chosen as minister of defence because he was a 'dolt' (his own description); Gennady Yanaev was a non-entity whose staff did his paperwork for him while he devoted himself to his twin passions: drink and women. Asked if he enjoyed good health, he quipped: 'My wife has no complaints'; Valery Boldin, his chief of staff, had been with him since 1978.

On 19 August, Yanaev became president but was in no fit state to carry out his duties as he had spent much of the night drinking with Valentin Pavlov, notorious for liking a tipple. Yazov told military officers that an attack on Soviet power was imminent. At 6 a.m., funereal music by Chopin alerted the public that something terrible had happened. A state of emergency had been introduced, and the motherland was in mortal danger, as Gorbachev's reforms had led the country into a cul-de-sac. Soviet institutions had been undermined by an unscrupulous minority bent on dictatorial power, and a tidal wave of sex and violence threatened to drown the motherland. Socialism, communism and the party were not mentioned.

One of the greatest mistakes perpetrated by the plotters was their failure to arrest Boris Yeltsin. The order was given and then cancelled. Why? Yeltsin was permitted to make his way to the White House, the Russian seat of government. Kryuchkov tried to convince him to join the Extraordinary Committee, but Boris sensed that his moment of destiny had arrived. As an instinctive politician, he seized the opportunity to lead the opposition to the attempted coup and was clever enough not to rally everyone behind the flag of Russia but to call for the reinstatement of Gorbachev as Soviet president. Yeltsin, the showman that he was, mounted a tank outside the White House and roared defiance at the self-appointed State Committee. Giving in would return the Soviet Union to the era of the Cold War and cut the country off from the outside world. Amazingly, communications from the White House had not been cut and Yeltsin was able to talk to world leaders, including President Bush.

Astonishingly, CNN continued broadcasting inside the Soviet Union, and this meant that republican leaders had another source of information. It often conflicted with the version being put out by the party in Moscow.

Most foreign leaders assumed that the coup had succeeded. President Mitterrand thought it was a fait accompli, but Margaret Thatcher did not. She had to break the news to Leonid Zamyatin, the Soviet ambassador in London. He later recalled:

> She called me at eight in the morning and said very angrily: 'Mister Ambassador, do you know what is happening in Russia?' 'I am sorry, madam, I don't.' 'Well, then turn on your TV set and see for yourself. I need permission for a flight of an English aircraft to Russia. You are flying with me. I will take a doctor along. Gorbachev must be sick. Maybe dying. I must be in Russia.'

(Service 2015: 491)

Thousands of Muscovites surrounded the White House and built barricades, but they would have been routed had the military attacked. The reason they did not was that Yazov had demanded a written order from the Extraordinary Committee, which never arrived.

Three young men were killed accidentally by tanks during the attempted coup. The troops returned to barracks on 21 August, and the same day a Russian parliamentary delegation, accompanied by two Gorbachev allies, Evgeny Primakov and Vadim Bakatin, flew to see Gorbachev at Foros. Kryuchkov suggested to Yeltsin that they should jointly go to see the Soviet president, but Boris suspected it was a plot to assassinate him. When Raisa heard that the plotters were on their way to see her husband, she feared the worst and had a 'massive fit . . . micro stroke . . . had a haemorrhage in both eyes. Her eyesight declined dramatically.' The Committee leaders arrived at 4 p.m., but Gorbachev would not speak to them. The Russian delegation arrived at 8 p.m. The president was already a free man and had been telephoning President Bush and republican leaders. About midnight, the plane with the Russian delegation and the Gorbachev family took off. Kryuchkov was with them to ensure that the KGB did not shoot down the aircraft. The plotters were in another plane.

Gorbachev arrived at Vnukovo airport about 2 a.m. and he headed straight for the microphones, but Evgeny Primakov cut in and stated that the president was too tired to comment. Primakov was speaking for Russia, and the Soviet president would have to play second fiddle to Russia from now on. At midday in the Kremlin, Gorbachev convened a meeting of his supporters and new appointments were announced. Then the Soviet president made for the White House and made the speech which effectively ended his political career. He talked about reforming the party, but he had not grasped that the party had betrayed him and could not be reformed. He talked about a new future, but the response was a torrent of abuse. Exasperated, he told journalists: 'You will never know the complete truth.'

On 24 August, he bitterly commented, 'I came from Foros to a different country and I, likewise, am a different person.' Boris Yeltsin was ready with the knife, and the president was forced to rescind the appointments he had made the day before. He was invited to the White House by the president of Russia to meet the Russian Supreme Soviet or Parliament. The Russian president humiliated the Soviet president at every turn as he stood above him and pointed the finger down at him. He forced Gorbachev to read the minutes of the government meeting of 19 August when all but two of the ministers had supported the coup. 'And you appointed that government,' Boris said gloatingly. 'Now on a lighter note, shall we sign the decree banning the Russian Communist Party?' All Gorbachev could splutter was: 'I haven't read the decree.' Yeltsin also signed a decree seizing the assets of the Communist Party of the Soviet Union on Russian territory.

On 25 August, Gorbachev resigned as General Secretary of the CPSU and its Central Committee was dissolved. The Communist Party, which had so triumphantly seized power on 7 November 1917, had expired in a whimper. The Bolshevik era was over.

Others died as well. Marshal Sergei Akhromeev, the top brain in the military, hanged himself in his office at the second attempt and there were several notes: one to pay an outstanding mess bill – roubles included. When they came for Boris Pugo, the minister of internal affairs, they were shocked by what they found. His wife lay dying with a bullet in her brain; he was dead with a bullet in his head and her aged father, in the final stages of dementia, was wandering around the apartment. Pugo's note read: 'Forgive me. It was all a mistake.' Others jumped out of windows to their deaths.

On 30 August, Gorbachev asked Shevardnadze to come to the Kremlin and the ensuing conversation was explosive. The latter accused Gorbachev of betraying his life's cause, betraying his allies and surrounding himself with mediocrities and flatterers. 'You became a person who – whether it was deliberately or involuntarily doesn't matter – provoked the coup. And I have every ground for supposing that you took part in the plot.' When he declined to become minister of foreign affairs again, Gorbachev asked why. Shevardnadze replied, 'I don't trust you' (Service 2015: 492).

The fifth and final session of the USSR Congress of People's Deputies was convened on 2 September in the Kremlin. As Estonia, Latvia, Lithuania, Moldova and Georgia had declared independence, they were not represented. Deputies agreed to dissolve the Congress and draft a new Union Treaty to establish a Union of Sovereign States. Gorbachev proposed a federation in which the centre would be responsible for defence and foreign policy. Yeltsin disagreed and stated that the president of the new Union would play a ceremonial role, 'similar to that of the Queen of England'. There was also talk of a confederation, and it might have kept twelve republics together (Estonia, Latvia and Lithuania were beyond the pale), but Gorbachev would have none of it. The model was obviously Switzerland, and Gorbachev was aware that the Swiss president enjoyed only a ceremonial role.

Plokhy (2014) calls the USSR the Soviet Empire, and he vividly brings out the seething resentment of many nationalities at Moscow rule. The Russo-Ukrainian treaty, signed in November 1990 by Yeltsin and President Leonid Kravchuk, guaranteed the existing boundaries, but all that changed after the failed coup. On 24 August, Yeltsin recognised the independence of Estonia, Latvia and Lithuania within their existing frontiers, and on the same day, Ukraine declared independence. Whereas the declaration of sovereignty had given precedence to republican laws over Soviet Union laws, independence meant that Union laws could be ignored completely. Contrary to the policy adopted towards the Baltic States, Russia did not recognise Ukraine's independence, or that of Georgia, which had proclaimed independence in April 1991.

When the Ukrainian declaration of independence was read out in the Soviet Parliament, Gorbachev, red-faced, stormed out of the chamber. Dmitry Likhachev, the doyen of academia, warned that the collapse of the Soviet Union would lead to border wars. The Russian Federation, hitherto leading the charge to drain the Union of its powers, was now faced with the problem of how to save the Union. Yeltsin told his press secretary, Pavel Voshchanov, to draft a statement saying that 'if any republic breaks off Union relations with Russia, then Russia has the right to raise the question of territorial claims' (Plokhy 2014: 176). When the statement was published, Voshchanov was asked which republics could face claims and he answered, Ukraine and Kazakhstan. He later expanded this to mean territories which had previously been part of Russia: Crimea and Donetsk oblast in Ukraine, Abkhazia in Georgia, and northern oblasts of Kazakhstan. Critics were quick to point out that Donetsk oblast (Donbas) had never been part of the Russian Federation. After 1917, it was included in the Republic of Ukraine and later incorporated in the Ukrainian Soviet Socialist Republic. Abkhazia, likewise, had never been part of Russian territory. It had either been independent or an autonomous Republic of Georgia. In 1917, northern Kazakhstan became part of the Russian Soviet Federative Socialist Republic (RSFSR). In the early 1920s, the autonomous Republic of Kazakhstan was proclaimed and declared to be part of the RSFSR. Kazakhstan became a Soviet Socialist Republic in 1936.

Gorbachev weighed in by stating that 'there cannot be any territorial claims within the Union, but their emergence cannot be ruled out when republics leave the Union' (Plokhy 2014: 177). The president's message was clear: stay in the Union or face dismemberment.

The Ukrainians hit back immediately and labelled the Moscow democrats imperialists in disguise. Yeltsin sent his emissaries to Kiev and they had to defend the indefensible, but it turned out that the territorial claims were merely a tactic to postpone Ukrainian independence. 'Do you think we need those territories?,' a member of Yeltsin's inner circle asked. 'We need Nazarbaev [president of Kazakhstan] and Kravchuk [president of Ukraine] to know their place' (Plokhy 2014: 179). Their place, of course, was in the Union and under Russia's control. The Russian delegation failed to find common ground with Kravchuk and the Ukrainian democrats, and it was plain to see that they were aiming for a 'civilised divorce'. On hearing the outcome of the failed talks, Nursultan Nazarbaev sent a message to Yeltsin asking for the Russian delegation to come to Almaty, the capital of Kazakhstan. At a joint press conference with Nazarbaev, Russian Vice President Aleksandr Rutskoi stated there were no territorial problems between Russia and Kazakhstan.

This disastrous démarche ended any trust that existed between Kiev and the new masters in Moscow. Gorbachev and Yeltsin wanted the same thing: Moscow rule. Kravchuk did not bother to turn up at the Novo-Ogarevo discussions about a successor state to the USSR. A more skilful politician than Gorbachev might have saved something from the flames, but he did try to play the ethnic card by warning that eleven million ethnic Russians in Ukraine would be difficult to swallow. How right he was. He also encouraged the autonomous republics within the Russian Federation to seek recognition as republics.

The parlous state of the Soviet economy after the attempted coup was graphically illustrated by Gavriil Popov, the mayor of Moscow, in a conversation with James Baker, the US secretary of state. Popov said there was no longer a central government and that republics and large cities, such as Moscow, were on their own. The food situation was so serious Moscow could not survive the winter. He asked for eggs, powdered milk and mashed potato mix. 'Some of this material is stored by your army, which throws it out after three years. But a three year shelf life is good enough for us.' What a humiliating position for a superpower to be in.

After meeting Russian democrats, Baker concluded that they were incapable of ruling the country without outside help. He wrote to President Bush proposing a new Marshall Plan to prevent a 'world which is more threatening and dangerous, and I have little doubt if they [democrats] are unable to deliver the goods, they will be supplanted by an authoritarian leader of the xenophobic right wing' (Plokhy 2014: 205). The timing was unfortunate because of the poor state of the US economy; it was in no position to fund a new Marshall Plan but President Bush strained every sinew to keep the Union afloat. The reason was the fear that the four nuclear republics – Russia, Ukraine, Belarus and Kazakhstan – could fall apart and nuclear weapons end up in the wrong hands. The continuation of the Union was in the US interest, but Bush failed to understand the power of nationalism once glasnost had uncorked the bottle of protest.

On 1 December 1991, Ukraine held a referendum on independence. In March, three-quarters of the electorate had voted for a 'renewed federation' and now 90 per cent favoured independence, but the Soviet Union could not survive without Ukraine. When Yeltsin arrived in Belavezha forest near Minsk on 8 December 1991, his first move was to offer Kravchuk the Gorbachev-approved plan for a reformed Soviet Union, but the Ukrainian president did not even consider the proposal. Gorbachev and Kravchuk agreed that a viable Union had to include Russia and Ukraine. Russia would not enter such a Union on its own as it would become responsible for weak Central Asian Muslim states. It should be pointed out that Ukraine vastly overestimated its economic potential as it thought it was the richest republic, which it was not. The Russian Federation was the richest. Had Kravchuk had a more realistic understanding of the Ukrainian economy he might have acted differently. Plokhy maintains that it was Ukraine and not Russia which determined the fate of the Soviet Union, with Kravchuk signing its death certificate.

So the heads of state of Russia, Ukraine and Belarus dissolved the Union of Soviet Socialist Republics and set up the Commonwealth of Independent States (CIS). Yeltsin then phoned President George H.W. Bush with the news, and it was left to Stanislau Shushkevich, the Belarusian leader, to inform Gorbachev. The latter had every right to feel insulted as he had been duped. A Russian put it graphically: 'After Foros, Yeltsin had Gorbachev by the balls.' The CIS would not have a president, and Gorbachev and Yeltsin shared the Kremlin as if they were dual monarchs. That came to an end on 25 December 1991, when Mikhail Gorbachev appeared on television to announce his resignation as president of the USSR. There had been an agreement between the two presidents that the Soviet Union would expire on 31 December 1991, but the red flag was taken down and replaced by the Russian tricolour on Christmas Day. The two were to meet to sign the documents which would transfer the nuclear briefcase to the Russian president, but in a fit of pique, Boris refused to go. He was so incensed by Gorbachev declining to say he was resigning – he stated he was laying down his responsibilities – that he ordered the TV to be turned off. Eventually, officials had to go from one president to the other to get the requisite signatures. There was no ceremony ending the existence of the Soviet Union, and it expired without a whimper.

14 The judgement

The US, in 1945, was a global economic and military power, and this combination made it possible for the American political leadership to begin dreaming of a new world order which would mirror American values. 'Man by nature is violent' is an old adage. There were over 2,000 civil wars in China before Qin Shi Huang established the first modern world state in 221 BC, ruling 90 million subjects or one-third of the world's population. The Roman Empire lasted a half millennium and had always to defend its territory and, if possible, extend it. The Religious Wars in Europe between Roman Catholics and Protestants lasted almost a century and a half. Spain, France and Britain fought one another to dominate the continent afterwards. Great empires rose and fell. Russia expanded to the Pacific in 1639; the Russians even acquired Alaska and had a fortress in California, Fort Ross (a corruption of Rossiya).

In 1945 the Americans thought it would be possible to put an end to the constant warfare and conflict which had blighted human history. If the major world powers – the US, the Soviet Union, Britain and China – could come together and agree a new world order, peace could reign. Sometimes dubbed the four policemen, they could patrol the planet and snuff out any conflict which threatened to disrupt the peace. The problem with this vision was that the four policemen were not equally strong. Britain and China were bankrupt, and the Soviet Union would take years to recover its former strength, which left the US as the dominant power. The concept of world government was a thinly veiled attempt for the US to take over the world. At least, that is how the other powers saw it. Because politics is about power, this vision was dead in the water from birth. Not only Britain was bankrupt but the whole of Europe was as well.

Had the world been wholly capitalist, a modus vivendi could have emerged. War was off the agenda as reconstruction had priority. However, the main military force in Europe, the Soviet Union, was not capitalist but communist. The European Enlightenment (1650–1780) had given birth to a revolutionary idea: man could shape his own destiny and had no longer to be subservient to God. In other words, man became God, and a product of this thinking was Marxism. Marx, following Hegel, put forward the intoxicating vision of the perfection of humankind, and it was not only possible, it was certain. This vision eliminated the market economy which, in Marx's view, was the source of all human evil because inequality led to the formation of classes. There were two main classes, the proletariat and the bourgeoisie. The workers produced the wealth, and the factory and landowners – the capitalists – expropriated it. So the solution was simple: abolish capitalism and the proletariat could rule the world. The first stage would be socialism, during which there would be inequality; this was because some would contribute more than others to human wealth. The second, higher stage, communism, would abolish inequality, and harmony would reign – conflict would be a thing of the past – and everyone's needs and desires would be satisfied.

This powerful narrative won many adherents worldwide. The message was quite simple: all the ills of the planet emanated from capitalism – the US was the leading capitalist state – so overturn capitalism, and the land of plenty was within reach. War arose because capitalists had to fight one another for markets, so abolish markets and thereby abolish war. No wonder Washington after 1945 found it difficult to come up with a competing narrative which was just as seductive. The capitalist world could preach freedom and democracy, but the communists could respond that freedom meant that people could become rich by exploiting others and democracy was a sham as it was the rule of powerful capitalist elites.

Russia before 1917 was a land with a mission. The Russian Orthodox Church regarded itself as a repository of a long Christian tradition. The first Rome was the centre of Christianity; then Constantinople became the Second Rome; then Moscow took on the mantle of the Third Rome when Constantinople succumbed to Islam; there would not be a Fourth Rome. This mythical progression was deeply embedded in Russian religious thought. The European Enlightenment did not embrace Russia so there was no debate about separating church and state, as the Tsar fused both in his person and answered for the whole Russian people at the Day of Judgement.

The secular reaction to this was Marxism, and religion was the opiate of the people, so they had to be liberated from it and the cloying power of the Church. Marx's ideas came late to Russia because industrialisation only got under way in the 1890s. So Russia was already half a century behind other Western European states such as Britain, France and Germany. Revisionism was creeping into Marxism there as Marx's theories, set out in *Das Kapital*, were proving inaccurate. He did not bother to publish volumes two and three of *Das Kapital*. After his death, in 1883, it was left to Friedrich Engels, his close associate, to edit and publish them, and it is fair to say that Engels did not always understand what he was editing. So Marxism was becoming less dogmatic by the end of the nineteenth century, and a fundamentalist interpretation was difficult to sustain.

Russians embraced Marxism with a religious fervour. At long last, they could escape from their economic backwardness and join the mainstream of European and world development. Russia was behind, of course, as it had yet to achieve a bourgeois revolution – industrialists taking power – whereas the other leading European powers were already well into that phase. Capitalism had to develop until it reached its zenith, and then would come the inevitable socialist revolution when workers would seize power from their bourgeois bosses and initiate progress which would end in an earthly paradise. Russia had now joined the mainstream of human development. There was no longer a Russian problem, and there was no need to feel inferior.

When the Bolsheviks took power in October 1917 they adopted a fundamentalist approach to Marxism and rejected the revisionism of Bernstein, Kautsky and the German social democratic party. Stalin penned the history of the Communist Party, in 1938, and it was the last word on the subject, and it could not be revised or amended, except by Stalin himself. He also published the *Foundations of Leninism*, in 1924, after Lenin's death which presented the basic tenets of the faith. Without the party – it was the proletarian vanguard – workers could not achieve socialism and communism. According to Stalin, the Soviet Union attained the socialist stage of development in 1936 and thereafter communism was being built.

Stalin achieved political dominance in 1929 and his power grew as time passed. According to Khlevniuk (2015), all his policies had one aim: to increase his personal security as leader, and foreign and domestic policies were two sides of a coin. The stronger the state, the stronger he became. His worldview was Marxist, he always saw problems from a class point of view, and he was strongly opposed to capitalism as it permitted the individual to act autonomously. From his point of view, everyone had to serve the state. He or she had to sacrifice all – even life – as the state could do no wrong; if harsh measures were needed, this was a function of historical necessity, and Stalin saw himself as the agent who fulfilled the demands of historical necessity.

The world outside Europe, later to be known as the Third World, was dominated by European Empires during the first half of the twentieth century. The largest was the British; then came the French, Dutch, Belgian, Portuguese, Spanish and Italian. Germany had lost its colonies after 1918. The Japanese came on the scene in the 1930s when they penetrated China. All these empires collapsed after 1945. In their place appeared a plethora of new states, many of them appearing on the world stage for the first time. Most of them were not nation states but groups of clans or tribes, but they all wanted their place in the sun and to escape from imperial influence. Because most of these states were unstable, they were fertile ground for the spread of communism. To the Soviet Union, these new states presented an unprecedented opportunity. If they adopted the Leninist brand of socialism, this would serve as the demonstration effect, and it would also subtract these states from the total of capitalist states. If the Third World turned socialist, capitalism, headed by the US, would be doomed. The Third World, the periphery for the superpowers, was to pay a high price for the Cold War as the Soviet Union and the US intervened in their own interests, not those of the locals.

Why did the Cold War between the superpowers emerge in the years to 1953?

The emergence of the Cold War was a slow process. It is normally dated from 1947, but all that says is that it was then out in the open. Even after the opening of the Soviet archives after 1991, it is still impossible to conclude who was more responsible: Stalin or Truman. One can plot Stalin's actions quite closely, and something he recognised as potentially fatal for the Soviet system was close association with capitalist powers. He labelled this 'kowtowing to the West', and the two competing systems had to keep their distance from one another otherwise Soviet society could be infected with Western ideas. The country was weak economically and needed all the aid and finance it could get from the West, but the goal was not a rapprochement between the two competing economies. Stalin never thought of changing the economic levers which had propelled the country forward in the 1930s, and drew no conclusions from observing the rapid growth of the American wartime economy. He held to his Marxist view that the US economy would suffer recession soon after the war ended and the capitalists would then fight one another for markets. He ignored the advice of Soviet economists that the capitalist states had learnt how to run a successful economy during the war and could put this experience to good use in peacetime.

During the autumn of 1945, Stalin was exercised by the effect of foreign praise of Soviet officials. He sent a letter denouncing unnamed 'senior officials' who 'were thrown into fits of childlike glee' by praise from foreign leaders. 'I consider such inclinations to be dangerous since they develop in us kowtowing to foreign figures. A ruthless fight must be waged against obsequiousness towards foreigners.' There was a risk that the country would develop an inferiority complex and that Western culture would 'contaminate' Soviet society. In August 1946, a Central Committee resolution was published attacking Leningrad writers. Spearheaded by Andrei Zhdanov, the campaign vilified them for 'kowtowing to the contemporary bourgeois culture of the West'. Musicians were also lambasted. Two scientists, developing a cancer drug, were baselessly accused of passing secrets to the West and 'servility to anything foreign' (Khlevniuk 2015: 265–6). Hence Stalin was trying to avoid any interaction between the two competing world systems, and keeping them at arms' length was his aim.

There were several démarches which annoyed Stalin. The Americans would not permit the Soviets to participate in the occupation of Japan, and he wanted a base in Libya which would give the Soviet Union a presence in the

Mediterranean. Again the answer was no. The Western Allies dragged their feet on German reparations, and a large loan from Washington was not forthcoming. Under pressure, the Soviet Army had to leave Iran in early 1946. Stalin offered a 'friendly' warning to the US ambassador after Churchill's 'Iron Curtain' speech in Fulton, Missouri. 'Churchill and his friends might try to prise the United States away from the USSR.' Stalin saw the Marshall Plan as American economic imperialism, as its aim was to draw Eastern Europe away from the Soviet Union. At the founding conference of the Cominform, Zhdanov divided the world into two camps, and comrades were instructed to stand up to 'international imperialism'.

On the Western side, meetings proved very frustrating. An example was the foreign ministers' conference in London in September 1945. Molotov agreed that France and China could participate in discussions about peace treaties with the defeated countries, but they could not vote on the final draft. On hearing this, Stalin became angry and demanded that Molotov rescind the agreement as he had exceeded his brief. The next day, Molotov duly reversed his approval, but he mentioned this was on Stalin's orders which made the *vozhd* even more angry. He was told that this was quite unacceptable behaviour, as Stalin always wanted Molotov to play the hard man while he could come in later and make some concession to save the day.

Another perennial problem was Poland. The Soviet Army needed to pass through the country to get to East Germany so Poland had to have a government friendly towards the Soviet Union. Stalin actually used the word 'satellite' to refer to the Eastern European countries in a note to Molotov. Hence he regarded the Soviet presence there as non-negotiable. Security was paramount.

In December 1945, with Stalin on vacation in the south, the foreign press began speculating about Molotov taking over. Stalin sent angry telegrams to top politicians but not Molotov. He talked of 'libels against the Soviet government' and wanted stricter censorship.

> I am convinced that Molotov does not care about the interests of our state and the prestige of our government . . . So long as he gains popularity within certain foreign circles, I can no longer consider such a comrade as first deputy [Prime Minister] . . . I have doubts about some of those close to him.
>
> (Khlevniuk 2015: 272)

No wonder it was extremely difficult to reach agreement with Molotov. A Damocles sword was always suspended over his head, and he was succeeded as foreign minister, in March 1949, by Andrei Vyshinsky; as the latter was terrified of Stalin, he was unlikely to stray from his brief.

Stalin also cut the Soviet military down to size as he was aware that they uttered disparaging remarks about him at reunions. Marshal Georgy Zhukov was withdrawn from Germany, and some other top military officers were shot. Stalin was aware that Zhukov and General Dwight Eisenhower were on very good personal terms, so he made sure they had little contact and that the Soviet military was not permitted to fraternise with their former Allied comrades.

Stalin committed some egregious mistakes, and the greatest was the Berlin Blockade. Coming after the Prague coup, in February 1948, it was Stalin throwing down the gauntlet, and the longer the airlift lasted, the closer the US and Western Europe were bound together. Without it, there would have been no NATO or the rapid founding of the Federal Republic of Germany and its integration in European political, economic and military structures.

Another blunder was to turn down the invitation to join the IMF and World Bank, and this cut off badly needed credit. The Marshall Plan was designed deliberately to exclude the Soviet Union, but Stalin could have negotiated to see if a deal was possible. Stalin also assumed the Americans would not intervene in Korea.

So what were Stalin's priorities? First and foremost, security – meaning primarily military security. He had to ensure that the West did not launch an attack to destroy the Soviet Union and its satellite states in Eastern Europe. He always asked for respect and a recognition that the Soviet Union and the US were equal powers, but America was quite unwilling to concede this. Then came ideological security because he recognised that Soviet society had not developed to the point where it could resist the seductions of capitalism. This also meant walling Soviet culture off from bourgeois culture, again because the latter could contaminate the former. This applied also to science and technology, even though there was a cost to pay by avoiding contact with the world's leading scientists and engineers, and Stalin even divided science into socialist and bourgeois science. For instance, he viewed much of Einstein's work as erroneous and rejected Mendelian genetics in favour of Lamarckian genetics – the latter believed in the inheritance of acquired characteristics. He dismissed Freud as a pervert. Khlevniuk sees Stalin's first priority as personal security, and all the aforementioned policies stemmed from this basic premise. If you like, Stalin was a control freak who had to control everyone and everything he encountered. It is possible to conceive of a post-war world which did not provoke a Cold War. The prerequisite was communist and capitalist worlds which had minimal contact with one another and could coexist without any meaningful interaction. The problem with this analysis is that it is not Marxist. Stalin took the view, as a Marxist, that capitalism had to attempt to destroy communism before communism destroyed it. The stronger communism became, the more desperate capitalism would be to destroy it. Hence conflict was inevitable but it must never be allowed to spiral into war.

Dr Myasnikov's assessment is that the Soviet Union was ruled by a sick man in the years before his death. He underlines his obstinacy and suspiciousness. When did his mental faculties begin to decline? Was his obstinacy one of the reasons for the length of the Berlin Blockade? His suspiciousness would have contributed to the Leningrad Affair, the Show Trials in Eastern Europe and the treatment of Molotov, Mikoyan and others because he appears to have believed that they were conspiring against him. The last foreigner to have an interview with Stalin was the Indian foreign minister, and he noted that Stalin was doodling while he was talking to him. Doodling what? Wolves. Did he see himself being attacked by wolves or was he planning to set the wolves on others? All in all, the second nuclear power was headed by a sick leader whose behaviour was quite unpredictable.

How does one recognise a psychopath? The traits of a psychopath include lack of empathy; no conscience; being a risk-taker; grandiosity; narcissism; sexual promiscuousness; superficial charm; being manipulative; possibly becoming very violent; ruthlessness; and unwillingness to admit guilt (but some are murderers but others are not). So was Stalin a psychopath? As he ticks many of the boxes listed here, he can be judged a psychopath. Many other world leaders were also psychopaths, including Hitler, Mao Zedong, Pol Pot and Muammar Gaddafi. It is striking that among Soviet leaders after Stalin – Khrushchev (but he was a high risk-taker), Brezhnev, Andropov (but he was addicted to conspiracy theories), Chernenko and Gorbachev – none was a psychopath. This is one of the reasons why there was no world war after 1953. In Eastern Europe, the psychopath was Romania's Nicolae Ceauşescu, but Enver Hoxha, the Albanian leader, may also qualify. Among US presidents the nearest to a psychopath was Richard Nixon, but he always knew when to draw back from nuclear Armageddon. This said, the North Vietnamese fell for his Madman act, and hence they adjudged him a psychopath.

Psychopaths are also to be found heading businesses, such as Robert Maxwell (Mirror Group), Fred Goodwin (who bankrupted the Royal Bank of Scotland) and Jeffrey Skilling (who destroyed Enron). Psychopathic tendencies help many politicians and businessmen get to the top where ruthlessness and total self-belief are often rewarded. One of their traits is not knowing when to stop expanding their empire, and this normally ends in disaster. Another trait is to see no difference between oneself and the state. Louis XIV famously said 'L'Etat, c'est moi' ('I am the state'); Stalin clearly identified himself with the Soviet state and Mao also fell into this category. In 1933 a Norwegian psychiatrist diagnosed Hitler as a psychopath and warned that there was trouble ahead, but he was ignored. As yet, there is no medical cure for psychopathy.

Why did the Cold War come to an end?

> What is socialism? The most difficult and tortuous way to progress from capitalism to capitalism.
>
> (Czech StB officer at the last meeting of Soviet bloc intelligence services in East Berlin, in October 1988)

The answer is quite simple: one of the main protagonists, the Soviet Union, collapsed. Why?

Domestic reasons

- The Soviet Union was dismantled by the ruling elites who decided that the system was no longer worth defending. They had concluded that a post-communist world would offer them greater rewards. Hence it was not the people below who overthrew the USSR but those on top.
- The attempted coup in August 1991 failed because society had changed radically; Gorbachev thought that had the coup been launched a year and a half or two years previously, it would probably have succeeded.
- Fear of the KGB declined to the point where, in August 1991, the statue of 'Iron' Feliks Dzerzhinsky in front of the Lubyanka was toppled.
- The Soviet Union proved incapable of inspiring and leading a world socialist revolution.
- Karl Marx, in *The Eighteenth Brumaire of Louis Napoleon*, posed the question: how was it possible for Louis Napoleon to dissolve the Legislative Assembly and negate the democratic achievements of the Second Republic and become Emperor Napoleon III in the 1851 coup? The answer was simple: the Second Republic was a premature revolution because it lacked the social substructure to sustain itself. The reason, applying Marx, why the Soviet experiment failed was because the October Revolution was a premature revolution. Russia in 1917 lacked the social substructure to build communism, and Lenin's belief that the party, as the vanguard of the proletariat, could compensate for this absence was misguided. Lenin simply ignored Marx's warning, and Russia paid a heavy price.
- It lacked intellectual and cultural prestige.
- This was present under Lenin, but Stalin concentrated on building socialism in one country and moved from ideological conviction to military and political pressure.
- This led to opposition within and outside the USSR.
- The Soviet standard of living did not keep pace with the aspirations of the Soviet people; they could see that living standards in the GDR and Czecho-slovakia, for example, were higher than in the Soviet Union; so Coca-Cola and jeans were more ideologically damaging than any capitalist propaganda.
- An inability to analyse the defects of the planned economy, which was accepted as the highest form of economic management. This led to a rash of conspiracy theories in which the malevolent influence of the US and the West was always present. Kryuchkov and Andropov were especially prone to blame Soviet economic failure on a Western conspiracy. In June 1991, Kryuchkov read out a 1977 report by Andropov to the Politburo claiming that the CIA, regardless of cost, was recruiting agents within the Soviet economy, administration and scientific research and training them to commit sabotage. Many of the Soviet Union's current problems, claimed Kryuchkov, derived from this sabotage offensive (Andrew and Mitrokhin 2005: 489–90). Valery Boldin, Gorbachev's chief of staff, took seriously Kryuchkov's claim that the KGB 'had inter-cepted certain information in the possession of Western intelligence agencies

concerning plans for the collapse of the USSR and steps necessary to complete the destruction of our country as a great power' (Boldin 1994: 263).

- Marxism-Leninism became wooden and was dismissed by most of the intelligentsia; when I asked a Russian once about ideology, she replied dismissively: 'Educated people do not discuss Marxism-Leninism!' Soviet youth (and some oldies as well) were enraptured by Western pop music.
- Gorbachev's new thinking unleashed nationalist aspirations in non-Russian republics.
- Glasnost undermined the authority of the CPSU.
- Heavy military expenditure deprived other sectors such as education, health, culture and social services of investment. Soviet industry could simply not compete with the US in the scientific and technical race for supremacy; one example of this was the small number of computers available, even to the military. A major weakness was that innovations in the defence sector were not transferred to the civilian economy.
- The country never solved the food problem, even with agricultural investment reaching 25 per cent of the budget; enormous amounts of food had to be imported.
- Gorbachev made a fatal mistake by engaging in political and economic reforms simultaneously.
- His economic reforms were haphazard, sowed confusion, lacked coherence and clear goals.
- He wanted to make the centrally planned economy more efficient and thought that by introducing capitalist reforms he could achieve this objective; this revealed he did not understand economics.
- Rise of Boris Yeltsin and Russian nationalism in the Russian Federation.
- Ukraine's decision to go for independence sealed the fate of the Soviet Union.
- The Russian Federation would only join a successor state if Ukraine joined it.

External reasons

- The Soviet Union could not compete economically and militarily with the US; however, Soviet military power was at its zenith when the state collapsed, but in many sectors technically it was slipping behind the US; the financial burden was simply too heavy. Reagan realised this and ratcheted up defence spending.
- The SDI programme could not be matched.
- Presidents Reagan and Bush always adopted policies which promised to force concessions out of the Soviet Union.
- Eastern Europe was a financial liability.
- Gorbachev told Eastern European leaders, in 1985, that they had to build communism on their own; there would be no more military interventions; this signalled that the Brezhnev Doctrine was dead.
- Gorbachev believed that because the Soviet Union and Eastern Europe had chosen socialism, this would never change; reverting to capitalism was inconceivable; it would mean going backwards socially.

- Collapse of communism in Eastern Europe was a shock and a bitter blow; it inspired those in the Soviet Union who wanted to see the back of the CPSU.
- The Eastern European example encouraged Estonia, Latvia, Lithuania, Georgia and Azerbaijan to go for independence.
- By the mid-1980s, the Soviet model had failed in the Third World; communism was often the result of military power but, in order to be sustainable, military force has to give way to consensus based on economic and social wellbeing; failure to achieve this resulted in the collapse of communist states. Efforts to copy Soviet industrialisation and the collectivisation of agriculture resulted in abject failure. The belief that the Third World was the battleground on which socialism would vanquish capitalism worldwide proved a chimera. During the Khrushchev era, the Soviet Union was involved in over 6,000 projects, not all economic. The continent which suffered the most was Africa; it is instructive that the states which received the greatest arms shipments suffered most; weapon exports to sub-Saharan Africa rose from $150 million in the late 1960s to $370 million in 1970–73 and $820 million in 1974–6, before reaching a peak in 1977–8 of $2.5 billion; during the years 1980–7, weapons exports averaged $1.6 billion annually, but fell dramatically to $350 million annually over the period 1989–93.

(Clapham 1996: 153–4)

Other reasons

- Détente was a milder form of liberation policy.
- President Kennedy's strategy of peace and Egon Bahr's concept of change through closer contacts in Germany and Eastern Europe bore fruit; they proposed closer contacts, information exchange and trade as ways of breaking down barriers.
- These were based on the magnet theory of liberation policy.
- The Helsinki Final Act had hidden dangers; the West could protest against human rights violations in the Soviet Union and Eastern Europe; the new electronic media promoted freedom of expression and contacts.
- The Soviet Union abjured the use of force outside its frontiers; the West was not going to attack.
- Gorbachev was radically different from previous Soviet leaders.
- He took risks, and when they did not achieve stated objectives, he took even greater risks; these led to the destruction of the Soviet Union.
- Hence he can be regarded as an 'accidental' leader.
- If this is so, the end of the Cold War was an accident, a stroke of luck.
- Changes in perception of Gorbachev in the outside world are critically important.
- He came to be regarded as a man of principle; one who could be trusted.
- Hence arms control and disarmament treaties could be signed.
- Both sides accepted that nuclear arms could not guarantee security; in fact, they increased tension because of the lack of trust between the two sides.

- The end of the Cold War revealed it to be a classic power struggle.
- Both sides held on tenaciously to their narratives.
- Gorbachev was removed from power by the attempted coup; no Soviet successor emerged, only Russian and Ukrainian leaders who wanted power for their republics.
- Central Soviet government and CPSU authority had vanished by late 1991.
- President Bush tried to keep the Soviet Union together as he feared the loss of control over the Soviet nuclear arsenal which was dispersed over four republics; he had no influence whatsoever over the final death agony of the USSR.
- Hence it was not a change in US policy which led to the end of the Cold War; it was a change in Soviet policy; this change was so radical that it led to the breakup of the Soviet Union; it is difficult to conceive of any other Soviet leader espousing the same policies; Gorbachev conceded one point after another to the US because of his desire to create a new world but also because of economic weakness; this is particularly evident in his negotiations with Helmut Kohl, the West German chancellor.

There were two main centres

- East and West;
- It was a total contest embracing politics, economics, social, culture, science and technology, sport, music, etc.;
- Because a nuclear war could not be fought, competition moved to other spheres; this resulted in proxy wars with conventional weapons; e.g. Korea and Vietnam;
- Space opened up for other powers to act: e.g. West Germany and its Ostpolitik; China, Vietnam, the UN and the Non-aligned Movement were influenced by the main actors but were able to find room to manoeuvre.

There was no reason for the CPSU to lose power or the Soviet Union to collapse; therefore, the demise of communist power was not inevitable; it resulted from misguided policies; Gorbachev let go of the usual levers of power and tried to 'modernise' the Soviet Union – in other words, to make it more like the US or a Western European state; the tragedy was that neither he nor anyone else knew how to transition from a centrally planned to a capitalist economy. Had he come to power a decade later, this conundrum would have been a no brainer; copy China's (and Vietnam's) move to a capitalist economy, guided by the Communist Party; China revealed that a Communist Party can reform successfully a centrally planned economy by moving to a capitalist economy.

The Chinese explanation

After the collapse of the Soviet Union in 1991, the Chinese Academy of Social Sciences embarked on two exhaustive studies: why did the Communist Party of the Soviet Union lose power and why did the Soviet Union collapse? The Soviet Party lost power because it departed from Leninist norms:

- Democratic centralism;
- A monopoly of political power;
- Unwillingness to use coercion to stay in power.

There is also the view that the Soviet communist culture was not robust enough to withstand Western 'infiltration'.

Xi Jinping, in early 2013, added his judgement which can be summed up as:

- Political rot;
- Ideological heresy;
- Military disloyalty.

Political rot set in when Gorbachev began his political reforms which were much too hasty, and although they aimed at strengthening the role of the party, they had the opposite effect. Economic reform undermined the leading role of the party. An example of what Xi calls ideological heresy was the removal of Article 6 of the Soviet Constitution which afforded the party a monopoly of political power in the state. Military disloyalty presumably refers to the reluctance of the military to become embroiled in domestic security after the Vilnius events of January 1991 and another example would be the botched coup in August 1991.

In December 2013, he stated that the CPSU had made a fatal error by denigrating Lenin and Stalin, and the result of unseating the founding fathers was that

Figure 14.1 Xi Jinping and Vladimir Putin
© ITAR-TASS Photo Agency/Alamy.

party members wallowed in historical nihilism. Their thoughts became confused, and party organisations at different levels were rendered useless.

What would have happened had Viktor Grishin, the Moscow Party leader, been elected to lead the Soviet Union, instead of Gorbachev, in 1985? Most likely, the USSR would still be in existence. He would not have embarked on political reform but would have been forced to introduce economic reform which would not have undermined the authority of the party. Given the loyalty of the KGB and the military to the party, it is difficult to see the country collapsing. Put another way, the Cold War that Gorbachev ended would still be with us.

Near misses

On 24 October 1973, US forces went over to DEFCON (Defense Readiness Condition) 3, two stages from nuclear war. This was in response to Soviet threats to send an airborne force to fight on the Arab side during the Yom Kippur War. The Soviet military favoured action, but Brezhnev did not accept their advice.

On 26 September 1983, Lieutenant Colonel Stanislav Petrov was on duty in the bunker near Moscow which monitored the Soviet Union's Oko early warning satellite system. Suddenly, just before midnight, the screen went red, and the alarm bells would have woken the dead. A satellite showed that the US had fired five ballistic missiles at the Soviet Union. Just a few weeks before, on 1 September, the Soviets had shot down a South Korean civilian airliner, killing 269 civilians, including a US congressman, as they had assumed it was a military aircraft. So tension was high.

Petrov should have passed the information on to higher command which could have set in motion a full scale nuclear alert and possibly war, but he decided not to do so because it struck him as odd that the Americans would launch an attack with only five missiles. He also did not trust the newly installed launch detection system, and the ground-based radars did not confirm the launch.

Later a satellite proved to be the culprit. It mistook the sun's reflection off the tops of clouds for a missile launch, and the computer system which was supposed to filter out such information did not do so.

Initially, he was praised for his judgement but later reprimanded, and he concluded that the bugs found in the early warning system and false alarms had embarrassed the top brass and scientists. He is to be commended for using his own judgement as there is no telling what would have happened had he confirmed to the high command that the US had launched a nuclear strike.

Needless to say, NATO was unaware of the scare. On 2 November 1983, it launched an exercise, codenamed Able Archer 83, covering the whole of Western Europe. It simulated a conflict escalation, culminating in a nuclear attack on the Soviet Union; the scale of the exercise was interpreted by Moscow that a nuclear war was imminent. It put its nuclear forces on alert and placed air units in Poland and East Germany on alert, but the threat of nuclear war ended on 11 September when the exercise ended.

These three cases, plus the Cuban Missile Crisis, could have escalated into nuclear war. As far as one knows, they are the closest the world came to nuclear Armageddon.

In 1987, the Soviets launched a submarine exercise off the US coast, but it took the US Navy five days to detect it. In case of war, this would have resulted in US cities being wiped out by nuclear missiles.

Why were Soviet submarines so advanced and increasingly difficult to detect? John Walker headed a spy ring which had been selling US naval secrets to the Soviets for twenty years before he was unmasked in 1985, with the information being incorporated in the newest Soviet submarines. In the late 1980s, the Soviets were designing a submarine which could stay submerged for seven years.

The enormous investment in submarines resulted in repairing and servicing being curtailed, and this led to tragedy, on 6 October 1986, when the K-219 nuclear submarine sank in the Sargasso Sea, in the Bermuda Triangle, with sixteen nuclear missiles and forty-eight warheads on board. A sailor sacrificed his life to shut down the nuclear reactor and thereby prevented a nuclear explosion; most of the submariners were rescued.

The Royal Navy's nuclear submarine fleet was much smaller than the American, and this meant it had to take more risks in shadowing Soviet nuclear subs. On one occasion, a submarine was within a few hundred yards of a Soviet sub but managed to remain undetected. An American, when asked to assess the performance of the Royal Navy captains and crews, said they had 'balls, balls'.

What about nuclear weapons on US soil? The Defense Atomic Support Agency has revealed that between 1958 and 1974 there were several hundred 'Accidents and Incidents Involving Nuclear Weapons', and these ranged from the ridiculous to the miraculous.

In 1960, a nuclear war with the Soviet Union was narrowly averted after a US Air Force computer had identified a rising moon over Norway as a '99.9 per cent certain' incoming Soviet nuclear missile. In 1961, a B-52 bomber broke up over North Carolina and dropped a four-megaton hydrogen bomb, but it failed to explode when it hit the ground because one switch (out of 10) remained in the safe position.

In 1966, a B-52 bomber refuelling over Spain exploded and dropped four hydrogen bombs, but they did not explode.

In 1968, a B-52 over Greenland caught fire. The crew bailed out, and the aircraft, carrying four hydrogen bombs, hit the ice at 600 mph. The explosion destroyed the USAF base and scattered plutonium over three square miles, but many bomb parts were never recovered.

Maryland, New Jersey, Louisiana, Kentucky, Texas, Morocco, Japan and RAF Lakenheath in Suffolk were scenes of further miraculous escapes.

In September 1980, in Arkansas, a Titan II, carrying a nine-megaton warhead with an explosive force three times as powerful as all the bombs dropped during the Second World War, ignited. It shot 1,000 feet into the air, but the warhead did not explode (Schlosser 2013: passim).

Graphs

Here is the superpower confrontation presented in graphic form:

Changing Levels of Tension Between the USA and the USSR During the Cold War

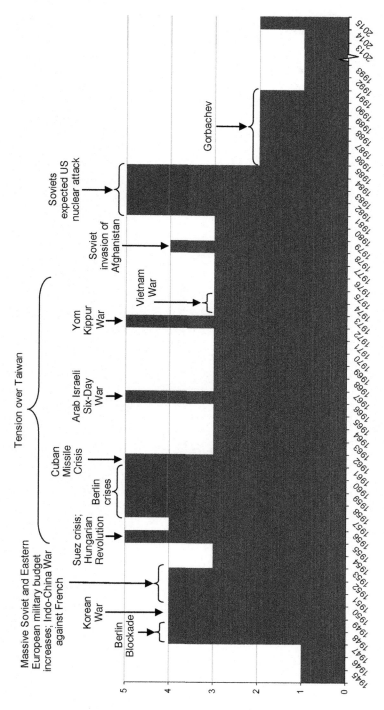

There were quite a few very dangerous years: the 1950s, 1962, 1967, 1973 and 1980–5.

Changing Levels of Tension Between China and the USSR During the Cold War

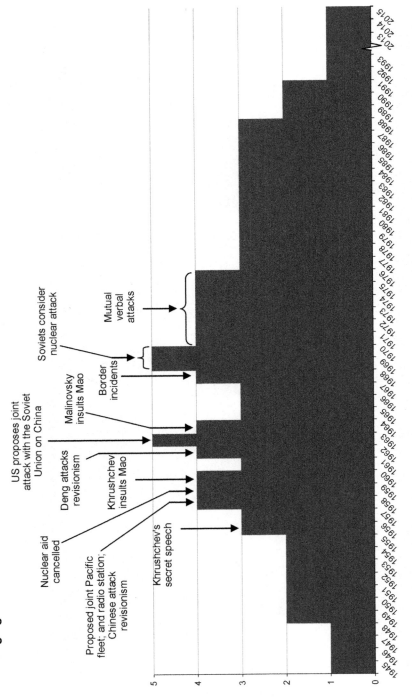

The most dangerous years were the 1960s.

Changing Levels of Tension Between the USA and China During the Cold War

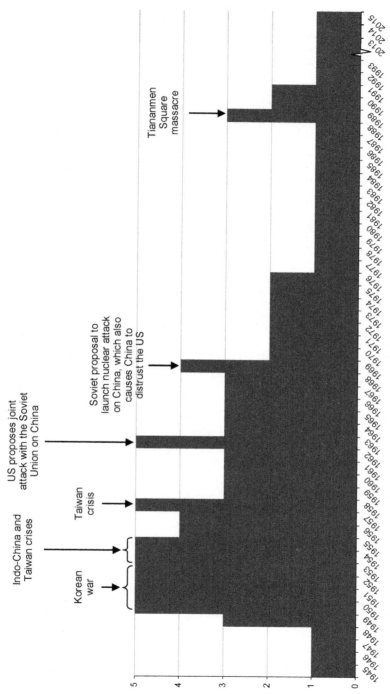

The most dangerous years were the 1950s and 1963.

15 The post–Cold War world

Russia

When the Soviet Union collapsed in 1991, the Russian Soviet Federal Socialist Republic (RSFSR) acquired the status of an independent nation and became known as Russia or the Russian Federation. The CPSU nomenklatura occupied all the new government positions in the autonomous republics and other non-Russian ethnic territories. Boris Yeltsin, himself a leading member of the old nomenklatura, did not have a team in waiting to rule Russia, and it was natural that he would turn to those who had experience of governing the Soviet Union. In a third of the eighty-nine territorial entities of the Russian Federation he appointed governors, heads of government and other top executives from the old nomenklatura. About one third had been 'red' directors of state-owned enterprises, but this did not reimpose the Soviet system. There were numerous amendments to the constitution, one of which defined Russia as a 'sovereign, federal state, created by the peoples historically united in it'. During 1990 and 1991, due to the weakness of the centre, power flowed to the regions and Yeltsin quipped: 'Take as much sovereignty as you can swallow.' This led to autonomous republics within the RSFSR declaring sovereignty even before the demise of the Soviet Union. The most striking examples were Tatarstan and Chechnya-Ingushetia which quickly split into two autonomous republics. Chechnya declared independence as its goal.

There was a real danger that Russia would fragment just as the Soviet Union had done. To overcome this, agreements were signed between the federal centre and the regions and those seeking independence. An 'asymmetric federation' had evolved by 1993, and each member gained significant de jure and de facto powers.

Map 15.1 Eastern Europe since communism

Conflict between Yeltsin and the opposition reached a point where a peaceful resolution, in the president's eyes, was no longer possible. In October 1993, he turned the instruments of coercion, the military and the police, on the opposition and attacked the White House, the parliament. Blood flowed and the first phase of Russia's post-1991 development was over. Force was deployed to resolve a political impasse. The new constitution conferred sweeping powers on the president and was dubbed a super-presidential constitution, but it stated that in dealing with the federal government 'all territories shall be equal.' Given the asymmetrical federation which existed, this did not reflect reality. Tatarstan, Bashkortostan, Yakutia-Sakha, Sverdlovsk oblast and St Petersburg enjoyed greater autonomy than the others and they also paid less federal tax; the reason for this was the clout of the regional leaders.

When Vladimir Putin became president in 2000 he set out to change the nature of Russian federalism and established seven (and then eight) federal districts, appointed members of his own clan as heads and endowed them with far-reaching powers. He launched a campaign against asymmetrical federalism by imposing the dominance of federal over local laws and ending the tax and other economic benefits which existed. A war was launched against the Chechen separatists in 1999 to bring that republic to heel.

On the face of it, therefore, Russia is now a unitary state where federalism only exists on paper, but this is only part of the story. The top-down or power vertical in Russia is a myth, and the role of Vladimir Putin, as the Father of the Nation, is kept alive by media propaganda which nourishes the belief in a strong leader to save Russia.

The huge windfall during the 2000s from oil, gas and commodity exports has been spent mainly on preserving the central government and on vanity projects such as the Sochi Winter Olympics. Much of it disappeared because of corruption, but some was channelled into a Reserve Fund and a National Wealth Fund. The opportunity to create development-promoting institutions in the economic, social and political spheres was missed, and reform is avoided because it could disturb the distribution of power at the top.

The de facto independence of governors breeds corruption. They suppress local opposition and any independent media, obtain rents from local businesses and are often involved in the running of these businesses. The term 'burness' or bureaucratic business has been coined to describe this phenomenon and, as a consequence, it is difficult for small- and medium-sized businesses to set up and develop in such an environment.

The most extreme case of the loss of central control is to be found in the North Caucasus, especially Chechnya. There Ramzan Kadyrov effectively runs the republic on his own terms, helped by federal subsidies. Some local laws are based on Sharia or Islamic law, and the largest mosque in Russia is in Grozny, the capital.

The conclusion is that no unitary state, in the classical meaning of the term, exists in Russia. What exists is a spontaneous confederation in a weak legislative framework, with common political and social institutions and different statuses enjoyed by the regions. Even the statement that the state is held together by 'securocrats' – the military, political police and the militia – is not accurate as corruption now reaches the top levels of the military.

Parliamentary and presidential elections in Russia since 1991 have always been rigged, and there have been protests, but these have little effect. This changed in 2011–12 when Muscovites, in particular, demonstrated against the blatant manipulation of the results.

Large cities are not as dependent on the state as the medium and small cities. The 319 monotowns – where there are only one or two industries, usually part of the military-industrial complex – are the most dependent, as without government contracts and subsidies they would collapse. They resent the advent of democracy and the market economy because they associate them with the loss of their traditional way of life where the state provided employment and social benefits. They are the heartland of support for Putin and look to him for survival. These people are conservative, patriotic and resistant to change.

All major publications and media are now run by those loyal to the Putin clan. The main message is that there is no alternative to Putin, but his popularity began to dip after 2010 because of declining incomes. In 2013 they were 62 per cent with the opposition climbing to 36 per cent.

Then the president had a great stroke of luck. The Maidan protests in Kyiv (Kiev in Russian) in February 2014 led to the flight of President Viktor Yanukovych and the election of a new pro-Western president and government. Moscow regarded its naval base in Sevastopol, Crimea, as of critical importance for national security. Crimea, with a majority ethnic Russian population, after a referendum, was annexed by Russia in March 2014. Conflict broke out in Donetsk and Luhansk oblasts – with large ethnic Russians populations – and they declared themselves people's republics. Insurgents attempted to expand their reach aided by 'volunteers' from Russia. A bloody civil war was the result, and about 1.3 million of the original 3.3 million inhabitants have fled – most to others parts of Ukraine but half a million to Russia and 100,000 abroad. The US and the EU imposed economic sanctions, and a new Cold War got under way. The annexation of Crimea was wildly popular in Russia and Putin's approval ratings – as high as 80 per cent – hit a level unseen since 2000.

Putin has worked tirelessly to forge closer ties with former Soviet republics. The Commonwealth of Independent States proved a disappointment, but the Customs' Union and the Eurasian Union promise more, and they consist of Russia, Belarus, Armenia and Kazakhstan. Does Putin want to recreate the Soviet Union? No. True, he has said that the collapse of the Soviet Union was the greatest geopolitical disaster of the twentieth century. On the other hand, he has expressed the view that anyone who does not mourn the passing of the Soviet Union has no heart but anyone who tries to recreate it has no head.

Putin has forged a close relationship with the Russian Orthodox Church. The Duma passed a law returning all Church property seized during the Soviet era, and this made the Orthodox Church one of the largest landholders in the state.

Over the past 15 years, Putin has ordered state-owned energy companies to contribute billions to the rebuilding of thousands of churches destroyed during the Soviet era, and around 25,000 churches have been built or rebuilt since the early 1990s. The church has the right to teach religion in schools and to review all draft legislation before the Russian Duma.

The election of Patriarch Kirill in January 2009 strengthened bonds as the Patriarch and Putin share a common vision of Russian national identity and exceptionalism. According to this vision, Russia is neither European nor Asian but rather a unique society representing a special set of values which are believed to be divinely inspired. The Church partners the state, and this is the ideological justification for Putin's crackdown on dissent and the repression of civil society and other religious groups.

The basis of Putin's legitimacy was, until recently, the increasing standard of living. Now with the economy flagging, emphasis has switched to Putin as the Father of the Nation who is defending it against a hostile West which is attempting to impose its will on Russia. Vyacheslav Volodin, deputy chief of staff of the presidential administration, coined the slogan: 'If there is Putin – there is Russia, if there is no Putin – there is no Russia.' In St Petersburg, he has been portrayed as an angel spreading out his hand to bless the city's inhabitants, and the same city has unveiled a statue of him as a Roman emperor. Vladislav Surkov, a close associate, has revealed that Putin is a 'man whom fate and the Lord sent to Russia'.

When Vladimir Putin was re-elected president in February 2012, the Patriarch acclaimed him with the words: 'He is a miracle of God.' In April 2015, the Patriarch consecrated a new church to the 'special forces', the KGB and FSB, who gave their lives for the Fatherland. When there were demonstrations against Putin because of the atrocities in Chechnya, the Patriarch's spokesman commented: 'Organised forces with foreign support are behind this.' Kirill maintains that 'in Russia a strong, centralised form of rule is typical: without this nothing gets done' (*The Times*, 9 May 2015).

The Russian mode of rule is referred to as *sistema*, the system. Alena Ledeneva (http://www.russia-direct.org, 4 May 2015) defines it as a network-based system of governance. Characteristics are the limited nature of property rights; the manner in which the legal system can be manipulated by the authorities to remove anyone they dislike; the double standards of the Russian Orthodox Church, which is involved in politics and which justifies the actions of corrupt officials; the all-embracing corruption which pervades power institutions; and the powerlessness of the individual vis-à-vis *sistema*.

It is based not on what you know but who you know, and another factor is doublethink. If a politician helps another to get a job it is corruption, but if you help a friend to get a job, it is friendship and mutual help. Politics is virtual – in other words, merely a façade. There are democratic elections, but the results are always rigged. *Sistema* exists in many countries such as Silvio Berlusconi's Italy and in Central Asia where it surfaces as clanism, neo-patrimonial power or patronal politics. Traditionally, proximity to the tsar meant proximity to power and wealth. Hence being near Putin opens up huge opportunities, and no other centre of power is permitted to emerge. Property rights are insecure (there is no freehold, only leasehold in Russian law), and even the wealthiest oligarch is ready to hand over his assets to the state without a whimper. In China, there is *guanxi* (system of social networks and informal relationships which facilitate business and other deals), and paying bribes is a way of life. However, it is not as suffocating as in Russia because small- and medium-sized businesses (SMEs) can prosper. A reason for this is that China does not have an abundance of oil and gas – the natural resource curse. Thus people there have to work hard to generate wealth. In Russia *sistema* has been remarkably successful and has ensured stability and if the country collapsed, new power holders would emerge who would most likely develop their own form of *sistema*.

There are about twenty million Muslims (95 per cent are Sunni) in Russia, and Moscow has the largest Muslim population of any European city. This is about one in seven of the population, but present trends indicate that some young Muslims are being radicalised and at least 3,000 are fighting with Islamic State in Syria and Iraq, the majority of whom come from the Caucasus. Russia, in common with many other European states, has to contend with Islamism in their midst.

On 28 December 2015, a 400-page tome of pronouncements by President Putin, *Words that Change the World*, was sent to about a thousand politicians and officials. It consists of nineteen speeches, articles and campaign pledges dating back to the president's appearance at the UN General Assembly in 2003. A letter accompanying the gift explains that the speeches would allow readers to understand the 'moral principles and reference points which led to extremely important domestic and foreign policy decisions'. The president constantly insists that the UN should be paramount in global decision making. The anthology includes the president's speech at the Munich security conference when he railed against US dominance, claiming it had 'overstepped its national borders in every way', and it also includes his speech in 2014 confirming Russia's annexation of Crimea which, he claimed, had been 'handed like a sack of potatoes' to Ukraine in 1954. Another striking comment, in 2012, was that 'any person living in our country should not forget his faith and ethnicity but before everything else, he must be a citizen of Russia and be proud.'

The economy

After the collapse of the Soviet Union, the Russian economy went into freefall. Egor Gaidar headed a team of economists who introduced shock therapy to reform the moribund planned economy. Hyperinflation wiped out savings, and privatisation of industry was set in train. The Central Bank engaged in quantitative easing, also known as printing money, as tax returns were very small. The oil industry was the biggest prize, and those who acquired major stakes became known as oligarchs, but Prime Minister Viktor Chernomyrdin made sure that the gas industry, Gazprom, remained nationalised. Yeltsin lurched from crisis to crisis and was kept afloat by IMF and other loans. The economy grew 1.4 per cent in 1997, which was quite an achievement given that the average annual decline between 1992 and 1996 had been 9.4 per cent, but the economy collapsed like a pack of cards in 1998, and Russia defaulted on its debts.

Then a miracle occurred as economic growth between 1999 and 2008 skyrocketed. Russia's per capita gross domestic product (GDP) doubled in constant prices (average annual growth of 7 per cent) and grew sixfold in nominal dollars – from $270 billion to $1.7 trillion in current prices as oil prices rose fivefold during these years. Then the global crisis of 2008–9 hit Russia very hard, and in 2009 the economy contracted by 8 per cent, more than any other major economy. The economy recovered and recorded 4 per cent growth in 2010 and in 2011 but then stagnation set in and there has been decline ever since. The slowdown occurred before the annexation of Crimea and the fighting in eastern Ukraine which exacerbated the economic situation (Aron 2015: passim). The economy declined by 3.9 per cent in 2015. The oil price is a key factor as oil and gas revenues made up 52 per cent of the budget and 68 per cent of export revenues in 2013. An oil price of $52 a barrel is needed to balance the 2016 budget, but the oil price at present is around $40. Military expenditure was cut 3.6 per cent in 2015 and 5 per cent in 2016.

One of the consequences of the downturn is capital flight and it reached $151.5 billion in 2014 or about 7.5 per cent of GDP. This was almost three times the previous year's amount.

Poverty has been increasing and embraced 22.9 million in the first quarter of 2015. In early 2016, the Russian Academy of Sciences estimated that 25 per cent of the population was below the poverty line. Russia's population, in January 2016, was an estimated 146.5 million.

Russia has been turning more and more towards China. A $400 billion gas deal was signed in November 2014. Trade turnover is rising rapidly, and the Russian Central Bank is to create a new funding instrument in yuan. However it can normally only be used in bilateral trade. Trade turnover with the Middle Kingdom is a key priority, but it declined 27 per cent in 2015 due to falling oil and commodity prices, and Chinese investment in Russia has been disappointing. President Putin and President Xi Jinping are forging a closer relationship and meet several times a year.

Economists have recommended structural reforms based on secure property rights, the rule of law and a reduction in the number of state-owned enterprises. These recommendations have fallen on deaf ears. Why? The political will is not there to reform because it would upset the balance of interests at the top. How did the Putin clan come to dominate the economy?

A few days after Vladimir Putin was inaugurated as president on 7 May 2000, he signed a decree creating Rosspirtprom (Russian alcohol industry). State shares in seventy alcohol enterprises were transferred to it, and it became a cash cow at a time when oil was cheap, and the state thus took over booze from the mafia. Putin established two groups: the economics group and a business group. The latter's function was to establish control over property and financial flows.

By spring 2008, according to Olga Kryshtanovskaya, a leading sociologist, the Putin clan made up about 80 per cent of the country's top political leadership. Most members were from the former KGB, GRU (military intelligence), the military and the Ministry of Internal Affairs (people with epaulettes), and about a quarter of the elite migrated from St Petersburg to Moscow with the president.

In January 2003, sixty-six of the largest companies in which the state held controlling stakes were placed under Putin's management. Four main sectors of the economy were chosen: finance; the fuel and energy complex; the military-industrial complex; and infrastructural enterprises – from transport to various forms of communication. One estimate is that the Putin clan controlled, in 2014, about 15 per cent of the Russian GDP which works out at about $280 billion. It can be understood as a vertical holding company, and it has its own credit facilities; its own oil and gas wells which provide a constant flow of cash; its own pipeline systems; its own transport services; its own media services; its own security services; and its own control system of parliament and of the electoral system. All this can be dubbed Rossiya Inc.

Foreign policy

Russia's goal after the demise of the USSR was to join the club of 'civilised nations'. It dreamed of becoming as rich as the leading Western countries and expected money and aid to achieve this, but the West did not reciprocate. Moscow waited for a new Marshall Plan but got only loans and, it must be confessed, poor advice from American and other experts. Andrei Kozyrev, the first post-communist foreign minister – he now suns himself in Florida – was sacked for being too pro-Western. In other words, Russia's kowtowing to the US had not paid off. Russia was dependent on IMF and other loans and could not pursue a foreign policy which reflected national interests.

Putin's foreign policy has much in common with that of Prince Alexander Gorchakov, the master diplomat of the nineteenth century:

*   *Realpolitik* (copying Bismarck);
*   Supreme self-confidence that Russia is one of the world's leading powers;
*   An unshakable belief in the utility of hard power;
*   The belief that Russia will always play a leading role in international affairs.

Putin has learnt from hard experience to cling to his own beliefs, reject foreign concepts of right and wrong, and defend national interests even in the face of overwhelming odds. He has a neo-Hobbesian vision of the planet where the strong dictate to the weak, and this flows from this conviction that small states have to concede to large states. He does not want to recreate the Soviet Union, but he claims a proprietorial right to decide what happens in the space occupied by the former Soviet Union.

Putin began as a pro-European committed to partnership with the European Union, the US and NATO but changed his mind as NATO and the EU expanded to Russia's borders. He favours a greater Europe – embracing Russia – and is multipolar and pluralist, but the EU prefers a wider Europe which would exclude states which do not conform to the Western model. Estonia, Latvia and Lithuania, former Soviet republics, and Poland, the Czech Republic, Slovakia, Hungary, Romania and Bulgaria, all former members of the Warsaw Pact, have joined NATO and the EU. Putin regards the EU's decision to oblige Ukraine to choose between closer ties with Russia or closer ties with it as the genesis of the present conflict.

The turning point in relations with the West was Putin's hard-hitting speech in Munich in February 2007, which was partly due to his exasperation at Western policies but also stemmed from his belief that he had little to lose by attacking Washington and its NATO allies (Lo 2015: 23).

While Putin was at the Olympic Games in Beijing, in August 2008, Georgia became embroiled in a conflict in South Ossetia. Russia responded and occupied Abkhazia as well, and ethnic Georgians were expelled from South Ossetia. These two regions were recognised by Russia and would have preferred to join Russia, but Moscow has not moved to incorporate them.

Putin was greatly offended by the US support of public demonstrations against him in 2011 and early 2012, and one can trace a hardening of attitudes towards the US from this date. During the 2012 presidential campaign, the US was pilloried as the fount of all evil. Until the world financial crisis of 2008, economic growth was the bedrock of his legitimacy, but it is now the renaissance of the Russian nation. One can characterise his foreign policy as an anti-agenda with Russia as the spoiler, but this changed dramatically in September 2013 when Putin intervened successfully in the dispute over Syrian chemical weapons.

The reset with the US from 2009 to 2011 promised much and eventually disappointed, but it did produce the START agreement of 2010 which was the most significant achievement since 1993. There is now an ideological divide or schism between Russia and the West with the former remaining conservative and traditional and the latter liberal; the gulf between these two is now as wide as between communism and capitalism. Russia does not believe it has anything to learn from the West but only craves one thing: advanced technology.

The increase in Russian defence spending added to the tension, and NATO responded with exercises near the Russian border. This was to reassure the Baltic States and Poland that NATO would come to their aid if attacked, and it was made clear to Moscow that Article 5 of the NATO Charter, which states that an attack on one member is an attack on all, was still in force. Russia's deputy minister of defence complained that the West was forcing Russia to engage in a new arms race.

During an interview with the German magazine *Bild*, published on 12 January 2016, Putin stated that there had been a conversation between Valentin Falin and

Egon Bahr, the father of Ostpolitik, in 1990, in which Bahr had proposed that a new alliance be formed in Europe, 'separate from NATO' that would include Central European countries, the US and the Soviet Union. Putin complained that, instead of pursuing the Bahr plan, NATO had expanded in Europe which was a grave mistake and a manifestation of Western post–Cold War triumphalism. 'Leading NATO member nations should have refused to accept new member states into the Alliance,' insisted Putin; 'you are not obliged to accept applications.' The vision of a neutralised Europe, with the US and Russia as equal partners, Moscow holding a recognised sphere of influence along with veto power on strategic decisions, and NATO pared down or fully disbanded, could perhaps have been achieved if Moscow had pressed harder, but the opportunity was lost and Putin still laments that. According to him, Russia's main mistake 'in the last 25 years' has been not to 'state our national interests from the very beginning: if we had, maybe today the world would look more balanced.' Putin made clear Russia does not want to play the role of a superpower because it is too expensive. According to the president, Russia 'is the fifth or sixth world economy – today in trouble but with good growth potential'. He angrily rejected President Obama's assertion that Russia is a 'regional power' as it is too big and present in too many regions – Europe, Asia, the Arctic and the Pacific – a world power by definition. Putin was signalling that present-day Russian ambitions are less than those of the Soviet Union during the Cold War, and a possible future 'Yalta 2.0' – an agreement to divide spheres of influence and settle scores to 'balance' the world and make it a safer place – would not cost that much. The entire West or possibly several leading European countries, including Germany, must take the offer and strike a deal, even when Moscow is slightly humbled by an economic downturn. There are conditions, of course, such as accepting the Crimean annexation as just and absolutely legal. Ukraine must be accepted as a Russian de facto protectorate and the government in Kyiv pressured to accept constitutional reform, transforming the country into a loose federation, and discouraged from seeking any form of integration in the EU. All sanctions imposed over Crimea must be lifted and fighting in eastern Ukraine stopped. The US and its allies must accept Bashar al Assad as the legitimate president of Syria, and Putin rejects all claims that he is responsible for massacres. 'He is defending his nation against outside aggression by armed terrorists. Any civilian casualties are collateral and are the ultimate fault of the armed opposition and those who support them' (*Eurasian Daily Monitor*, 14 January 2016).

Putin's statement that Russia was the 'fifth or sixth world economy' was correct in 2015, but the situation has changed. The rouble fell from thirty-three to the dollar, in June 2014, to eighty-four roubles, in January 2016. This resulted in GDP shrinking from $2.1 trillion, in June 2014, to under $1 trillion, but it recovered to sixty-eight to the dollar in April 2016.

On another occasion, ruminating about Russian rulers – his heroes are Peter the Great and Catherine the Great – Putin commented that the 'greatest criminals in our history were those weaklings who threw power to the ground – Nicholas II and Gorbachev – and allowed power to be picked up by hysterics and madmen'. On the October Revolution:

> Letting your rule be guided by an idea is right but only when it leads to the right results, not like it did for Vladimir Ilich [Lenin]. In the end, that idea led to the fall of the Soviet Union. We did not need a global revolution. They [the Bolsheviks] placed an atomic bomb under the building that is Russia and the bomb exploded.

On balance, has foreign policy been a success or a failure under Putin? According to Bobo Lo, it has been 'outstandingly successful'. The humiliated nation of the 1990s has transformed itself into a 'resurgent global power' and 'one of the influential and competitive poles in the modern world. It is more independent, more indispensable, more self-confident and more influential than at any time since the fall of the Soviet Union' (Lo 2015: 199). The West needs Russia more than ever, and this implies it must treat Russia with respect and as an equal. Russia backs Syria's President Bashar al Assad with weapons and diplomatic support in the UN and elsewhere. The Russian relationship goes back to the 1950s, and Moscow is keen to retain influence there. Russia has the ability to surprise, and this was illustrated in September 2015, when Sukhoi jets and attack helicopters arrived in Syria and engaged in combat missions as did ground forces. Russia thereby influenced the course of the civil war, but Moscow engaged in a 'partial withdrawal' of its forces in March 2016. A ceasefire and talks in Geneva held out hopes of an end of the war.

The downing of a Russian passenger plane, en route from Sharm el Sheikh, Egypt, to St Petersburg on 31 October 2015, resulted in Russia engaging in a bombing campaign directed at Daesh or Islamic State but also against opponents of al Assad. Relations between Moscow and Ankara plummeted after a Turkish F-16 shot down a Russian Su-24 bomber on 24 November 2015, accusing it of violating Turkish airspace. Moscow maintained that the jet had not strayed into Turkish airspace.

Japan

Russia has been trying to improve relations with Japan for a long time, but the main sticking point is the status of the Kurile Islands. Japan has accused Russia of boosting military infrastructure in the South Kurile Islands of Kunashir and Iturup and has made clear that it wishes Moscow to discuss the sovereignty of all the South Kurile Islands. In 1945, the Soviet Union acquired the South Kuriles after Japan capitulated, but Tokyo and Washington have never legally recognised the Southern Kuriles as part of the Soviet Union or Russia, and no peace treaty between the two countries has been signed since 1945. The Moscow Declaration of 1956 ended the state of war and re-established full diplomatic relations between Moscow and Tokyo. According to the declaration, Moscow promised, after a peace treaty had been concluded, to transfer sovereignty of the islands of the Lesser Kurile Chain – Shikotan and the uninhabited Habomai Islands – to Japan. President Putin has renewed the offer, but Tokyo flatly rejects it.

Prime Minister Dmitry Medvedev has stated that seventy billion roubles ($1 billion) will be invested in the South Kurile Islands to develop them and improve living standards there. Of the eighteen major Kurile Islands, only four are inhabited, and of these, three are in the south. The entire population of the Kuriles is under 20,000 so the investment per capita is huge. Medvedev declared that

> we are rebuilding not only the civilian but also the military infrastructure of the Kuriles. The build-up began some time ago and is now well under way. The Kuriles are strategically important for the defence of Russia and our military presence will be enhanced.

On 22 October 2015, Sergei Shoigu, minister of defence, announced that a military base is to be built in the Kurile Islands. Russia's interest is not only military and political. The world's 'richest known deposit of rhenium, a rare earth element used in alloys to create components for missiles and supersonic aircraft technology is on Iturup, near the Kudryavy volcano. Besides rhenium, there are thousands of tonnes of titanium, iron ore, gold and silver in the Kuriles.'

Two nuclear-armed submarines will patrol from Kamchatka into the Russian-controlled Sea of Okhotsk. Keeping control over the entire Kurile chain, including Kunashir and Iturup, is regarded as essential to keep US and allied naval anti-submarine forces out of the Sea of Okhotsk. The Lesser Kuriles – Shikotan and Habomai – are viewed as strategically less important, and Putin appears disposed to handing them back to Japan, but Tokyo will not settle for these two and wants all of the islands back. Tension between Tokyo and Moscow is set to continue (*Eurasia Daily Monitor*, Vol. 12, no. 138, 23 July 2015).

Now for some good news. In July 2015, the US and Russia introduced visa-free travel for indigenous inhabitants of Chukotka and Alaska. The passports of Alaskan natives will contain an insert to that effect. It only applies to those who have relatives living in Chukotka or Alaska. This term applies to those who have blood relatives, a member of a tribe or those who share a linguistic or cultural heritage with indigenous peoples of the neighbouring territory. Inhabitants need an invitation and can stay up to 90 days in the neighbouring country. Russians have been able to enter parts of the US without a visa since 2012, and a visa-free regime exists for the American island of Guam and the Mariana Islands in the Pacific Ocean.

The US

President George H.W. Bush received an unexpected present on Christmas Day 1991: Gorbachev's head on a platter. Well, not quite. The Soviet leader had just announced he was stepping down as president, and the end of Gorbachev was the end of the Cold War. Bush went on television to explain to the American people the significance of the event. The collapse of communism meant the end of the Cold War and that the US had won, and he congratulated the people on the victory of their values. The language became more grandiloquent in the Union address in January 1992. 'Changes of biblical proportions' had occurred and 'by the grace of God, America won the Cold War.' A new era had dawned. A 'world once divided into two armed camps', he declared to the US Senate and House of Representatives, 'now recognises one sole and preeminent power, the United States of America'. The audience roared its approval.

This was in marked contrast to the language used at the Malta summit in December 1989, when it was stated that the Cold War had ended in cooperation with Gorbachev. Just a few hours before Bush's Christmas message, the White House declared: 'Working with President Reagan, myself, and other allied leaders, President Gorbachev acted boldly and decisively to end the bitter divisions of the Cold War and contributed to the remaking of a Europe whole and free' (Plokhy 2012: xiii–xv).

Throughout 1991, Bush had downplayed his influence and been very modest about his contribution to events. Suddenly this all changed, and grandiloquent language took over and framed the narrative which the American people internalised about the ending of the Cold War. In reality, the Soviet Union had imploded, but the story now was that US policies had played a decisive role in bringing communism to an end and the Soviet Union to its knees. This was writing history in dreamland. We now know that Bush's preferred scenario was for the CPSU to continue to exist. The main reason for this was the fear that the four Soviet republics with nuclear weapons could lose control of them.

America was now the sole superpower, and the myth that it was omnipotent, omniscient and omnipresent took hold and led to terrible consequences. The exceptionalism of the Soviet Union had turned to ashes, but the exceptionalism of the US had triumphed. Exceptionalism was missionary and both superpowers believed it was their duty to spread their values to all corners of the earth, but now America had no competitor when it came to spreading the gospel of the good life.

How was Russia to be treated? It was there for the taking, politically and economically. Russia expected a grand partnership which would elevate the country to the pinnacle of the civilised world. The US had no intention of according Russia star treatment and so began the bitter disillusionment with the brave, new post-communist world. Russia was humiliated time after time as it came begging for money to Washington to keep afloat, but the dream was still there when Vladimir Putin became president in 2000. He expected respect and got very little. Gradually things turned sour and have ended in a new Cold War. How did this happen?

The exit of the Soviet Union from Afghanistan was followed by the defeat of the Taliban. Washington regarded this as a job well done and left. This permitted the Taliban to regroup and out of this came al Qaeda and Osama bin Laden. The attack on the World Trade Center in New York and the Pentagon on 9/11 by al Qaeda was an existential shock to Americans. How could such a thing happen on US soil? The response by President Bush was the war on terror, but at the best of times this is a very vague concept. How can one launch a war against such an intangible opponent as terror?

So it was back to Afghanistan to wipe out al Qaeda there, but after fifteen years and counting, the Taliban have still to be beaten. A primary objective was nation building. The tribes could be brought together and a Western-style state created with free and fair elections, a parliament and a free market economy. Just like America, in other words. Did the Afghans want to become like Americans? No one stopped to ask this simple question. It was assumed that outsiders knew best what was good for the Afghans.

The biggest international intervention of the last fifty years saw over a million troops, which cost more than $1 trillion, left 3,500 foreign dead and tens of thousands injured. Britain declared the war over in 2014 but still has 500 troops there and the US still there as well. Out of the Afghan Taliban came the even more aggressive Pakistan Taliban.

By far the greatest blunder was relations with Pakistan and, especially the Inter-services Intelligence Agency (ISI). The West gave Pakistan $20 billion to wean it away from the Taliban but, in reality, Pakistan created, nurtured, trained and funded the Taliban which became America's number one enemy after 9/11. Thus Pakistan was playing a double game, and an inner core, the S division of ISI, helped the Taliban undermine the government in Kabul. Their aim was for the Taliban eventually to take control, a scenario which Pakistan always favoured. Indian influence had to be kept out of the country, but China may be the big winner in the end.

The next big nation building project was Iraq, and it was invaded in 2003 on the pretext that Saddam Hussein had weapons of mass destruction, but they had been removed before the invasion. The reasons for invasion were flimsy, but that was ignored and the advice of Middle East experts – don't invade – was ignored. After taking Baghdad the Iraqi army and police were disbanded.

The invasion also ended the 'covenant of security' that forbade Muslims in non-Muslim countries from harming those who provide them with protection. The first attack in Europe soon followed: the Madrid bombings of 2004. Then in November came the murder, in Amsterdam, of the film-maker Theo van Gogh. The covenant was officially renounced in the UK by Omar Bakri Muhammad in January 2005, and six months later came the 7/7 attacks. It is not surprising that Europe is the target of many attacks as it is home to the greatest number of jihadi veterans or radical preachers, and the world centre is London. These veterans 'groom' foot soldiers to carry out their missions, most of whom are 'misfits' or those with a grievance.

On 1 May 2003, George W. Bush delivered his 'Mission Accomplished' speech on board the USS *Abraham Lincoln*. He appeared quite unaware of the fact that he had presented the Iranian regime with the victory over Iraq which they had failed to achieve in eight years of brutal fighting. With the Iraqi army pulverised, the way was open for a pro-Iranian Shiite regime to take over in Baghdad which would profoundly alter the geopolitics of the Middle East. George H.W. Bush had established links with Saddam to ensure a balance of power there, viewing him as the best bulwark against an ambitious Tehran. When the US pulled out of Iraq in December 2011, Iranian leaders must have felt deep satisfaction that Washington had done their work for them as Iraq was now weak, divided and open to Iranian influence. It had taken thirty-one years of struggle and sacrifice, from 1980 to 2011, to secure the victory the leadership had craved, and the greatest irony of all was that its greatest foe, the Great Satan, had enabled it to celebrate this sweet victory.

Donald Rumsfeld, US secretary of defense from 2001 to 2006, ruminating about Iraq has concluded:

> I'm not one who thinks that our particular template of democracy is appropriate for other countries at every moment of their histories. The idea that we could fashion a democracy in Iraq seemed to me unrealistic. I was concerned about it when I first heard these words.

That is putting it mildly and is reminiscent of Robert McNamara's comments about the Vietnam War: we should never have been there in the first place, and we are abysmally ignorant of foreign cultures. Rumsfeld went on to mention that NATO and the UN are no longer fit for purpose. The West should start a new Cold War–style offensive against Islamic State, and removing Colonel Gaddafi from power in Libya left the region more dangerous. President Obama has abdicated leadership and opened the door to Russian expansionism (*The Times*, 6 June 2015).

The US has spent billions of dollars training an Iraqi army, but it is mainly Shia and is reluctant to defend Sunnis. The quagmire of Iraq has spawned Islamic State (also called Daesh, ISIS [Islamic State in Iraq and Syria] and ISIL [Islamic State in Iraq and the Levant]), a Sunni fundamentalist group, determined to take over Iraq and Syria. The rise of IS has drawn in Shia Iran and Shia Hezbollah in Lebanon. They also want to keep President al Assad, an Alawite Shia, in power in predominantly Sunni Syria. The US, under the cautious President Obama administration, provides aid, training and air power in the fight against al Assad. Boots on the ground is not an option after the coruscating experiences of Afghanistan and Iraq.

China

Economic growth widened the gulf between the coastal cities, and the rest of China and cities, towns and villages began to manage their own local economy. Those which could attract foreign investment became richer and richer and, inevitably, corruption and crime flourished. The 'princelings', the sons and daughters of the party-state elite, have built up their own business empires, and these included members of Deng's family. Bandit gangs became a major problem, and smuggling contraband goods, especially drugs, became enormously lucrative. The mayor of Beijing became involved in a massive scandal in 1989 and was expelled from the Politburo and sent to jail for eighteen years. Jiang Zemin's ideology became nationalism, and the nation's ire was turned on Japan. 'Spiritual pollution [Western ideas]' was not to infect China. Inflation reached 22 per cent in 1994, but Zhu Rongji managed to bring it down. He was formally made prime minister in 1998 and was popularly known as the 'economic emperor'.

Deng's model can be seen as three rungs of a ladder. The coastal region would develop first, then the central region and the western region last, and this meant that the coastal region received huge benefits initially. By 2005, the coastal region accounted for more than 90 per cent of exports and imports, and it received 85 per cent of foreign investment which exceeded $70 billion annually. Public capital expenditures being channelled to the coastal provinces increased from 50 per cent in the mid-1980s to 65 per cent in the mid-1990s.

The inner group in the Politburo, the Standing Committee, runs the country. Each member is responsible for a sector of the economy or the state, and they work behind closed doors and attempt to be invisible. The Central Military Commission, always headed by the party leader, ensures that the military remains loyal to the party. Double-digit increases in the annual military budget are now a feature of Chinese life. In order to ensure that the military concentrates on purely military affairs and does not become a state within a state, it was forced to give up almost all its economic interests and hand its enterprises over to the state. The fear was that it would slip out of party control. Despite this, many military officers have extensive economic interests.

News or information is of critical importance as Beijing has to ensure that it tells the story. The Central Propaganda Department of the CC contains a formidable army of officials to ensure that editors and authors understand where the red line of permissible comment is. Ideology is functional and hence is infinitely flexible, but there is one chink in the armour: Hong Kong. The colony retains a special status, and it is possible to publish radical books there – for example, a book on the number of deaths during the Great Leap Forward (a taboo subject) was published there.

How were relations with the sole superpower to develop? Beijing was nervous about the future, meaning the ability of the Communist Party to retain power. There was the view after the collapse of the Soviet Union that nation states were giving way to globalisation. President Clinton spelled out his vision at the UN General Assembly in September 1993. The goal of the US was to expand the number of states which were market-based democracies until humanity achieved a 'world of thriving democracies that cooperate with each other and live in peace'. Promoting human rights aggressively was to become the cornerstone of American policy, and this was based on the belief that democracies do not go to war but autocracies are violent and often export terrorism. Chinese leaders perceived Clinton's vision as an attempt to subvert their state and keep it weak. Washington proposed dialogue on many issues, but no one seems to have realised that this implied the Chinese should gradually negotiate away the pillars of their own system. Beijing's response was predictable: it would never give in to pressure from abroad. It never had and never would. Washington thought of the post-Soviet world as unipolar, but Beijing wanted it to be multipolar. Relations reached an impasse in March 1994, when Secretary of State Warren Christopher met Li Peng, the Chinese prime minister. The exchanges were brutal as Li made clear that Chinese human rights policy was not the business of the US, and that the US should address its own human rights problems before criticising China.

The US got the message and placed less emphasis on forcing human rights concessions out of the Chinese; this led to Jiang Zemin visiting the US in 1997, and President Clinton visiting China a year later.

Hong Kong, Britain's richest colony, returned to Chinese sovereignty on 1 July 1997. Jiang Zemin beamed as the Chinese flag was raised and the Union Jack was lowered, but Hong Kong will retain its separate identity within China for fifty years. British citizens, for example, do not need a visa to visit the former colony. Chris Patten, the last governor, ruffled some feathers by attempting to introduce democracy shortly before the handover. Called a 'sinner for a thousand years', Patten was doing something that Britain had always refused to do, but British businessmen did not side with him. Li Peng, the chief Chinese negotiator, confided that his main objective had been to reassure local business leaders that their wealth was safe under Beijing rule as a massive outflow of money was the last thing China wanted, and the ex-colony retained its own currency, the Hong Kong dollar. Consultative democracy will be practised. In other words, Beijing will decide who rules, and there was talk of Hong Kong residents choosing their leader in 2017. If elected, he will be acceptable to Beijing as well. The People's Republic cannot countenance the democracy bug entering from the former colony. In 1997, over 800,000 Hong Kong citizens left, clutching British passports, but since then over half a million have returned as they believe they can make more money there. Another reason for returning is that they found the work ethic in Canada, the US and Australia too laid back. The Chinese like to work hard.

Macau returned to the Motherland in 1999, and it is the gambling capital of China, with the state taking 90 per cent of the profits. China now has native speakers of Portuguese which is very good for business with Brazil, Angola and other former Portuguese colonies. Jiang could derive great satisfaction from the fact that China had managed to drive away all the foreign 'devils': Russian, French, German, Italian, British, Portuguese and Japanese. There was only one territory left, Taiwan, to complete the restoration of 'one China'. It had been ruled by Japan from 1895 to 1945 and thereafter by Chiang Kai-shek's Guomindang as the Republic of China. Chiang ruled with an iron fist until his death in 1975 at age 87; his son, Chiang Ching-kuo, continued Guomindang rule until his death in 1988. Taiwan became an Asian 'tiger' economically and gradually acquired its own identity. Democratically elected presidents engaged in negotiations with Beijing, and a cautious rapprochement has been evident. Taiwan's business community invests heavily in the People's Republic. As long as the US provides a security umbrella, Taiwan will prosper and will retain its independence.

At the 17th Party Congress in 2007, Hu Jintao was voted another five years in power, and he talked of 'scientific socialism' and defended the party's monopoly of power. Social harmony was a goal in a country in which the gulf between the rich and poor continued to widen. Two members of minority parties were made ministers in 2007 but, as in other communist countries, this was merely a token gesture. The eight minor parties, disrespectfully dubbed 'flower pot' parties, are controlled by the CPC. There are contested elections at village level, but local activists complain that communists ensure that they dominate the lists.

The 2008 Olympic Games were a great triumph for Beijing. The city was cleared of dissidents, factories were relocated to cut down on pollution and China won most gold medals. The Middle Kingdom's message to the world was 'we've arrived.'

The sixtieth anniversary of the People's Republic on 1 October 2009 was marked by an extravaganza which showed the world China's military and economic might.

A scandal occurred when Bo Xilai, the flamboyant party leader in Chongqing, was sacked. As head of the self-governing municipality – it counts thirty-two million inhabitants – Bo had been aiming high. He had wanted to become one of the members of the Politburo Standing Committee at the 18th Party Congress. He was promoting a Mao cult with red songs, statues and eulogies to the Great Helmsman; in other words, he wanted to ride to power on the back of Mao. Unwisely, he fell out with his chief of police, Wang Lijun, who eventually sought asylum in the US consulate in Chengdu. The Americans debriefed him and then handed him over to the Ministry of State Security – the secret police.

Bo's wife, Gu Kailai, was accused of murdering Neil Heywood, a British businessman. She was found guilty and received a suspended death sentence. One of Heywood's roles was apparently to move large amounts of the family cash abroad. Gu was a prominent lawyer whose company oversaw every important contract with a foreign firm. Their son attended the British public school Harrow and Oxford, Harvard and Columbia Universities, and wealth oozed from the family.

The 18th Party Congress finally met a month late, in November 2012, due to infighting over who would be promoted. Xi Jinping became secretary general of the party and also assumed the roles of president and chair of the Central Military Commission. Li Keqiang became prime minister in March 2013. The Politburo Standing Committee was reduced from nine to seven members. Xi and Li are the Fifth Generation leaders born in the 1950s, but the other five members are all members of the Fourth Generation leaders born in the 1940s. So Xi and Li will have to wait until the 19th Party Congress, in 2017, to renew the Standing Committee with their nominees, as the other five will all be near or past the age of retirement, which is 70 years.

The rising standard of living has seen the emergence of a Chinese middle class. Credit Suisse, in its 2015 Global Wealth Report, estimates that China has now surpassed the US as the country with the largest middle class. It defines members of the middle class as those with wealth (not income) of between $50,000 and $500,000; almost 110 million people now fit this criterion compared to 92 million in the US, and this figure is expected to grow substantially by 2025. It could represent about a half of the urban population by that date. China's population is expected to level off at about 1.5 billion. Traditionally, an expanding middle class develops a thirst for capital, information and consumer choice. China's response is to strengthen its control over traditional media to counter the increasing number of bloggers who have millions of followers between them. The CPC now counts about eighty-eight million members or 13 per cent of the adult population. An official report stated that in 2007, 88 per cent of those with personal fortunes of over $14 million were children of top party and government officials. One can assume that many of them found their way into the party, and this means that the CPC is already a middle-class party. Students are joining the party in growing numbers. Less than 1 per cent of students were members in 1990 but in 2011, this had risen to 11 per cent.

Some analysts regard the new middle class as consisting mainly of members of the political elite who have been able to convert their patronage into economic wealth, and the term 'black collar class' has been coined to describe them. They dress in black, drive luxury black cars, have hidden incomes and links to organised crime, live with mistresses and lead secret lives. It all sounds like a James Bond movie! The private wealth of members of the elite has become a thorny problem. Just before the Party Congress, the *New York Times* reported on the wealth of the leading families with the information coming from a Chinese source. For instance, the family of Wen Jiabao was estimated to be worth $2.7 billion.

It is instructive that the teachings of Confucius (551–479 BC) are now being studied. Confucius did not found a religion; his values are secular and aim at creating a harmonious and happy society. There are no classes, so class conflict is absent and all people are equal. When communist leaders claim that their goal is a harmonious society in which everyone is happy, they are echoing Confucius; in January 2011, the rehabilitation of the sage was complete when his statue was unveiled on Tiananmen Square.

Xi Jinping is concerned that the core Marxist ideology has suffered a meltdown in the course of the country's reforms. During the summer of 2014, the party started an 'ideological education' programme in rural areas. Training young Marxists is something which has not been done for quite a few years, and the goal is to produce young cadres who will continue the cause and apply Marxism in their practical work. Xi is also concerned by university lecturers criticising China's development, so he has ordered them to defend the 'moral bottom line' and resist the corrosive creep of Western values. Foreign textbooks are to be strictly limited and Marxism and Chinese values funnelled directly 'into the heads of students'. Any sort of discussion which includes blaming party leaders is to be 'banished from the classroom'. Some universities have been told closed-circuit television cameras will be installed in the lecture theatres. The crackdown on academic freedom has seen many academics suspended, sacked and in two cases sentenced to long periods in prison. Those teaching law, economics and history are under the greatest scrutiny, but one lecturer got round the prohibition of teaching comparative constitutional law by sharing discussions in his car.

How does one explain this policy? Xi Jinping is facing the same problem as Mao, Jiang Zemin and Hu Jintao: the fundamental problem that the state does not wither away after the workers take power. Interest groups emerge under socialism. Jiang Zemin talked about the three represents:

- The party should embrace advanced social production forces;
- Advanced culture;
- Represent the overwhelming majority.

Hu Jintao evolved the concept of the harmonious society. Nowadays, hundreds of thousands of Chinese study abroad, millions learn English and millions travel abroad, so why tell universities to cut back the number of foreign textbooks at a time when China is catching up with the outside world? The case of the teacher of constitutional law provides a clue. The party is fearful of foreign ideas ('spiritual pollution') entering China's mainstream. Traditionally, the party solution is to accentuate ideological education and insist that cadres and others study set texts. At present, that means chiefly Xi Jinping's writings and he articulates the Chinese Dream or becoming number one in the world, but there is a contradiction here. The party has already dumped Marx's economics so that means only parts of Marx's opus are relevant to China today.

How is the Chinese Dream to be achieved if foreign ideas are shut out? This only applies to culture and especially the social sciences. Every Chinese girl aspires to have a Gucci handbag or a Versace dress, and that is fine as it strengthens the legitimacy of the party because everyone is getting richer. The Chinese Dream underlines Chinese exceptionalism, but it is different from American exceptionalism as it does not proselytise; it does not claim that its contemporary institutions are relevant outside the Middle Kingdom (Kissinger 2012: xiv).

The US discovered that soft power or cultural influence was a powerful weapon and contributed to the demise of the Soviet Union. As regards China, it can stress the rule of law, human rights, democracy, the accountability of officials and so on, and the American argument is that if China is to become the leading power in the world, it can only do so by becoming more like the US. China is a middle-income country, but no country, as yet, has become an advanced country without first adopting democracy understood in the Western sense, and this deeply worries the Communist Party.

Relations with the US have two faces. Keep out American ideas on society but welcome American technology and science; Beijing cannot afford to fall out with Washington and vice versa. America does not fear Chinese cultural influence, but

China does fear American cultural influence. The party has a powerful weapon which it can deploy when under pressure: nationalism. Every child learns about the century of humiliation. The sign: 'No dogs or Chinese' is trotted out when Shanghai is mentioned, but the problem is that there never was such a sign in Shanghai so it is a cleverly crafted cultural myth. The party can turn the tap of nationalism on at a moment's notice – after all, it controls the narrative – and provide one that suits itself. Xi's goal is to ensure that a Chinese political culture evolves which is devoid of foreign influence, and he can point to the fact that the American economic model or Washington Consensus has failed. Is the American political model heading for the rubbish bin of history? The Chinese Party will do all in its power to achieve this, but will it succeed?

The crisis in the West

How did Beijing react to the financial meltdown in the West in 2008? It launched a huge fiscal stimulus package amounting to about 16 per cent of GDP to ensure that the economy grew by at least 8 per cent in 2009. (Investment forms part of GDP.) Eight is a lucky number in Chinese. Add to that bank lending to state corporations of about 25 per cent of GDP and one can grasp the impact of state direction of the economy. In 2010, it was estimated that the top 1 per cent of Chinese society had a net worth of between $3 trillion and $5 trillion, and this means that there is surplus capital looking for investment opportunities. There are an estimated sixty-four million empty apartments in China, but this does not mean they are unsold as they have been bought as an investment and left empty.

Astonishingly, Mao Zedong Thought made a comeback during the sixtieth anniversary celebrations of the founding of the People's Republic on 1 October 2009. Banners proclaiming Mao Zedong Thought were carried by students from Beijing University and others during the parade, and this began a trend. Statues of Mao began appearing in various cities and towns, including his birthplace. One, in Chongqing, was seven storeys high.

Why should the egalitarian Mao make a comeback among elite students? It had to do with the factional struggle among the leaders of the party and government. There are three main factions in the party leadership. President Hu Jintao (until 2012) is patron of the Communist Youth League (CYL) faction; as a former leader of the CYL he has been promoting former CYL cadres to top party and government posts. Another faction, called the princelings or offspring of former leading party, government and military officials, is headed by President Xi Jinping. The third faction is the Shanghai group.

In August 2011, Xi delivered a remarkable speech to students. He told them that the world ultimately belonged to them: 'The world is yours and it is also ours; but ultimately the world belongs to you. Young people are like the sun at eight or nine in the morning. The future rests with you.'

What is remarkable about this speech? Xi was echoing Mao word for word, but the Great Helmsman was addressing a group of Chinese students at Moscow

University on a visit to the Soviet Union in 1957, and this underlined Xi's commitment to aspects of Maoism. The military was one of his power bases, and it is no surprise to find that he wholeheartedly supports the modernisation of the Chinese military. His military supporters prefer the more aggressive foreign policy stance of Mao to Deng Xiaoping's policy of 'biding one's time and hiding one's talents'.

Riots in Tibet and Xinjiang in 2008 revealed that Beijing has failed to integrate these Buddhist and Muslim areas into the mainstream of Han Chinese culture. There is a growing concern that these border regions are becoming more and more alienated from Beijing rule. A problem for Han Chinese is that the thin air of Tibet means that cadres have to be rotated every three years.

Religion

An increasingly educated population will expect a greater say in how China evolves, and this is already occurring as the Internet flourishes and spreads ideas. There is the Great Chinese Firewall which attempts to exclude access to many sites, but the IT literate can find ways round it.

One of the striking features of modern Chinese life is the revival of religion. Why is this? Daoism is one of the traditional religions, and one can observe numerous restored temples throughout China; many Chinese make the traditional pilgrimage to a temple at New Year. Among the five religions officially recognised by China are Catholicism and Christianity or Protestantism. They are differentiated in the Chinese mind by different terms for God, different transliterations of the names of the Apostles and so on. Protestantism is now regarded as 'post-denominational', and Presbyterian, Lutheran, Methodist, Anglican and Baptist are labels which no longer are relevant. Chinese believers always wanted a unified Christian church which was authentically Chinese. A National Christian Council was set up in 1922 to foster unity but did not make much headway. Under Mao all foreign missionaries were expelled.

Protestantism, however, enjoys no unity of doctrine, and many indigenous churches, such as the True Jesus Church and the Little Flock, sprang up. These were often founded by breakaway groups from other churches. Eventually Western denominations were channelled by the state into the Three-Self Patriotic Movement. These are the churches which Western leaders attend on Sunday mornings when visiting China. Those who refused to join the new union were mercilessly persecuted and went underground. The Cultural Revolution closed down all churches for a decade. There had been about 20,000 churches open in the late 1960s, but the Red Guards burned all the Bibles and Christian literature they could lay their hands on. A new China Christian Council was established in 1980, and it became a member of the World Council of Churches. Pentecostalism, which had appeared at the beginning of the twentieth century, proved very popular. Arguably it is the fastest growing part of Protestantism in China today.

Churches have many fine buildings and provide a social venue for local believers. Underground or unregistered churches are also expanding rapidly, and their pastors are routinely jailed but they grasp the opportunity to engage in pastoral work there. There were an estimated one million believers half a century ago, and this has now swelled to about 130 million with the Three Self-Patriotic Movement claiming twenty million. Many of the underground churches are vociferously supported by the Chinese diaspora in the US and Taiwan, who advocate a more aggressive stance vis-à-vis the state. All believers are conservative and regard the Bible as the literal truth and have little time for the niceties of biblical criticism. In other words, they are fundamentalists. The new emerging middle class is attracted to Protestantism, and Western observers are astonished to observe young, well-dressed Chinese in Shanghai heading for church on Sunday mornings. Many find the underground churches the most attractive.

The Roman Catholic Church – the faithful are estimated at twenty-five million – has survived and is attracting converts. New churches are also being built and are easily recognised with their bell towers and crosses.

So what is the appeal of Christianity? Christian churches appeal to three social groups: those who have lost their family connections and are lonely; those who find it difficult to cope with the rigours of the new China with its emphasis on self-help and individual success; and the new, educated middle class. The church provides a new family and a sense of belonging for the first two groups with many coming to faith through dreams, visions and miraculous healings.

Buddhism and Islam are widely practised. Muslims are mainly concentrated in Xinjiang, but they can be observed in many parts of China wearing their distinctive skull caps.

Women

Women have gained most under communism and China's market economy. In two generations, they have left the back-breaking work in agriculture – face to the ground and back to the sky – and become urban dwellers. They are no longer sentenced to a life of drudgery, bearing and raising a family under the heel of their mother-in-law, who made clear to them that they were the property of their husband and family. Now educated, they can pick and choose who they wish to marry in the cities, and they feel liberated and regard the future as theirs. They negotiate how free they will remain during the marriage and if they are not satisfied, divorce is easy. There is only one problem: Chinese husbands expect their wives to be less intelligent but also to obey them. There is nothing worse for the male ego than being contradicted in bed. This reveals that many have not yet adjusted to the new norms of Chinese life but some have altered their ways; I have been in Chinese families where the husband was as tame as a pussycat. Every wife's goal – pregnancy outside marriage is still frowned upon – is to have a son, and he is treated like a 'little emperor'. Now the one-child policy has been relaxed (it never applied to ethnic minorities); if both spouses have no siblings, they can have two children. This applies to an estimated ninety million families, but experience in other countries reveals that this policy may have little effect.

Arguably, the one-child policy revolutionised the role of females. The brainchild of Chinese rocket scientists, the only technical group to survive the Cultural Revolution unscathed, it was introduced in September 1980. The trigger was Mao's comment that 'mankind must control itself and reach a planned increase,' trumpeted far and wide during the Cultural Revolution. This led to over a million abortions in Shandong province in 1971 alone. The policy was also part and parcel of the desire to plan everything from Beijing. Female infanticide was traditional in a China which regarded the continuity of the family as imperative and only in the male line. The son was to support the parents in their old age and bury them when they died. The tragedy of the one-child policy which caused endless misery (a girl could only marry at twenty and have a child at twenty-four) as enforcers aborted foetuses deemed outside the plan, was that the policy – which, according to official sources, prevented the birth of an extra 400 million babies – was a tragic mistake, as the best contraceptive is capitalism. Rising incomes result in falling birth rates as can be observed in Thailand and Taiwan. A county in a poor province was kept as a test case, and the one-child policy did not apply to it. The result? Birth rates there are now lower than the Chinese average.

The one-child policy spawned a huge bureaucracy of over fifty million officials as there was one spy per ten households. An extra child could cost between two and ten years' annual salary, and obviously, few families could afford this. Female fertility in the 1960s was 6 but is now down to 1.7, which is below the 2.1 needed to reproduce the population. This has led to a gender imbalance which will result in about forty million males in 2020 incapable of finding a wife. Kidnapping of girls and selling them on to prospective husbands is common. Over 100,000 North Koreans girls have sought refuge in China and, it is said, were sold on to sex-starved males for $1,500 each. Another alternative is to purchase an expensive life-size sex doll, modelled on porn stars with real hair and indestructible nipples, and make love to it – or should this be her? The country's total working age population peaked in 2015, and the number of rural workers between the ages of twenty and twenty-nine, in 2030, may only be half its present level. Now, ten million retire each year while the total workforce shrinks by seven million. China currently has five working adults to every pensioner, but this will gradually change to two adults struggling to support one child and four elderly parents who are living longer due to modern medicine. The number of over-60s, in 2015, was over 200 million, but by 2050, it is estimated that a quarter of the population will be sixty-five or older. There are now over a million families who have lost their son; they face a bleak future and will find it difficult to gain admission to a care home or even get a burial plot. These situations will have momentous consequences for the world economy and the Middle Kingdom's role in the world.

One of Chairman Mao's goals after 1949 was to bring about the equality of males and females. Females say they can make money from a stone and are better than males at accumulating wealth. There are now 145 female billionaires (expressed in US dollars), an almost sevenfold increase in the past twenty years, outpacing the fivefold expansion of their male counterparts over the same period. However, there are 1,202 male billionaires. That said, females have yet to climb the tree of political power. The female revolution has been astonishing and climbing the Communist Party ladder may be their next challenge.

Overview

So how does one explain China's astonishing economic performance over the last thirty years? Is there such a thing as a China model? Is China's experience unique? No, it is not. Other countries have recorded very rapid growth – such as Japan, Brazil, Singapore and South Korea – but they have never maintained it for so long. So what is China's secret? It is based on several pillars. One is the huge population which has permitted a flow of rural migrants to augment the labour supply, and then there is the fact that household incomes are deliberately depressed. The undervalued yuan means that foreign goods cost more. Chinese put their savings in banks, and the government sets the borrowing and the savings rates. Borrowing by state enterprises (80 per cent of investment comes from bank loans) is set about 4 per cent below the equilibrium rate, and correspondingly household savings are reduced by that amount; this means that households are subsidising banks and industry. The economy in China is capital-intensive, not labour-intensive. Domestic consumption in China in 2000 amounted to about 45 per cent of GDP, but in 2008 this was down to 35 per cent – an astonishingly low figure – but some economists think the rate is higher. US domestic consumption may be as high as 70 per cent.

Growth has slowed, and this was inevitable. The official figure for 2015 was 6.9 per cent, but according to the Li Keqiang index, which measures electricity consumption, credit growth and rail cargo – it is named after the Chinese prime minister, who devised it when he was a provincial governor – the present growth is between 3 and 4 per cent. Chinese fixed investment is now $5 trillion a year, as much as North America and Europe combined. Capital outflows are climbing to 10 per cent of GDP as China's real effective exchange rate has moved upwards by 30 per cent since 2012. Wages have also been rising as the flow of cheap labour from the villages dries up; this has led to lower corporate profits, and some shipbuilding companies have gone bankrupt. Vast road and rail building projects are under way to keep construction companies employed. There are ghost cities, which are immaculate because they are empty.

The new five-year plan (2016–20) envisages growth of 6.5 per cent with fifty million new jobs being created and the urban population swelling to 60 per cent. These appear to be overambitious targets.

Seeing into the future is a futile business. In the early 1960s, Paul Samuelson, the Nobel Prize-winning economist, predicted that the Soviet economy would overtake the American as the world's largest economy in the 1980s or 1990s. Ouch! According to Michael Pettis, of Peking University,

> there have been 30 or 40 growth miracles since 1945 and every single one has ended either in a debt crisis or a lost decade or two of very low growth. The only different thing about China is that the level of indebtedness and economic imbalances are greater than anything witnessed before.
>
> (Ed Conway, *The Times*, 30 September 2015)

The yuan has dropped its peg to the dollar and is now valued against a basket of currencies which includes the dollar. Beijing is now attempting to achieve a minor miracle: control domestic monetary policy; keep its exchange rate fixed; and permit money (capital) to flow in and out of the country at will. However, international experience has shown that a government can only control two of these three at any one time. In order for the People's Bank of China to control monetary policy, it needs to allow the yuan to float against other currencies. The IMF has recently added the yuan to a basket of leading world currencies. London is bending over backwards to accommodate China in an effort to become the world's main offshore centre for trading the yuan, and Zimbabwe has even made the Chinese currency legal tender in return for writing off $40 million of its debt. As Beijing unpegs its link to the dollar, interest rates will have to rise to attract foreign capital and prevent money flowing out of the country. The problem is that no country has managed a transition of its monetary system, such as China is at present undergoing, without inflicting pain on its own citizens and the rest of the world. The way ahead is going to be rocky (Ed Conway, *The Times*, 19 January 2016).

Xi Jinping is amassing more power than any leader since Mao and Deng, and he has used this to remove those who oppose him. For instance, about forty generals and 40,000 officers have been cashiered for corruption, but because corruption is endemic in society, this charge can be levelled at anyone. Xi's anti-corruption drive has penetrated all sectors of the party and government, and tens of thousands of party, government and business officials have been imprisoned and ruined. Even minor party officials have been caught in the net. The highest ranking casualty is Zhou Yongkang, the former security chief, becoming the first member of the Politburo Standing Committee to be disgraced. Another target are the managers of SOEs. Over a hundred officials did not wait to be charged and moved to the US and Canada, as these countries have no extradition treaties with China. These officials shifted money offshore in the past and then their families, and over a trillion dollars has been squirreled out of China illegally.

In October 2014, the 'Spirit of Xi Jinping' was elevated to the same level as the teachings of Mao and Deng, and it is now placed on a par with Marxism-Leninism, Mao Zedong Thought and Deng Xiaoping Theory. The party newspaper, *People's Daily*, claimed that Xi's 'brilliant talks and instructions represent a new way of thinking, new perspectives, new conclusions and new demands . . . Xi has grasped the new demands of the era as well as the new expectations of the masses'. A Hong Kong critic wrote that 'Xi, the new emperor, is wielding the knife to stifle Western ideas and to impose orthodoxy . . . The clock is being turned back and we seem to be in the midst of a quasi-Cultural Revolution' (*China Brief*, Vol. 15, no. 5, 6 March 2015). Xi shocked many economists by claiming that communism is an 'attainable goal', and this reverses Deng Xiaoping's assertion that China was only in the first stage of building socialism and the process could take a hundred years. He has also revived Mao's policy of tight party control of literature, the arts and all creative work. Democratic centralism has been re-emphasised, and party members have been warned not to engage in 'groundless criticism of major Party policies'.

In December 2015, Xi went one step further and declared himself the 'Core of the Leadership'. The party now expects cadres to demonstrate 'absolute loyalty'. In March 2016, an article by Mao titled 'Work Methods of Party Committees' was circulated. The message was simple: there is only one big boss and he is Xi. The media was warned to reflect truthfully party policy, and total loyalty was demanded of the military. No wonder many assumed that Xi saw himself as the Mao of the twenty-first century. Party leaders, according to the constitution, only serve ten years, but Deng Xiaoping omitted to write this into party statutes. Xi could stay longer than ten years. Another way of reading Xi's démarche would be to regard him as a nervous leader who is expecting troubled times ahead.

The preceding analysis concentrates on domestic issues. How do these impinge on foreign policy? The first thing that is obvious is that the growth of the economy was given top priority, and this involved attracting foreign investment and know-how, including technology transfer. The SEZs were a great success and would not have been possible without good relations with the US, which opened its markets to Chinese goods. Cheap Chinese goods keep down prices and inflation in the US and the European Union.

So the most valuable Chinese export may well turn out to be no inflation. The Chinese producer price index reveals that prices have been falling for four years. Wholesale prices were down 4.8 per cent in 2015 compared to the year before, one of the largest annual falls ever recorded. Deflation in Chinese factories has a worldwide impact. After the global financial crisis of 2008, Chinese state and private enterprises invested heavily and gross capital formation, compared to 2006, has risen threefold. This splurge has been financed by debt: Beijing's total social financing (total credit) rose from 120 per cent of GDP in 2008 to 250 per cent in 2014 ($26 trillion).

The result of this investment surge is that Chinese industry has overcapacity. So China has too many factories producing too many goods, and world demand cannot keep pace. The solution adopted has been to slash prices, and practically no one now pays full price for Chinese goods. Overcapacity is most serious in the fashion industry. Cheaper Chinese goods have led to factory gate prices falling in the US, Germany and Japan. Producer prices in the US are down by 0.7 per cent year on year, in Japan by 2.4 per cent and in Germany by 1.3 per cent, and this is a completely new phenomenon.

Why are manufacturers able to reduce their prices? One reason is that oil is cheaper. The Chinese domestic market is not developed to the point where it can absorb the overcapacity of Middle Kingdom industry. So China can be thanked for ensuring that inflation rates in the developed world stay low. This situation is likely to continue for some time because of China's overcapacity (*The Times*, 20 July 2015).

Although China has a centrally planned economy, part of the economy is acting strangely. One of the reasons for the rapidly expanding debt mountain is shadow or black banking. The borrowed money found its way into assets, and the stock market skyrocketed over the year to 2015 by 150 per cent. Inevitably, the bubble burst, and some 13.5 trillion yuan (£1.4 trillion or $2.17 trillion) was wiped off the value of shares on the Shanghai and Shenzen stock exchanges from mid-June to 8 July 2015. There are over ninety million Chinese investing (speculating would be a more precise term) in the stock exchanges and were encouraged to do so by the party daily, and stocks were a safer bet after the housing bubble burst, according to conventional wisdom. Beijing reacted by ordering state-owned companies not to sell shares, and it became illegal to buy large numbers of shares. Pension funds and the social security fund were forced to buy more shares. The regulators then encouraged investors to borrow even more (against their apartments, if necessary) and buy shares, but the vast majority did not. These panic moves were an attempt to regulate the market, but Beijing discovered that in a market economy this is extremely difficult to achieve. The party has now realised that it cannot run the market as if it were a football team as too many players do not obey orders.

Another concern for Beijing is that the yuan has risen by about 20 per cent against the euro. Meanwhile, Japan is trying to force down the value of the yen, and as a consequence the yuan rose 16 per cent in 2015. With wages rising, some specialists believe that China has lost its competitiveness. The yuan has now joined the IMF's elite group of major currencies (US dollar, pound sterling, euro and yen) held as global reserves, and this is called the special drawing rights basket. The fund deems the currency to be 'freely usable' but not fully convertible, and this means that the decision was not an economic but a political decision, designed to draw China into global governance. Li Keqiang is behind the move and hopes to use the prestige which will flow from joining the world's elite currencies to overcome vested interests in the Communist Party and promote free market reforms. It is a huge risk for Beijing as there are $17.3 trillion in Chinese deposit accounts, and a large proportion is held by rich Chinese who will be permitted to switch half their assets into foreign stocks and property under the new rules. The yuan weighting in the SDR will be 10.92 per cent.

Stable relations with Washington were and are of critical importance in the development of modern China, and Beijing avoids any overt confrontation with the US. Gone are the days when there was brinkmanship over Taiwan. Deng's foreign policy consisted of the Middle Kingdom keeping its head down, as foreign policy consisted of fostering good commercial relations with the world. However, foreign trade always has another dimension: security. The 'string of pearls' bases from China to Myanmar (Burma), Bangladesh, Sri Lanka and Pakistan are just the beginning. The Middle Kingdom is becoming a naval power and wishes to expand its 'string of pearls' around the world. How does it proceed? It offers loans and builds infrastructure. In Sri Lanka's case it provided the military might which permitted Colombo to defeat the Tamil Tigers in 2009 after a twenty-six-year conflict. In Pakistan, China is developing the port of Gwadar and from there is building roads, rail links and pipelines to Xinjiang.

At present, China is becoming more self-confident on the international stage and is pushing its own agenda. The days when Beijing kept its head down are in the past, and now it is raising its head above the parapet higher and higher. It is no longer a game player but becoming a game changer.

BRICS

Brazil, Russia, India, China and South Africa make up the trading organisation BRICS. It has a total GDP of $32 trillion, occupies 26 per cent of the earth's surface, accounts for 16 per cent of world trade and 42 per cent of global population, but China has emerged as the dominant partner. Now Brazilian and Peruvian trade turnover with China is larger than that with the US. A $10 billion transcontinental railway from Peru to Rio de Janeiro, Brazil, is being built and will cut the cost of exporting Brazilian maize, soya bean, oilseeds, iron and other products to China. China has native Portuguese speakers in Macau. In July 2015, a New Development Bank, with an initial capital of $50 billion, and a Currency Reserve Fund, with capital of $100 billion, were established – China is to contribute $41 billion, Russia, Brazil and India $18 billion each and South Africa $5 billion. The reserve fund is to help members and other states which encounter short-term liquidity problems.

China in Africa

China was extraordinarily lucky that the moment it launched its expansion overseas globalisation was just beginning. From being a bit actor on the African and Asian stage, it has become a leading actor. The rules of globalisation were set by the rich countries, the US and the EU in particular, but China is now rewriting those rules and jettisoning many of the norms and conventions adopted by the West. For the first time, there is a new kid on the block which is challenging successfully the hitherto unchallenged dominance of the West in the Third World.

This has been achieved by putting together a barter system in which China gets hydrocarbons, minerals, timber and other materials and, in return, African states get new dams, railways, airports, hospitals, ports and schools. The Chinese companies go for large projects which few international firms would contemplate. A major reason is that they are state-owned, so if they lose some money, the state pays the bill. The Chinese Export-Import Bank and other state banks offer to fund projects which involve Chinese companies, Chinese materials and Chinese labour.

Africa was forgotten by the West after the Cold War, so China seized the opportunity to enter the continent and learn international business. There was also the fact that Africa was a vast treasure trove of raw materials and energy which were greatly in demand for China's rapid economic growth. Xi Jinping visited the continent shortly after becoming leader, and other top leaders visit annually. Few Western leaders bother to go there, but the Chinese understand the value of personal contacts with national leaders. Trade turnover has exploded and reached $200 billion in 2012, up twentyfold since the beginning of the millennium, and is now way ahead of the US and the EU.

China is building the continent's infrastructure, but roads lead to mines, railway lines to ports, and ports where exports to China are possible. Along with the engineers and labourers come the entrepreneurs and small traders. There are at least a million Chinese now in Africa, and they are to be found everywhere working from dawn to dusk to make money. For instance, in Zambia they are chicken farmers, and in Mozambique they farm large areas of the country. Timber is illegally felled and shipped to the Middle Kingdom. Money talks. In Ghana, China put together a $13 billion loan package with the first tranche of $3 billion, and this was more than the country had received from Western sources during fifty years of independence. This permitted the Bui Dam, under way for forty years, to be developed. In 2011, the World Bank loaned all African countries a total of $2.2 billion (French 2014: 187–8).

Africa has notched up some world firsts: Luanda, the capital of Angola, is now the most expensive city in the world because almost everything has to be imported, and Luanda also has the largest shopping mall in Africa, staffed by Chinese.

Not everything has gone according to plan. After Colonel Gaddafi was ousted in Libya, Beijing, in February 2011, arranged for 36,000 Chinese workers to be evacuated. The operation went smoothly because of China's good relations with Greece and Malta. Greece supplied two boats, and when the Chinese landed in Crete, the prime minister welcomed them.

Natural resources make up two-thirds of Africa's exports, but in Nigeria and Angola oil and gas constitute 97 per cent with most of the rest diamonds, but this puts them at the mercy of commodity prices. Nigeria used to have a vast textile industry employing 350,000 workers. Imports are banned, but they have come in from China and elsewhere and almost wiped out the indigenous producers. The Western oil majors have linked up with the Chinese to control the African oil industry. Shell companies in Hong Kong control the trade through Moscow, London, New York, Pyongyang and Shanghai, and then money is then transferred into numbered bank accounts (Burgis 2015: 226–30). The average African sees little of this wealth.

China is shaping the future of Africa whose population is expected to double from one to two billion by mid-century and 3.5 billion by the end of the century.

That will be more than double China's population. For the Chinese the future is bright: the future is black.

Chinese decision making

The Chinese understanding of *Realpolitik* and strategy differs from that of the West. They have learnt from historical experience that not every problem has a solution and not to concentrate on one specific aspect of a problem. China has always been surrounded by enemies with greatly differing traditions and aspirations. This has led the Chinese to avoid an all-or-nothing approach and to elaborate a multilayered, long-term approach to security.

Chinese are much taken by *wei qi* (a game of surrounding pieces) which is based on strategic encirclement. The board has a grid of 19 by 19 lines. Each player has 180 pieces, or stones, each is of equal value, and the objective is to encircle the opponent's stones in various parts of the board. Each player reacts to the other's move. At the end, the margin of advantage is small, and the identity of the winner is not always obvious.

Chess – the national passion of Russia – on the other hand, is about total victory. The vast majority of games end in victory by attrition or, perhaps, by a swift dramatic gambit, but it is also possible to settle on a draw. Chess is about a decisive battle, and *wei qi* is about a protracted campaign. The chess player aims for total victory, but the *wei qi* player strives for relative advantage. The chess player sees all the pieces the adversary has, but the *wei qi* player has to take into account not only the stones on the board but also the reinforcements the adversary may deploy. Chess teaches the Clausewitzian concepts of 'centre of gravity' and 'decisive point' whereas *wei qi* teaches the art of encirclement. The good chess player tries to eliminate his opponent's pieces by a head-on attack, but the *wei qi* player scores by moving into empty spaces. Chess teaches single-mindedness and *wei qi* strategic flexibility.

Chinese military doctrine avoids head-on confrontations and concentrates on psychological advantage to achieve victory. The key text is Sun Tzu's *The Art of War*, originally published in 513 BC. It consists of observations on strategy, diplomacy and war, and found expression in the tactics and strategy of Mao Zedong during the Chinese Civil War and Ho Chi Minh during the Vietnam War. Vo Nguyen Giap adopted Sun Tzu's principles of indirect attack and psychological warfare against the French and Americans; the French, Americans and Soviets paid a heavy price for ignoring Sun Tzu's opus (Kissinger 2012: 22–6). An example of this was when Khrushchev ruefully admitted that the Soviets did not understand the Chinese at all.

The Russian and American pivots to Asia

Russia's foreign policy has always been to balance relations with the US, Europe and China, but now Moscow is moving closer to China, and a Eurasian political, economic and military grouping is forming from St Petersburg to Shanghai.

In 2013, the EU accounted for about 50 per cent of Russia's foreign trade – some $417 billion – and about 30 per cent of Europe's energy came from Russia. Germany has about 6,000 companies engaged in business there, but Europe joined the US in applying sanctions to Russia, and twenty-five years of Russian-Western cooperation began to unravel. Putin favoured a 'greater Europe' from Lisbon to Vladivostok which would embrace economics, culture and security. Russia would have provided Europe with natural resources and a pathway to Asia and the Pacific. The key player, Germany, eventually turned this opportunity down.

The shooting down of a Malaysian Airlines passenger plane over Ukraine in July 2014 was a turning point. Russia blamed the Ukrainians for the disaster and the Ukrainians blamed Russia. Germany blamed Russia and hardened its attitude towards sanctions. Mikhail Gorbachev's idea of a 'common European home' led to a closer relationship between Russia and Europe, centred on Germany, but in 2014 divorce was looming on the horizon.

The US expected China to strongly condemn the annexation of Crimea and involvement in eastern Ukraine based on the principles of territorial integrity and non-interference in domestic affairs, but China chose to abstain in the UN Security Council vote in March 2014 along with fifty-seven other states. Why did China abstain? It viewed the Western-backed colour revolution in Kyiv as a greater threat to its security than Russia's actions. Russia's falling out with the US left it with little option but to seek a closer relationship with Beijing, but the Chinese were faced with a dilemma. Under no circumstances could they fall out with the Americans as the two countries were forging a 'new type of great power relationship', to quote Xi Jinping. Beijing expects a long period of peaceful competition with Washington which would eventually tilt in China's favour.

As it turned out, China has been the greatest beneficiary of Russia's falling out with the West and was the largest economy outside the anti-Russian coalition. Trade turnover in 2014 was $95 billion. At the Asia-Pacific Economic Cooperation summit in Beijing in November 2014, Xi placed himself physically between Obama and Putin. The message was clear: the Cold War triangle of Washington, Moscow and Beijing is a thing of the past. Now the relationship has changed with China at the top and enjoying better relations with the other two than they have with one other.

China's relations with the US are becoming more competitive. Sino-Russian relations are laid down in a treaty signed in 2001 and the border issue was settled in 2004.

The Russian Navy took part in joint naval exercises with the Chinese Navy in the East China Sea, and the two countries engaged in a celebration of Japan's defeat in 1945. Russia's relations with South Korea have not been materially damaged by the fallout over Ukraine. Other US allies in the region, Taiwan and Singapore, place good relations with Washington ahead of relations with Moscow.

The Eurasian Economic Union embracing Russia, Belarus, Armenia, Kazakhstan and Kyrgyzstan promotes, from 2015, the free movement of goods and common policies. Russia would like it to become a political, military and cultural union as well, but Kazakhstan will only agree to an economic union as it wishes to remain a sovereign state.

Both Russia and China view Western campaigns to promote democracy and human rights in their countries as attempts to destabilise them, and they resent Western criticisms and regard Western media as biased. In 2011–12, Vladimir Putin blamed street protests on American support for Russian civil society, and Beijing saw a foreign hand behind the protests in Hong Kong in 2014.

With Moscow no longer having a foot in the Western camp, the two countries' assessment of world events is converging. China's ambition – the Chinese Dream – is to return to its natural position of dominance in Asia and then eventually the world. Russia's vision is much more modest, and it would like to establish itself as a leading great power in Eurasia and further afield. Beijing reads American pressure on Russia as an attempt to force it to obey its rules, and it is also seen as a warning and a deterrence to China. Beijing does not expect the US to subjugate Russia, and a pro-Western or chaotic Russia is not in its interest. Russia and China regard American dominance of the world to continue for several more decades but see that power gradually weakening; this will afford China greeter room for manoeuvre and Russia more freedom of action.

Putin and Xi are closer than previous leaders and expect to be in power into the early 2020s. This adds greater continuity to their policies.

Greater Europe from Lisbon to Vladivostok has been replaced by Greater Asia from St Petersburg to Shanghai. China became an importer of Russia's natural gas for the first time in 2014 (hitherto almost all had been exported to Europe) and is developing a greater appetite for Russian oil. In February 2015, Russia stated that Chinese companies could acquire majority stakes in Russia's strategic oil and gas fields, except those on the continental shelf. The sanctions have reduced the influence of Britain's BP and the US's ExxonMobil, and Chinese companies are likely to take advantage of this. The EU is also pursuing a policy of less reliance on Russian energy imports.

China is investing in high-speed rail links to Moscow via Kazakhstan and modern sea ports in Primorsky *krai* on the Pacific coast. The Northern Sea shipping route from Asia to Europe across the Arctic is another project.

China's Silk Road Economic Belt (SREB, also known as One Belt [sea], One Road), a regional trade and transport system which eventually will see trains running from Beijing to London, is a natural partner for Putin's Eurasian Economic Union. The SREB will run for over 8,000 miles from Beijing to St Petersburg. The twenty-first-century Maritime Road will start in Beijing, then down to the South China Sea, South Pacific Ocean, Indian Ocean, through the Suez Canal, the Mediterranean Sea and then up the Danube. A $40 billion fund is available for projects along the route.

China is wooing the EU to link up with the SREB. A proposed $358 billion Investment Plan for Europe is on the table, but Brussels is proceeding slowly as it is aware that EU companies encounter considerable difficulties in China and are excluded from certain sectors and projects.

The Shanghai Cooperation Organisation (SCO) comprises Russia, Kazakhstan, Kyrgyzstan, China, Tajikistan and Uzbekistan, with Afghanistan, Iran, Mongolia and Pakistan having observer status. Belarus, Turkey and Sri Lanka are partners in dialogue. India and Pakistan are expected to become full members soon. The SCO will oversee the Silk Road development and has become the centrepiece of Beijing's foreign and trade policy towards countries along the route. Latin America is left out, but a canal is being built in Nicaragua which will rival the Panama Canal.

China wants advanced Russian military technology transfers, especially in air and missile defence. Traditionally, Moscow has hesitated to provide Beijing with cutting-edge technology but appears now to have concluded it has no other choice. There have been regular joint military exercises, and in 2015, they held joint naval exercises in the eastern Mediterranean.

The relationship between Russia and China is not an equal one. Economically, the Middle Kingdom dwarfs Russia, with some Beijing commentators already referring to Russia as the junior partner. Russia was a vassal state under the Mongols from 1240 to 1480, and it does not wish to repeat the experience. Khrushchev would not treat Beijing as an equal, and this led to decades of enmity. The boot is now on the other foot, and Xi needs to be sensitive to Putin's needs. Russia dominated relations with China from the Treaty of Nerchinsk in 1689 until recently, and it will be difficult for Russians to accept a junior role.

When Xi attended the seventieth anniversary celebrations of victory over Germany in Moscow on 9 May 2015 – Chinese units also marched in the parade – he signed thirty-two agreements, and large yuan loans were extended to Russian banks. It will become easier for Russian companies to invest in China and Chinese companies in Russia. The Russian rouble is too weak to become a major international currency, but the yuan has that potential.

When the IMF was set up in 1944, President Roosevelt was determined that the Big Four – the US, UK, Soviet Union and China (in that order) – would have greatest control over it and the World Bank. To justify this political decision, an economic rationale had to be devised. A young American economist, Ray Mikesell, was given the task of turning economic statistics about the Allied economies into a ranking which would place the Big Four at the top. There was a problem: based on economic criteria, the Soviet Union and China did not qualify for a top-table place. France's trade turnover was greater than that of the USSR and China combined, but because Roosevelt and de Gaulle did not see eye to eye, France had to be excluded. Eventually Mikesell devised a set of equations which did the job. They were so abstruse that the delegates could not understand them and consequently were voted through. Hence the Big Four got the lion's share of the voting rights at the IMF and World Bank. When the French delegate realised what had happened, he created such a fuss that France was given a seat at the top table. Several months later, Mikesell's equations were used to determine voting rights and national contributions at the United Nations. The US, UK, Russia, China and France are still the five permanent members of the UN Security Council and have the right of veto.

There were repeated efforts to update the formula, and the latest was in 2010 which gave emerging economies more voting power and relegated Old World economies to second place. The IMF proposed raising China's voting shares from 3.8 per cent to 6 per cent. This was well below the US's 16.7 per cent and the right to veto decisions it does not favour. China felt insulted given its economic rise. In December 2015, the US Congress ratified it (*The Times*, 22 December 2015).

In 2015, China's response was to set up the Asian Infrastructure Investment Bank (AIIB) with capital of $50 billion and invited other countries to join as shareholders. The Obama administration tried to dissuade countries from joining, but this backfired spectacularly. Allies such as the UK and Australia ignored Washington's pleas and were among the fifty-seven founding members. Russia initially declined to join but eventually did. The AIIB will develop into a strong competitor for the World Bank, the IMF and the Asian Development Bank – all dominated by the US. Xi maintained in 2014 that it was for the people of Asia to run Asian affairs, and Chinese money is to promote this. An estimated $8–10 trillion is needed to develop Asian infrastructure between 2010 and 2020.

America's answer is the Trans-Pacific Partnership (TPP) which will set rules for an estimated 40 per cent of world trade. China has mentioned it may join. There is also the Transatlantic Trade and Investment Partnership with the EU and the goal is a free-trade area.

China's main competitor in Asia is India. Prime Minister Narendra Modi visited the Middle Kingdom in May 2015. The Chinese foreign minister talked about a 'Chinese whirlwind' sweeping the world, and Xi said a waking China is a 'peaceful, amiable and civilised lion'. When Xi visited India in September 2014, lots of business initiatives were signed which included Chinese investment of $20 billion. Since then progress has been slow with the Chinese complaining about Indian red tape and the Indians complaining of import barriers.

In April 2015, Xi pledged $45.6 billion over fifteen years while on a visit to Pakistan to build roads, railways, oil, gas, fibre-optic cables and power generation plants to create an 'all-weather strategic partnership of cooperation'. The plan is to link Kashgar in Xinjiang with Gwadar Port in Pakistan. The money is a loan and interest will have to be paid on it. The Chinese project dwarfs the US loan of $7.5 billion over five years in 2009 to Pakistan, but it was spread too thin and proved ineffective.

In September 2014, Modi was in Japan and a Beijing newspaper commented that he wanted to work with Japan to contain China. Barack Obama was also in India; he and Modi issued a statement on their 'strategic vision for Asia-Pacific and the Indian Ocean region'. There is an unresolved territorial dispute in Arunachai Pradesh bordering on Tibet which flares up from time to time when Chinese troops appear in what India regards as its domain. Chinese GDP is over seven times that of India, but India's population is already 1.25 billion and will surpass China's during the next decade. Militarily, India is no match for the Middle Kingdom, so it must balance relations with the Middle Kingdom and the US and gain concessions from both.

The South China Sea

It is not surprising that Washington views relations with China as of primary importance in the near and long term. It appears to be gradually withdrawing from Europe and the Middle East and focusing on Asia, especially East Asia. Beijing has made no secret of the fact that it regards a US presence in the region as illegitimate, and America may be a Pacific power, but this does not extend to East Asia. China has laid claim to the South China Sea and is claiming an area equivalent to one and a half times that of the Mediterranean Sea. But this is not new as Chiang Kai-shek expressed the same sentiments. A nine-dash line has been drawn which overlaps with the Exclusive Economic Zone claims of Brunei, Indonesia, Malaysia, the Philippines, Singapore, Taiwan and Vietnam. It is thought there are large reserves of hydrocarbons under the sea. The Spratly and Paracel Islands are the subject of bitter disputes. China claimed the Scarborough Shoal which the Philippines regarded as its territory; China took it over in 2012, but the US Navy did not come to Manila's assistance, and it is now de facto Chinese territory. The situation has now changed, and the Obama administration is playing a much more active role. Its main point is that it wishes to ensure free navigation of vessels in international waters and air travel. China wishes to resolve disputes on a one-to-one basis and rejects international arbitration. Its view is illustrated by a comment that the Philippines is a small nation, implying that small nations should concede to large nations. The littoral states want the US Navy to protect them. China's naval ambitions do not stop in the East China Sea, and maps have appeared which reveal that its maritime zone of influence extends to Hawaii.

Another problem is the building of Chinese bases on islets which have been expanded to take jet aircraft. One estimate is that they have created about 2,000 acres of new territory. The Subi Reef is claimed by the Philippines, Taiwan and Vietnam, but China has effectively taken it over. Other areas in dispute by China, the Philippines, Vietnam and Taiwan are the Duncan, Woody, Thilu and Itu Aba Islands; the Southwest Cay and the Mischief, Fiery Cross, Hughes, Swallow and Johnson South Reefs. According to the UN Convention of the Law of the Sea, the right to twelve nautical miles (one nautical mile = 1.15 miles) of maritime territory can only be claimed around true islands, not man-made structures on submerged objects such as Subi Reef. China is not observing this law at present.

The conflict with Japan over the Diaoyu-Senkaku islands in the East China Sea in 2014 almost boiled over. The dispute is about eight uninhabited islands near Taiwan, and nationalist feelings in both countries were ramped up by the respective governments. As a result, Japan is increasing its defence budget and views China as a potential aggressor.

China and America – Chimerica – are now in a symbiotic relationship, and they form the G2 which will dominate the world stage. America has a huge trade deficit with China and China, in turn, buys US bonds to make it possible for the US to continue importing so many goods from the Middle Kingdom.

President Barack Obama's first official visit to China took place in November 2009. The body language underlined the fact that the Chinese, for the first time since 1949, felt themselves in the ascendancy. If China becomes too aggressive it will provoke a response from Uncle Sam. Contiguous states, such as Vietnam, were historically vassal states of China and have no wish to return to this status. They will rely on the US to resist Chinese domination. All this has the makings of a slow-burning Cold War in Asia.

North Korea

The collapse of the Soviet Union was a disaster for the Democratic People's Republic of Korea (DPRK). Deprived of spare parts and oil and power, most of the industry stopped. One estimate is that industrial output in 2000 was half of that in 1990 and factory managers began selling their machinery to China as scrap metal.

Agriculture suffered more than industry, as chemical fertiliser was used liberally, but factories depended on Soviet inputs. There was extensive irrigation supported by pumping stations, and when power failed, the pumps stopped. Torrential rain in 1995 and 1996 led to a collapse of state agriculture, and the public distribution system stopped functioning, and even privileged elites failed to get their rations on occasion. The famine of 1996–9 led to many deaths, and the lowest estimate is about half a million or 2.5 per cent of the population.

How did people survive? They rediscovered capitalism. One estimate is that between 1998 and 2008 income from the shadow market economy accounted for 78 per cent of total household income. The same pattern observed in China occurred in North Korea as reform came from below. Unlike China, however, the state refused to disband the grossly inefficient state farms. Farmers, therefore, had to find virgin and abandoned land to till, and mountain slopes were brought into cultivation.

In cities, barter appeared but money soon took over, and huge markets were visible in 1995. Most market traders were female, and this was because all able-bodied males had to work in a state enterprise. Married women could stay at home and look after the children, so the main breadwinner was female. Most restaurants are now privately owned, and sometimes the capital comes from relatives in China. Technically the restaurant is state-owned and managed by an official agency, and the private owner agrees to pay the municipal authority a rent or bribe and everyone is happy. The retail sector follows the same pattern. Over half of the shops are, in reality, private businesses, and private transport has developed rapidly. The best guarantee of unrestricted trading is to register the vehicles as belonging to the military. China accounts for 90 per cent of imports and exports, but minerals are handled by the state whereas other goods, especially food, are private (Lankov 2013: 202–6).

The collapse of the command economy led to a weakening of the state as lower-level officials turned a blind eye to illegal activities in return for a bribe. Travel controls melted away, and passports were issued for the first time in 2003 to regulate travel to China. Women took to wearing trousers and riding bicycles in cities – previously banned activities.

Kim Jong-il was known for his love of Western luxury, and among his treasures was a cellar with 10,000 bottles of the finest wines. Kim the elder decided to sacrifice living standards in his bid to acquire an atomic bomb and the country is now a nuclear state. Five rounds of talks by the People's Republic of China, the US, Russia, Japan, the Republic of Korea (South Korea), and North Korea, between August 2003 and February 2007, resulted in the Yongbyong nuclear reactor being closed down. In February 2005, North Korea stated it had nuclear weapons for 'self-defence', and in September 2015 the Yongbyong nuclear plant was again in operation.

The DPRK economy is in a parlous state, but aid from China will ensure that the state does not collapse; it supplies 90 per cent of its energy and 80 per cent of its consumer goods. One way of grasping how crippled the DPRK has become is to observe a satellite picture at night of the Korean peninsula. The north is almost entirely black while the south is bright with lights.

As the food situation stabilised, the authorities decided to introduce reforms in 2002. Consumer prices rose sharply and enterprises were permitted to acquire inputs and sell their output and wages depended on performance. Private markets were sanctioned, but the more conservative elements in the leadership lobbied for capitalism from below to be reined in. In 2005 it was announced that the public distribution system would be restored. The state grain monopoly was reimposed but soon failed as lower-level officials declined to implement it. In 2006 males were banned from engaging in private trade, but this had little effect as females dominated market trading. So the following year, women under fifty were forbidden to trade, but this led to riots and the ban being ignored. There was draft legislation, to be introduced in 2009, to permit market activity only three days a month and to ban the sale of industrial goods, but the law was never enacted. In order to eliminate profits from private trade, a currency reform was introduced in 2009, and this echoed the currency reform in 1947 in the Soviet Union. Stalin's aim was to wipe out black market profits made during the war and after, and it was effective. However, in North Korea it resulted in rapid inflation as workers and officials were awarded huge wage increases, but the supply of goods did not increase.

Kim Jong-il was succeeded by one of his sons, Kim Jong-un, on 13 April 2012. He had been a pupil at the Liebefeld Steinhölzli School outside Bern, Switzerland, between 1998 and 2000. He was presented to the nation at a massive military parade, in October 2010, marking the sixty-fifth anniversary of the Korean Workers' Party. Significantly, on the reviewing stands were Korean generals but also Zhou Yongkang, head of China's domestic security apparatus. The symbolism was evident: the leader was supported by the army, party and China.

Kim Jong-un also has a magical touch. During an inspection, he miraculously created a new synthetic fertiliser which can produce 15,000 tonnes of wheat on a 9,000 m² piece of land. The problem of hunger has been solved!

He has a beautiful wife, Ri Sol-ju, who appears with him on occasion, but he has a ruthless streak, and there have been public executions of criminals, those caught watching South Korean DVDs and USBs, and Christians. This reveals that many, perhaps half a million, watch foreign videos and a million may listen to foreign broadcasts. There are now about 20,000 North Koreans in the South, and they prepare DVDs to be smuggled into the North. Balloons containing US dollars are released near the Demilitarised Zone to float into the North.

Kim Jong-un decided, in December 2013, to humiliate publicly his uncle and second in command, Chang Sung-taek. He was removed from a meeting by guards on live TV and accused of being 'idle, womanising and ideologically sick . . . of gambling, taking drugs and counter-revolutionary factional acts'. Never before has a top official been dismissed in this fashion. He was then shot, and his entire family, including North Korea's ambassadors to Cuba and Malaysia with their wives and children, were wiped out. The minister of defence, Hyon Yong-chol, was executed in front of a crowd of officials by a four-barrel anti-aircraft gun. Kim Jong-un has been photographed riding a Ferris wheel, on a ski lift, watching a missile

Figure 15.1 Kim Jong-un

© Xinhua/Alamy.

test at sea and inspecting fish, fowl or cattle. He has decreed that all males copy his hair style with monitors cutting off locks if they are longer than two centimetres (0.8 inches). They are to imitate his bouffant which emerges upwards from shaved patches above his ears. Women have been told to adopt a bob similar to that of Ri Sol ju, Kim's wife; the only people excluded are performers. Kim has adopted the same hairstyle as his grandfather, the founder of the state, and there have even been rumours that he has undergone plastic surgery to make him resemble his grandfather more closely.

Xi Jinping and Kim Jong-un have still to meet, and Kim defied China by staging North Korea's third nuclear test in 2013. That said, the Treaty of Friendship, Co-operation and Mutual Assistance between China and the DPRK, signed in 1961, which contains a clause on mutual defence against foreign aggression, is still in force. Then Kim broke UN resolutions by testing missiles. In March 2015, Beijing replaced its ambassador with a senior Communist Party official, but it is not certain if he has met the 'Great Marshal' yet. Kim was expected to turn up in May 2015 at the seventieth anniversary celebrations of Germany's defeat in Moscow, but he cancelled at the last moment. China is not keen on Russia improving relations with Pyongyang. The Chinese news agency Xinhua reported that relations with the DPRK were 'as close as lips and teeth' (*Sunday Times*, 17 May 2015).

When Liu Yunshan, a member of the Politburo Standing Committee, visited Pyongyang in October 2015, he failed to extract from Kim Jong-un an explicit promise to desist from testing nuclear weapons and missiles. In January 2016, Pyongyang announced an underground hydrogen bomb test and a month later the launch of a nuclear satellite. China's response was acerbic. An editorial stated that nuclear tests were a deep-seated deformity of the DPRK's security policy and nukes 'could not compensate for the weak national economy as well as critical deficiencies in other areas of defence'. The article concluded that North Korea was using nuclear weapons as a ticket to a nuclear club to force other states to pay it tribute. It 'believed that they would guarantee the country would have every resource and opportunity brought to its door . . . this is completely unrealistic' (*Huanqiu Shibao*, 6 January 2016). Kim Jong-un has threatened South Korea, Japan and the US with nuclear strikes if they attack his country.

Pyongyang is slowly becoming like any other East Asian city, which is a startling change from a decade ago. There is a property boom, and the nouveau riche are indulging in cars, clothes, perfume and chocolate biscuits. Property prices are thought to have risen thirtyfold this century, with the most expensive costing £130,000 in a country where the average wage is £1 a month. All property is owned by the state, so how do people acquire apartments? By 'swapping'. The person moving to a less desirable property is compensated in US dollars with a bureaucrat arranging all the paperwork for an agreed bribe. Who are the new rich? State enterprise managers who effectively run their companies as private businesses, and then there are the merchants who buy and sell food and household items. The banks do not pay interest, so the only way to spend large amounts of money is to invest in property. Refrigerators and computers are all the rage, but the Internet is off limits for all except a small elite. Professor Andrei Lankov, regarded as the leading specialist on the country, puts it succinctly: 'Kim Jong Un has no choice, He's like a man on the fourth floor of a burning building. If he jumps, he may well be killed but if he doesn't jump, he will certainly die'. Another trend can be observed which is typical of East Asia, especially China. Every successful man has to have a few mistresses, and the richer he becomes, the greater the number of beautiful girls in his harem (*The Times*, 18 April 2015).

Cuba

In 1989, on his last visit to Havana, Gorbachev declared that the Soviet Union opposed theories and doctrines justifying the export of revolution and counter-revolution. Castro was apoplectic in public and private and mocked the Soviet worker's fear of unemployment and lack of sugar (Cuba's main export).

However, Cuba surprised the world after the collapse of the Soviet Union in 1991 by continuing as a communist state. As in other communist states, the party proved to be the most effective institution backed up by the instruments of coercion – the military and political police – and about a fifth of the population is trained to bear arms. The key to retaining power was to ensure that the ruling elite remained united. Cuba is dominated by Fidel and Raúl Castro, and the charismatic figure of Fidel with his cap, beard, cigar and fatigues is central to the survival of a system which is neither democratic nor economically successful. Fidel loves to talk and is in his element in his interminable monologues. I find them very good practice for honing my Spanish, but if one does not understand a sentence or idiom, he comes back time and again to the same theme. In other words, he repeats himself ad nauseam, and if one listens to him for fifty hours, one has heard his complete vocabulary. On the podium, waving his hands and gesticulating, Castro gave the impression of being another Moses leading the children of Israel to the Promised Land. Moses did not make it, but neither will Fidel get to full communism.

> *Castro to his doctor: 'Doc, I am suffering from insomnia.' 'Try reading your own speeches.'*

The other aspect to retaining power is to imprison and kill opponents. Fidel will not enter into a dialogue about policy because he is aware his own position is weak, and the more eloquent opponents are shot. Another reason why opposition is not more manifest is that hundreds of thousands of Cubans have left the island illegally for the US, Latin America and Europe. There is now a Cuban community on Lanzarote, in the Canary Islands, for instance.

The mass base of support is among the poor. Without communism, a proportion of the population would feel marginalised. Literacy rates before the revolution, at 75 per cent, were among the highest in Latin America. Control of the media means that there is no political or cultural debate which challenge accepted norms. This had led to the emigration of a large number of Cuban writers and artists. Science and engineering education have been promoted but, as one graduate engineer informed me in the late 1990s, she had no intention of working as an engineer because the pay was little better than that of an ordinary worker. She said that many graduate girls preferred to work as prostitutes because they could earn much more. Castro, on one occasion, said that Cuba had the most highly educated prostitutes in the world, but this should not be revealed to the outside world!

Cuba has a large black population, and they were enthusiastic supporters of the regime in the early days, but only one black, Juan Almeida Bosque (died 2009), became a member of the ruling elite. He took part on the storming of the Moncada fortress and was imprisoned afterwards; he was one of eighty-two insurgents who sailed on the *Granma* from Mexico to Cuba. He proved himself an able military commander as leader of the Third Eastern Front and was vice president and a member of the Politburo of the Communist Party of Cuba. He was said to mediate on occasion between Fidel and Raúl Castro, both strong-willed comrades, but real power rested with Fidel Castro, el Comandante en Jefe or the boss.

The collapse of the Soviet Union in 1991 was a disaster for Cuba. The sugar industry could no longer compete and began to decline rapidly. Life is hard for most Cubans, and one told me that it is usual for family rations to run out in the third week of every month. Traffic is light compared to other capital cities. Old bangers, dating from the 1950s, dominate. Another striking feature about the capital is the total absence of commercial advertising.

A bonus for the Castros (Raúl is now in command as Fidel is incapable physically of running the country on a day to day basis) was Hugo Chávez of Venezuela. He took up the baton of anti-Americanism in Latin America and attempted to forge an alliance of left-wing states including Venezuela, Bolivia, Argentina and Ecuador, but Brazil declined to join. Venezuela provides oil at discounted prices, and Cuba sends medical professionals, among others, to Venezuela, and this continues under President Maduro.

A bitter Cuban joke sums this up:

What are the Cuban revolution's three greatest failures? Breakfast, lunch and dinner.

In September 2010, Fidel came to a stunning conclusion: 'The Cuban model does not even work for us anymore.' Later he warned that Cuba was 'on the edge of a precipice' and the fifty-year battle to produce a successful, communist Cuba had failed. A Party Congress in April 2011, the first in fourteen years, began reintroducing capitalism. Barbers, plumbers, locksmiths and others in the service sector will now be working for themselves, and the list of permitted trades totals 151. Restaurants have sprung up, and entrepreneurship, suppressed for half a century, has reappeared. A typical burger and salad costs a week's wages, but business is booming. Doctors are only paid $25 a month, which is not enough to live on, so they must find a secondary occupation. The buying and selling of cars, houses and apartments (but not land) is permitted once again, and transactions are in US dollars. Estate agents have reappeared, and commission for a $50,000 apartment is $300. Farmers may lease land and employ labour, and many have grasped the opportunity to farm on their own account again. Needless to say the flesh business is expanding all the time, but the girls pay a tax.

Cuban Americans can now visit and bring in huge quantities of goods, which can be sold in the markets. They also provide capital to help their relatives start businesses, and this is already worth billions a year. Foreign tourism is booming and bringing in billions of dollars annually. It is like going back fifty years, and there are even steam trains to transport the people.

Havana, once a beautiful city replete with colonial architecture, is falling down and crumbling away. The state does not have the resources to repair buildings, so the private sector will have to step in. Painful decisions about loss-making industry and agriculture have still to be taken. Cuba has revealed that the old adage 'abolish capitalism and fail economically' is true.

Where has the inspiration for the second Cuban revolution come from? China, of course. Beijing has shown that a Communist Party can retain power while running a capitalist economy. Havana hopes that taxes from private businesses and tourism can fund healthcare (the best in Latin America), education and pensions.

Communism in Cuba is solid and is likely to remain while Raúl is in power, but when he goes, the risk is that it may fragment. The equation 'Cuban Communism = Castroism' may turn into reality. In December 2014, President Obama announced that diplomatic relations with Cuba would be re-established, and they were on 20 July 2015. Many in the million-strong Cuban exile community in Florida were not amused. On 21 March 2016, Obama became the first US president to visit Cuba since Calvin Coolidge in 1928. Will the embrace of American capitalism prove fatal for Cuban communism?

Addendum

Current communist states

- People's Republic of China: October 1949–
- Republic of Cuba: January 1959–
- Democratic People's Republic of Korea: September 1948–
- Lao People's Democratic Republic: December 1975–
- Socialist Republic of Vietnam: July 1976–

Former communist states

- Democratic Republic of Afghanistan: April 1978–April 1992
- Socialist People's Republic of Albania: January 1946–March 1992
- People's Republic of Angola: November 1975–August 1992

- Azerbaijani People's Government: November 1945–December 1946 (in present-day Iran)
- People's Republic of Benin: November 1975–March 1990
- People's Republic of Bulgaria: September 1946–December 1990
- People's Republic of the Congo: January 1970–March 1992
- Czechoslovak Socialist Republic: July 1960–March 1990 (People's Republic of Czechoslovakia: February 1948–July 1960)
- People's Democratic Republic of Ethiopia: September 1987–May 1991
- German Democratic Republic: October 1949–October 1990
- Political Committee of National Liberation (Greece): December 1947–August 1949
- People's Revolutionary Government of Grenada (West Indies): March 1979–October 1983
- People's Republic of Hungary: August 1949–October 1989 (Republic of Hungary: May 1945–August 1949)
- Democratic Kampuchea (Cambodia): April 1976–January 1979
- People's Republic of Kampuchea: January 1979–October 1991
- Republic of Mahabad (Iran): January 1946–December 1946
- Mongolian People's Republic: November 1924–February 1992 (Communist from July 1921)
- People's Republic of Mozambique: June 1975–December 1990
- Republic of Nicaragua: July 1979–April 1990
- People's Republic of Poland: June 1945–July 1989
- People's Republic of Romania: December 1947–65; Socialist Republic of Romania: 1965–December 1989
- Somali Democratic Republic: July 1976–January 1991
- Union of Soviet Socialist Republics (Soviet Union): December 1922–December 1991; Soviet Russia: October 1917–December 1922
- Tuvan People's Republic: August 1921–October 1944
- Democratic Republic of Vietnam: September 1945–July 1976
- Provisional Revolutionary Government of the Republic of South Vietnam: April 1975–June 1976
- People's Democratic Republic of Yemen: November 1967–May 1990
- Democratic Republic of Yemen: May 1994–July 1994
- Socialist Federal Republic of Yugoslavia: November 1943–October 1991/April 1992

There are states which declare themselves socialist but not Marxist-Leninist

- People's Republic of Bangladesh: 16 December 1971–
- Multinational State of Bolivia: July 2006–
- Great Socialist People's Libyan Arab Jamahiriya: September 1969–September 2011

- Democratic Socialist Republic of Sri Lanka: September 1978–
- Syrian Arab Republic: 1961–
- United Republic of Tanzania: April 1964–
- Bolivarian Republic of Venezuela: 1999–
- People's Republic of Zanzibar: 1964 (now part of Tanzania)

States which formerly declared themselves socialist but not Marxist-Leninist

- People's Democratic Republic of Algeria: September 1963–February 1989
- Burkina Faso
- Republic of Cape Verde
- Republic of Ghana
- People's Revolutionary Republic of Guinea: 1958–84
- Guinea-Bissau
- Republic of Iraq: July 1958–July 1979
- Democratic Republic of Madagascar: December 1975–August 1992
- Republic of Mali: December 1968–January 1992
- Republic of Nicaragua
- Portuguese Republic: April 1974–July 1976
- Democratic Republic of São Tomé and Príncipe
- Republic of Senegal
- Republic of Seychelles
- Democratic Republic of Sudan: 1969–85
- Republic of Suriname
- Tunisian Republic
- Republic of Uganda

Note: The first socialist republic in history was the Paris Commune (March–May 1871). It was inspired by many socialist thinkers, including Karl Marx, and it introduced many policies which later were regarded as Marxist. Lenin drew the important conclusion that in order to succeed, the revolution had to use terror to annihilate its enemies to retain power.

Estimated deaths as a result of attempting to establish a communist society

- **Soviet Union**
  Civil War (1918–21): 9 million
  Collectivisation and gulag: 22 million (includes famines)
  Total: 31 million
- **Eastern Europe**
  1.5 million
- **People's Republic of China**

Civil War (1945–49): 3 million
Imposing communist rule (1949–51): 3 million
Great Leap Forward (1958–61): 45 million of whom 2.5 million were executed
Cultural Revolution (1966–76): 1 million
Labour camps: 27 million
Total: 79 million

- **Democratic People's Republic of Korea**
  2 million
- **Republic of Vietnam**
  1 million
- **Kampuchea (Cambodia)**
  2 million
- **Afghanistan**
  1.5 million
- **Africa**
  1.7 million (the greatest bloodletting was in Ethiopia)
- **Latin America**
  150,000
  The gross total comes to about 120 million

The numbers of deaths caused by the phenomenon of communism vary widely, but it is not possible to calculate the exact number of fatalities. The preceding numbers are simply an estimate, and they do not include the civil wars before the communists came to power.

Further reading

The most comprehensive treatment of the Cold War is Melvyn P. Leffler and Odd Arne Westad (eds.), *The Cambridge History of the Cold War*, 3 vols. (Cambridge: Cambridge University Press, 2012). It consists of articles by leading scholars. See also the stimulating overview by Marc Trachtenberg, *The Cold War and after: History, Theory, and the Logic of International Politics* (Princeton, NJ: Princeton University Press, 2012).

An excellent analysis of the Cold War is Bernd Stöver, *Der Kalte Krieg: Geschichte eines radikalen Zeitalters, 1947–1991* (Munich: C. H. Beck, 2011); also very useful is John W. Young, *The Longman Companion to America, Russia and the Cold War, 1941–1998* (Harlow: Longman, 1999).

See also Odd Arne Westad, *Reviewing the Cold War Approaches, Interpretations, Theory* (London and Portland, OR: Frank Cass, 2000). A detailed, comprehensive study of the imposition of communism in Eastern Europe is Anne Applebaum, *Iron Curtain: The Crushing of Eastern Europe, 1944–1956* (London: Allen Lane, 2012).

A still valuable analysis is Adam Ulam, *Expansion and Coexistence, Soviet Foreign Policy, 1917–1973*, 2nd edn (New York: Holt, Rinehart & Winston, 1974).

The founding father of post-revisionism, John Lewis Gaddis, has rethought his position, and the result is *We Now Know: Rethinking Cold War History* (Oxford: Oxford University Press, 1998). He concludes that ideology is the central theme, and this is an indispensable source.

Among the best overviews of the Cold War are Richard Crockatt, *The Fifty Years War: The United States and the Soviet Union in World Politics, 1941–1991* (New York: Routledge, 1995); J.P.D. Dunbabin, *The Cold War: The Great Powers and Their Allies*, 2 vols. (Harlow: Longman, 1994); Ralph B. Levering, *The Cold War: A Post–Cold War History* (Arlington Heights, IL: Harlan Davidson, 1994); Ronald E. Powaski, *The Cold War: The United States and the Soviet Union, 1917–1991* (New York: Oxford University Press, 1998); Martin Walker, *The Cold War: A History* (New York: Henry Holt, 1993). See also Douglas Brinkley, *Dean Acheson: The*

Cold War Years, 1953–1971 (New Haven, CT: Yale University Press, 1992); Gabriel Gorodetsky (ed.), *Soviet Foreign Policy, 1917–1991: A Retrospective History* (London: Frank Cass, 1994); John W. Young, *Cold War Europe, 1945–1989: A Political History* (London: Edward Arnold, 1991). A good selection of articles is Klaus Larres and Ann Lane (eds.), *The Cold War: The Essential Readings* (Oxford: Blackwell, 2001).

A fine study concentrating on the actions of Roosevelt and other US politicians in the immediate post-war period is Frank Costigliola, *Roosevelt's Lost Alliances: How Personal Politics Helped Start the Cold War* (Princeton, NJ: Princeton University Press, 2013). See also J. Robert Moskin, *Mr Truman's War: The Final Victories of World War II and the Birth of the Postwar World* (New York: Random House, 2002); Melvyn P. Leffler, *A Preponderance of Power: National Security, the Truman Administration, and the Cold War* (Stanford, CA: Stanford University Press, 1992).

On Russian nationalism, see David Brandenberger, *National Bolshevism: Stalinist Mass Culture and the Formation of Modern Russian National Identity, 1931–1956* (Cambridge, MA: Harvard University Press, 2002).

The most stimulating accounts of Soviet policy are Vladislav Zubok and Constantine Pleshakov, *Inside the Kremlin's Cold War: From Stalin to Khrushchev* (Cambridge, MA: Harvard University Press, 1996) and Vladislav M. Zubok, *A Failed Empire: The Soviet Union in the Cold War from Stalin to Gorbachev* (Chapel Hill: University of North Carolina Press, 2007). See also Vojtech Mastny, *The Cold War and Soviet Insecurity: The Stalin Years* (New York: Oxford University Press, 1996). Hannes Adomeit, *Soviet Risk-Taking and Crisis Behavior: A Theoretical and Empirical Analysis* (London: Allen & Unwin, 1982) is a thought-provoking and stimulating study. On Khrushchev's foreign policy see Aleksandr Fursenko and Timothy Naftali, *Khrushchev's Cold War: The Inside Story of an American Adversary* (New York: W.W. Norton, 2006).

On nuclear weapons, see John Lewis Gaddis, Philip Gordon, Ernest R. May and Jonathan Rosenberg, *Cold War Statesmen Confront the Bomb: Nuclear Diplomacy since 1945* (New York: Oxford University Press, 1999). See also Francis J. Galvin, *Nuclear Statecraft: History and Strategy in America's Atomic Age* (Ithaca, NY: Cornell University Press, 2012); Raymond Garthoff, *Reflections on the Cuban Missile Crisis*, rev. edn (Washington, DC: Brookings Institution, 1989). A critical account of US military and foreign policy is Chalmers Johnson, *The Sorrows of Empire Militarism, Secrecy and the End of the Republic* (London: Verso, 2004); the most detailed and authoritative study of Britain's nuclear submarine service is Peter Hennessy and James Jinks, *The Silent Deep: The Royal Navy Submarine Service since 1945* (London: Allen Lane, 2015). Stories of some of the Cold War patrols will make your hair curl.

On Western Europe, see the stimulating books by Geir Lundestad, *'Empire' by Integration: The United States and European Integration, 1945–1997* (Oxford: Oxford University Press, 1998); *The United States and Western Europe since 1945: From 'Empire' by Invitation to Transatlantic Drift* (Oxford: Oxford University Press, 2003). On détente, see Richard Davy, *European Détente: A Reappraisal* (London: Sage, 1992); John van Oudenaren, *Détente in Europe: The Soviet Union and the West since 1953* (Durham, NC: Duke University Press, 1991); Odd Arne Westad (ed.), *The Fall of Détente: Soviet-American Relations during the Carter Years* (Oslo: Scandinavian University Press, 1997).

On Eastern Europe, see Odd Arne Westad, Sven Holtsmark and Ivor B. Neumann (eds.), *The Soviet Union in Eastern Europe, 1945–1989* (New York: St Martin's Press, 1994). One of the best accounts of the collapse of communism in Eastern Europe is Victor Sebestyen, *Revolution 1989: The Fall of the Soviet Empire* (London: Weidenfeld & Nicolson, 2009).

On Bulgaria, see Vesselin Dimitrov, *Stalin's Cold War Soviet Foreign Policy, Democracy and Communism in Bulgaria, 1941–1948* (Basingstoke: Palgrave Macmillan, 2008); see also Norman Laporte, Kevin Morgan and Matthew Worley (eds.), *Bolshevism, Stalinism and the Comintern: Perspectives on Stalinization, 1917–1953* (Basingstoke: Palgrave Macmillan, 2008).

On Britain, see Sean Greenwood, *Britain and the Cold War, 1945–1991* (Basingstoke: Macmillan, 2000).

The best book on Italy is C. J. Duggan and C. Wagstaff (eds.), *Italy in the Cold War: Politics, Culture and Society, 1948–1958* (Oxford: Berg, 1995).

On the Korean War, see William Whitney Stueck, *The Korean War: An International History* (Princeton, NJ: Princeton University Press, 1997).

On the Middle East, see Galia Golan, *Soviet Policies in the Middle East from World War Two to Gorbachev* (Cambridge: Cambridge University Press, 1990) and Rajan Menon, *Soviet Power and the Third World* (New Haven, CT: Yale University Press, 1986).

On Vietnam, see Ang Cheng Guan, *Ending the Vietnam War: The Vietnamese Communists' Perspective* (London: Routledge Curzon, 2005).

On Laos, the outstanding book is Martin Stuart-Fox, *Buddhist Kingdom, Marxist State: The Making of Modern Laos* (Bangkok: White Lotus Press, 2002). The section on Laos is based mainly on this study.

On Japan, see Walter LaFeber, *A History of US-Japan Relations* (New York: Norton, 1997); William R. Nester, *Power across the Pacific: A Diplomatic History of American Relations with Japan* (Basingstoke: Macmillan, 1996); Michael Schaller, *Altered States: The United States and Japan since the Occupation* (Oxford: Oxford University Press, 1998).

The standard biography of Khrushchev is William Taubman, *Khrushchev: The Man and His Era* (London: Free Press, 2003). This is a monumental study which provides an enormous amount of information on Khrushchev as a person and his relationship with the US and the West, among other things. See also Sergei N. Khrushchev, *Nikita Khrushchev and the Creation of a Superpower* (University Park: Pennsylvania State University Press, 2000). His son reveals much about the private life and thinking of his father. See also Michael R. Beschloss, *Kennedy v. Khrushchev, the Crisis Years, 1960–1963* (London: Faber & Faber, 1991).

Khrushchev was loquacious, and there are various volumes of his reminiscences, including Nikita Khrushchev, *Khrushchev Remembers*, vol. 1, trans. and ed. by Strobe Talbott (Boston, MA: Little, Brown, 1970).

Nikita Khrushchev, *Khrushchev Remembers*, with an introduction, commentary and notes by Edward Chankshaw, trans. by Strobe Talbott (London: Sphere Books, 1971).

Nikita Khrushchev, *Khrushchev Remembers: The Glasnost Tapes*, with a foreword by Strobe Talbott, trans. and ed. by Jerrold L. Schecter and Vyacheslav V. Luchkov (Boston, MA: Little, Brown, 1974).

Nikita Khrushchev, *Khrushchev Remembers: The Last Testament*, vol. 2, trans. and ed. by Strobe Talbott (Boston, MA: Little, Brown, 1974).

Worth consulting is Cyrus Vance's memoirs, *Hard Choices* (New York: Simon & Schuster, 1983).

Simon Hall, *1956: The World in Revolt* (London: Faber, 2015) has a chapter on Poland and one on Hungary.

On Eisenhower, see Stephen E. Ambrose, *Eisenhower, Vol 2: The President* (New York: Simon & Schuster, 1984); Robert R. Bowie and Richard H. Immerman, *Waging Peace: How Eisenhower Shaped an Enduring Cold War Strategy* (New York: Oxford University Press, 1998); Kenneth Osgood, *Total Cold War: Eisenhower's Secret Propaganda Battle at Home and Abroad* (Lawrence: University of Kansas Press, 2006); Evan Thomas, *Ike's Bluff: President Eisenhower's Secret Battle to Save the World* (New York: Little, Brown, 2012) and Yanek Mieczkowski, *Eisenhower's Sputnik Moment: The Race for Space and World Prestige* (Ithaca, NY: Cornell University Press, 2013); on Kennedy, see Alan Brinkley, *John F. Kennedy: The American Presidents Series: The 35th President, 1961–1963* (New York: Henry Holt, 2012); on the Bay of Pigs, see Jim Rasenberger, *The Brilliant Disaster: JFK, Castro and America's Doomed Invasion of Cuba's Bay of Pigs* (New York: Scribner, 2011); on Nixon, see Stephen E. Ambrose, *Nixon, Vol. 1: The Education of a Politician, 1913–1962* (New York: Touchstone Books, 1987) and *Nixon, Vol. 2: The Triumph of a Politician, 1962–1972* (New York: Simon & Schuster, 2014) and also R.S. Litwak, *Détente and the Nixon Doctrine: American Foreign Policy and the Pursuit of Stability, 1969–1976* (Cambridge: Cambridge University Press, 1984); Richard M. Nixon, *RN: The Memoirs of Richard Nixon* (New York: Simon & Schuster, 1992).

On Johnson, the magisterial volumes of Robert A. Cato, especially *The Years of Lyndon Johnson: The Passage of Power*, vol. 4 (New York: Knopf Doubleday, 2012); see also Charles Peters, *Lyndon B. Johnson, the American Presidents Series: The 36th President* (New York: Henry Holt and Times Books, 2010).

On Dean Rusk, see Warren I. Cohen, *Dean Rusk* (Totowa, NJ: Cooper Square, 1980) and Dean Rusk, *As I Saw It*, ed. by Daniel S. Papp (New York: W.W. Norton, 1990).

On the Berlin crises, see H.M. Harrison, 'Ulbricht and the concrete "rose": New archival evidence on the dynamics of Soviet-East German relations and the Berlin crisis, 1958–1961', *Cold War International History Project*. Woodrow Wilson Center, Washington, DC, no. 5, May 1993, and H.M. Harrison, 'New evidence on Khrushchev's 1958 Berlin Ultimatum', *Cold War International History Project Bulletin*. Woodrow Wilson Center, Washington, DC, no. 4, Autumn 1994.

On the Cuban Missile Crisis, the must-read is Ernest R. May and Philip D. Zelikow (eds.), *The Kennedy Tapes: Inside the White House during the Cuban Missile Crisis* (Cambridge MA: Belknap Press of Harvard University Press, 1997).

On the Middle East, see G. Lenczowski, *American Presidents and the Middle East* (Durham, NC: Duke University Press, 1990).

On Shevardnadze, see Carolyn McGiffert Ekedahl and Melvin A. Goodman, *The Wars of Eduard Shevardnadze* (London: Hurst, 1997).

On the reunification of Germany, see Philip Zelikow, *Germany Unified and Europe Transformed: A Study in Statecraft* (Cambridge, MA: Harvard University Press, 1997).

The best source on culture during the Cold War is David Caute, *The Dancer Defects: The Struggle for Cultural Supremacy during the Cold War* (Oxford: Oxford University Press, 2003). See also Frances Stonor Saunders, *Who Paid the Piper? The CIA and the Cultural Cold War* (London: Granta, 2000).

Sergei I. Zhuk, *Rock and Roll in the Rocket City: The West, Identity, and Ideology in Soviet Dniepropetrovsk, 1960–1985* (Baltimore: Johns Hopkins University Press, 2010) is a very readable and entertaining account of pop culture in a Soviet city.

An excellent source for Soviet and Russian foreign policy is Robert H. Donaldson, Joseph L. Nogee and Vidya Nadkarni, *The Foreign Policy of Russia: Changing Systems, Enduring Interests*, 5th edn (London: Routledge, 2014).

On Soviet nationality policy, see S. Seweryn Bialer, *Politics, Society, and Nationality inside Gorbachev's Russia* (Boulder, CO: Westview, 1989).

Harry Gelman, *The Brezhnev Politburo and the Decline of Détente* (Ithaca, NY: Cornell University Press, 1984) is a stimulating account.

The leading book on the arms race is David Holloway, *The Soviet Union and the Arms Race*, 2nd edn (New Haven, CT: Yale University Press, 1984).

On Soviet espionage, the most revealing sources are Christopher Andrew and Vasili Mitrokhin, *The Sword and the Shield: The Mitrokhin Archive and the Secret History of the KGB* (New York: Basic Books, 2000) and *The Mitrokhin Archive II: The KGB and the World* (London: Allen Lane, 2005).

On the Gorbachev years, see the revealing memoirs of Jack F. Matlock Jr, *Autopsy on an Empire* (New York: Random House, 1995); Mikhail Gorbachev, *Memoirs* (London: Doubleday, 1996) reveals much but not all.

Pierre Razoux, *The Iran-Iraq War* (Cambridge, MA: Belknap Press of Harvard University Press, 2015) is outstanding and an indispensable guide to the Middle East today.

On the end of the Cold War, see Beth A. Fischer, *The Regan Reversal: Foreign Policy and the End of the Cold War* (Columbia: University of Missouri Press, 1997); Raymond L. Garthoff, *The Great Transformation: American-Soviet Relations and the End of the Cold War* (Washington, DC: Brookings Institution, 1994). Two first class studies are Sergii Plokhy, *The Last Empire: The Final Days of the Soviet Union* (London: One World, 2014) and Robert Service, *The End of the Cold War, 1985–1991* (London: Macmillan, 2015). The latter is the most scholarly, detailed account available of US-Soviet relations during this period.

On espionage, see the very revealing Christopher Andrew and Oleg Gordievsky, *KGB: The Inside Story of Its Foreign Operations from Lenin to Gorbachev* (New York: HarperCollins, 1990). See also Richard J. Aldrich, *The Hidden Hand: Britain, America and Cold War Secret Intelligence* (London: John Murray, 2001), which reads, at times, like a James Bond novel. The authoritative account of MI5 is Christopher Andrew, *The Defence of the Realm: The Authorized History of MI5* (London: Allen Lane, 2009). MI6 is revealed in Keith Jeffery, *MI6: The History of the Secret Intelligence Service, 1909–1949* (London: Bloomsbury, 2010). We shall have to wait some time for the next volume! The leading study of espionage during the Second World War is Max Hastings, *The Secret War: Spies, Codes and Guerrillas, 1939–1945* (London: William Collins, 2015) is essential background reading for an understanding of the emergence of the Cold War. Two very interesting studies of members of the Fab Five are Geoff Andrews, *The Shadow Man: At the Heart of the Cambridge Spy Circle* (London: I. B. Tauris, 2015) and Andrew Lownie, *Stalin's Englishman: The Lives of Guy Burgess* (London: Hodder, 2015). The best source on Philby is Ben Macintyre, *A Spy among Friends: Philby and the Great Betrayal* (London: Bloomsbury, 2015).

A revealing account of the collapse of the Soviet Union and the emergence of Russia is Yegor Gaidar, *Days of Defeat and Victory* (Seattle: University of Washington Press, 1999). See also Andrei Grachev, *Final Days: The Inside Story of the Collapse of the Soviet Union* (Boulder, CO: Westview Press, 1995). A much more detailed account of the Cold War and after is Andrey Grachev, *Le Passé de la Russie est Imprévisible: Journal de bord d'un enfant de dégel* (Paris: Akma Editeur, 2014).

The outstanding source on the Cold War in the Third World is Odd Arne Westad, *The Global Cold War: Third World Interventions and the Making of Our Times* (Cambridge: Cambridge University Press, 2005).

Norman Stone, *The Atlantic and Its Enemies: A Personal History of the Cold War* (London: Allen Lane, 2010) is an entertaining and instructive analysis.

The best source on Britain's poison war is Ulf Schmidt, *Secret Science: A Century of Poison Warfare and Human Experiments* (Oxford: Oxford University Press, 2015).

On a lighter note, see Bruce Adams, *Tiny Revolutions in Russia: Twentieth-Century Soviet and Russian History in Anecdotes* (London: Routledge Curzon, 2005).

China

An instructive and entertaining account of modern China is Jonathan Fenby, *Tiger Head, Snake Tails: China Today, How It Got There, and Where It Is Heading* (New York: Simon & Schuster, 2012). Also very informative is Timothy Beardson, *Stumbling Giant: The Threats to China's Future* (New Haven, CT: Yale University Press, 2013).

The most informative biography of Mao is Jung Chang and Jon Halliday, *Mao: The Unknown Story* (London: Jonathan Cape, 2005); see also Andrew G. Walder, *China under Mao* (Cambridge, MA: Harvard University Press, 2015), who lays bare the sufferings of the Chinese population and shows that in the decades after Mao 'China began the long process of recovering from his misrule.'

On Chiang Kai-shek the most detailed study is Jay Taylor, *The Generalissimo: Chiang Kai-shek and the Struggle for Modern China* (Cambridge, MA: Harvard University Press, 2009).

See also D. Borg and W. Heinrichs, *Uncertain Years: Chinese-American Relations, 1947–1950* (New York: Columbia University Press, 1980); see also Margaret MacMillan, *Nixon and Mao: The Week That Changed the World* (New York: Random House, 2007).

The best book on the Chinese economy and transition to capitalism by far is Ronald Coase and Ning Wang, *How China Became Capitalist* (Basingstoke: Palgrave Macmillan, 2012).

Three outstanding studies of the early years of the People's Republic are Frank Dikötter, *The Tragedy of Liberation: A History of the Chinese Revolution, 1945–1957* (London: Bloomsbury, 2013); *Mao's Great Famine: The History of China's Most Devastating Catastrophe, 1958–1962* (London: Bloomsbury, 2010) and *The Cultural Revolution: A People's History, 1962–1976* (London: Bloomsbury, 2016). They are a stunning achievement.

The best biography of Deng Xiaoping by far is Alexander V. Pantsov and Steven I. Levine, *Deng Xiaoping: A Revolutionary Life* (New York: Oxford University Press, 2015) and is scholarly, detailed and thoughtful, revealing his Marxism and his ruthlessness. See also Ezra F. Vogel, *Deng Xiaoping and the Transformation of*

Modern China (Cambridge, MA: Harvard University Press, 2013) which concentrates heavily on the post-1978 period; and Michael Dillon, *Deng Xiaoping: The Man Who Made Modern China* (London: I. B. Tauris, 2015).

The best source on the Communist Party of China is Richard McGregor, *The Party: The Secret World of China's Communist Rulers* (London: Allen Lane, 2010).

On the rise of religion in China, see Bob Fu and Nancy French, *God's Double Agent: The True Story of a Chinese Christian's Fight for Freedom* (Grand Rapids, MI: Baker Books, 2013).

An eye opening account of the one-child policy is Mei Fong, *One Child: The Story of China's Most Radical Experiment* (Boston, MA: Houghton Mifflin Harcourt, 2016).

On ping-pong diplomacy, an excellent source is Nicholas Griffin, *Ping-Pong Diplomacy: Ivor Montagu and the Astonishing Story behind the Game That Changed the World* (New York: Simon & Schuster, 2015).

The best book on the early stages of the Sino-Soviet relationship is Zhihua Shen and Yafeng Xia, *Mao and the Sino-Soviet Partnership, 1945–1959* (Lanham, MD, and London: Lexington Books, 2015). It is by two Chinese scholars who have had access to Chinese Party and government archives. A companion volume covering the years 1960–73 is in preparation. See also Thomas P. Bernstein and Hua-Yu Li (eds.), *China Learns from the Soviet Union, 1949–Present* (Lanham, MD: Lexington Books, 2010); Jeremy Friedman, *Shadow Cold War: The Sino-Soviet Competition for the Third World* (Chapel Hill: University of North Carolina Press, 2015); Dieter Heinzig, *The Soviet Union and Communist China, 1945–1950: The Arduous Road to the Alliance* (New York: M. E. Sharpe, 2004); Austin Jersild, *The Sino-Soviet Alliance: An International History* (Chapel Hill: University of North Carolina Press, 2014); Mercy Kuo, *Contending with Contradictions: China's Policy toward Soviet Eastern Europe and the Origins of the Sino-Soviet Split, 1953–1960* (Lanham, MD: Lexington Books, 2001); Lorenz M. Lüthi, *The Sino-Soviet Split: Cold War in the Communist World* (Princeton, NJ: Princeton University Press, 2008); Sergey Radchenko, *Two Suns in the Heavens: The Sino-Soviet Struggle for Supremacy, 1962–1967* (Washington, DC, and Stanford, CA: Woodrow Wilson Center and Stanford University Press, 2009); Odd A. Westad (ed.), *Brothers in Arms: The Rise and Fall of the Sino-Soviet Alliance, 1945–1963* (Stanford, CA: Stanford University Press, 1998); Elizabeth Wishnick, *Mending Fences: The Evolution of Moscow's China Policy from Brezhnev to Yeltsin* (Seattle: University of Washington Press, 2001); Chen Jian, *Mao's China and the Cold War* (Chapel Hill: University of North Carolina Press, 2001).

On Sino-American relations, see Chen Jian, *China's Road to the Korean War: The Making of the Sino-American Confrontation* (New York: Columbia University Press, 1994); Shu Guang Zhang, *Mao's Military Romanticism: China and the Korean War, 1950–1953* (Lawrence: University Press of Kansas, 1995); Shu Guang Zhang, *Deterrence and Strategic Culture: Chinese-American Confrontations, 1949–1958* (Ithaca, NY: Cornell University Press, 1991); Qiang Zhai, *China and the Vietnam Wars, 1950–1975* (Chapel Hill: University of North Carolina Press, 2000); Henry Kissinger, *On China* (London: Penguin, 2012) is a valuable, learned analysis of modern China and Sino-American relations; and Bobo Lo, *Axis of Convenience Moscow, Beijing, and the New Geopolitics* (London: Chatham House, 2008).

On Cambodia, see William Shawcross, *Sideshow: Kissinger, Nixon and the Destruction of Cambodia* (New York: Simon & Schuster, 1987).

The leading study of North Korea is Andrei Lankov, *The Real North Korea: Life and Politics in the Failed Stalinist Utopia* (New York: Oxford University Press, 2013).

The most informative and instructive analysis of what it was like to prepare for nuclear war in Britain is Peter Hennessy, *The Secret State: Preparing for the Worst, 1945–2010* (London: Penguin, 2010).

On the West's defeat in Afghanistan there is a revealing and instructive study by Christina Lamb, *Farewell Kabul: From Afghanistan to a More Dangerous World* (London: William Collins, 2015).

Two excellent surveys of communism are Archie Brown, *The Rise and Fall of Communism* (London: Bodley Head, 2009) and Robert Service, *Comrades: Communism: A World History* (Basingstoke: Macmillan, 2007).

References

Alenius, Kari (2014) *Unselfishly for Peace and Justice – and against Evil: The Rhetoric of the Great Powers in the UN Security Council, 1946–1956*, Tornio, Tornion kirapaino.

Alexander, Andrew (2011) *America and the Imperialism of Ignorance: US Foreign Policy since 1945*, London, Biteback.

Alperovitz, Gar (1985) *Atomic Diplomacy: Hiroshima and Potsdam*, rev. edn, New York, Penguin.

Andrew, Christopher and Vasili Mitrokhin (2005) *The Mitrokhin Archive II: The KGB and the World*, London, Allen Lane.

Aron, Leon (2015) 'Putinology', *American Interest*, Vol. 11, no. 1.

Banac, Ivo (ed.) (2003) *The Diary of Georgi Dimitrov, 1933–1949*, New Haven, CT, Yale University Press.

Beschloss, Michael R. and Strobe Talbott (1993) *At the Highest Levels. The Inside Story of the End of the Cold War*, Boston, Little, Brown.

Boldin, Valery (1994) *Ten Years That Shook the World: The Gorbachev Era as Witnessed by His Chief of Staff*, New York, Basic Books.

Boukovsky, V. (1995) *Jugement à Moscou – un dissident dans les archives du Kremlin*, Paris, Robert Laffont.

Burdick, Eugene and Willian Lederer (1958) *The Ugly American*, New York, W. W. Norton.

Burgis, Tom (2015) *The Looting Machine: Warlords, Tycoons, Smugglers and the Systematic Theft of Africa's Wealth*, London, William Collins.

Burr, William and Jeffrey P. Kimball (2015) *Nixon's Nuclear Specter: The Secret Alert of 1969, Madman Diplomacy, and the Vietnam War*, Lawrence, University Press of Kansas.

Byron, John and Robert Pack (1992) *The Claws of the Dragon: Kang Sheng – The Evil Genius Behind Mao and His Legacy of Terror in People's China*, New York, Simon & Schuster.

Caute, David (2003) *The Dancer Defects: The Struggle for Cultural Supremacy During the Cold War*, Oxford, Oxford University Press.

Chandler, Alfred D. (1981) *The Papers of Dwight D. Eisenhower*, Vol. 11, Baltimore, MD, Johns Hopkins University Press.

Chang, Jung and Jon Halliday (2005) *Mao: The Untold Story*, London, Jonathan Cape.

Chen, Jian (1994) *China's Road to the Korean War: The Making of the Sino-American Confrontation*, New York, Columbia University Press.

Clapham, Christopher (1996) *Africa and the International System: The Politics of State Survival*, Cambridge, Cambridge University Press.

Coase, Ronald and Ning Wang (2012) *How China Became Capitalist*, Basingstoke, Palgrave Macmillan.

Cohen, W.I. (1993) *America in the Age of Soviet Power, 1945–1991*, Cambridge, Cambridge University Press.

Cohen, W.I. and A. Iriye (eds.) (1990) *The Great Powers in East Asia, 1953–1960*, New York, Columbia.

Costigliola, Frank (2012) *Roosevelt's Lost Alliances: How Personal Politics Helped Start the Cold War*, Princeton, Princeton University Press.

Dikötter, Frank (2010) *Mao's Great Famine: The History of China's Most Devastating Catastrophe, 1958–62*, London, Bloomsbury.

Dikötter, Frank (2013) *The Tragedy of Liberation*, London, Bloomsbury.

Dikötter, Frank (2016) *The Cultural Revolution: A People's History, 1962–1976*, London, Bloomsbury.

Dobrynin, A. (1995) *In Confidence: Moscow's Ambassador to America's Six Cold War Presidents*, New York, Random House.

El Sadat, Anwar (1978) *In Search of Identity*, London, Collins.

Evans, Alfred B. Jr (1993) *Soviet Marxism-Leninism: The Decline of an Ideology*, Westport, CT, Praeger.

Ferguson, Niall (2015) *Kissinger 1923–1968: The Idealist*, London, Allen Lane.

French, Howard W. (2014) *China's Second Continent: How a Million Migrants Are Building a New Empire in Africa*, New York, Alfred A. Knopf.

Gaddis, J.L. (1987) *The Long Peace: Inquiries into the History of the Cold War*, Oxford, Oxford University Press.

Gaddis, J.L. (1990) *Russia, the Soviet Union and the United States*, 2nd edn, New York, McGraw-Hill.

Gaddis, J.L. (1998) *We Now Know: Rethinking Cold War History*, Oxford, Oxford University Press.

Gaidar, Yegor (2007) *Collapse of an Empire: Lessons for Modern Russia*, Washington, DC, Brookings Institution Press.

Gaidar, Yegor (2012) *Russia: A Long View*, Cambridge, MA, MIT Press.

Garthoff, R.L. (1994) *Détente and Confrontation, American-Soviet Relations from Nixon to Reagan*, rev. edn, Washington, DC, Brookings Institution.

Gerard, Emmanuel and Bruce Kuklick (2015) *Death in the Congo: Murdering Patrice Lumumba*, Cambridge, MA, Harvard University Press.

Goldman, Marshall (2010) *Oilopoly, Power and the Rise of the New Russia*, London, One World.

Goldman, Stuart D. (2012) *Nomonhan 1939: The Red Army's Victory That Shaped World War II*, Annapolis, MD, Naval Institute Press.

Gorbachev, Mikhail (1987) *Perestroika: New Thinking for Our Country and the World*, London, Collins.

Gorbachev, Mikhail (1996) *Memoirs*, London, Doubleday.

Halliday, F. (1983) *The Making of the Second Cold War*, London, Verso.

Haslam, Jonathan (2011) *Russia's Cold War from the October Revolution to the Fall of the Berlin Wall*, New Haven, CT, Yale University Press.

Hastings, Max (2015) *The Secret War: Spies, Codes and Guerrillas, 1939–1945*, London, Collins.

Hatherley, Owen (2015) *Landscapes of Communism: A History through Buildings*, London, Allen Lane.

Hayton, Bill (2010) *Vietnam: Rising Dragon*, New Haven, CT, Yale University Press.

Khlevniuk, Oleg V. (2015) *Stalin: New Biography of a Dictator*, New Haven, CT, Yale University Press.

Khrushchev, Nikita (1971) *Khrushchev Remembers*, Vol. 1, New York, Little, Brown.

Kissinger, Henry A. (1969) 'The Viet Nam Negotiations', *Foreign Affairs*, January.

Kissinger, Henry A. (1979) *The White House Years*, London, Weidenfeld & Nicolson.

Kissinger, Henry A. (1982) *Years of Upheaval*, London, Weidenfeld & Nicolson.

Kissinger, Henry A. (2012) *On China*, London, Penguin.

Kolko, Joyce and Gabriel Kolko (1972) *The Limits of Power: The World and United States Foreign Policy, 1945–1954*, New York, Harper and Row.

Kotkin, Stephen and Bruce A. Elleman (eds.) (1999) *Mongolia in the Twentieth Century Landlocked Cosmopolitan*, Armonk, NY, M.E. Sharpe.

Kryuchkov, Vladimir V. (1996) *Lichnoe Delo*, Vol. 1, Moscow, Olimp.

LaFeber, Walter (1993) *America, Russia, and the Cold War, 1945–1992*, 7th edn, New York, McGraw-Hill.

LaFeber, Walter (2006) *America, Russia and the Cold War, 1945–2000*, Oxford, Oxford University Press.

Lankov, Andrei (2013) *The Real North Korea: Life and Politics in the Failed Stalinist Utopia*, New York, Oxford University Press.

Larres, Klaus (2002) *Churchill's Cold War: The Politics of Personal Diplomacy*, New Haven, CT, Yale University Press.

Lo, Bobo (2015) Russia and the New World Disorder, Chatham House, London, and Brookings Institution Press, Washington DC.

Lüthi, Lorenz M. (2008) *The Sino-Soviet Split: Cold War in the Communist World*, Princeton, NJ, Princeton University Press.

MacArthur, Douglas (1965) *Reminiscences: General of the Army*, New York, Fawcett World Library.

Malraux, André (1967) *Anti-memoirs*, translated by Terence Kilmartin, New York, Henry Holt.

McNamara, Robert (1999) *Argument without End: In Search of Answers to the Vietnam Tragedy*, New York, Times Books.

McNamara, Robert and Brian VanDeMark (1995) *In Retrospect: The Tragedy and Lessons of Vietnam*, New York, Random House.

Milanovic, Branko (2011) *The Haves and the Have Nots: A Brief and Idiosyncratic History of Global Inequality*, New York, Basic Books.

Miscamble, Wilson D. (2011) *The Most Controversial Decision: Truman, the Atomic Bombs, and the Defeat of Japan*, Cambridge, Cambridge University Press.

Mosley, Leonard (1978) *Dulles: A Biography of Eleanor, Allen and John Foster Dulles and Their Family Network*, London, Dial Press.

Nixon, Richard M. (1967) 'Asia after Viet Nam', *Foreign Affairs*, October.

Oberdorfer, D. (1992) *The Turn: From Cold War to the New Era: The United States and the Soviet Union, 1983–1990*, London, Cape.

O'Clery, Conor (2011) *Moscow, December 25, 1991: The Last Day of the Soviet Union*, London, Transworld Ireland.

Pantsov, Alexander V. and Steven I. Levine (2015) *Deng Xiaoping: A Revolutionary Life*, New York, Oxford University Press.

Pikhoya, R.G. (1998) *Sovetskaya Soyuz: Istoriya Vlasti, 1945–1991*, Moscow, Izdatelstvo RAGS.

Priestland, David (2009) *The Red Flag Communism and the Making of the Modern World*, London, Allen Lane.

Primakov, Yevgeny (2004) *Russian Crossroads: Towards the New Millennium*, New Haven, CT, Yale University Press.

Razoux, Pierre (2015) *The Iran-Iraq War*, translated by Nicholas Elliott, Cambridge, MA, Belknap Press of Harvard University Press.

Sakharov, Andrei (1990) *Memoirs*, New York, Alfred A. Knopf.

Schlosser, Eric (2013) *Command and Control*, London, Penguin.

Schram, Stuart (1989) *The Thought of Mao Tse-Tung*, Cambridge, Cambridge University Press.

Service, Robert (2015) *The End of the Cold War, 1985–1991*, London, Macmillan.

Shen, Zhihua and Yafeng Xia (2015) *Mao and the Sino-Soviet Partnership, 1945–1959*, Lanham, MD, and London, Lexington Books.

Shepilov, Dmitrii (2007) *The Kremlin's Scholar: A Memoir of Soviet Politics under Stalin and Khrushchev*, New Haven, CT, Yale University Press.

Shultz, G.P. (1993) *Turmoil and Tragedy: My Years as Secretary of State*, New York, Charles Scribner's.

Sisman, Adam (2015) *John Le Carré: The Biography*, London, Bloomsbury.

Spence, Jonathan (1999) *The Search for Modern China*, New York, W.W. Norton.

Stöver, Bernd (2011) *Der Kalte Krieg Geschichte eines radikalen Zeitalters 1947–1991*, Munich, C.H. Beck.

Swanson, Vern G. (2008) *Soviet Impressionist Painting*, Suffolk, Woodbridge, Antique Collectors' Club.

Talbott, Strobe (trans. and ed.) (1974) *Khrushchev Remembers: The Last Testament*, Boston, Little, Brown.

Taubman, W. (2003) *Khrushchev: The Man and His Era*, New York, Norton.

Toranska, Teresa (1987) *'Them': Stalin's Polish Puppets*, New York, Harper and Row.

Trachtenberg, Marc (1991) *History and Strategy*, Princeton, NJ, Princeton University Press.

Tschernajew, Anatoli (1993) *Die letzten Jahre einer Grossmacht: Der Kreml von innen*, Munich, C.H. Beck.

Westad, Odd Arne (2005) *The Global Cold War Third World Interventions and the Making of Our Times*, Cambridge, Cambridge University Press.

Wolfe, Alan (1984) *The Rise and Fall of the Soviet Threat*, Cambridge, MA, South End Press.

Žižek, Slavoj (2007) *On Practice and Contradiction Mao Tse-Tung*, London, Verso.

Index